THE GREENHAVEN ENCYCLOPEDIA OF

ANCIENT EGYPT

5/04

THE GREENHAVEN ENCYCLOPEDIA OF

ANCIENT EGYPT

Patricia D. Netzley

Michael Berger, *Consulting Editor*

Daniel Leone, *President*
Bonnie Szumski, *Publisher*
Scott Barbour, *Managing Editor*

**GREENHAVEN
PRESS ®**

THOMSON

GALE

REF
932
NET

San Diego • Detroit • New York • San Francisco • Cleveland • New Haven, Conn. • Waterville, Maine • London • Munich

© 2003 by Greenhaven Press. Greenhaven Press is an imprint of The Gale Group, Inc., a division of Thomson Learning, Inc.

Greenhaven Press® and Thomson Learning ™ are trademarks used herein under license.

For more information, contact
Greenhaven Press
27500 Drake Rd.
Farmington Hills, MI 48331-3535
Or you can visit our Internet site at http://www.gale.com

LIBRARY OF CONGRESS CATALOGING-IN-PUBLICATION DATA

Netzley, Patricia D.
    Encyclopedia of ancient Egypt / by Patricia D. Netzley.
        p. cm. — (Greenhaven encyclopedias)
Summary: An alphabetical presentation of definitions and descriptions of terms and events associated with ancient Egypt.
Includes bibliographical references and index.
    ISBN 0-7377-1150-7 (hard : alk. paper)
    1. Egypt—Civilization—To 332 B.C.—Encyclopedias, Juvenile. 2. Egypt—Civilization—332 B.C.–A.D. 638—Encyclopedias, Juvenile. [1. Egypt—Civilization—To 332 B.C.—Encyclopedias. 2. Egypt—Civilization—332 B.C.–A.D. 638—Encyclopedias.] I. Title. II. Series.
    DT58 .N48 2003
    932' .003—dc21
                                                                2002006965

Printed in the United States of America

CONTENTS

PREFACE

Around 3000 B.C., a complex civilization began to develop in Egypt. Over the next two thousand years Egypt became the cultural and political center of much of northeastern Africa. By 30 B.C., however, when the Romans completed their conquest of the region, the ancient Egyptian culture had all but disappeared. The pyramids and other colossal monuments that ancient Egyptian kings had built remained, but all memory of the purpose of these ancient structures had been lost. Inscriptions found on the walls of these monuments were of no help since nobody knew how to interpret them.

Since the late eighteenth century, scholars have learned how to translate ancient Egyptian writings, but much is still unknown about ancient Egyptian history and culture. Over the millennia many records and artifacts have been lost, destroyed, or stolen, leaving large gaps in the record of Egypt's past. In addition, the ancient Egyptians sometimes distorted their own history, as when some kings obliterated all references to their predecessors and/or exaggerated their own accomplishments, skills, and physical prowess.

As a result of these gaps and distortions, modern scholars cannot be sure that all of their conclusions about ancient Egyptian kings and their reigns are correct. Scholars have faced similar difficulties in their attempts to understand ancient Egyptians' religious beliefs. However, enough ancient texts have survived to shed light on what Egyptians believed about the Afterlife and about the many deities they worshiped. Scholars have had even greater success in determining how ancient Egyptians lived because works of art found in tombs and other structures typically depict scenes from everyday life. In addition, tools, furniture, personal items, funerary goods, and other artifacts uncovered by archaeologists have provided insights into the ancient Egyptians' daily activities, their values, and their customs.

Scholars continue to study ancient Egyptian artifacts and archaeological sites in an effort to learn more about ancient Egyptian culture and history. Excavations of tombs and other structures are ongoing at many sites in Egypt. These include Saqqara and other cemeteries located along the banks of the Nile River, which, because it was the primary source of life-giving water, was where most of ancient Egyptian civilization was concentrated.

The *Greenhaven Encyclopedia of Ancient Egypt* was written to present the most up-to-date information available. This volume includes details relating to important people and places in ancient Egypt as well as material on ancient Egyptian customs, religious beliefs, artwork, literature, and other aspects of society. It also discusses the work of the archaeologists and other scholars who founded the discipline of Egyptology, as the academic study of ancient Egypt is known. In addition, the encyclopedia offers an extensive bibliography that will help readers find more information on all aspects of ancient Egyptian civilization.

Abbott Papyrus

The Abbott Papyrus is a Twentieth Dynasty document produced by officials from the court of Ramses IX that reports the details of a lengthy investigation into a series of tomb robberies that took place during the king's reign. The investigation was launched at the behest of Paser, the mayor of eastern Thebes, who suspected that certain government officials were involved in the crimes. According to the report, several people were tried and convicted of tomb robbing, although apparently none of them were high-ranking government officials. As part of the investigation, a number of tombs were inspected; those found to have been raided or damaged were repaired and resealed. The papyrus identifies the location of the royal tombs of Seventeenth Dynasty kings Intef VII, Sobekemsaf II, Tao II, and Kamose, among others. In 1923, archaeologist Herbert Winlock used this information to find these tombs. **See also** Paser; Ramses IX; robbers, tomb.

Abu Ghurob

Located near the city of Giza, Abu Ghurob is known as the site of six Fifth Dynasty temple complexes created to honor the sun god Re and the kings who built them. However, only two such temples have been found, one constructed at the behest of King Userkaf and the other of King Neuserre (also known as Izi).

King Userkaf's was apparently the first sun temple built in ancient Egypt. Although today it is greatly deteriorated, it once featured a squat obelisk (which was a common symbol for the sun), a sun altar, and a causeway leading to a mud-brick boat said to belong to Re. The temple complex of King Neuserre was far more elaborate than Userkaf's. Built in approximately 2400 B.C., it had an upper temple and a lower temple linked by a causeway that some archaeologists believe symbolized one's passage through life. The lower temple was located next to a canal, so that boats could dock beside it. The upper temple had a chapel, an eighteen-foot-by-nineteen-foot sacrificial altar of alabaster blocks, and an obelisk, among other structures. The temple complex also apparently had a solar bark (a boat associated with the sun god) made of brick and nearly one hundred feet long. This boat's purpose was to carry the king's spirit across the sky in the Afterlife. Reliefs on walls in the temple complex depicted Neuserre engaged in activities like hunting or battling enemies or participating in a religious festival. Other reliefs, in a room that archaeologists call the Room of the Seasons, show scenes involving farming, plants, animals, and the Nile River floods.

Most of the artwork, however, was removed by German archaeologists Ludwig Borchardt, Frederick von Bissing, and Heinrich Schäfer, who first excavated Neuserre's temple from 1898 to 1901. Today, many of the temple reliefs are in museums in Cairo and Berlin. Others, however, were destroyed in the Allied bombing of Germany during World War

II and have therefore been lost forever. **See also** barks of the gods; Neuserre; Userkaf.

Abu Roash (Abu Rowash; Abu Rawash)

From the First Dynasty on, the village of Abu Roash was the site of a large burial area, or necropolis, serving nearby Memphis. As such, it was part of a string of Memphis cemeteries that included the sites of el-Aryan, Saqqara, Abusir, Giza, and Dashur. Archaeologists excavating Abu Roash, including one French team in 1922–1923 and another French and Swiss Team in the 1990s, have discovered many tomb complexes for royals and those who served them, dating from various dynasties. Abu Roash is also the site of the barely begun pyramid of King Djedefre of the Fourth Dynasty, who died only eight years into his reign. **See also** Djedefre; Memphis.

Abu Simbel

Located more than 150 miles south of modern-day Aswan near the west bank of the Nile River, Abu Simbel was the site of two rock temples built in Nubia by Nineteenth Dynasty king Ramses II. Together, these two temples served as a center where various religious ceremonies were conducted by numerous priests and their assistants. According to some ancient records, this center was so important to Ramses II that, when it was severely damaged by an earthquake shortly before its completion, the king spared no expense in restoring it.

The first and largest of the Abu Simbel temples was created to honor the sun gods Amun-Re and Re-Horakhty and King Ramses II in anticipation of his attaining divinity in the Afterlife. The temple was carved into a cliff and is famous for its façade, which features four colossal statues of a seated Ramses. Each

Four giant statues of Ramses II flank the entrance to the main temple of Abu Simbel, built about 1250 B.C. to honor Ramses himself and the sun gods Amun-Re and Re-Horakhty.

statue is approximately sixty-five feet high, and located between these statues' legs are smaller statues of the king's loved ones, including his wife Queen Nefertari, his mother Queen Muttuya, his son Prince Amenhirkhepshef, and several of the king's daughters. There are also several statues of baboons, which the Egyptians associated with the morning sun (probably because of the screeches they make at sunrise).

Another dramatic feature of this temple is that twice each year, on approximately April 22 and October 22 (one month after the spring and autumnal equinox, respectively), a shaft of light from the rising sun passes through the temple entrance, down a corridor, past eight floor-to-ceiling pillars, and into a niche at the far end of the sanctuary, a distance of roughly 180 feet back into the rock. There the sun illuminates four statues normally in darkness: likenesses of King Ramses II and the gods Ptah, Amun-Re, and Re-Horakhty, the three most important deities during Ramses II's reign.

In addition to the sanctuary are numerous small chambers that were probably used as storerooms, as well as a number of large halls. These rooms feature wall reliefs depicting the king's military campaigns in Palestine (to the east of Egypt), Libya (to the west), Syria (to the north), and Nubia (to the south). Since the king campaigned elsewhere as well, archaeologists generally believe that these locations were chosen to symbolize the extent of the king's power. Other reliefs depict the king engaged in various ceremonies, including ones that suggest he was actually deified during his lifetime rather than after death.

One aspect of the temple proved helpful to archaeologists in learning how to read hieroglyphs, the form of writing used by ancient Egyptians. In September 1822, a scholar named Jean-François Champollion was studying a then-incomprehensible inscription over the temple's door when he realized that the hieroglyphs might represent sounds. Champollion's hunch proved correct: The sounds that the pictures suggested composed Ramses II's throne name, Usermaatre. Champollion's work paved the way for deciphering many other previously unreadable inscriptions.

The second, or lesser, temple at Abu Simbel is a smaller version of the first. Archaeologists sometimes refer to it as the Temple of Nefertari because it is dedicated to Ramses II's chief wife Queen Nefertari and the goddess Hathor. Its rock façade has six huge statues of standing figures, four depicting the king and two the queen, accompanied by smaller statues of their children. (As large as these statues are, they still are only half the size of those in the façade of the greater temple.) Inside this temple is a niche containing a statue of the goddess Hathor, as well as wall reliefs showing the queen participating in ceremonies alongside her husband. An underground portion of the temple contained numerous chambers for conducting rituals to honor Hathor, a hall, and vestibules.

King Ramses II's Abu Simbel temples were first discovered by archaeologist Johann Ludwig Burckhardt in 1813. Four years later, archaeologist Giovanni Battista Belzoni had excavated enough of the larger temple to allow scholars to enter the structure. For many years thereafter, the temples at Abu Simbel were a major tourist attraction. However, they are no longer at their original site, which is now under the waters of Lake Nasser (a reservoir created by the building of the Aswan High Dam). Between 1964 and 1968, both temples were painstakingly dismantled and moved to higher ground approximately 230 yards away. As part of this endeavor, the temples' massive façades were cut from their rock cliffs into blocks that could be moved. Both the exteriors and the interiors of the two temples were then reconstructed, and the greater temple was oriented on its new site so that the sun would still illuminate its interior on April 22 and October 22. The total cost of the temple relocation project, which was supervised by an international team of archaeologists, was more than $90 million. **See also** Belzoni, Giovanni Battista; Champollion, Jean-François; Nefertari; Ramses II.

Abusir

Abusir was one of a string of cemeteries serving the city of Memphis. As such, it contains numerous tomb complexes, monuments, and temples. In fact, Abusir contains the earliest solar temple in Egypt, an unfinished pyramid begun by the Fifth Dynasty king Userkaf. The pyramids of other Fifth Dynasty rulers were built at Abusir as well. Still surviving, although ravaged by time, are those of Kings Sahure, Kakai, and Neuserre (also known as Izi), as well as the pyramid of Queen Khentkawes I, the unfinished pyramids of King Neferirkare and Reneferef and King Shepseskhaf and other structures. The most elaborate pyramid appears to have been that of King Sahure. Constructed of red granite from Aswan as well as both local limestone and limestone from the quarries at Tura, across the Nile River from Abusir, the pyramid featured black basalt flooring and a copper drainpipe over three hundred yards long. Some of the pyramid's limestone blocks weighed as much as 275 tons, the largest being 35-by-9-by-12 feet in size. However, all but two of these blocks have been destroyed, probably as a result of an earthquake that shook the area in antiquity.

Artwork found at Abusir has yielded important information about life during the Fifth Dynasty. For example, on the inner walls of a causeway that once connected Sahure's pyramid with other royal tombs and pyramids, reliefs depicted a variety of Fifth Dynasty scenes, including people dancing, wrestling, and shooting bows and arrows as part of military training. Reliefs and paintings inside the temple show the king engaged in such activities as hunting and include the earliest depiction of Egyptian ships meant for ocean voyages (as opposed to Nile River travel). Other Abusir temples, including the pyramid complex of King Neuserre and the pyramid of Queen Khentkawes I, have yielded ancient papyrus columns and scrolls, providing archaeologists with descriptions related to the day-to-day management of Old Kingdom pyramid complexes.

Abusir also contains numerous royal and nonroyal tombs, many of which are of a rectangular Old Kingdom style known as mastaba (Arabic for bench). These mastaba tombs include several built for royal princesses, as well as one of the largest Old Kingdom nonroyal tombs, that of Ptahshepses, who was married to a daughter of King Neuserre and who served as vizier. So grand was this tomb that its ruins were mistaken by archaeologist Karl Richard Lepsius for those of a royal pyramid. Archaeologists restored the Ptahshepses tomb during the 1970s and 1980s, and excavation and restoration of other tombs in the area is ongoing.

Some of the tombs that have been excavated in modern times are Twenty-sixth and Twenty-seventh Dynasty shaft tombs, which are tombs located at the bottom of a vertical shaft cut deep into the earth. One of these, the tomb of a priest named Iufa who served in the temple of the goddess Neith in the town of Sais, escaped the ravages of tomb robbers and has therefore yielded numerous artifacts, including statues and personal items.

There is another Egyptian town named Abusir that is located near the city of Alexandria in the Delta region of Lower Egypt. Originally called Taposiris Magna by the ancient Greeks, its ruins date from the beginning of the Greco-Roman Period.

This town is famous for a limestone unfinished temple of Osiris that archaeologists have been unable to date and a burial site for sacred animals. **See also** Lepsius, Karl Richard; mastaba tomb; Userkaf.

Abydos

Called Abedju by the ancient Egyptians, the city of Abydos (a Greek name) was located north of Dendera in Upper Egypt, near modern-day el-Araba. During the Predynastic Period, this city became an important burial site and remained prominent throughout ancient Egypt's history. In fact, its necropolis area was patronized by most of Egypt's kings. During the Middle Kingdom, Abydos also became a cult center (a religious center dedicated to a particular deity or family of deities) for the god Osiris and eventually the principal religious center for all of Egypt. Consequently, Abydos had many temples, monuments, tombs, cenotaphs (false tombs), and other structures.

The most famous archaeological discovery in Abydos was evidence that, during the First Dynasty, servants were sometimes sacrificed so they could accompany their masters to the Afterlife. Between 1900 and 1901, British archaeologist Sir William Matthew Flinders Petrie excavated numerous First Dynasty royal tombs and cenotaphs in the area and found that they were surrounded by the graves of people who were servants; those found near the tomb complex of First Dynasty king Aha had clearly been killed. Several young lions were sacrificed and buried near the king as well, although Egyptologists disagree on whether these animals were Aha's pets or were captured, killed, and buried for some other ritual purpose.

The largest monument in Abydos, however, was not Aha's tomb but apparently the temple of Nineteenth Dynasty king Seti I. Initial construction of this structure took place while the king was still living, but it was probably completed by Seti I's successor, Ramses II. Within this temple is a shrine with a gallery now known as the Gallery of Lists because of its wall reliefs consisting of lists of various facts, including lists of the kings who ruled prior to the temple's construction. Archaeologists refer to the list of rulers as the Abydos King List. There are other halls in the temple as well, some of which served purposes as sacred as sheltering the barks (boats) of the gods while others served purposes as mundane as housing the temple butcher.

Behind the Temple of Seti I is a cenotaph built by Seti I (but perhaps completed by his grandson Merneptah). Inside is the Island Hall and Room, so named because the sarcophagus-shaped room once contained a mound of earth that was surrounded by a moat supplied by canals cut through the walls from outside. Archaeologists disagree on the purpose of this mound. At one time, most thought that it held the canopic jars and perhaps also the sarcophagus of Seti I (which would mean that the building was a real tomb, not a cenotaph). Most now believe that the mound was a place where temple priests grew barley as a symbol of the resurrection of Osiris, who was honored in many Abydos ceremonies. The cenotaph of Seti I also contains a ceiling depicting the stars and the signs of the zodiac.

Just northeast of the cenotaph, the Temple of Ramses II has a granite statue of Seti I as well as similar statues of Ramses II, the god Amun, and various other deities. Its limestone walls also have numerous carved wall reliefs depicting scenes from events in Ramses II's reign, including the Battle of Kadesh.

Near the Temple of Ramses II is the Temple of Osiris, once one of the focal points of Abydos religious activities. Some Egyptologists speculate that one reason Abydos was associated with Osiris had to do with a moaning sound that could be heard near a cenotaph built there by First Dynasty king Djer. Caused by desert winds, this sound would have suggested that the land of the dead was close at hand. In fact, Thirteenth Dynasty priests declared that this cenotaph was actually Osiris's tomb and incorporated the site into rituals intended to honor the god. For example, mummies of prominent people were taken there by boat to "witness" an annual water festival, and pots of offerings to Osiris were left near the site—so many in fact that, by the New Kingdom, the surrounding area had become known as Mother of Pots.

Many other important structures are located in the Abydos area. For example, at a desert site called Shunet el-Zbib (Storehouse of Dates), there is a Second Dynasty necropolis that contains a mortuary structure that is the largest mud-brick building still standing (and perhaps ever built), with walls approximately thirty-three feet high. Also in the Abydos area are the Temple of Senwosret III (a Twelfth Dynasty king), a mortuary complex of Seventeenth Dynasty queen Tetisheri, and a pyramid possibly constructed by Eighteenth Dynasty king Ahmose I. The latter is particularly significant because it contains battle scenes with a picture of a horse, the first known appearance of the animal in Egyptian art. **See also** Aha; Osiris; Petrie, William Matthew Flinders; Ramses II; Seti I.

admonitions and instructions

Admonitions and instructions were two types of ancient Egyptian literature that were educational in purpose. Specifically, they were meant to guide young men in regard to their behavior and/or choice of career. Usually the author was purportedly an older and wiser man, such as a king, a vizier, a father, or a teacher, writing to his son or heir, his student, or some other young man. Sometimes the comments made by this adviser were sin-

cere and upbeat, encouraging good behavior; others, however, were cynical and negative, warning that the adoption or continuance of certain bad behaviors would surely bring disaster.

In either case, during the Old and Middle Kingdom, texts of this type were usually intended for the upper classes and generally stated that certain behaviors were good because they would bring rewards in the form of wealth and status. By the New Kingdom, the intended audience included the middle class and the message was that certain behaviors were good not just because they brought wealth and status but, more importantly, because they were morally correct. However, New Kingdom admonitions and instructions also suggested that correct behavior did not come automatically. In the New Kingdom work *Instructions of Any,* for example, a father offers advice to his argumentative son, who accepts this advice only after much debate.

Also by the New Kingdom, admonitions and instructions were being included in educational materials presented to schoolboys. Called "instructions in wisdom," these manuals were intended to be copied as well as read, because it was thought that one of the best ways of mastering any literary work was by writing it over and over again. Perhaps the first instruction in wisdom was *The Instruction of Hardadef* (also called *The Instruction of Djedefhor*), which claimed to be advice given by Prince Hardadef (also known as Djedefhor), the son of Fourth Dynasty king Khufu, to his own son, Prince Auibre. Hardadef had gained a reputation as a sage during the Old Kingdom, and his advice included admonitions regarding how to lead a good life and raise exemplary sons. A similar work of the period was *The Instruction of Ptahhotep,* credited to Fifth Dynasty vizier Ptahhotep. Among many other pieces of advice, the author says that a good son lives his life according to his father's wishes.

Another early work in the genre is *Instructions of Kagemni,* in which Kagemni (a Sixth Dynasty vizier) is being offered advice as a young man on how to become successful. The author offering the advice is unidentified, and Egyptologists have long debated who it might have been. Some believe that it was the vizier of an Old Kingdom king, perhaps Huni of the Third Dynasty. Others, however, think that *Instructions of Kagemni* was written long after Kagemni's death and that its author was someone from the Middle Kingdom trying to show that Kagemni's acceptance of good advice led to his success.

Other instructions and admonitions from various periods include the *Instructions for Merikare, Amenemhet's Instructions, The Admonitions of Ipuwer,* and a text that no longer exists but is mentioned in several Middle Kingdom documents, written by Third Dynasty vizier Imhotep to advise his king, Djoser. **See also** *Admonitions of Ipuwer, The; Amenemhet's Instructions; Satire on Trades, The.*

Admonitions of Ipuwer, The

Also called *The Admonitions of a Prophet* or *The Admonitions of an Egyptian Sage, The Admonitions of Ipuwer* is an Old Kingdom or perhaps early Middle Kingdom text warning Egypt's king that certain practices and policies will lead the nation to ruin. Specifically, it purports to be the words of Ipuwer, a sage who visited an unidentified Egyptian king at court to tell him of problems within Egypt. Among these problems were too many foreigners moving into Egypt, particularly in the Delta region where they were taking jobs away from native Egyptians; insufficient trade with other countries; unpoliced roads plagued by robbers; and civil wars in the south. In addition, Ipuwer reported that Egypt was experiencing a weakening of religious beliefs that was leading not only to improper burial practices but also, in his opinion, to widespread infertility and general misery among the populace. Unless the proper worship of gods was restored, Ipuwer argued, conditions in Egypt would continue to worsen. Moreover, unless the king acted to expel foreigners, fight his enemies more effectively, and strengthen Egyptian society, Ipuwer predicted there would be anarchy throughout the land and the king would be overthrown.

Egyptologists disagree on which king Ipuwer was addressing. The most likely candidate is Sixth Dynasty king Pepy II, but several Seventh and Eighth Dynasty kings have been named as possibilities as well. In any case, the document does seem to describe many problems that developed as the Old Kingdom gave way to the Middle Kingdom.

The Admonitions of Ipuwer includes some comments made by the unnamed king, but they are incomplete because the original version of the text no longer exists. The only version known today is a copy made by Nineteenth Dynasty scribes who apparently omitted some material while writing it on a papyrus that modern scholars call the Leiden Papyrus. Because this papyrus has sustained heavy damage over the years, the text lacks its introduction and conclusion, and many snippets in between are missing as well. **See also** admonitions and instructions; Leiden Papyrus; Pepy II.

Afrocentrism

For much of their history, ancient Egyptians were Afrocentric, meaning that they were highly prejudiced against anyone who came from outside of Africa. In fact, they were prejudiced against anyone who came from outside of Egypt, as evidenced by the fact that all ancient Egyptian words referring to human beings were applied only to Egyptians. Reflecting this attitude was the fact that rulers of foreign lands were referred to as chiefs to avoid suggesting equality to Egyptian kings.

Because of their attitudes, the ancient Egyptians did not hesitate to try to take over whatever lands they wanted, believing not only that they were better equipped to control them but that the gods had chosen them to rule all the world. This belief was particularly strong during Egypt's early history, when its civilization was far wealthier and more advanced than any other in the region. Conversely, when foreigners began moving into Egypt to live and work, the Egyptian people generally became upset. For example, a late Old Kingdom or early Middle Kingdom text, *The Admonitions of Ipuwer,* complains that foreigners are ruining Egypt by taking jobs away from Egyptians and negatively affecting Egyptian culture.

Afrocentric attitudes meant that initially foreigners were allowed to hold only menial jobs. However, under Eighteenth Dynasty king Amenhotep II people from some regions of Syria and Palestine, known as Asiatics, were permitted to work as skilled craftsmen. Nonetheless, the average Egyptian clearly reviled Asiatics, whom some texts refer to as "abominations of Re." Faced with such prejudice, these foreigners primarily kept to themselves, and for many this isolationism continued even after they achieved better positions in society. Large numbers of Asiatics lived in separate areas of various cities; those who served in Egypt's army worked in separate garrisons, meaning that they socialized only with their own countrymen. This was generally true of other foreigners within Egypt as well. At the same time, some foreigners abandoned their own cultures and by both belief and behavior became assimilated into Egyptian society, a process that modern scholars call Egyptianization.

By the Nineteenth Dynasty, foreigners' situations in Egypt had improved dramatically, largely because contributions by foreign mercenaries had enabled Egypt to achieve some major military victories. Impressed by these mercenaries' fighting skills, the government rewarded them with titles, property, and positions of power. For example, a Nineteenth Dynasty soldier named Urhiya, whom Egyptologists believe was of Hurrian, Canaanite, or Palestinian descent, was able to work his way up to the position of general under King Seti I and then become a steward for Seti's successor, King Ramses II.

As the New Kingdom progressed, the government recruited foreign soldiers in increasing numbers—so much so, in fact, that some Egyptologists believe that the majority of New Kingdom soldiers were foreign born. The government seemed to give preferential treatment to foreign-born soldiers over native Egyptians. Eventually, resentment of foreigners caused by such favoritism resulted in a civil war during the rule of Twenty-sixth Dynasty king Apries. At that time, native Egyptian soldiers openly expressed hatred for the many Greek mercenaries that King Apries brought into Egypt to supplement his forces. In approximately 570 B.C., after returning to the city of Memphis from a battle in a foreign land, the Egyptian soldiers in the king's garrison at Elephantine attacked the Greek mercenaries. During the resulting civil war, now called the Battle of Memphis, the Egyptian soldiers declared their general Ahmose II (also known as Amasis) to be the king of Egypt. Shortly thereafter, Ahmose II met Apries in combat at Memphis and killed him. Even though the native-born soldiers now had their king on the throne, they were unable to stem the growing influence of foreigners in Egypt. Mercenaries existed in too large a number to suppress, and in any case Egypt's ability to wall itself off from people of other countries was weakening because it was preoccupied with a variety of internal social and political problems. **See also** Ahmose II; Apries; mercenaries; military; Seti I; Urhiya.

Afterlife

To ancient Egyptians, the Afterlife was an experience much like life. If their bodies had been properly preserved, Egyptians believed, they could continue to engage in the same activities after death that they had practiced during life. This meant, for example, that peasants in the Afterlife would continue to harvest crops, although their lands—believed to lie below the western horizon in the land of the dead— would be eternally bountiful and they would experience no personal hardships. Meanwhile, the upper classes would be able to use whatever luxury items had been placed in their tombs. In addition, the dead could receive nourishment from offerings left for them on altars in tombs or temples.

During the early Old Kingdom, the ancient Egyptians also believed that people entered the Afterlife regardless of their behavior while they lived, and that they would continue that behavior in the Afterlife. For example, a criminal would continue committing crimes in the Afterlife. By the New Kingdom, the prevailing belief was that only the most deserving people were welcome in the land of the dead. Over time, a complex mythology developed regarding how a person was judged worthy of being in the Afterlife. The deceased would come before Osiris, chief god of the dead, in his judgment hall, where he and forty-two judges would ask the deceased whether he or she had committed various wrongs. As this was taking place, the heart of the deceased was being weighed by Anubis, a god associated with embalming who was also said to help guide the dead to the Judgment Hall of Osiris. Anubis placed

the deceased's heart on one side of a scale and the feather of Ma'at, a goddess of Truth, on the other, with the result of the weighing recorded by the god of scribes, Thoth. Those whose hearts balanced Ma'at's feather could remain in the realm of Osiris, becoming an aspect of the god but retaining individuality at the same time. If the heart did not balance with Ma'at's feather, however, a beast sitting beside the scale would swallow both the heart and the deceased. To ensure that the heart behaved properly during this procedure, therefore, bodies were mummified with a heart scarab, an amulet with inscriptions intended to magically influence the heart's behavior in the Afterlife.

Just getting to this moment of judgment, however, was a difficult task for the deceased. After death, a person's spirit would have to travel to the Judgment Hall of Osiris through a complicated maze of corridors, passing a variety of monsters and other dangers. At certain points along this journey, the deceased would be stopped by gatekeepers demanding that certain passwords be spoken. In order to know the right words to state at the right times, the deceased was believed to consult a guide (which Egyptologists call a mortuary text) to the Afterlife that had been left in his or her tomb. In the New Kingdom one such guide was the *Book of the Dead,* which advised people of all social classes on how to reach the Afterlife. In the Middle Kingdom, the mortuary texts known as the Coffin Texts addressed the Afterlife needs of the nobility; the mortuary texts of the Old Kingdom, the Pyramid Texts, addressed the needs of the king.

As these texts illustrate, beliefs about the criteria for entering the Afterlife gradually changed. In later years, behavior during life counted more, while social class counted less. Therefore, whereas in predynastic times the Egyptians believed that only the king went to the Afterlife (in which he became a god), by the Old Kingdom the Egyptians had begun to believe that the king could bring selected companions into the Afterlife, providing that his tomb and body had been prepared properly and the correct rituals had been conducted. Tomb workers, artisans, and others who had contributed to these details were usually included among those chosen to enjoy an Afterlife. By the Middle Kingdom, the nobility was thought to have the same access to the Afterlife as the king, although they would not have the same access to the gods that he, as a deity himself, would have.

In the New Kingdom, everyone, even the poor, was believed to have access to the Afterlife, and with this belief came concerns among those in the lower classes that only the upper classes might be judged worthy when they appeared before Osiris. As a result, people in the lower classes began looking for ways to influence Osiris's decision. They came to believe that priests could provide them—for a price—with magical words that would allow them to remain with Osiris even if they had behaved badly in life.

Meanwhile, the upper classes rejected the notion that they could buy and conjure their way into the Afterlife, although they did believe that their success after death was dependent on having the right tomb, a properly preserved body, and the correct mortuary rituals. **See also** *Book of the Dead;* Coffin Texts; mummification; Pyramid Texts.

agriculture

The first Egyptians were hunter-gatherers rather than farmers. During predynastic times, they developed the practice of agriculture in the Faiyum (a western oasis) and Delta regions, and thus were able to establish permanent settlements in these regions. Farming soon spread to other parts of Egypt—primarily in oases and along the Nile River and its tributaries, because of the water available in these places for growing crops—and with farming came more and more permanent settlements.

From the Early Dynastic Period on, the majority of Egyptians were farmers, working either for themselves or for someone else. In working a field, most

The Egyptians were practicing farming by 3000 B.C. In this scene from the Book of the Dead, *a worker plows a field behind a pair of oxen.*

farmers plowed with oxen. Men usually worked in pairs, one leading and one steadying a plow made of lightweight wood. Both men and women might work to hoe the plowed land in preparation for planting. Seeds were then scattered on the soil, after which pigs and other domestic animals were herded through the area to trample the seeds into the ground.

The main crops planted were two varieties of wheat, spelt and emmer, which were used to make bread, and barley, which was used to make beer. Other common crops included lentils, lettuce, chickpeas, and onions, while trees provided pomegranates, dates, carob, and a variety of other fruits. Grapes were grown, primarily for wine, in desert oases and in the western Delta; oil-producing plants like sesame were grown much more widely. Spices were grown throughout Egypt as well, often in a garden just outside a home's kitchen, and many people kept beehives (although wild honey was harvested as well) so that they could sweeten certain drinks and foods. In addition, flax was grown to provide linen, papyrus plants—wild or cultivated—provided writing material, and, beginning in the third century, cotton was grown as well.

When the crops were ready to be harvested, farmers gave thanks to the god Min, who was associated with agriculture as well as fertility. The crops were then harvested by hand—in the case of grain, using a wooden sickle with flint teeth. The stalks were bundled into short sheaves and taken by donkey to a threshing area. There the donkeys were made to trample the stalks, which would separate the grain from the stalks and loosen the husk of the grain. Workers then used wooden scoops to toss the grain into the air so that the chaff, or straw and husks, would blow away, leaving the grain to fall on the ground, a process called winnowing. The straw was then gathered and saved for making bricks, while the grain was sent to a central granary. Scribes would record how much grain each farmer contributed. Grain and other crops were stored for the community's use, but a portion was always sent to the capital city for the king to use to pay his workers. To ensure that farmers paid this tax, the king sent assessors to farming communities on a regular basis. However, temples—which often had their own vast fields—were sometimes exempt from paying this tax.

Once the crops had been harvested, animals were allowed to graze in the fields to consume any plant material that had been left behind. This helped ready the fields for the next growing season by clearing them of plant debris and weeds. Occasionally, however, a field was allowed to rest for a growing season in order to improve its fertility for the next one. **See also** Amenemhet III; food; gardens; Nile River; taxation.

Aha (ca. 3065–ca. 2986 B.C.)

Also known as Hor-Aha (the "Fighting Hawk"), Aha (the "Fighter") was either the first or second member of the group of kings now said to constitute Egypt's First Dynasty (3000–2890 B.C.), depending on whether his predecessor, King Narmer, is included in the First Dynasty. Aha might have been King Narmer's son, perhaps by Queen Nithotep. (Also known as Neithotepe, this woman is thought by some Egyptologists to have been Aha's wife instead of his mother.) Much of what is known about Aha (and other First Dynasty kings as well) comes from ivory and wooden tomb labels, which archaeologists call plaques, that were created to record in words and/or pictures the outstanding events in a king's reign, such as battles that were fought and structures that were built.

According to much later accounts from the Greco-Roman period, Aha ruled for sixty-two or sixty-four years, during which many changes took place in Egypt, including the introduction and development of writing. In addition, Aha's reign was marked by many military campaigns north and south of the Nile Valley. He apparently conducted raids on the Sinai Peninsula and Libya, quelled rebellions in Nubia, and greatly expanded Egypt's territory along the Nile River. Some scholars credit him with building the cities of Crocodilopolis and Memphis. According to legend, in founding Memphis, Aha built a dam to redirect a branch of the Nile and form a flat plain where he could construct the city. There is some evidence that Memphis was indeed created in this fashion; scientists from the Egypt Exploration Society recently discovered that the course of the Nile River near Memphis is significantly east of its original location.

Some historians further credit Aha with uniting Upper and Lower Egypt. (Others believe that Narmer deserves this distinction, as well as the credit for founding Memphis.) As evidence for Aha's role as unifier, scholars point to the fact that during the first part of his reign he ruled from the Upper Egypt city of Abydos and during the second part from the Lower Egypt city of Memphis, which then appears to have become the capital of both Upper and Lower Egypt. In addition, the fact that Aha took Mena ("Establisher") or Men as his *nebti,* or second royal name, has led some scholars to believe that he is the Menes who Greco-Roman period historians such as Manetho and Herodotus said was the first king of a unified Egypt.

Aha does have the distinction of being the first of many kings to build his tomb at the cemetery of Abydos. Although his remains have never been found, twelve boats were found buried at Abydos, some as long as one hundred feet, that scholars suspect were connected to royal funerary rituals performed during Aha's burial. Aha's tomb at Abydos, apparently the first monumental funerary complex in Egypt, also contained the remains of several people, none of whom were over the age of twenty-five at death. Scholars suspect that these people were Aha's servants, killed so they could continue to serve their master after death. The remains of some young lions, perhaps once pets of the king, were found there as well.

The circumstances of Aha's death are uncertain. By some accounts, most notably Manetho's, Aha was killed by a hippopotamus while hunting. Whether or not Aha was actually killed by a hippopotamus, some scholars believe that he was at least attacked by one. According to legend, Aha was once attacked by wild dogs in the Faiyum (a large oasis west of the Nile) but was saved by a crocodile. Since many Old Kingdom tomb reliefs show hippopotamuses being attacked by crocodiles, some scholars believe that the dog attack actually refers to the hippopotamus incident instead. **See also** Abydos; Faiyum; Manetho; Narmer.

Ahhotep I (ca. 1590–ca. 1530 B.C.)

Queen Ahhotep I is best known as the mother of Eighteenth Dynasty king Ahmose I, serving as his regent during the early years of his reign. (By various accounts, Ahmose was either five or ten years old when he assumed the throne, although it is widely agreed that he did not begin ruling independently until age sixteen.) While functioning as Ahmose's regent, Queen Ahhotep I personally led an army from Thebes into battle against the Hyksos, a group of foreigners from the east who had conquered parts of northern Egypt one hundred years earlier. Because of her actions during this and subsequent battles, she received several awards for bravery known as the Gold of Valor. Given by royal decree, this award took many forms but was most typically a necklace made of gold.

When Ahhotep I died, probably at age ninety, Ahmose honored her by erecting a stela or inscribed stone pillar at Karnak to commemorate her military accomplishments. He then had her buried beside his brother Kamose at Thebes. Afterward, Ahhotep I was considered divine, and a cult was established to honor her. She was revered in Egypt for many years after her death. **See also** Ahmose I; Hyksos; Kamose.

Ahmose I (ca. 1550–ca. 1525 B.C.)

Also known by his throne name of Nebpehty-re ("The Lord of Strength Is Re") or his Greek name Ahmosis I, Ahmose I ("The Moon Is Born") was the first king of the Eighteenth Dynasty and the founder of the New Kingdom. He was the son of Seventeenth Dynasty king Seqenenre Tao II and Queen Ahhotep, and he was preceded on the throne by his older brother King Kamose. Ahmose I was either five or ten years old, depending on which ancient records one reads, when Kamose was killed in a battle against a group of invaders known as the Hyksos. Ahmose I then assumed the throne, but because of his youth, his mother became his regent. King Ahmose I appears to have begun ruling independently at the age of sixteen and remained on the throne until his death at approximately age twenty-five. His principal wife during this time was his sister, Queen Ahmose-Nefertiry, but he also had at least two other wives, Inhapi and Kasmut.

Ahmose I focused his energies on expelling the Hyksos from his country, leading his army in military campaigns that eventually pushed the Hyksos forces back to their capital, Avaris, and laying siege to their city by both land and water. This siege was interrupted by a rebellion around Thebes instigated by supporters of the Hyksos, but within a short time Ahmose I had quelled the rebellion and returned to Avaris to renew his siege. Those holding the city finally surrendered in approximately 1532 B.C., and the Hyksos nobles fled to the city of Sharuhen in southern Palestine. Ahmose I pursued them there, laying siege to Sharuhen just as he had Avaris. Three years later, Sharuhen fell as well, and the Hyksos fled to Syrian territories. Historians estimate that all Hyksos had been expelled from Egypt by the sixteenth year of Ahmose I's reign.

Once the Hyksos had been expelled from Egypt, Ahmose I turned his attention to strengthening his government and its forces so that it would be less vulnerable to invasion. In doing so, he gave his relatives and most loyal supporters powerful positions in his administration, granting many of them land as well. He also reorganized the system for assessing and collecting taxes; rebuilt canals, dikes, and irrigation systems; and sponsored the building of many monuments and temples throughout his lands. To increase the supply of building materials, he encouraged trade with Crete, Byblos, and Nubia. To decorate many monuments, he acquired a great deal of lapis lazuli, a decorative stone, through trade with Asia.

As his country grew stronger, Ahmose I launched military campaigns that gained him more territory south into Nubia and the Levant (a term historically applied to the countries along the eastern Mediterranean shores and still sometimes used to denote Syria and Lebanon). After these successes, the king established administrative offices at Aswan and Elephantine in Nubia, giving one of his officials, Ahmose Sitayet, the responsibility of ruling the Aswan region and all Egyptian lands below the First Cataract of the Nile. This position, known as the Viceroy of Nubia (also called the King's Son of Kush), was continued by many of the king's successors.

In keeping with customs of the time, after he died Ahmose I was buried with objects that were believed to be necessary for his happiness in the Afterlife. These included a ceremonial battle-ax and the oldest known *shabti* (also known as a *shawabti* or *ushabti,* or "answerer"), which was a small figurine placed in a tomb for the purpose of answering for and serving the deceased during the journey to the Afterlife. After King Ahmose I's death, he and his mother were honored jointly with their own cult. The king was succeeded on the throne by his son Amenhotep I. **See also** Ahhotep I; Avaris; Hyksos; Kamose.

Ahmose II (Amasis; Amosis; Khnemibre) (?–ca. 526 B.C.)

The fifth king of the Twenty-sixth Dynasty, prior to ascending the throne Ahmose II was a popular general known as Amasis. He assumed the throne after defeating King Apries (also known as Wahibre) during a civil war in 570 B.C. As soon as he became king, Ahmose II worked to quell civil unrest. In particular, he gave foreigners living in Egypt more rights and spoke out against racism. He also allowed foreigners to establish temples dedicated to their own gods. In addition, Ahmose II built up trade between Egypt and various nations in the Mediterranean region, especially Greece. However, throughout his reign his influence on the public was apparently rivaled by the Divine Adoratrice of Amun, Princess Ankhesneferibre, who was the daughter of one of the king's predecessors, King Psamtik II. **See also** Psamtik II.

Ahmose Meryt-Amon (or Meritamun) (ca. 1536–ca. 1504 B.C.)

Ahmose Meryt-Amon was an Eighteenth Dynasty queen who was married in succession to two kings of Egypt: her brother, King Amenhotep I, and Tuthmosis I. Some scholars believe that Tuthmosis I was actually the queen's stepson (a son of Amenhotep I perhaps by a commoner named Senisonb). Ahmose Meryt-Amon herself had two children during her lifetime. The first, conceived with

Eighteenth Dynasty queen Ahmose Meryt-Amon, as depicted on her mummy case.

Amenhotep I, was a son who apparently died in infancy. The second, conceived with Tuthmosis I, was a daughter, Hatshepsut, who eventually ruled Egypt as queen-pharaoh.

Scholars know from tests on her mummified remains that Meryt-Amon died in her early thirties, although the exact cause of her death remains a mystery. From her remains experts can also tell that she suffered from scoliosis, which is a curvature of the spine, and arthritis—two conditions found in several other royal mummies as well, including that of King Ahmose I. In addition, archaeologists know that even though the queen's mummy was found at Deir el-Bahri (across the Nile River from the temples at Karnak), this was not her original resting place; records show that Meryt-Amon was reburied there during the Twentieth Dynasty after her tomb was robbed and her mummy damaged. **See also** Amenhotep I; Deir el-Bahri; Hatshepsut; Tuthmosis I.

Ahmose-Nefertiry (ca. 1570– ca. 1505 B.C.)

The daughter of Tao II and Queen Ahhotep, Eighteenth Dynasty queen Ahmose-Nefertiry was the wife and most likely also the sister of King Ahmose I, and probably the wife of his predecessor, King Kamose, as well. She served as regent to her son Amenhotep I until he was old enough to assume the throne, probably when he turned sixteen. In both positions—wife to one king and regent to another—Queen Ahmose-Nefertiry was one of the most influential women of the New Kingdom.

In particular, the queen worked closely with King Ahmose I to rebuild Egypt after the defeat of the Hyksos, invaders from the east who had controlled northern Egypt for years. In return for her help, the king created a new title specifically for her: God's Wife of Amun, which came with lands and political power. Associated with the Temple of Amun at Karnak in the city of Thebes, this position also came with religious duties, such as making offerings to the gods and participating in certain rituals to honor the god Amun and his role in maintaining the world. Eventually, Ahmose-Nefertiry herself became an object of worship, revered along with her son in religious ceremonies.

After the queen's death, a cult was established in her honor at Thebes. It remained prominent there for many years, particularly among artisans who built and decorated temples because in life Ahmose-Nefertiry had been a great supporter of the arts. In fact, for years the queen was revered as the patron of necropolis workers throughout all of Egypt. Ahmose-Nefertiry's mortuary temple was on the west bank of the Nile near the entrance to the Valley of the Kings. Archaeologists suspect that it was intended to house the mummies of Ahmose-Nefertiry and Amenhotep I alone, even though the queen had another son and four daughters as well.

However, no mummies have been found in this structure.

Another legacy of the queen is a stela at Karnak that shows her with Ahmose I, and her name is mentioned in many inscriptions on other monuments. Some of these monuments date from the reign of Ahmose I, others from the reign of his successor, Amenhotep I. It appears that Ahmose-Nefertiry continued to be honored long after her death.

In 1881, archaeologists discovered Ahmose-Nefertiry's mummy in another tomb in the Valley of the Kings that was part of a royal cache of New Kingdom coffins that priests had relocated in approximately 1000 B.C. to protect the mummies from tomb robbers. Ahmose-Nefertiry's coffin still bore a gilded likeness of her face, although because her mummy had been improperly reembalmed prior to being reinterred, when it was unwrapped, it gave off a terrible odor and some of its blackened flesh dissolved. **See also** Ahhotep I; Ahmose I; Amenhotep I; caches, royal.

Ahmose Pen-Nekhebet (Pennekheb) (ca. 1550– ca. 1525 B.C.)

Ahmose Pen-Nekhebet was a soldier of noble birth who served in the armies of three pharaohs, Ahmose I, Ahmose II, and Amenhotep I, and the Queen-Pharaoh Hatshepsut at the beginning of the Eighteenth Dynasty. Under Ahmose I, he fought the Hyksos and might have been present when their capital city, Avaris, was captured by the Egyptians. He also campaigned with Ahmose I in Palestine and Syria. Under Amosis and Amenhotep I, Ahmose Pen-Nekhebet fought in Nubia. Inscriptions in his rock tomb at el-Kab, near King Ahmose I's tomb, also tell of a military campaign for Hatshepsut. These and other inscriptions there have provided historians with valuable information about how military campaigns were conducted during the Eighteenth Dynasty. In the final years of his life, Ahmose Pen-Nekhebet served as tutor to Hatshepsut's daughter Neferure. **See also** Ahmose I; Ahmose II; Amenhotep I; Hatshepsut; Hyksos.

Ahmose Son of Abana (dates unknown)

An Eighteenth Dynasty nobleman and military hero from the Upper Egyptian city of el-Kab, Ahmose Son of Abana (who is commonly referred to in this way to distinguish him from King Ahmose I), was most active around approximately 1540 B.C. He served in the armies of Kings Tao II, Ahmose I, and Tuthmosis I and fought in several important campaigns against foreign invaders from the east known as Hyksos. Although he was a soldier, he spent much of his time on the Nile River aboard a boat that was both a transport ship and a warship. During one battle, he leaped into the Nile to capture an enemy soldier, thereby earning himself the Gold of Valor, an award for bravery. He received this award seven times during his career, as well as grants of land near his hometown of el-Kab and several slaves taken in battle.

Ahmose Son of Abana was also present during the siege of Avaris, the Hyksos stronghold in Egypt, and at Sharuhen in Palestine, to which the Hyksos nobles fled after being expelled from Egypt. In addition, he sailed south of the Second Cataract of the Nile with King Amenhotep I (the son and heir of King Ahmose I) against the Kushites of Nubia. After this battle, Ahmose Son of Abana was named Warrior of the Ruler, one of the highest military ranks. Later, he sailed farther south with King Tuthmosis I in yet another campaign against the Nubians. This time, Ahmose Son of Abana commanded the ship's crew while helping the king bring back the bodies of several deceased Nubian chiefs.

Ahmose Son of Abana provides details of his military campaigns in inscriptions and painted reliefs on the walls of his tomb in the limestone cliffs of el-Kab. His first-person account of his experiences has given modern historians many insights into the workings of Eighteenth Dynasty military forces. **See also** Ahmose I; military; Tao II; Tuthmosis I.

akh

According to ancient Egyptian beliefs regarding the Afterlife, the *akh* is a form of the spirit that survives after death, along with two other forms called the *ba* and the *ka*. The *akh* is a luminous spirit capable of interacting with the living. Symbolized by the figure of a mummy, the *akh* was believed to be formed upon the moment of death, and afterward it allowed the deceased to communicate with loved ones and perhaps intercede in events on their behalf. **See also** Afterlife; *ba; ka;* religion.

Akhenaten (ca. 1369– ca. 1336 B.C.)

Akhenaten, or "He Who Serves Aten," was the name that King Amenhotep IV of the Eighteenth Dynasty took when he decided to adopt the deity Aten as the only true god. This decision was so unpopular that when Akhenaten died, his name was eradicated from many monuments by his former subjects, who were angered over his decision to set aside Egypt's traditional gods. **See also** Amenhotep IV; Aten.

Akhmim

Called Ipu or Khent-min by the ancient Egyptians and Panopolis or Khemmis (from which its modern name was derived) by the Greeks, the town of Akhmim on the east bank of the Nile River was once the capital city of the ninth nome (an administrative district) of Upper Egypt and a cult center dedicated to Min, a god of travel and fertility. Tait, a goddess of linen weaving, was worshiped there as well.

Only the necropolis (cemetery and worship) area of the once-thriving ancient capital remains in modern times; most of the temples and other buildings from this period have been destroyed, apparently by people in later times seeking building materials. However, ruins of an Eighteenth Dynasty temple still exist, and in 1981 archaeologists also discovered one corner of a temple from Greco-Roman times, apparently dedicated to Min, in the area. Nearby were two fallen colossal statues carved from limestone, one of King Ramses II and the other of Queen Ahmose Meryt-Amon, which were subsequently restored to their original condition. Archaeologists have also discovered the ruins of a rock chapel dedicated to Min in nearby el-Salamuni, a site that is often considered part of Akhmim. According to an inscription at this site, the chapel was built by the high priest of Min, Nakhtmin, during the Eighteenth Dynasty reign of Ay. **See also** Ahmose Meryt-Amon; Min; Ramses II.

Alexander the Great (Alexander III) (356–323 B.C.)

The son of King Philip II of Macedonia, Alexander the Great (also known as Alexander III) became the ruler of Upper and Lower Egypt in 332 B.C. when the Persians, who were controlling Egypt at that time, surrendered the country to him. The Egyptians were pleased about this event, because they had disliked their Persian overlords and considered Alexander to be the son of the god Amun. Alexander encouraged this view, saying that the gods had chosen him to rule Egypt just as they had chosen Egyptian kings in the past. Paintings from the period typically depict Alexander wearing a set of horns associated with Amun. Alexander was crowned at Memphis but decided to build a new city, Alexandria,

on the Mediterranean Sea to function as his capital. He also provided the funds to build temples at Karnak and Luxor. However, Alexander died before his new city and temples could be finished, succumbing from a fever while on a military campaign in Babylon in June 323 B.C. His body is now housed in a mausoleum in Alexandria. **See also** Alexandria; Ptolemaic kings.

Alexandria

Located where the Nile River empties into the eastern Mediterranean Sea, the city of Alexandria was Egypt's administrative and trading center under the Ptolemaic kings. It was founded on the site of the ancient Egyptian town of Raqote (which was destroyed in the process) by King Alexander III of Macedonia, also known as Alexander the Great, in approximately 331 or 332 B.C. However, Alexander died before his new city was finished.

Upon its completion, Alexandria had two harbors and a lighthouse, the Heptastadium, whose base connected the island of Pharos to the mainland. Alexandria's most important buildings included a museum, a library, a palace, a necropolis, and a temple known as the Serapaeum, built by King Ptolemy III to honor the god Serapis (a god who embodied several Greek and Egyptian gods but was primarily a god of healing). Egyptologists believe that the library was designed by King Ptolemy I but was built by Ptolemy II, who filled it with Greek, Egyptian, and Near Eastern literature. Historical records indicate that the library once held approximately nine hundred thousand manuscripts of different types, including seventy thousand papyrus scrolls. However, the library was destroyed in a fire during the time of Roman emperor Julius Caesar, and although the Romans immediately restocked the library, many irreplaceable texts were lost. By this time, the museum had become a center for scientific research and intellectual discussion. Many great Greek and Roman scholars worked there, including the mathematician Euclid, who established the principles of geometry.

Despite Greek dominance in the city, remnants of the ancient Egyptian culture remained, as evidenced by the fact that Alexandria's necropolis has many first- and second-century catacombs and tombs containing both Greek and Egyptian paintings, reliefs, and statues. However, the Egyptians were far outnumbered by Greeks and other foreigners and confined themselves primarily to two sections of the city, the island of Pharos and a district called Rhakotis.

The lighthouse that linked Pharos to the mainland was one of the most sophisticated structures in Alexandria. Over three hundred feet tall, its mirrors reflected the light from a huge fire at its base up to its top so that the light could be seen far out to sea. Eventually, however, the lighthouse tower fell to ruins. There is also evidence that at some point after the Greco-Roman Period the waters of the Mediterranean rose and covered part of the ancient city. In the 1990s, archaeologists found numerous ruins on the seafloor off the coast of Alexandria, including thousands of columns and a variety of statues and obelisks. **See also** Alexander the Great; Ptolemaic kings.

Amarna (Akhetaten)

The modern city of Tell el-Amarna is typically called simply Amarna by Egyptologists. Located in Middle Egypt just north of Asyut beside a bay on the east bank of the Nile River, the city is best known for a type of artwork now called Amarna art, which was produced during the Eighteenth Dynasty and was a radical departure from previous artistic styles in Egypt. Specifically, whereas artwork of previous periods had depicted members of the royal family as perfect physical specimens, Amarna art depicted them realistically, including so many physical deformities that some modern scholars have labeled the representations caricatures. For example, in one painting, the king Akhenaten is shown with an extremely bloated belly and arms as thin as sticks. Amarna art also features realistic depictions of birds, flowers, animals, and other natural elements. Perhaps its most famous piece of art, however, is a realistic painted bust of Queen Nefertiti, which was discovered by archaeologist Ludwig Borchardt.

The city of Amarna was built by Eighteenth Dynasty king Akhenaten (originally known as Amenhotep IV) to honor a sun god, Aten, whom the king believed surpassed all other gods. Akhenaten called his new city Akhetaten, or the "Horizon of Aten," perhaps because it offered a view of a flat horizon across the desert. Egyptologists speculate that Akhenaten chose to build Akhetaten in large part because people in the city of Thebes, the Egyptian capital when he assumed the throne, did not approve of his worship of Aten; in fact, there is evidence that residents of Akhetaten secretly worshiped other gods (particularly Bes and Taweret) as well.

Just east of Akhetaten are the remains of a village that housed the workers who constructed the city. It once had approximately seventy-four houses, and the many personal items, artwork, and other artifacts the various workers left behind have allowed archaeologists to learn the names and occupations of the inhabitants of various homes. For example, one house belonged to a sculptor named Thutmose and another to a vizier named Nakht.

In addition to homes, the town had studios and workshops for various craftspeople as well as government buildings. According to records found at the site, during the construction of Akhetaten, its workers lived in their village only on their two consecutive days off. Otherwise—for eight days straight—they lived in huts at the building site.

When it was completed, Akhetaten contained private residences for both rich and poor, administrative buildings, palaces, temples, and other structures constructed of brick, wood, and stone. There were also agricultural lands around the city that archaeologists have estimated could have supported a population of forty-five thousand. However, most believe that the city held only thirty thousand at its peak.

In designing the city, royal architects grouped most of the temples at its center, with the largest being the Per-Aten-em-Akhetaten, or Temple of the Aten in Akhetaten. Near the city's center was a secular building that archaeologists refer to as the Great Palace, which included paintings of scenes from Egyptian life. Despite its name, the Great Palace was not the king's residence but a state building with rooms for official business and living quarters for the king's advisers and courtiers; the king's residence was across the road from this structure. Another set of structures, apparently with a religious purpose, was a complex known as the Maru-Aten. Located at the south end of the city, it also had an artificial lake and island.

The city also had monuments with inscriptions explaining Akhenaten's purpose in building the city (to glorify Aten) as well as numerous tombs, including Akhenaten's and others for some of his retainers. However, archaeologists do not know how many of these tombs were actually used because most of their contents are missing. In fact, few buildings of Akhetaten survive today, largely because the Egyptians destroyed them following Akhenaten's death. The king's subjects so disliked him and his god that they defaced the king's monuments and buildings throughout Egypt and abandoned

Akhetaten even though it had been in use for only fifteen years.

A few years later, during the reign of Ramses II, the city was further damaged when the king dismantled its buildings and used the materials to build Hermopolis, a city across the river from Amarna. Amarna was then forgotten until the 1880s, when it was rediscovered by archaeologists excavating a collection of clay tablets found in an unoccupied area of Tell el-Amarna. Known as the Amarna Letters, these tablets provided details about Amarna that led archaeologists to begin uncovering the ancient city. **See also** Amarna Letters; Amenhotep IV.

Amarna Letters

The Amarna Letters are a collection of more than three hundred ancient Egyptian clay tablets with cuneiform writing on them. Archaeologists excavating the location where the tablets were found soon uncovered a building that they named the Record Office and learned that it was part of an ancient, long-forgotten city named Amarna. Had the Amarna Letters not been discovered, archaeologists still might not know that Akhetaten (or Eighteenth Dynasty king Akhenaten also known as Amenhotep IV, who built the city) ever existed.

Scholars who have studied the content of the Amarna Letters say they comprise an ongoing correspondence between the Egyptian royal family and the family of the rulers of Mitanni (also known as Naharin), a country across the Euphrates River from Syria. The two families had been united earlier when King Tuthmosis IV married a daughter of the Mitanni ruler. Another king, Amenhotep II, married Mitanni princesses as well, and apparently the two royal families remained close for quite some time thereafter, because some of the Amarna Letters clearly refer to the death of Tuthmosis IV's successor, Amenhotep III. Other of the Amarna Letters include diplomatic correspondence between Egypt's kings—Amenhotep III, Akhenaten, and a subsequent king, Tutankhamun—and the rulers of Palestine, Syria, Mesopotamia, and other lands.

The discovery of the Amarna Letters attracted several archaeologists to the area. The first was Urbain Bouriant (1849–1903) who wrote a book called *Two Days' Excavation at Tell el Amarna* to describe his excavation at the site. In 1891–1892, British archaeologist Sir William Matthew Flinders Petrie oversaw another excavation; a team of German archaeologists in 1911–1912 did further work, followed by German archaeologist Ludwig Borchardt (1863–1938) in 1913–1914. Several American archaeologists dug there during the late 1970s and early 1980s, and work by archaeologists of various nationalities continues. **See also** Amenhotep IV; Petrie, William Matthew Flinders.

Amenemhab (Amenemheb) (ca. 1479–ca. 1400 B.C.)

Amenemhab was an Eighteenth Dynasty army officer whose tomb in Thebes features mortuary reliefs depicting battles he fought. From these scenes, Egyptologists have learned much about the military campaigns of King Tuthmosis III, whom Amenemhab served. Amenemhab also went hunting with Tuthmosis III and his son and successor, Amenhotep II, for whom he fought as well. Ancient Egyptian tomb writings suggest that Amenemhab saved the king from an elephant attack, although Egyptologists disagree on whether the king referenced was Tuthmosis III or Amenhotep II. **See also** Amenhotep II; Tuthmosis III.

Amenemhet I (Sehetepibre) (ca. 2002–ca. 1956 B.C.)

Amenemhet I, the first king of the Twelfth Dynasty, was one of Egypt's most successful kings, in large part because during his approximately thirty-year reign he reorganized his government to increase his control over his administrators. He also launched several successful military campaigns to subdue the people of Sinai, began building fortresses and garrisons all along Egypt's east and west borders, and built a fortress and a trading post to the south in Nubia. Amenemhet I moved Egypt's capital from Memphis to what is now the city of el-Lisht because it was centrally located between Upper and Lower Egypt. He named his new capital Itj-tawy, or "The Seizer of the Two Lands," to reflect the high level of control he had over both parts of Egypt.

Despite his firm grip on the throne, Amenemhet I was the first king to share the throne with his heir in a coregency prior to his death. His coregency with his son, Senwosret I, lasted ten years, during which Senwosret I was a military commander in charge of maintaining Egypt's borders. In addition to this prince, who was the child of Amenemhet I's principal wife, Nefrutotenen, the king had at least three daughters, Nyetneb, Nenseb-Djebet, and Nefrusheri. Amenemhet I had numerous wives, including Sit-Hathor, Sobeknefru, and Dedyet (who was also his sister).

Most Egyptologists believe that Amenemhet I succeeded to the throne not by birth but because he was the vizier of his predecessor, King Montuhotep IV, who probably named him as heir. Under this scenario, Amenemhet I would have assumed the throne after the king's death. However, some Egyptologists believe that Amenemhet usurped the throne, either before or after Montuhotep's death, perhaps even killing the king in the process. Amenemhet I himself was later killed, probably as a result of an assassination plot hatched by the members of his large harem.

Amenemhet I left behind a mortuary pyramid at el-Lisht, which subsequently became the site of other royal burials. The pyramid had a limestone core made of blocks salvaged from damaged Old Kingdom buildings elsewhere, and an exterior of white limestone quarried at Tura. Over time, the chambers at the lowest levels of this pyramid suffered from groundwater seepage, filling with water. As a result, nobody has been able to enter the burial chambers to see whether the king's funerary goods are still present.

Amenemhet I left a significant religious legacy by moving Egypt away from the worship of Mont, a god of war, as its primary deity, and instead promoting Amun, a solar deity, as Egypt's chief god. After the king's death, this emphasis on Amun worship strengthened; eventually the Temple of Amun became the wealthiest temple in Egypt and the position of High Priest of Amun became the most powerful priesthood. Amenemhet I is also famous among Egyptologists for inspiring two literary works in which he is the central figure: *Amenemhet's Instructions,* in which after his death he tells his son how to be a good king, and *The Tale of Sinuhe,* which mentions a failed assassination plot against the king. Some scholars believe that Amenemhet I wrote *Amenemhet's Instructions,* perhaps as part of a deathbed will, while others think this work was written by someone else in the king's name. **See also** *Amenemhet's Instructions;* Amun; el-Lisht; *Sinuhe, The Tale of.*

Amenemhet II (Nubkaure) (ca. 1924–ca. 1877 B.C.)

Twelfth Dynasty king Amenemhet II reigned for at least thirty-four years, during which he apparently encouraged diplomatic and trade relations with the people in the Levant (a region along the eastern Mediterranean that includes modern Lebanon and Israel), Babylonia, Mesopotamia, and elsewhere. Evidence for such trade comes from an archaeological discovery called the "Treasure of Tod," a collection of valuable goods from

various foreign lands that were found in a temple built by Amenemhet II at Tod, just south of Luxor.

Amenemhet II himself went on a trading expedition along the Red Sea in the twenty-eighth year of his reign. He also went on a military expedition to Nubia during his first three years on the throne. Otherwise, Amenemhet II seems to have remained close to home. However, he did visit construction sites within Egypt, having initiated many building and engineering projects. Perhaps the most significant was the enlargement of a tributary called the Bahr Yusef that brought water to the Faiyum (a desert oasis) from the Nile River. Amenemhet II built his pyramid near the site of this project, at Dashur, where he was entombed following his death.

Amenemhet II's successor to the throne was his son, Senwosret II, by his principal wife, Mereyet. Amenemhet II had at least one other wife, Kemanub, as well as six daughters: Ata, Atuart, Khnumt, Sit-Hathor, Sit-Hathor Hormeret, and Sit-Hathor Meryt. **See also** Dashur; Faiyum; Senwosret I; Senwosret II.

Amenemhet III (Nimaatre) (ca. 1844–ca. 1786 B.C.)

The son of King Senwosret III and Queen Sebekshedty-Neferu, King Amenemhet III of the Twelfth Dynasty reigned for at least forty-five years, although for the first few years he coruled with his father. During his time alone on the throne, Amenemhet III launched numerous building projects, and in order to have enough materials for them he established new quarries in Egypt and more heavily exploited existing ones. In addition, he sent workers to the Sinai to mine copper and turquoise. According to more than fifty inscriptions cut into rocks at various Sinai locations, the king's workers mined the region from the second year of his reign to its end. In return, he built houses for the workers and protected them against the hostile Bedouin tribesmen who lived in the region.

Perhaps the most interesting of Amenemhet III's building projects was the Labyrinth, located at Hawara. Made of mud brick cased in limestone, it received its name from classical authors like Herodotus and Strabo, who described it as a two-story complex (with the first floor underground) of more than three thousand rooms joined by a maze of corridors. Herodotus also reported that crocodiles were entombed in certain rooms in honor of the crocodile god Sobek. By the time archaeologist William Matthew Flinders Petrie excavated the site in 1888–1889, the structure had become so eroded that he doubted such descriptions were accurate, but subsequent investigation showed that the Labyrinth had indeed once been large, perhaps 1,000 by 800 feet or larger, and the mummified remains of crocodiles were found at the site. Because of the mummified crocodiles, some archaeologists have labeled the Labyrinth a temple complex or cult center dedicated to Sobek. Others, however, believe it was a mortuary complex, a palace, or an administrative center.

Amenemhet III also built a pyramid at Hawara, as well as one at nearby Dashur. The pyramid at Hawara had an underground burial chamber carved from a block of quartzite that was then lowered into the earth. The king's sarcophagus, also made of quartzite, rested inside, beside a similar sarcophagus made for his daughter Neferu-Ptah. Even though a nearly fifty-ton slab of rock covered this chamber, the royal pair's remains and the chamber itself were damaged by tomb robbers.

Amenemhet III is also noted for his contribution to Egyptian agriculture. He constructed a canal in the Faiyum that directed the floodwaters of the Nile River into Lake Moeris. By regulating the flow of these and other waters in the area, the king was able to drain marshes and reclaim over 150,000 acres of the Faiyum. As a result, Egypt gained more agricultural land and the country prospered from it.

Amenemhet III was able to accomplish such ambitious projects because his reign was peaceful. The king apparently did not have to undertake any military actions except for a brief expedition south to the Third Cataract of the Nile River, which was primarily a show of force to strengthen Egypt's hold on its southern lands. **See also** Faiyum; Hawara; Herodotus; Strabo.

Amenemhet IV (Maakherure) (?–ca. 1777 B.C.)

Twelfth Dynasty king Amenemhet IV probably became the ruler of Egypt fairly late in his life and reigned less than ten years. Egyptologists know little about Amenemhet IV's rule, even though he left several monuments behind, including a temple in the Faiyum dedicated to the goddess Renenet, a goddess of good fortune. However, they suspect that part of the king's reign might have been shared with his predecessor Amenemhet III, whom most Egyptologists suspect was Amenemhet IV's father. Amenemhet IV himself had no son, so when he died, his sister Sobeknefru (also known as Nefru-Sobek) assumed the throne. Some Egyptologists, however, believe that Queen Sobeknefru was Amenemhet IV's regent before his death and simply continued ruling after his death; under this scenario, Amenemhet IV would have been a young boy rather than an old man when he became king. **See also** Amenemhet III; Faiyum.

Amenemhet's Instructions (The Instructions of King Amenemhet I; Testament of Amenemhet)

Amenemhet's Instructions is a Twelfth Dynasty literary text of approximately eighty-eight lines of verse addressed to Senwosret I, the son and heir of King

Amenemhet I. The authorship of this work is a matter of controversy. Some Egyptologists believe that King Amenemhet I wrote *Amenemhet's Instructions* as a last will and testament, while others believe that some as yet unidentified person in court wrote the verse to commemorate the king after his death and perhaps guide Senwosret I in his new role as king.

In either case, the work is in the form of a message sent by the king after his death to his son, advising him on how to be an effective king. In this regard, it is an important document for modern scholars, because it was apparently the first literary work in the ancient world to outline the duties and responsibilities of a king. Specifically, the text admonishes Senwosret I to think about and try to meet the needs of his subjects while not allowing them to become too close to him personally, even though this destined the king to lead a lonely life of self-sacrifice. Because of the didactic tone of *Amenemhet's Instructions,* schoolboys of the Ramessid Period were required to copy it over and over, both to learn its content and to master writing and grammar. *Amenemhet's Instructions* is just one of a number of texts used for these purposes. Egyptologists have found copies of *Amenemhet's Instructions* in two papyri, the Milligan Papyrus and the Papyrus Sallier II.

Another important aspect of *Amenemhet's Instructions* is the fact that it mentions the possibility of a king being assassinated, describing an attempt on Amenemhet I's life. The text not only suggests that a king must be vigilant to prevent such attacks but also portrays the royal palace as a place of treachery. The forcefulness of this description has led many Egyptologists to believe that Amenemhet I feared for his life during the latter part of his reign and perhaps was assassinated. **See also** admonitions and instructions; Amenemhet I; Senwosret I.

Amenhirkhepshef (Amon-Hir Khopsef) (?–ca. 1153 B.C.)

A Twentieth Dynasty prince, Amenhirkhepshef, was the son of Ramses II. He was heir to the throne until he died suddenly, although how old he was is uncertain. Some scholars believe that the prince died when he was quite young, while others think that he served in his father's military campaigns and therefore probably died from battle wounds. Regardless of how he died, Amenhirkhepshef is known today primarily for his tomb in the Valley of the Queens, which contains vivid paintings with subject matter typical of the artwork of the Ramessid period. In one painting, the prince is led by his father to the god Ptah and two sons of the god Horus, Amset and Duamutef, who then lead father and son before the goddess Isis. In another painting, father and son are led to the goddess Hathor, then to Horus's other two sons, Hapy and Qebsennuf, and then to the god Shu and the goddess Nephthys. **See also** Ramessid Period; Ramses II; Valley of the Queens.

Amenhotep I (Amenophis I; Djeserkare) (ca. 1549– ca. 1504 B.C.)

Later known as Amenophis I by the Greeks, Amenhotep ("Amun Is Satisfied") I was an Eighteenth Dynasty king who apparently ruled for nearly thirty years. He was the son of King Ahmose I and Queen Ahmose-Nefertiry, and apparently he only became king because his older brother, Ahmose Sipar, died before he could assume the throne.

Although there are few records related to his reign, Amenhotep I's years on the throne seem to have been quite successful, particularly in regard to strengthening Egypt militarily. The king moved his forces into new regions in Nubia, pushing south to the Third Cataract, and later dealt with a Nubian uprising swiftly and fiercely. At the same time, he built and repaired strongholds along the western borders when a Libyan uprising twice threatened to destabilize the region. He was equally aggressive in the north and east, fortifying his lands to make foreign invasions far less likely to succeed.

Amenhotep I was greatly concerned with his country's architectural legacy as well. He restored many of his predecessors' monuments, including the tomb of Eleventh Dynasty king Montuhotep II at Deir el-Bahri, as well as a series of shrines along the Nile River that were dedicated to various deities. He also built many new structures, such as the temple complex in Karnak (a religious center associated with the city of Thebes), and was the first king to build his mortuary temple in a place separate from his tomb. Unfortunately, many of these buildings were destroyed by succeeding kings in need of building materials for their own projects.

Amenhotep I had at least two wives, Ahhotep II, who was also his sister, and Ahmose Meryt-Amon. Ahhotep II gave Amenhotep I a son, Amunemhet, but the boy lived only a short time. Apparently the king had no other children, since he named his senior military commander, Tuthmosis I, as his heir.

When Amenhotep I died, he was declared a god by the Priests of Amun and then placed in a tomb that has never been positively identified. Archaeologists suspect, though, that it might have been a tomb discovered at Dra Abu el-Naga (a Theban burial town) or another uncovered in the Valley of the Kings. In either case, Amenhotep I's mummy was moved sometime after the reign of Ramses IX. Egyptologists know this because the Abbott Papyrus, a report on an inspection of royal tombs that was conducted during that reign, lists Amenhotep I's tomb as being undisturbed, yet the king's remains were found in 1881 among a cache of royal mummies in the Valley of the Kings. One of the best-preserved mummies ever found, its flower-covered wrappings included the remains of a wasp that was accidentally trapped there. By analyzing his mummy, archaeologists determined that Amenhotep I died at approximately the age of forty-five, but they are uncertain as to the cause of his death. **See also** Abbott Papyrus; caches, royal; Ramses IX; Valley of the Kings.

Amenhotep II (Amenophis II) (ca. 1445–ca. 1400 B.C.)

The son of King Tuthmosis III and Queen Meryt-Re Hatshepsut, Amenhotep ("Amun Is Satisfied") II was an active Eighteenth Dynasty king whose approximately twenty-seven-year reign was marked by a number of military campaigns. He was highly skilled in all activities related to war, such as archery (he could shoot an arrow accurately both on foot and on horseback), and he so enjoyed battle that he let out war whoops whenever he was about to engage in any kind of combat. As a young man, he was a passionate sportsman and horseman. In fact, he was the first king to own horses throughout his life, and he eventually became an expert in horse breeding.

Amenhotep II became coruler of Egypt during the last few years of his father's reign. During that time, he was in charge of the country's naval base at Peru-Nefer, at the same time managing extensive estates in nearby Memphis. Two years after Amenhotep II began ruling alone, he was faced with an uprising in Syria that threatened Egyptian holdings there. Amenhotep II immediately launched a military campaign to quell the uprising, leading troops into Palestine and across the Orontes and Euphrates Rivers into Syria. After much fighting, Amenhotep II's forces succeeded in capturing seven Syrian princes, whom he brought back to Egypt for beheading as part of a religious ceremony in the Temple of Amun at Karnak.

The following year, according to stelae he left on Elephantine Island and at Amada, he killed seven more princes, this time during a similar campaign in Nubia. The bodies of six of these princes were brought down the Nile River tied to the prow of Amenhotep II's ship, then displayed at a temple in Thebes; the body of the seventh prince was left in Nubia, as a warning to others who might rise up against the king. Six years later, Amenhotep II again waged war, quelling uprisings in Palestine. Yet this king had less fear of foreigners than did his predecessors. He allowed Syrians to come into Egypt to work as craftsmen or engage in trade, whereas prior to this time foreigners had been generally kept out.

The remainder of Amenhotep II's reign was apparently without conflict, the king having exerted enough force initially to discourage further rebellion. However, a minority view among Egyptologists is that Amenhotep II dealt with another uprising in Nubia shortly before his death.

Amenhotep II was only forty-five when he died, and he was entombed in the Valley of the Kings. Sometime later, the mummies of several other kings were placed in the same tomb. This royal cache, which was uncovered by archaeologist Victor Loret in 1898, was the result of a Twenty-first Dynasty attempt to protect the mummies from tomb robbers. An analysis of Amenhotep II's mummy has shown that the cause of death was most likely a massive systemic bacterial infection, probably originating within the king's severely decayed teeth.

Amenhotep II left behind two temples dedicated to Amun and other deities. One of these temples was at Aswan on Elephantine Island, and the other was at Amada in Nubia; both had been begun by the king's father. Amenhotep II also ordered the creation of a statue that depicts the king drinking from the udder of Hathor the cow goddess. Now one of the most famous works of art from ancient Egypt, this statue is currently in the Cairo Museum. **See also** caches, royal; Hathor; Tuthmosis III.

Amenhotep III (ca. 1407–ca. 1352 B.C.)

Amenhotep ("Amun Is Satisfied") III, the ninth king of the Eighteenth Dynasty, enjoyed a reign of approximately forty years. During this time, Egypt was at peace except for some minor rebellions in Nubia. Consequently, the king was free to engage in numerous building projects. In particular, he ordered the restoration of several important temples, although on some occasions he dismantled other structures to acquire the necessary building materials. For example, stones from shrines built by Amenhotep I and Senwosret I have been found in the foundations of temple pylons at Karnak. Amenhotep III spent years restoring and adding to Karnak's structures. Among his additions were a hypostyle hall and numerous shrines.

Amenhotep III also began construction on a temple complex at Luxor. Although later kings, including Ramses II, Nectanebo II, and Alexander the Great, each added to this complex, it still provides considerable information about Amenhotep III. For example, one of the sections built by Amenhotep III includes numerous sphinxes with faces in the king's likeness. In addition, the temple complex includes a room dedicated to the god Amun in which wall scenes depict the king's birth. One of these scenes shows the creation god Khnum fashioning the king and his *ka* (spirit) on a potter's wheel; another shows the god Amun nursing Amenhotep III.

Amenhotep III also built a large palace on the western bank of the Nile River at Thebes, his capital city. The palace had its own lake, which was constructed over a period of just fifteen days on orders of the king, that was used both for pleasure boating and for religious ceremonies featuring the ceremonial boat of the sun god Aten. The palace was also the residence of the king's harem, which included his principal wife, Queen Tiy, and several foreign princesses, including at least two from Mitanni and one from Babylonia.

Amenhotep III took a large number of wives because he wanted to have as many sons as possible. However, it appears that he only ended up with two sons, one who succeeded him as Amenhotep IV, and Merymose, who was sent to manage Egyptian lands in Kush (a region of Nubia) as its viceroy. Amenhotep III also had several daughters, including Ast, Hentmerheb, Hentaneb, Baketamon, Isis, and Sitamun. He married the latter two as soon as they reached maturity, at the urging of Queen Tiy. She supported his desire to have many male heirs to the throne, probably to secure her own position once her husband was dead.

Egyptologists believe that Queen Tiy had enormous influence over her husband, and it appears that toward the end of King Amenhotep III's life it was really she who was running the country, perhaps along with her brother Anen, who held many of the most prestigious titles in Egypt. Queen Tiy's name appears as the official signature on many royal documents of the period, including announcements of her husband's various marriages. In addition, it was Tiy who apparently arranged for the occasional distribution of commemorative scarabs (representations of beetles believed to be associated with protective magic, the Afterlife, and the sun god) to celebrate her husband's marriages and other successes.

One reason for the queen's heavy involvement in Egypt's affairs might have been King Amenhotep III's declining health. Records show that he was sickly for several years before his death, and at a *sed* festival he attended toward the end of his life, he asked a goddess of healing, Istar of

The towering sandstone Colossi of Memnon, located at Luxor, were just one of Amenhotep III's many building projects.

Nineveh, to ease his suffering. Amenhotep III was approximately fifty-five years old when he died, whereupon he was entombed in the Valley of the Kings. **See also** Anen; Karnak; Luxor; Tiy.

Amenhotep IV (Akhenaten) (ca. 1369–ca. 1336 B.C.)

An Eighteenth Dynasty king and the son of Amenhotep III, Amenhotep ("Amun Is Satisfied") IV changed his name to Akhenaten ("He Who Serves Aten") in the fifth year of his reign when he decided that the sun god Aten was superior to all other deities, even other sun gods. Egyptologists believe that Akhenaten's mother, Queen Tiy, influenced her son in this regard, since she had been involved with an Aten cult earlier. Akhenaten imposed the new religion on the rest of Egypt, shutting down temples to other gods and destroying their statues while building temples to Aten in his religious center and residential city of Thebes. When he encountered resistance among Theban priests, nobles, and administrators, he built a new city and moved his royal residence there, along with his secular capital, which was formerly in Memphis. Called Akhetaten, or the "Horizon of Aten," to honor his god, the king's new city (now called Tell el-Amarna or simply Amarna) became the center of Aten worship.

After the king's death Akhetaten was abandoned, as was Akhenaten's new religion, because despite the king's efforts Aten worship never became popular in Egypt. (In fact, there is evidence that even the king's workers in Akhetaten kept worshiping their old gods, although the king was surely unaware of this.) One reason for the new religion's unpopularity was the fact that Akhenaten tried to do away with not only Egypt's traditional gods but also long-held concepts regarding the Afterlife. Osiris, the god of the dead, was banned along with other deities, and with him went all customary

mortuary rituals. Moreover, the king decreed that he was in charge of the Afterlife as well as Egypt, and therefore he could keep all but his favorite subjects from enjoying eternal life. Consequently, most people refused to accept Akhenaten's new beliefs, and Egypt's priests continued to encourage rebellion against Aten worship.

Nonetheless, the religion might have continued if the king had had a forceful male heir to enforce his policies after his death. However, Akhenaten and his wife apparently had only daughters (as many as six by some accounts), and Akhenaten's successor, Smenkhkare, not only failed in attempts to promote Aten worship but lasted on the throne only a few months. Egyptologists disagree on how Smenkhkare was related to Akhenaten. Some believe he was a son not mentioned in records; others believe he was a brother or half-brother; still others think that "he" was really a "she," Akhenaten's wife Nefertiti, ruling under an assumed name. Support for the latter theory stems in part from the fact that Smenkhkare was apparently coruler with Akhenaten for approximately two years prior to the king's death, yet during this time the king appears to have lived the life of a recluse with only his immediate family nearby.

Also unclear is how and when Akhenaten died. At some point after the seventeenth year of his reign, he was apparently buried in a tomb at Akhetaten, but his mummy was later removed from there and has never been found. Some Egyptologists believe that Smenkhkare's successor, King Tutankhamun (who returned the country to its old religion), moved the mummy to the Valley of the Kings. Others believe that Egyptians who were angry with Akhenaten over his approach to religion destroyed the mummy, just as they destroyed most other traces of Akhenaten after his death. Indeed, this destruction was so effective that, until the mid–nineteenth century, when Egyptologist Karl Richard Lepsius uncovered references to Akhenaten in Amarna, scholars did not even know that a king of that name had ever existed. However, ancient records elsewhere in Egypt told of a king called "the Blasphemer"; today archaeologists know that this was the name used to refer to Akhenaten after his death. **See also** Amarna; Aten; Smenkhkare; Tiy.

Amenhotep, Son of Hapu (ca. 1480–ca. 1350 B.C.)

An Eighteenth Dynasty royal scribe, Amenhotep, Son of Hapu, was credited with authoring numerous proverbs and words of wisdom that brought him fame during his lifetime. He was apparently considered such a sage that people around the country sought him out for advice. Eventually, he was awarded the titles King's Scribe, Scribe of Recruits (which came with military duties), and Overseer of All Works of the King (which gave him responsibility over all architectural plans). Some Egyptologists believe that in the latter capacity he oversaw the construction of King Amenhotep III's pyramid. Ancient records suggest that Amenhotep, Son of Hapu, might also have been a priest at a temple at Athribis, where he apparently gave speeches. As a result of his prominence, when he died a cult was established to honor him, and by the Ptolemaic Period he was considered a god of healing and wisdom. **See also** Amenhotep III; Ptolemaic Period.

Amenmesses (Amunmesse; Menmire) (?–ca. 1200 B.C.)

A king of the Nineteenth Dynasty, Amenmesses assumed the throne by means still unknown. When his predecessor, King Merneptah, died in approximately 1203 B.C., the natural successor to the throne would have been the king's eldest son, Crown Prince Seti-Merneptah. Why Amen-

messes became king instead is a matter of dispute. Some modern scholars think that the crown prince died before he could assume the throne and that Amenmesses was Seti-Merneptah's younger brother and therefore the legitimate heir. Others believe that Seti-Merneptah was not dead but away in a foreign war when his father died and Amenmesses usurped the throne in his older brother's absence. Still others believe that Amenmesses did not succeed King Merneptah directly but reigned at some later time, perhaps usurping King Seti II between the third and fifth years of that king's reign. Such theories have support because the details of Amenmesses' reign are vague; his unfinished tomb in the Valley of the Kings was destroyed, and he apparently erected only one monument during his brief time on the throne.

Scholars disagree on what Amenmesses' relationship was to other members of the Nineteenth Dynasty. Specifically, although most scholars agree that Amenmesses had some kind of family tie to King Ramses II, they do not know what this tie was. The most prevalent theory is that Amenmesses was Ramses II's grandson, possibly through the woman who was most likely Amenmesses' mother, Queen Takhaet.

How Amenmesses' life ended is as much of a mystery as other aspects of his life. Because of King Amenmesses' brief reign and the fact that his tomb was unfinished at the time of his death, some historians have suggested that the king was murdered, possibly by the supporters of Seti-Merneptah. However, the mummy found in that tomb and suspected of being King Amenmesses' shows no evidence of foul play. Most scholars believe that one of two other mummies found in Amenmesses' tomb is that of Queen Takhaet. **See also** Merneptah; Ramses II; Seti II.

Amenmose

Several prominent ancient Egyptians share the name Amenmose: an Eighteenth Dynasty prince, a Nineteenth Dynasty scribe, a Nineteenth Dynasty vizier, and a Twenty-second Dynasty priest. Of these, the two Nineteenth Dynasty Amenmoses were the most influential during their lifetimes.

The Nineteenth Dynasty scribe called Amenmose (?–1213 B.C.), also known as Amenmessu, was designated the Royal Scribe of the Two Lands during the reign of Ramses II. Most scholars do not know how he achieved this position, but he was probably related to the royal family, given that his parents were the subjects of many statues. Figures of his mother, Mutemonet, were sometimes the focus of prayers and offerings intended to convince her spirit to intercede with the gods on the petitioners' behalf. A bust of his father, Pa-en-djerty, was found in Amenmose's tomb in the Theban necropolis.

The Nineteenth Dynasty vizier named Amenmose (?–1196 B.C.) served King Amenmesses. The vizier is known for having judged a legal case in which his own stepfather and fellow scribe, Neferhotep, was accused of some kind of wrongdoing by a rival, Paneb. Amenmose not only found in favor of his stepfather but later convinced King Amenmesses to remove Paneb from his job as foreman of the builders of the Theban necropolis.

The Eighteenth Dynasty prince Amenmose, son of King Tuthmosis I and Queen Ahmose Meryt-Amon, died before he could assume the throne, probably as a result of battle wounds; he was buried in a royal necropolis on the western shore of the Nile River at Thebes.

Amenmose the Twenty-second Dynasty priest (?–715 B.C.) was known for being a healer of snakebites, perhaps because he was priest of the snake goddess Serquet (also known as Selket). He was stationed in the temple at Deir el-Medina, where he treated many of the builders of the necropolis there. **See also** Ahmose Meryt-Amon; Ramses II; Tuthmosis I.

Amenpanufer (?–ca. 1108 B.C.)

A Twentieth Dynasty stone carver, Amenpanufer was put on trial during the reign of Ramses IX for robbing the tomb of Seventeenth Dynasty king Sobekemsaf II. Amenpanufer confessed to the crime during an investigation instigated by the mayor of eastern Thebes, Paser, who accused his rival Pawero, the mayor of western Thebes, of being involved in a widespread tomb-robbing ring along with other high-level government officials. As a result of this investigation, forty-five robbers, including Amenpanufer, were found guilty of various incidents of theft, but there has been no proof that a tomb-robbing ring existed. It is also unclear how Amenpanufer was punished for his crime; modern scholars are unsure whether his fate was impalement (the customary punishment for acts against the gods) or something less extreme. **See also** Paser; Ramses IX.

Amherst Papyrus

Discovered in the city of Thebes, a document known as the Amherst Papyrus has provided Egyptologists with information about tomb robbing in ancient Egypt. Specifically, it discusses a trial that took place during the Twentieth Dynasty in which a group of approximately forty-five robbers was convicted of violating tombs. A similar document, the Abbott Papyrus, contains information about the same event, but the two documents complement rather than duplicate each other. Whereas the Abbott Papyrus concentrates on the robbery investigation and the inspection of tombs, the Amherst Papyrus concentrates on the trial and its outcome. **See also** Abbott Papyrus; Paser.

amulets

Amulets were small objects that the Egyptians believed would magically protect the person carrying them in some specific way. Called *sa, meket,* or *nehet* in ancient Egyptian (all words related to the concept of protection), these objects were believed to be effective even after death. As a result they were often placed within a mummy's wrappings to protect it and its spirit from harm.

Amulets might be made of metal, wood, faience (a type of glazed pottery), glazed stone, terra-cotta, lapis lazuli, turquoise, or other semiprecious stones, or other materials such as shells or animal parts like claws or teeth. The type and degree of power exerted by an amulet were thought to vary according to its composition, shape, color, and markings. Certain amulets could protect against poor health, for example, while others were effective against famine or animal attacks. Frog-shaped amulets were believed to protect against infertility, and amulets shaped like body parts were believed to strengthen and protect those parts. Amulets with markings representing offerings to the gods, such as wine, were believed to bring prosperity. Those with symbols of power, such as representations of gods or crowns, were believed to enable the bearer to overcome danger or adversity. At the end of the New Kingdom, another type of amulet appeared as well: scraps of papyri with magical spells written on them, worn around the neck within a tiny tube hung on a cord. However, these amulets never replaced the traditional ones.

Among the symbols considered the most powerful were the Sacred Eye of Horus, the ankh, the scarab, and the *djed* pillar. Also known as the Wedjat, the Eye of Horus represented wholeness, contentment, and healing. The ankh represented life. The scarab, or dung beetle, was a symbol of creation, renewal, and the solar deity Re. The *djed* pillar, resembling a tree, was associated with the god Osiris and symbolized rebirth, strength, and stability. Amulets bearing such symbols usually had a general purpose, offering overall protection and good health. Oth-

ers, however, were designed for a specific need or problem. For example, a woman giving birth might have an amulet fashioned to look like the god Bes, who was believed to protect both mother and child during labor. To prevent miscarriage, a pregnant woman might carry a knot-shaped amulet called a *tyet,* associated with Isis, who was a goddess of magic, marriage, and fertility.

At one time, Egyptologists thought that amulets were carried openly on cords around their owners' necks. Now, however, most experts believe that amulets were hidden in clothing, with cords sometimes wrapped and knotted around them because knots were associated with magic. However, common amulet symbols, such as the ankh, often appeared openly on jewelry, furniture, and other personal items. **See also** ankh; jewelry; magic; scarab.

Amun (Amon; Amun-Re)

A solar deity, Amun was the principal god of the New Kingdom, worshiped throughout Egypt. Prior to that time the god was worshiped mainly in Thebes, but thanks to that city's use as the capital by a number of Egypt's kings, Amun worship received royal support that encouraged its spread. In fact, most New Kingdom rulers carried banners dedicated to Amun (or Amun-Re, the manifestation of the god associated with kingship) whenever they went to war, and whenever they won a battle, they lavished gifts and land on the priests of the Temple of Amun in Thebes. Consequently, the position of high priest of Amun was one of the most powerful in Egypt, by some estimates controlling 10 percent of Egypt's land, including 40 workshops, 400,000 animals, and 90,000 priests and workers.

Amun was also associated with the royal household through the position of Divine Wife of Amun, or Amun's Wife, which was established by King Ahmose I of the Eighteenth Dynasty to honor his queens Ahhotep and Ahmose-Nefertiry. With this position came wealth, property, and a role in various religious ceremonies dedicated to Amun at the god's temples at Karnak and Luxor, where Amun's Wife was seen as being symbolically married to the god. From this point on, it was customary for at least one wife of every king to hold the title, and beginning in the Twenty-first Dynasty, royal princesses might be named Amun's Wife as well.

Once Egypt's kings elevated Amun to a national god, his powers were elevated as well. Initially, he was just one of several equally important deities, but by the Twelfth Dynasty, inscriptions were referring to Amun as the king of all other gods. By the New Kingdom, Amun was said to be the creator of all other gods, having brought himself into being first, and by the end of this period, all other gods were called manifestations of Amun. In addi-

tion, Amun was thought to have destructive power, and according to the *Book of the Dead* he would one day decide to send the world into the watery void of the goddess Nun. After this event, only he and Osiris, chief god of the dead, would remain.

However, beliefs about Amun's form and his associations with other gods varied according to place. At Thebes, for example, the god was worshiped either alone or with his consort, a sky goddess called Mut (in the Fifth Dynasty, he was said to have another consort, Amaunet, as well), and his son, Khons, a lunar deity and god of healing. In various other places, Amun was worshiped as Amun-Min (a combination of the essences of Amun and the fertility god Min) or Amun-Re (combination of Amun and Re, the solar deity of Heliopolis), and Mut and Khons might not be mentioned. Similarly, depictions of Amun varied—

Columns at a temple of the god Amun. By the New Kingdom, Amun had risen to such prominence that he was known as the creator of the other gods.

sometimes he was a man with a double-feathered headdress, sometimes a goose (the Great Cackler), and sometimes a ram. The goose association was derived from the concept of Amun as creator, the one who laid and hatched the earth. The ram was associated with Re and with kings as a symbol of power and leadership. The Egyptians explained these differences in ideas about the god by saying that the true nature of Amun was unknowable.

In most Egyptian myths, however, Amun was depicted in human form as the god of the sun, traveling in a boat across the sky to create the passage of a day. Consequently, golden boats believed to belong to the god were featured prominently in Amun worship. One such vessel, called Amun's Bark (also known as Userhetamun, or "Mighty of Brow Is Amun"), was used as a floating temple in Thebes and traveled to stations along the Nile River during certain holidays. On the bark was a shrine with a statue of the god Amun inside. The bark was also taken from Karnak to Luxor and back again during a festival known as the Feast of Opet (a goddess who was the patroness of Thebes), and at other festivals it traversed a sacred lake. During the festival known as the Beautiful Feast of the Valley, the bark was taken to the Nile to carry the statue across the river to the western shore at Thebes, where it participated in various rituals and visited various tombs.

When King Amenhotep IV (also known as Akhenaten) ordered that all Amun worship be replaced with the worship of another solar god, Aten, such rituals ended. In order to enforce his decree, the king shut down all of Amun's temples. However, people continued to worship Amun in secret, and as soon as Amenhotep IV died, they returned to worshiping Amun openly. **See also** barks of the gods; Karnak; Luxor; Re.

Amunnakhte's Instructions

Found within a papyrus that modern scholars call the Chester Beatty Papyrus IV, the literary text now known as *Amunnakhte's Instructions* is a work in which a scribe, Pir Ankh, tells a young man about the opportunities afforded by being a scribe. From this and other records, Egyptologists know that the profession of scribe was considered a lofty one and therefore provided social as well as economic benefits. In addition, Pir Ankh, who was a scribe of an educational facility in Thebes called the House of Life, outlines the duties of a scribe, which include collecting taxes, keeping records, and overseeing court activities. For performing these duties, Pir Ankh explains, the scribe will always eat well, have nice clothing, and receive the respect of others. **See also** admonitions and instructions; papyrus; scribes.

Anastasi Papyrus

The Anastasi Papyrus is actually a collection of several papyri from many different sources and eras, although most are from the Ramessid Period (ca. 1295–ca. 1069 B.C.). These documents were assembled by representatives of the Swedish government living in Egypt during the nineteenth century. **See also** papyrus; Ramessid Period.

Anen (Onen) (ca. 1390–1352 B.C.)

Anen was the high priest of the temple complex at Heliopolis and at the temple of the god Re at Karnak during the Eighteenth Dynasty reign of Amenhotep III. He might also have been an astronomer, because a statue of him (now in the Turin Museum in Italy) shows him not only in the garb of a priest but also holding what might be astronomical instruments for viewing and measuring the heavens. In addition, Anen evidently held the titles "second prophet of Amun," "chancellor of the king of Lower Egypt," and "divine father," among others. Anen's success was apparently due in large part to the fact that, as the sibling of Queen Tiy, he was the king's brother-in-law. He also might have been the brother of a later Eighteenth Dynasty ruler, King Ay. Anen was entombed in western Thebes after his death. **See also** Amenhotep III; Ay; Tiy.

Anhur (Onuris)

Called Onuris by the Greeks, Anhur ("Sky Bearer") was worshiped by the ancient Egyptians as a god of the sun, or, more accurately, of the sun's creative power and its manifestation among men. At first Anhur was linked with Shu, a god of the air who was sometimes depicted with a solar disk on his head. Gradually, however, Anhur was associated with Re instead, and by the New Kingdom he had come to be seen as Re's warrior form. Later still, Anhur was called the god of war. Consequently, at festivals dedicated to Anhur battles were typically staged in the god's honor, and in art Anhur was often depicted wearing a warrior's headdress. He was also called on to protect Egyptians from their enemies and from annoying or poisonous insects and vermin. **See also** Re; Shu.

Ani (dates unknown)

Ani was a royal scribe of the Nineteenth Dynasty who in approximately 1250 B.C. commissioned a version of the *Book of the Dead,* now known as the Ani Papyrus. This painted papyrus, which is still in relatively good condition, is over 175 feet long and includes New Kingdom mortuary texts, various religious and secular myths and legends, information about the gods and their origins, comments about educational facilities for priests, and numerous illustrations. Some of this material is not found in any other version of the *Book of the Dead.* **See also** *Book of the Dead;* New Kingdom; papyrus.

animals

Animals fulfilled important roles in ancient Egyptian life. They provided not only food but material goods and labor. Animals were the focus of various religious rituals, sometimes sacrificed to the gods and other times kept in lavish quarters and cared for by priests as physical manifestations of the gods.

The most important domesticated animals in daily life were goats, sheep, and oxen, which provided meat, milk, wool, and leather. (In addition, cattle, oxen, and donkeys were used as beasts of burden and transportation, pulling carts and wagons.) Beef, mutton, and goat meat might be served as part of festivals, rituals, and offerings, but otherwise they were not typically eaten. In fact, only the wealthiest people could afford to dine on beef, since cattle were expensive to feed and the government heavily taxed owners based on the size of their herd. Pigs were probably not eaten either (indeed, some Egyptologists believe that there was a religious taboo against their consumption), although they were used to trample seeds into the soil. Instead, the main source of protein in the ancient Egyptian diet came from birds, primarily pigeons and waterfowl such as cranes, geese, and ducks, all of which were either hunted or bred and fattened for slaughter. Birds were also used for sacrificial purposes, along with a variety of other animals such as gazelles, oryx, and goats.

Animals performed significant work in ancient Egypt as well. For example, the Egyptians sometimes hunted with dogs, although they kept these animals as pets as well. Egyptologists disagree on when horses were first introduced into ancient Egypt, but the earliest artwork they have found depicting the horse in battle dates from the Eighteenth Dynasty. By this time, however, horses were already being bred in great numbers, and most of them were descended from animals captured in foreign wars. King Amenhotep II of the Eighteenth Dynasty was the first king to grow up with horses, and as an adult he became one of Egypt's most knowledgeable horse breeders, also expanding the animals' use in warfare. Still, Egyptologists believe that the ancient Egyptians had no cavalry. In fact, horses were not typically ridden in any context, except by messengers, and instead were used to pull carts and chariots. Moreover, they were owned only by royalty and the highest levels of the nobility and royal court. Other people used donkeys for transportation.

In addition to their connections to agriculture, animal husbandry, and warfare, certain animals were associated with certain deities. The ancient Egyptians worshiped not animals but rather the deities or truths they represented, considering animals to be possible manifestations of a deity's essential characteristics or aspects. In other words, the animals' images were viewed as symbols of something greater, but the animals themselves were not deserving of veneration. Because they represented the gods, however, animal forms could be used as conduits for the gods' powers. For this reason, clay figurines fashioned to look like animals were used as amulets to confer certain benefits to their owners. Amulets shaped like frogs, for example, were believed to be connected to those aspects of the gods associated with fertility, so these amulets might be carried by women attempting to become pregnant or by farmers wanting to increase the yield of their fields. By the same reasoning, animals were sometimes mentioned in magical spells or featured in religious rituals.

In certain religious rituals, animals were seen as stand-ins for deities, because some gods were thought to take animal form on occasion. For example, the deities Shu, Bastet, and Sekhmet might manifest themselves as a lion or cat, while Horus might appear as a mouse (although he was more commonly associated with the hawk), Thoth as a baboon, and Seth as an oryx, hippo, or pig. The mongoose, or ichneumon, was often said to be Khaturi, a form of the solar deity Re.

The solar deity Amun, ancient Egypt's principal god during the New Kingdom, was often depicted as a ram; this animal was also considered a form that was sometimes taken by the creator god Khnum. The ram was therefore viewed as a symbol of both power and creation (i.e., fertility). To honor Amun, an ancient Egyptian cult center at Mendes (once the capital of the sixteenth nome of Lower Egypt, now the modern town of Tell el-Ruba) dedicated to the god kept a sacred ram, the Ram of Mendes.

Another animal commonly considered sacred was the bull. Bulls were not only viewed as manifestations of the gods' powers but were sometimes thought to be the form taken by deified kings. Such animals, including the Apis bull, A'a Nefer bull, and Mnevis bull, were worshiped at shrines along the Nile River, and upon death they were mummified and buried or entombed at special sites.

Archaeologists have found cemeteries with the remains of dogs, jackals, sheep, cows, and other animals associated with specific deities. For example, hundreds of mummified crocodiles have been found in areas where the god Sobek was venerated, because the reptile was thought to be a manifestation of the god and therefore sacred to him. Sobek was typically depicted in the form of a crocodile, and live crocodiles were featured in temple rituals dedicated to Sobek in the Faiyum and at Kom Ombo in Upper Egypt.

Similarly, live cobras were sometimes used in religious ceremonies dedicated to deified kings. The cobra (*wadjet*) was viewed as a manifestation of such kings and therefore became the symbol of royalty and of Upper Egypt, where most of

Egypt's rulers had their capital cities. Consequently, the reptile's image often appeared on royal jewelry and other adornments. Other animals, such as the turtle (*shetiu*), were considered to be manifestations of harmful spirits rather than gods, and many people considered it to be unlucky to feature them on jewelry.

Because of their associations with the gods, many animals figured prominently in ancient Egyptian myths. Among the most significant were two serpents, Methen and Apophis. In a story explaining the cycles of day and night, Methen guarded one of the sacred boats of the sun god Re, and Apophis tried to swallow Re each night to keep the sun from rising the next morning. In other myths, the scorpion was featured as an assistant to the goddess Isis.

Ancient Egypt had entirely mythical animals as well, usually described as having parts of various existing animals. For example, Saget was a beast that had the head of a hawk and the body of a lion, with a lotus flower as a tail. Egyptologists do not know what role this beast played in the ancient Egyptian worldview because it was not mentioned in texts but only shown in artwork that gives no clue as to its purpose. However, Egyptologists do know the role of another beast, the Anemait. With the head of a crocodile, the body of a hippopotamus, and the paws of a lion, the Anemait sat beside the scales in the Judgment Hall of Osiris, ready to devour those whose hearts did not measure up to the standards of truth and honesty necessary to remain in the Afterlife. **See also** Apis bull; crocodiles; food; hunting and fishing; Sobek.

ankh

The ankh was one of the most pervasive hieroglyphic symbols in ancient Egyptian art. Shaped like a capital letter "T" with an inverted teardrop atop it, the ankh is actu-

A statue clutches two ankhs, the hieroglyphic symbol of life.

ally a combination of two other hieroglyphic symbols: those of air and water. Therefore, the ankh represented life, because the ancient Egyptians believed that air and water were the two elements necessary to create life. The ankh was also the symbol for the giving of life, which is why when painters in ancient Egypt depicted a man holding an ankh up to a woman's nose and vice versa, that act symbolized a fertile sexual union.

Ankhs most typically appeared on amulets and other pieces of jewelry intended to magically confer long life on the wearer. When found on royal necklaces, bracelets, and other pieces, the ankh is often in the company of two other symbols, *djed* and *was,* with their combined meaning being "life, stability, and power." The ankh was also featured in rituals related to royal cults as well as to the gods Isis and Osiris, beginning in the Early Dynastic Period. In addition, ankhs appeared on coffin decorations and on furniture and other objects found in royal tombs. **See also** amulets; *djed; was* scepter.

Ankhaf (Ankhkhaf) (?–ca. 2550 B.C.)

Ankhaf was a vizier serving Fourth Dynasty king Khafre and a prince, either the son of King Snefru or his sibling. Ankhaf held the title "King's Eldest Son" during King Snefru's reign, but this was a title given to honor favorites of the king and did not denote kinship. Most Egyptologists believe that Prince Ankhaf received his position as vizier by supporting King Khafre in his bid to wrest the throne from King Djedefre.

Prince Ankhaf's tomb in Giza is of a type known as mastaba. Archaeologists excavating this tomb found a painted plaster bust made in the prince's likeness. This work of art is now in the Museum of Fine Arts in Boston, Massachusetts. **See also** Djedefre; Khafre; mastaba tomb; Snefru.

Ankhesenamun (Ankhesenamon; Ankhesenpaaten) (ca. 1350– 1327 B.C.)

Eighteenth Dynasty queen Ankhesenamun was a daughter of King Akhenaten (also known as Amenhotep IV) and Queen Nefertiti. The king was determined to get his subjects to worship a relatively obscure god, Aten, which he had elevated to national status. He changed his name from Amenhotep IV to Akhenaten in order to honor Aten, and he renamed his daughter Ankhesenpaaten for the same reason.

In keeping with the ancient Egyptian practice of royals marrying only close relatives, Ankhesenamun became her father's wife at a very young age. When he died, she married her brother or half-brother Tutankhaten. When he assumed the throne, Tutankhaten was only eight and Ankhesenamun was thirteen. The two children were under the control of two men: Ay, an elderly official who was probably Ankhesenamun's grandfather on her mother's side, and Horemheb, a very powerful general. It was these two men who convinced the young king and queen to renounce their father's unpopular new religion and replace the "aten" in their names with "amun" to show their support for still-popular god Amun. As a result, Ankhesenpaaten became Ankhesenamun.

Ankhesenamun was married to Tutankhamun for nine years, until his death in approximately 1327 B.C. During this time, she apparently gave birth prematurely to two girls; neither survived, and their mummified bodies were placed in King Tutankhamun's tomb.

After Tutankhamun's death, Ankhesenamun was forced to marry Ay, who then became king even though he was a commoner. Ankhesenamun had tried to avoid this by sending a desperate message to Suppiluliumas, the king of the Hittites, begging him to send one of his sons to become her husband. The Hittite king responded by sending Prince Zennanza, but when the young man reached Egypt's border he was killed, probably on orders of General Horemheb.

Whether Ankhesenamun actually married Ay is uncertain. A cartouche (a line encircling certain types of names in hieroglyphic writing) with their two names side by side, which usually indicated marriage, adorned a ring that archaeologist Percy Newberry reported seeing in Cairo, Egypt, in the 1920s. He was unable to acquire the ring and Newberry's claim was never corroborated; nonetheless, most Egyptologists accept his report as fact. Nothing more about Ankhesenamun's fate is known, although many Egyptologists suspect that she died early in Ay's reign. **See also** Amenhotep IV; Ay; Horemheb; Tutankhamun.

Ankhnesmery-Re I (Ankhenesmeryre I; Ankhesenpepy I) (?–2287 B.C.)

A queen of the Sixth Dynasty, Ankhnesmery-Re I was married to King Pepy I, as was her younger sister Ankhnesmery-Re II. According to a tablet found in the city of Abydos, the two were daughters of a noble family; their father, Khui, and their brother, Djau, were prominent officials from Abydos. Ankhnesmery-Re I died either during childbirth or a few months after giving birth to a son, possibly the future king Merenre I. **See also** Ankhnesmery-Re II; Merenre I.

Ankhnesmery-Re II (Ankhenesmeryre II; Ankhesenpepy II) (ca. 2321 B.C.–?)

A queen of the Sixth Dynasty, Ankhnesmery-Re II was married to King Pepy I, as was her older sister Ankhnesmery-Re I. Ankhnesmery-Re II and her brother, Djau, acted as coregents for her son, King Pepy II, since the boy assumed the throne at the age of six. At first, Egyptologists thought that Ankhnesmery-Re, also known as Ankhesenpepy ("She Lives for Pepy"), was an ordinary queen. Recent excavations of her tomb at Saqqara, however, have uncovered the hieroglyphs of the Pyramid Texts on the walls, suggesting that she had the status of a king. In addition, inscriptions state that after Pepy I died, she married her nephew Merenre and bore his heir, Pepy II. Thus she continued being the power behind the throne. **See also** Ankhnesmery-Re I; Pepy II; Pyramid Texts.

Ankhnes-Pepy (?–ca. 2161 B.C.)

A queen of the Sixth Dynasty, Ankhnes-Pepy was one of the many wives of King Pepy II. As such, she is believed to have been either the mother or grandmother of at least one king of the Eighth Dynasty.

Her remains were found in the sarcophagus of a man believed to be a friend of the royal family who labeled the sarcophagus as his own but apparently donated it for the queen's burial. **See also** Pepy II.

Ankhtify (?–ca. 2025 B.C.)

During the First Intermediate Period, Ankhtify was a powerful nomarch (a provincial ruler) and possibly a prince who controlled the cities of Edfu and Hierakonpolis and forged an alliance with the nome of Elephantine. Eventually, he decided to lead his troops in an attack on Prince Intef of Thebes. Intef defeated Ankhtify, driving him back to his own lands; nonetheless, Ankhtify included boasts of his greatness in the tomb he built for himself at el-Moalla, approximately twenty miles south of Thebes. Inscriptions there call him, among other things, a royal seal bearer, a general, and chief of foreign regions. There is also a record of his feeding starving people during a famine. However, he apparently did this not out of charity but on the orders of a Ninth Dynasty king, Kaneferre. **See also** First Intermediate Period; Intef.

Antefoker (Intefoker) (ca. 1985–ca. 1960 B.C.)

Antefoker was the vizier for two Twelfth Dynasty kings, Amenemhet I and Senwosret I. However, all information about him, including his portrait, was eradicated from the tomb of his mother, Senet (although some references to him appear elsewhere). For this reason, Egyptologists suspect that Antefoker committed some act of wrongdoing that would have caused his relatives to disassociate themselves from him. The prevailing theory is that Antefoker was charged with participating in the assassination of King Amenemhet I. However, he may have eventually been exonerated, because his name survives at his cenotaph (a ceremonial burial site containing no body) at el-Lisht and at his tomb in Thebes. **See also** Amenemhet I; Senwosret I; viziers.

Antony, Marc (Marcus Antonius) (ca. 82–30 B.C.)

Marc Antony was a prominent Roman statesman and general and a lover of Queen Cleopatra VII of Egypt. Following the assassination in 44 B.C. of Roman emperor Julius Caesar, Antony briefly coruled Rome with Caesar's nephew Octavius (also known as Octavian) and another Roman general named Marcus Aemilius Lepidus. Antony's prominence helped secure Cleopatra politically, but when Antony lost a power struggle with his corulers, Cleopatra's position as Egypt's queen became vulnerable, and eventually this situation led to both her and Antony's death.

The story of these deaths has been the subject of many literary masterpieces. The story underlying these works is that Marc Antony allied with Egyptian forces to fight Octavius at sea, but Rome's forces eventually trapped Antony at the Egyptian city of Alexandria. While Antony was on the battlefield in the summer of 30 B.C., he heard a false report that Cleopatra had been killed in her palace, and rather than live without her he committed suicide using his own sword. Upon hearing of Antony's death, Cleopatra committed suicide as well, some say by allowing a poisonous snake to bite her. Afterward, Octavius had the two lovers entombed together in Cleopatra's royal mortuary complex at Alexandria. **See also** Caesar, Julius; Cleopatra VII.

Anubis (Anpu; Anup)

Anubis (a Greek version of the ancient Egyptian Anpu or Anup) was the ancient Egyptian god of mummification, embalmers, funeral rites, and cemeteries. He was also believed to open the gates of the Afterlife for the dead, guiding the deceased to their destination (usually said to be the Judgment Hall of Osiris, the chief

In this Nineteenth Dynasty painting, Anubis, god of mummification and funeral rites, prepares a body for the tomb.

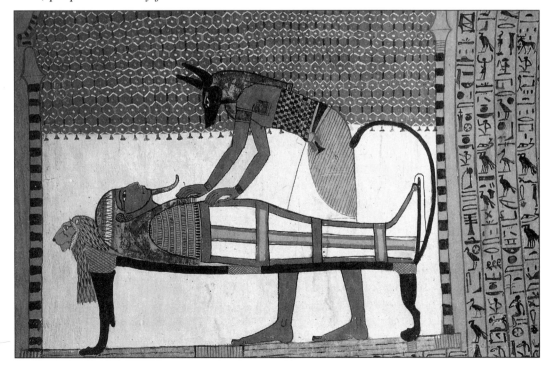

god of the dead), and to listen to prayers made on behalf of the dying. In some myths, Anubis helped Osiris judge the deceased's character by weighing the hearts.

Anubis was said to be the son of Osiris and Nephthys, abandoned by his mother at birth to be raised by her sister Isis. According to mythology, Anubis helped Isis mummify the body of Osiris when that god was killed by his own brother, Seth. In this way, Anubis became the god of mummy wrappings, and his other associations with funerary practices were soon added. Inscriptions in Fifth and Sixth Dynasty pyramids, however, collectively known as the Pyramid Texts, describe Anubis as the son of Re, a god of the sun associated with Creation, reflecting the Egyptians' belief in a cycle of death and rebirth (creation). In any case, Anubis was typically depicted as a jackal, probably because these animals scavenged Egyptian burial sites for bodies and body parts. Priests conducting funeral rites sometimes wore jackal masks. **See also** funerals; mummification; Osiris; Pyramid Texts.

Apepi I (Apep; Aphophis; Awoserre; Auserre Apepi I) (ca. 1606–ca. 1550 B.C.)

Also known by his throne name of Auserre ("Great and Powerful Like Re"), Apepi I was a Hyksos king who ruled northern Egypt during what Egyptologists call the Fifteenth Hyksos Dynasty, which coexisted with the Seventeenth Theban Dynasty ruling southern Egypt. Apepi I's rivals during this period were the Theban king Tao II and his successor, Kamose; the former officially declared war on Apepi I and the latter escalated the conflict.

Despite the war with his southern neighbor, Apepi I managed to hold on to his kingdom throughout his forty-year reign. During this time he exchanged some of his Hyksos ways for Egyptian ones, although he also introduced some of his traditional gods (such as Astarte, goddess of the moon) into the Egyptian areas under his control. His main god, however, appears to have been the Egyptian deity Seth, a god of desert wastelands.

Apepi I died of natural causes in his capital city, Avaris, in approximately 1550 B.C. He left his crown to his son Apepi II Aquenienre. **See also** Hyksos; Kamose; Tao II.

Apis (Hep; Hapi) bull

Considered a physical manifestation of the god Ptah, the Apis bull was a living sacred animal to the people of the city of Memphis. It was kept in a special stall in the Temple of Memphis and lavished with the best food and care. However, the bull also had certain duties. Specifically, it was featured in parades honoring Ptah, during which it was draped in gold cloth, and worked as the temple oracle, answering questions posed to it. To provide an answer, the bull would walk through one of several doorways in a special temple chamber; each doorway was labeled with a symbol representing one of the possible responses, and the door the bull chose indicated the answer.

According to various Egyptian records, including the Palermo Stone, the Apis bull was honored with its own festival at least once a year. However, when it reached the age of twenty-five, it would be killed by drowning. (Egyptologists are unsure of why this age and manner of death were chosen.) Once it had died, the bull's body would be mummified (although many Egyptologists believe that some parts of it were first eaten, probably by priests), placed in a stone coffin, and taken to Saqqara, where it was left in a subterranean room of a tomb now known as the Serapeum.

Each time an Apis bull died, a new one was chosen to take its place, but each candidate had to have either a white crescent on its side or a white triangle on its forehead. Possibly, Egyptian priests bred certain cattle in an effort to produce animals with these markings; any bull in Egypt displaying them could be selected as the new Apis bull. **See also** bulls, sacred; Memphis; Ptah; Saqqara.

Apophis

In Egyptian mythology, Apophis was a giant snake that tried to swallow the sun god Re each night as he passed through the Underworld or the celestial waters of Nun, depending on the version of the myth. In some versions, Apophis was considered another manifestation of Re and therefore his equal. Because of his power, his danger to the sun was severe, and when Egyptians awoke to the rare sight of a stormy dark sky, they feared that Apophis had overcome Re. **See also** Overthrowing Apophis; Re; Underworld.

Apries (Wahibre) (?–570 B.C.)

A Twenty-sixth Dynasty king, Apries assumed the throne in approximately 589 B.C. after the death of his father, King Psamtik II. He is best known for his military victories, particularly against the Babylonians.

Under King Apries, Egypt's forces controlled much of the eastern Mediterranean, but trouble eventually broke out among the king's troops. His native Egyptian soldiers resented the preferential treatment given to the many Greek mercenaries that King Apries brought into Egypt to supplement his forces. In approximately 570 B.C., after arriving at the city of Memphis from a battle in a foreign land, Egyptian soldiers from the garrison at Elephantine attacked the Greek mercenaries. During the resulting civil war, now called the Battle of Memphis, the Egyptian soldiers declared their general Ahmose II (also known as Amasis) king. Shortly thereafter, the two rival monarchs met in combat at Memphis and Ahmose II killed Apries. Apries was buried at Sais, a site that seems to have served as a royal cemetery for much of the Twenty-sixth Dynasty. **See also** Ahmose II; Elephantine; Memphis; mercenaries; Psamtik II.

archaeological expeditions

Egypt has been the focus of numerous archaeological expeditions since the seventeenth century, but the purpose of these expeditions has changed over the years. The goal of the earliest expeditions was simply to determine why the ancient Egyptians built their great monuments.

One of the first scholars to study ancient ruins, John Greaves, was an English mathematician and astronomer who wanted to prove that the pyramids had some kind of significance related to mathematics or astronomy. In 1638–1639 he attempted to measure the Great Pyramid of Giza to show that the ancient Egyptians had known and incorporated the earth's circumference into the design of their pyramids. However, his attempt failed because rubble at the base of the pyramid prevented him from taking precise measurements.

Other scholars of the period focused on deciphering ancient Egyptian hieroglyphics, the meanings of which had been forgotten centuries earlier. One of the first people to study hieroglyphs was a German Jesuit priest named Anthanasius Kircher who believed that the ancient Egyptian texts would contain cosmic truths. Like many people of his time, he was more focused on learning about ancient Egyptian beliefs and knowledge than about ancient Egyptian history.

This approach to the study of Egypt began to change in the eighteenth century after Europeans began to chart the ancient ruins and view them with a more scientific eye. For example, between 1714 and 1726 a French Jesuit priest named Claude Sicard created the first map showing the locations of important temples and tombs as well as the cities of Thebes and Memphis. Similarly, in 1743 Richard Pococke, the bishop of Ossory in Ireland, published *Observations on Egypt* to describe sites he visited on an earlier trip to Egypt, providing a description of the Valley of the Kings, the location of eighteen of its tombs, and a map of the Giza pyramids. Another important publication on Egyptian sites was the 1755 work *Travels in Egypt and Nubia* by Danish naval architect Friderik Norden; the book not only told about what Norden observed during extensive travels in Egypt but also provided accurate plans and drawings of various sites and monuments.

All of these works, combined with descriptions from earlier travelers to Egypt such as fifth-century B.C. historian Herodotus, proved invaluable in helping the first large-scale archaeological expeditions locate ancient sites in Egypt. The first such expedition was launched by General Napoléon Bonaparte of France in 1798 as part of a military expedition intended to create a French stronghold in Cairo. Dozens of archaeologists, architects, artists, surveyors, engineers, mathematicians, botanists, and other scholars accompanied Napoléon to Egypt and spent three years studying the nation's culture, history, flora, fauna, monuments, artifacts, and other features. They also mapped the location of both contemporary and ancient cities, buildings, and monuments, among other things. Between 1809 and 1828, the results of their work were published in France in twenty volumes collectively titled *Description de l'Egypte* (*Description of Egypt*), which included elaborately engraved illustrations. One of the expedition's artists, Baron Dominique-Vivant Denon, published his own book on his observations in Egypt, *Voyages dans la Basse et la Haute Égypte* (*Travels in Lower and Upper Egypt*), in 1802 in French, German, and English.

Napoléon Bonaparte in Cairo. Napoléon's military expedition to Egypt also included archaeologists and other scholars.

Expeditions like Napoléon's brought scientific study to Egypt but also resulted in numerous ancient Egyptian artifacts being taken out of the country. Some of these artifacts, like the Rosetta Stone (which eventually helped linguists decipher ancient Egyptian hieroglyphic writings), were the object of serious study. Others, however, were acquired for their beauty, their uniqueness, or simply because they could be sold. As demand for Egyptian antiquities grew, many expeditions were launched more out of a desire to find antiquities to sell than to advance the world's knowledge of ancient Egypt. For example, Bernardino Drovetti, a colonel in Napoléon's expedition who became the consul general of Egypt in

1810, participated in several archaeological excavations for the purpose of profiting from the sale of any antiquities he found. Henry Salt, the British consul general, did the same, assisted by antiquities collector Giovanni Battista Belzoni.

Some who did the actual collecting of antiquities made little or no effort to keep artifacts sorted according to their historic context. For example, one of the most aggressive procurers of Egyptian antiquities, Giovanni d'Anastasi, employed several agents to amass artifacts from all periods of Egyptian history, which he then sold in four batches, the first in 1826, the second in 1828, the third in 1839, and the fourth in 1857 (this sale took place after d'Anastasi's death). Sometimes artifacts were broken up and sold in parts. For example, d'Anastasi sold one papyrus in two halves, one in 1828 and the other in 1857.

Such practices compromised the serious study of ancient Egyptian artifacts, making it more difficult for scholars to date and understand the purpose of documents and other objects. As the nineteenth century progressed, however, a few serious, less profit-minded scholars became involved in Egyptian archaeology, and they increasingly recognized the importance of recording where an artifact was found and how it appeared at its original site. For example, Sir John Gardner Wilkinson, while studying archaeological sites in Egypt and Nubia (including Karnak, Beni Hasan, and the Valley of the Kings) between 1821 and 1833, made copies of ancient inscriptions before any of them were removed from the sites, thereby preserving the original form of these inscriptions for posterity. Similarly, Karl Richard Lepsius, who led expeditions to Egypt in 1842 and 1866, accurately described the country's monuments and produced on-site casts of ancient Egyptian inscriptions and reliefs—although he also took numerous antiquities back to the Berlin Museum.

Around this time, the general public became involved in efforts to study artifacts on-site, largely as a result of the work of British writer Amelia Edwards. After traveling to Egypt in 1873–1874 and writing a book (*A Thousand Miles Up the Nile*) about what she saw there, Edwards established a foundation called the Egypt Exploration Fund, later renamed the Egypt Exploration Society, which collected donations to fund archaeological expeditions to Egypt. These expeditions, which began in 1882, did not have antiquities-gathering as their goal, but rather sought to learn as much as possible about certain Egyptian sites before they were lost to collectors or simply destroyed by natural elements. Among the group's efforts was the Archaeological Survey, a project launched in 1890 to identify as many ancient Egyptian sites as possible and record their state of deterioration.

Along with such excavations and surveys came the recognition of Egyptology as a separate branch of scientific study. As the twentieth century approached, expeditions were increasingly being launched by major universities employing teams of scholars, usually under the supervision of the head of the university's Egyptology department. One person at the forefront of these scholarly efforts was Sir William Matthew Flinders Petrie, the first professor of Egyptology at the University College in London, England. Often called the father of modern Egyptology, Petrie established excavation guidelines and admonished other archaeologists not to use dynamite and other destructive methods to remove debris but rather to treat archaeological sites with care.

As a result of Petrie's efforts and those of the Egypt Exploration Fund, the archaeological expeditions that took place between the 1880s and World War I were increasingly academically oriented, and after a hiatus during the war they began again with even more emphasis on the scholarly approach. In fact, by this time archaeological expeditions were largely staffed by specialists in Egyptology; amateurs were rarely found on digs any longer. Moreover, the pace and purpose of excavations began to change. Archaeologists began working even more slowly and painstakingly, and they increasingly focused on uncovering facts that would answer specific questions regarding Egypt's past. For example, in the 1920s archaeologist Howard Carter led several expeditions to Egypt's Valley of the Kings specifically to prove the existence of King Tutankhamun by finding his tomb.

Carter's discovery of this tomb in 1922 unexpectedly led to a renewed interest in launching archaeological expeditions for the purpose of finding valuable antiquities rather than for advancing Egyptology, because Tutankhamun had been buried with thousands of treasures. As a result, archaeologists who were more profit-minded than scholarly again began launching expeditions. However, this situation was short-lived for two reasons. First, most of Egypt's most valuable treasures had already been excavated in previous years. Second, the Egyptian government had put in place measures to prevent the removal of artifacts without official permission. This meant that the most valuable artifacts found at a site would usually remain in Egypt, reducing the profit motive of expeditions.

Moreover, the Egypt Exploration Society continued to publicize the importance of scholarship in excavations. Also, whereas some of the foundation's previous expeditions had aimed to locate sites referred to in the Bible, now it turned to excavating a variety of sites in order to develop theories about ancient Egyptian life. As a result, the Egypt Exploration Society sponsored excavations of ancient cities,

English archaeologist and Egyptologist Sir William Matthew Flinders Petrie (1853–1942). Petrie's excavation methods became standard practice among Egyptologists.

including Tell el-Amarna (also known as Amarna), from various periods of history and later moved on to fortresses, workers' villages, agricultural communities, and other types of sites. In addition, it also sponsored efforts to repair ancient Egyptian structures and sites that had sustained damage over the centuries.

After World War II, the prevailing approach to Egyptian archaeology became one of restoration as well as discovery. By this time, many sites had been seriously damaged, not only by the ravages of time but by the clumsy excavations of previous archaeologists. Consequently, many scholars became involved in efforts to preserve various ancient structures that were threatened with destruction. For example, between 1964 and 1968 a massive project was undertaken to save two temples at Abu Simbel due to be submerged under the rising waters of Lake Nasser. An international team of archaeologists painstakingly dismantled and moved these temples to higher ground approximately 230 yards away. The total cost of this temple relocation project was over $90 million.

Even though restoration efforts are a major part of modern archaeological expeditions, attempts to make new discoveries are still an important part of these undertakings as well, even at sites that have already been explored. For example, at the city of Alexandria, excavations in the 1990s uncovered the ruins of a Roman house, complete with mosaic floors, and exploration of the waters offshore has yielded numerous columns, statues, and obelisks from the Greco-Roman Period. **See also** Abu Simbel; Carter, Howard; Egypt Exploration Society; Lepsius, Karl Richard; Petrie, William Matthews Flinders.

architecture

Architecture in ancient Egypt was of two types, secular and religious. Religious structures—temples, tombs, pyramids, and other buildings intended to honor gods and the deceased—were built to last for eternity, while secular structures were built with little consideration of posterity. Consequently, Egyptologists know little about ancient Egyptian houses because they were not constructed to last.

Scholars speculate that prior to 3400 B.C., homes were made of bundles of reeds and other plant materials and that mud bricks were incorporated into construction sometime during the Predynastic Period. Also during this period, the basic shape of a house appears to have been round or oval, with few rooms inside. By the Middle Kingdom, the rectangle seems to have been a more common shape, and houses of the upper classes had two or three stories, many rooms, staircases, gardens, and outbuildings. From references in art and literature, archaeologists know that such homes existed in the New Kingdom as well, but actual specimens of these and earlier versions of domestic architecture have not survived.

However, archaeologists have found ruins of New Kingdom palaces, which served as both royal residences and administrative centers. These structures had rooms related to government work around their perimeter, and the inner area was reserved for the private use of the king and his family. These and other secular buildings often had strategically placed air vents to promote air circulation that would keep them cool; they lacked windows because glass would have trapped heat inside.

The many existing examples of ancient Egyptian religious structures demonstrate that certain aspects of their design changed over time. In the Early Dynastic Period, the predominant type of tomb was the mastaba, a rectangular structure whose burial chamber was subterranean beside storerooms of goods intended for use by the deceased in the Afterlife. Each of these tombs had a shaft leading to an above-ground offering chapel shaped like a mound, probably as a symbol of the primordial mound from which all life was said to have arisen.

Over time, the mounds of royal mastaba tombs were slightly terraced to resemble steps to suggest that the deceased king would be ascending to the heavens. This led to the creation of the Step Pyramid, which was designed by Third Dynasty vizier and architect Imhotep for King Djoser. In creating Djoser's pyramid, Imhotep began with the mastaba design but made more pronounced steps and a much taller structure overall.

Many subsequent pyramids were built during the Old Kingdom, generally as part of complexes that included causeways, temples, and other buildings. Despite all of these accompanying structures, however, the main focus of the pyramid complex was the pyramid itself. During the Middle Kingdom, though, the temples within these complexes became more prominent and more ornate, with columned courts and numerous chambers, halls, and sanctuaries, and sometimes a sacred lake as well.

By this time, columns had become an important architectural feature for the ancient Egyptians, representing nature in general and trees in particular, and they tended to appear in groups resembling a grove of trees. Many bore carved inscriptions and reliefs, which over time became more ornate. Most columns were made of stone, although a few were made of wood.

The trend of producing ever more ornate structures continued into the New Kingdom for mortuary temples, with the exception of a few kings who either preferred more modest structures or could not afford something lavish. Meanwhile, tombs were increasingly carved out of living rock, as in places like the Valley of the Kings, and their location was kept secret to foil tomb robbers. Near these tombs and other construction sites throughout ancient Egypt, the king often built villages to house tomb workers and their families.

The building of tombs and other monuments was closely supervised by architects. These men had to be on hand constantly because, given the massive size of many building stones, it would have been very difficult to correct mistakes. Working from drawings done by a draftsman called the scribe of forms, the architect, called the overseer of works, would direct every effort on-site, including the work of sculptors and painters. Meanwhile, priests were on hand to conduct rituals at various points during construction to ensure that the project experienced good fortune.

Religious concerns were also taken into account during the building's design, when its orientation was determined based on astronomy. For example, ancient Egyptian architects used the North Star to find true north because each of a pyramid's sides had to face one of the four cardinal directions—north, south, east, and west. In addition, many temples were apparently oriented in accordance with whatever star was associated with the deity they were honoring.

The architectural tools used for building projects included the plumb bob, measuring line, level, and various carving tools of flint, hard stone, and (during later eras) copper or bronze. Stones were moved into place via ropes, levers, and brick, earth, and wooden ramps. However, some Egyptologists suspect that, given the fact that they were able to create such massive structures with relatively few workers, the ancient Egyptians might have had more sophisticated devices and methods for construction that have yet to be discovered. **See also** astronomy; building materials; construction rituals, temple; temples; tombs.

art

Beginning in predynastic times, the ancient Egyptians decorated pottery and other functional items with designs and images, but they primarily used art as a way to preserve the idealized representations of events and people for eternity. Therefore, the majority of their artwork appears in forms that were intended to endure, such as stone statues and wall reliefs and paintings in tombs, pyramids, and temples.

Artisans carved statues using a variety of tools, including stone hammers, chisels, drills, and saws whose blades or tips had been rubbed with wet sand to make them more abrasive. The largest statues, which were created from huge blocks, were crudely carved where their stone was quarried and then transported to their display site to be finished.

Artists' styles and techniques for creating their works varied little over the ages. Statuary typically showed figures at rest, with no attempt to suggest movement even if the depiction was of a person engaged in some ordinary daily activity. In carvings and paintings, human figures were typically shown in profile, facing right, although the eye and eyebrow on that side were often shown in full view. The more important the subject was, the larger he or she was portrayed, regardless of perspective, meaning that a king might be depicted as being many times larger than his family members, and still larger than his enemies, even if this created a visual distortion of a nearby figure appearing smaller than a distant one. The ancient Egyptians also traditionally depicted certain objects in paintings and reliefs in relatively consistent ways. For example, crocodiles were shown in profile, lizards were shown from above, and containers were often given a false transparency so that the things inside of them could be seen. A cooking pot, for instance, might be only an outline, with its interior showing the ladle dipped inside. The colors chosen to represent various items had symbolic meaning as well. For example, the traditional color of deification was blue, so gods and goddesses were often painted blue.

The ancient Egyptians preferred carving over painting because they knew that carved scenes were far more durable than painted ones. However, when interior rock was unsuited to carving or to save time and money, some interior walls were painted. To prepare a wall for painting, the artist might first coat it with mud and fine gypsum plasters. He would then draw grids on the walls as guidelines to help determine where each figure would go in relation to all others. Only when the artist was certain of the entire composition would he begin painting figures.

The same type of grids would be drawn on walls in preparation for carving either raised or sunken reliefs. In raised reliefs, the main figures are slightly higher than the background, whereas in sunken reliefs, the main figures are slightly recessed into the background. Because in raised reliefs all of the background has to be shaved down, these required far more work than sunken reliefs. The ancient Egyptians primarily used raised reliefs on inside walls and sunken reliefs on outside walls; some Egyptologists speculate that this was because raised reliefs show up better in dim light while sunken reliefs show better in strong sunlight.

Beginning in the Old Kingdom, wall carvings were smoothed and finished after completion to eliminate tool marks and then coated lightly with stucco. Afterward, paint might be applied if desired. Initially, on a sunken-relief carving only a few details, such as the eyes, might be painted. By the New Kingdom, however, reliefs might be extensively painted, and in the most lavish tombs colored stones and/or glass might be inlaid into the carvings for details like eyes. **See also** colors; painting; statues.

Asasif

Asasif is the site of numerous cemeteries, tombs, and mortuary complexes. Located on the western shore of the Nile River at Thebes near the Seventeenth Dynasty palace complex of Deir el-Bahri, Asasif was most heavily used as a necropolis during the Eleventh and Twenty-sixth Dynasties. However, the structure that is best known at the site today is an Eighteenth Dynasty tomb built by Kheruef, royal steward to Eighteenth Dynasty queen Tiy. Though unfinished, this structure contains many murals of such scenes as a *sed* festival and a dance viewed by the goddess Hathor. Another unfinished structure in the area is a Twentieth Dynasty temple of Ramses IV. **See also** festivals; Hathor; Ramses IV; Tiy.

Asiatics

Ancient Egyptian texts often refer to a group of foreigners from the east called Asiatics, whom Egyptologists generally believe were people from parts of Syria and Palestine. These foreigners were clearly reviled; in some texts, they are called "abominations of Re," and many texts refer to Asiatics in other derogatory terms. One popular Old Kingdom or early Middle Kingdom text, *The Admonitions of Ipuwer,* even suggested that the Asiatics would eventually lead to Egypt's ruin. **See also** *Admonitions of Ipuwer, The;* Afrocentrism; mercenaries.

Assyria

The ancient country of Assyria was one of Egypt's Near East neighbors that was located just north of another ancient country, Babylonia. (Both Assyria and Babylonia were situated along the Tigris River in what is now Iraq.) Assyria took its name from its first capital, Ashur, but during much of its early history it was under the control of others, first the Sumerians and then the Hurrians. As these two empires declined, the fortunes of Assyria rose. Finally, during the reign of Assyrian king Adad-nirari I (1308–1276 B.C.), Assyria became an independent power. Its influence subsequently spread, and during the reign of King Tiglath-pileser I (1116–1078 B.C.) the Assyrian empire encompassed much of Syria, Phoenicia, Anatolia, and Babylonia. At this time, the Assyrians developed an aggressive military stance, launching many unprovoked attacks on their neighbors.

Three centuries later, King Sargon II, who ruled from approximately 722 to 705 B.C., succeeded in unifying what had been a collection of semiautonomous states. This unity, coupled with Assyria's size, made the empire Egypt's rival, and King Sargon II's son and heir, Sennacherib (705–681 B.C.), was determined to take over some or all of Egypt's land. He made repeated attacks on the Egyptian frontier before his assassination in 681 B.C., whereupon his son and heir, Esarhaddon, took over the campaign and managed to capture the Egyptian city of Memphis.

Having established his forces in Memphis, in 669 B.C. Esarhaddon decided to return to Assyria, but he died before arriving home. His son, Ashurbanipal, took over his empire and expanded Esarhaddon's conquest by taking over Thebes. The Assyrians' control of Egyptian territory, however, declined over the next thirty to forty years. Opposition from Egyptians coupled with unrest at home forced Ashurbanipal to turn his control of Egyptian lands over to local rulers who were loyal to him. When Ashurbanipal died in 627 B.C. even this limited level of Assyrian control ended. A civil war soon led to the decline of the Assyrian empire. **See also** Babylonia and Chaldea; Nubia; Psamtik I; Saite Period.

astronomy

The ancient Egyptians developed a wealth of astronomical observations as a result of a need to keep track of when the Nile River flooded. Observing that the stars were in roughly the same place in the sky before each flooding, Egyptians learned to time their agricultural activities according to the positions of the stars and planets. Because the movement of the heavens was thought to be controlled by the gods, during the Old Kingdom priests were charged with the responsibility of memorizing and mapping the movements of the stars, moon, sun, and planets, and reporting on the positions of these objects when called upon. This connection between religious belief and the heavens eventually led to the common practice of putting star charts on the ceilings of tombs and temples.

The most important star was Sirius, called Sopdet or Sopdu by the Egyptians, because it appeared on the horizon right before the inundation, or flooding of the Nile, began in June. The North Star, on the other hand, had a different use. Called one of the Ikhemu-Seku, the Stars That Never Fail, because it was always visible in the night sky, it helped Egyptians orient their pyramids. Each of a pyramid's sides had to face one of the four cardinal directions—north, south, east, and west—so the North Star helped ancient Egyptian architects establish this alignment. Other stars were used to orient temples. In fact, some Egyptologists believe that many temples were oriented in accordance with whatever star was associated with the deity they were honoring.

Planets were also significant in ancient Egyptian astronomical observations, but there is no evidence that the ancient Egyptians could discern the difference between planets and stars as they appeared in the night sky. In any case, some planets were closely linked to deities. For example, three planets were associated with the god Horus: Jupiter, or Hor-tash-tawy (Horus Who Binds the Two Lands); Saturn, or Hor-ka-Pet (Horus the Bull of Heaven); and Mars, or Horus-Desher (Red Horus).

The sun was the most important celestial body, but prior to the Twenty-sixth Dynasty it was associated only with ancient Egyptian religion, not astronomy. In other words, the sun was not part of astronomical calculations related to architecture, agriculture, or other practical applications. The sun was instead worshiped as a god with many forms, which varied according to the prevailing mythology of a region or era. For the most part, however, the sun took the form of a winged scarab, or beetle, named Khepri in the morning as it arose, the sun god Re during the day, and the sun god Atum at night. Despite all their accurate observations, the ancient Egyptians envisioned the sun traveling in a circle around a flat earth that sat atop an orb of water.

The ancient Egyptians also believed that things that occurred on earth were mirrored in the heavens. Consequently, order in one place meant order in the other. However, this belief did not translate into a belief in astrology, the idea that the position of the stars influences things that happen on earth, until the Greco-Roman Period. At that time, ancient Egyptian versions of Babylonian and Greek signs of the zodiac began to appear in tomb, temple, and coffin decorations. **See also** Horus; Nile River; scarab.

Aswan (Sunnu)

Located at the north end of the First Cataract of the Nile River, Aswan was a center for trade that linked Egypt with Nubia and the African interior. In fact, the ancient Egyptian word from which Aswan was ultimately derived was *swenet,* or trade. (Ancient Egyptians called the town Sunnu, and Greeks called it Syene.) Because it was at a cataract that impeded river navigation, Aswan was also strategic militarily, and as such was the site of a garrison and fortress that protected the southern border of Egypt from invasion. However, other than soldiers, most people in the area lived on an island called Elephantine in the middle of the Nile. Aswan's bleak terrain was primarily the site of the graves of the many government officials who lived on the island and were responsible for administering the region. **See also** Elephantine; fortresses; trade.

Asyut (Assiut)

Called Lykopolis or Lyconpolis by the ancient Greeks, Asyut was once the capital of the thirteenth nome of Upper Egypt and a key stop on north-south trade routes. Travelers coming from below the First Cataract of the Nile would typically stop at Asyut, located on the eastern banks of the Nile just south of the ancient city of Hermopolis, en route north to the Kharga Oasis. Perhaps because of its strategic location, Asyut was home to many famous military figures who not only defended their own nome but also helped Egyptian kings deal with various civil and foreign wars. In particular, during the tumultuous Ninth and Tenth Dynasties when control of Egypt was split between royal families in Heracleopolis and Thebes, armies from Asyut fought for the Heracleopolitan king against the Theban one. The tombs of some of these armies' leaders were carved into the cliffs above Asyut. From inscriptions and other records, Egyptologists also know that Asyut was a center for the worship of the god Wepwawet. **See also** Heracleopolis; Kharga Oasis; Thebes; Wepwawet.

Aten

Aten was an ancient Egyptian solar deity that some Egyptologists believe was a form of Re-Horakhty, another solar deity. However, Aten was very specifically associated with the sun's rays rather than

with its other attributes and was therefore often depicted as a shining solar disk with rays as arms. The ends of these rays were the god's hands, which typically held the ankh, symbolic of life.

Aten was first worshiped during the Old Kingdom, but at that time he was a relatively minor god. During the New Kingdom, however, Aten began to rise to prominence, and by the Eighteenth Dynasty reign of Amenhotep III he was worshiped by an Aten cult supported by the king's wife Tiy. When Amenhotep III's son Amenhotep IV took the throne, he changed his name to Akhenaten, or "He Who Serves Aten," to honor the god and then decreed that only Aten should be worshiped throughout Egypt. By Akhenaten's command, temples dedicated to other gods were closed and sometimes damaged or even destroyed. However, the priests of these temples were not asked to serve the new religion, because Akhenaten declared himself the sole intermediary between Aten and humans.

Modern scholars consider the worship of Aten one of the earliest versions of monotheism, the belief in one supreme god. However, household shrines dedicated to Aten, where offerings of fruit or bread could be made to the god, featured figurines of not only Aten but also the king, his family members, and some of the most beloved personal gods in Egypt, such as Bes. This suggests that, although Akhenaten's subjects might have adopted Aten as their one god in public, they continued to worship multiple gods in private. As further evidence of this, as soon as Akhenaten died the Egyptian people abandoned Aten worship and returned to worshiping their traditional gods. **See also** Amenhotep III; Amenhotep IV; ankh; Re; Tiy.

Atum

Atum was an ancient Egyptian god of the earth and of creation who was apparently first worshiped in predynastic times. During the Old Kingdom many of his characteristics were attributed to Re, who then became known as Atum-Re. In his original form, Atum was said to have either created himself from his own seed or been created by the waters of Nun, a goddess of primordial chaos. As a result, his name has been translated as "the Completed One" (i.e., one who can create himself), "the Undifferentiated One" (i.e., one who was part of Nun's waters), or "the All" (reflecting his role as creator). After becoming associated with Re, Atum was considered an aspect of the sun, usually in its setting form.

Atum was associated with kingship as well. Initially, he was thought to protect only the king, who was then believed to ascend to the heavens to join Atum after death. Eventually, however, Atum was seen as the protector of all deceased who were attempting to reach the Afterlife. His cult center was at Heliopolis, but he was worshiped in many other places as well.

Atum was usually depicted as a human king wearing the Double Crown of Upper and Lower Egypt. However, he was sometimes shown as a snake, and in various places he was associated with the lion, the bull, or the scarab, all said to be sacred to him. **See also** Nun; Re.

Avaris

Located in the eastern Delta on a branch of the Nile River, Avaris was the capital city for the Hyksos kings of the Fifth Dynasty, who were constantly warring with Egyptian kings from Thebes. In the First Intermediate Period, foreigners from Asia began settling in the city, and by the Second Intermediate Period their numbers had grown to the point where they could take control of Avaris and the surrounding area. The Theban king conquered Avaris in approximately 1532 B.C. Archaeologists studying this site have found that the walls of the Hyksos palaces have been seriously damaged not just by erosion but by impact blows, suggesting that the battle to take the city must have been fierce.

Following this conquest, the Theban victors apparently destroyed all Hyksos records and monuments in the city. In the subsequent Ramessid Period, Ramses I and his successors rebuilt much of Avaris, adding new temples, shrines, and other structures, including a palace now known as Per-Ramses. Avaris became their capital city, and Per-Ramses was the official royal residence of all Nineteenth Dynasty rulers. **See also** First Intermediate Period; Hyksos; Second Intermediate Period.

Ay (Aya) (?–ca. 1323 B.C.)

During the Eighteenth Dynasty, Ay became king after the death of King Tutankhamun, possibly by marrying Tutankhamun's widow, Ankhesenamun (who might also have been his own granddaughter). However, Ay was related to several members of the royal family through his sister, Queen Tiy, and perhaps also Queen Nefertiti, who might have been his daughter. Despite these connections, Ay was of common birth and was assigned to oversee the horses and horsemen of kings Amenhotep III and Amenhotep IV as master of the horse, a position his father, Yuya, held before him.

During Tutankhamun's reign, Ay apparently acted as the young king's adviser; by this time, he was an old man and undoubtedly a father figure to the boy. Under Ay's guidance, Tutankhamun restored certain religious traditions and worship practices that had been abandoned by his father, Akhenaten, returning the country to the worship of the god Amun rather than Aten.

By the time he ascended the throne, Ay was elderly and lived only four more years. During this brief reign, he built a mortuary temple without a tomb at Medinet Habu in western Thebes; prior to this, a tomb had been prepared for him in King Akhenaten's city of Akhetaten (also known as Amarna). However, Akhetaten had been abandoned during Tutankhamun's reign, so Ay decided to take over a tomb that was probably intended for King Tutankhamun but was left unfinished at the time of his sudden death. Ay ordered his artisans to put representations of himself on the walls of this tomb, and interestingly this artwork features Ay's wife Tiy II (who was once Queen Nefertiti's nursemaid) rather than Ankhesenamun.

Ay's tomb shows evidence of having been brutally attacked sometime after he was placed there: Its wall art and texts have been defaced, its sarcophagus shattered, and its mummy removed. Some Egyptologists believe that this damage was done on the orders of Ay's successor, General Horemheb. Others think that it was committed by Egyptians who were angry with Ay because of his earlier association with King Akhenaten and his unpopular religion. In either case, Ay's mummy has never been found. **See also** Amarna; Amenhotep III; Amenhotep IV; Amun; Ankhesenamun; Aten; Horemheb; Tutankhamun.

ba

According to ancient Egyptian beliefs regarding the Afterlife, the *ba* is one of three elements or forms of the spirit that survive after death. (The others are the *ka* and the *akh.*) Although there is some disagreement among scholars regarding the *ba*'s nature, the predominant view is that the *ba* is the aspect of humanity that provides each person's unique personality and morality, both in life and after death. Apparently, even a god had a *ba,* and those gods that appeared in many forms were said to have many *bas.*

The ancient Egyptians believed that the *ba* was allowed to leave the body at the moment of death. The *ba* was said to spend each day traveling across the sky with the sun god and return each night to the entombed mummy from which it came. It was therefore through the *ba* that the deceased's spirit was supposedly able to move wherever it wished. However, the *ba* could not long be separated from the *ka;* if it was, the *ba* would cease to exist. The ancient Egyptians performed rituals intended to help the *ba* find its way back to the *ka* and its mummy, believing that evil spirits were always at work to prevent this reunion. The symbol of the *ba* was the stork or ram, the latter of which was also associated with the god Khnum, who was often said to be the *ba* of the sun god Re. **See also** *akh; ka;* Khnum; Re.

Babylonia and Chaldea

A neighbor of Egypt, the country of Babylonia was a trading partner with Egypt during the Middle Kingdom, and its chiefs sent lavish gifts as tribute to Eighteenth Dynasty kings. During this dynasty, Babylonia was on very good terms with Egypt, and at least one Egyptian king of this period, Amenhotep III, married a Babylonian princess. Over time, a people living in southern Babylonia, the Chaldeans, came to dominate Babylonia's affairs to the point that that country became known as Chaldea. At this point, relations with Egypt deteriorated, and during Egypt's Third Intermediate Period, the Chaldeans quickly became one of Egypt's most powerful enemies. In the Twenty-sixth Dynasty, after the Egyptians under King Necho II invaded their territory, the Chaldeans defeated Egyptian forces in the Battle of Carchemish (605 B.C.). In subsequent years the Chaldeans attempted to invade Egypt but were repelled on numerous occasions. Then in 559 B.C. when Persia posed a greater threat to the region, the Chaldeans and Egyptians banded together with the lands of Sparta and Lydia to fight against the forces of the Persian king Cyrus the Great. Despite this alliance, however, King Cyrus's armies destroyed Lydia in 546 B.C., captured the Chaldean capital, Babylon, in 538 B.C., and took over Egypt in 525 B.C. **See also** Amenhotep III; Necho II; Persia and Persian Periods; Third Intermediate Period.

Badarian culture

The Badarian culture was one of the first and most influential ancient Egyptian cultures. It formed during the Predynastic

Period in Upper Egypt at least as early as 4400 B.C. Its name comes from the site of el-Badari, where archaeologists first found signs of this culture at the foot of some cliffs. Evidence of the Badarian culture was subsequently found at or near the Egyptian towns of Qau el-Kebir, el-Hammamiya, el-Matmar, and el-Mostagedda.

The people of the Badarian culture, or Badarians, were employed in agriculture, growing barley, castor beans (for oil), flax (from which they wove linen), and a few other crops. They also kept sheep, goats, and cattle, which provided fur and leather, and apparently did not hunt large game, although they did have flint arrowheads with which they killed small game. Their primary tools were the throwing stick (used to disable game birds), the sickle (used to harvest crops), and the ax.

Despite their rudimentary agriculture, the Badarians were seminomadic, periodically moving their villages short distances. Some archaeologists believe that the Badarians developed this practice to protect their homes and livestock from the regular Nile River flooding. Others, however, believe that villages were moved whenever the surrounding fields needed to lie fallow to restore their fertility. In either case, villages were easy to move because the Badarians lived in impermanent structures such as reed and/or pole huts or animal-skin tents.

The Badarians also made pottery, shaping it by hand from Nile clay. Containers and bowls had simple shapes and very thin walls (in fact, the thinnest of the period), often with a rippled surface created by combing the wet clay. Since this pottery resembles that of another, older Predynastic Period culture, the Tasian, some archaeologists believe that the two groups associated with one another and that the Badarians learned how to make their pottery from the Tasians. Others, however, believe that the Badarian culture was not distinct from the Tasian culture but instead a later and/or regional variation of it.

The Badarians made items of adornment, such as hairpins and bracelets, as well, and sometimes they employed ivory and hammered copper in making these objects. Such artifacts have been found in the ancient Egyptian cities of Hierankopolis and Erment, over one hundred miles away, leading some archaeologists to believe that the Badarians were traders as well as farmers. The fact that copper ore would have been extremely scarce, if not nonexistent, for the Badarians supports the idea that they traded with other people in the region. In fact, a few Egyptologists argue that the Badarians traded with people from as far away as the Red Sea and the Sinai, though this theory is much in dispute.

The Badarian culture apparently had a class structure that divided the rich from the poor. Archaeologists have surmised this by studying Badarian cemeteries, where the graves of wealthier individuals are separated from those of the poor. The Badarians buried their dead lying on mats within pits; the bodies were placed on their left sides in the fetal position so that their heads were always pointed south and their faces turned west. This practice was apparently connected to the later ancient Egyptian belief that the land of the dead was located west of Egypt. **See also** Predynastic Period.

Bahariya Oasis

The Bahariya Oasis is about 125 miles west of the Nile River in Libya's Western Desert. Its necropolis site, near the town of Bawit, still has the remains of tombs that were built during the New Kingdom, as well as one temple built by the Twenty-sixth Dynasty king Apries and another by the Macedonian king Alexander the Great in around 331 B.C. Near Alexander's temple, archaeologists have found a cemetery with hundreds or perhaps thousands of well-preserved mummies from various periods of ancient Egyptian history, which they have grouped into four styles: mummies wrapped in linen stiffened by plaster and then painted, mummies wrapped in unstiffened linen decorated with gilded masks and other objects, mummies wrapped in unstiffened linen with no decorations, and mummies wrapped in unstiffened linen with no decorations and no coffin. The painted mummies feature depictions of the gods Horus, Osiris, Isis, Thoth, and Anubis. **See also** oases.

Bakenkhons (Bakenkhonsu) (ca. 1310–ca. 1220 B.C.)

A Nineteenth Dynasty high priest, Bakenkhons left behind a block statue of himself inscribed with his life story. From this, Egyptologists have learned that Bakenkhons was a stableboy at the Temple of Amun at Karnak during the reign of King Seti I when he came to the attention of the priests there. They educated him in their profession, and gradually he became so well respected and influential that the next king on the throne, Ramses II, appointed him the high priest of Amun at Thebes, a position that Bakenkhons held for twenty-seven years. Bakenkhons also oversaw the construction of Ramses II's temple at Karnak, erected bark shrines at Thebes to honor the gods, and served as a judge in the Egyptian court system. Because of his prominence during the reign of Ramses II, Bakenkhons's name appears on several statues, as well as in the Berlin Papyrus (a collection of papyri related primarily to literature and medicine). Some records suggest that Bakenkhons was related to Ramses II's wife Queen Nefertari. After Bakenkhons's death, his son Roma-Roy was appointed to succeed him as high priest of Amun at Thebes. **See also** Amun; bark shrines; priests; Ramses II.

Bakenrenef (?–715 B.C.)

Bakenrenef was a king of the Twenty-fourth Dynasty. His father, Tefnakhte, claimed to have unified all of Lower Egypt, although his influence was probably confined to the Nile Delta. Bakenrenef inherited his father's realm. He had been on the throne for only six years when the Nubian king Shabaka swept north to conquer his land and others. Upon defeating and capturing Bakenrenef, Shabaka ordered him burned alive. **See also** Saite Period.

bark shrines

A bark (or barque) shrine was a type of ancient Egyptian shrine that housed a cult statue of a god. The shrine was constructed so that it could be carried on a boat; such boats were called the barks of the gods. However, sometimes barks of the gods were called bark shrines as well. **See also** barks of the gods.

barks of the gods

Barks (sometimes spelled *barques*) of the gods were full-size or miniature boats used in ancient religious ceremonies to represent the boats supposedly used by the gods to travel across the sky or through the Underworld, both regions the ancient Egyptians believed were made of water. The barks were made of various materials, such as brick or wood, depending on whether they were actually intended to float on water. All of them, though, were fairly ornate, with well-decorated cabins to hold the gods' shrines and perhaps flags, obelisks, or other adornments as well. Barks of the god Osiris were the most lavishly decorated, covered with a great deal of gold and jewels.

Barks specific to certain gods were often housed in special temples, where they were maintained and used as floating shrines in ceremonies dedicated to those gods. For example, the bark of the god Amun was housed in a special temple in Thebes until it was needed for Amun-related ceremonies. Typical of these ceremonial occasions was the Feast of Opet (or Festival of Opet), which was held annually at the time of the Nile River inundation, when the water level rose to its

This tomb painting, created between 664 and 525 B.C., depicts a solar bark carrying Egyptian gods and goddesses.

highest point. When this occurred, priests in Amun's sanctuary at Karnak bathed and dressed a statue of the god and placed it in an enclosed shrine atop his ceremonial bark, which was named the Userhetamun or Weseghatamun ("Might of Brow Is Amun"). This bark was on poles so that the priests could carry the boat by lifting the poles onto their shoulders. To begin the festival, they transported the bark from their Karnak temple to the Temple of Amun at Luxor about one and a half miles away. In the early years of the festival, the priests carried the bark the entire route; later, however, the priests carried the bark only to the Nile River, where it was placed on a barge for its trip to Luxor. In either case, once in Luxor, the bark was taken inside the inner sanctuary of the temple, where Amun's figure was removed for use in various rituals. Afterward the god and his bark were returned to Karnak along the same route and in the same manner as they were brought to Luxor. **See also** Amun; deities; Osiris; temples.

basketry

Throughout their history, the ancient Egyptians fashioned grass, palm leaves, reeds, and rushes into various items, including mats, ropes, sandals, and baskets. To make baskets they used several techniques. The simplest technique was to make coils of fibers that were then spiraled and stacked to shape the basket; rows of coils were fastened together with thin fiber strands. More complicated techniques involved weaving or sewing strands or plaits of fiber into desired shapes. Baskets were usually left in their natural color, although occasionally some dyed strands were incorporated into the piece as decoration. Baskets were primarily used as containers for household goods and produce, but among the poor, large baskets were also commonly used as coffins. **See also** coffins.

Bastet

An ancient Egyptian goddess, Bastet was associated with dancing, music, and pregnancy and was called upon to ward off demons and prevent serious illness. From the Third Intermediate Period on, she was most commonly depicted as a cat or as a woman with the head of a cat, and she typically held a sistrum (a type of rattle used in religious ceremonies) and/or an ankh, the ancient Egyptian symbol for life.

Worship of Bastet originated in the town of Per-Bastet (located north of modern-day Cairo). Once the capital of the eighteenth nome of Lower Egypt, this town—in modern times called Tell Basta—contains the remains of a Sixth Dynasty shrine and a Ramessid Period temple complex both dedicated to the goddess. North of the main temple is a Birth House (a small temple where a god or goddess was supposedly born) dedicated to the son of Bastet, the god Mihos. At one time, the temple complex also had a series of water channels that fed a sacred lake. Because of Bastet's association with cats, these animals apparently figured prominently in ceremonies honoring her. Excavations of Tell Basta, which began with French archaeologist Edouard Naville in 1887–1889, have uncovered numerous catacombs holding mummified cats, as well as extensive burials of cats and other animals. **See also** Birth House; Ramessid Period.

Bayenemwast (?–ca. 1155 B.C.)

During the Twentieth Dynasty reign of Ramses III, Bayenemwast, who was the captain of the Nubian Archers in the Egyptian military, apparently became involved in a plot to kill the king and replace him with the king's son Pentaweret. There were nearly thirty people involved in this plot, including the boy's mother, Queen Tiy; several women in the king's harem, including Bayenemwast's sister; and government and military officials. According to an ancient Egyptian papyrus now known

as the Judicial Papyrus of Turin, as well as other records of the period, the conspirators were caught and put on trial. There is no specific information about what happened to every defendant, but at least some of those who were found guilty were sentenced to death and then allowed to commit suicide rather than be executed. Bayenemwast was most likely among those deemed guilty, because he is referred to as the "Evil in Thebes" in many ancient records. **See also** harem; Ramses III.

beer

The ancient Egyptians considered beer to be one of the two most important elements in their diet, bread being the other. Both adults and children drank beer daily, and the drink was brewed throughout the country.

The main ingredient in ancient Egyptian beer was fermented barley or wheat. Prior to fermentation, the grain was crushed, steeped in water, germinated, and dried (a process called malting). The resulting material was thoroughly ground and then mixed in warm water; the mash was pressed through a sieve and left to ferment. In an alternative method, leftover pieces of stale barley bread were crumbled and soaked in water mixed with various sweeteners and left to ferment. Once fermentation occurred, the liquid was squeezed and separated from the bread by pressing it through a cloth. If sweeteners (such as honey, dates, or spices) had not been added to the bread prior to fermentation, they were often added afterward.

Beer making was such a vital part of ancient Egyptian life that steps were taken to make sure that it continued to take place in the Afterlife as well. Scenes related to beer making were painted on many tomb walls, and small wooden models of people engaged in beer making were placed in tombs and temples, because such depictions were said to magically ensure that a particular activity would go on through eternity. Beer also figured prominently in Egyptian myths, in which certain deities, particularly Hathor and Sekhmet, were sometimes depicted as drinking to excess. In addition, beer and wine were part of certain temple rituals and offerings, and festivals for Hathor often involved drunken revelry. The patron deities of beer were Menqet and Tenemyt. Some Egyptian records indicate that Menqet was also the name for beer jars and Tenemyt for a variety of beer.

Beer was a part of Egyptian magic and medicine as well. The ancient Egyptians believed that a dream featuring beer would bring good luck—unless the beer was warm or bitter, in which case bad luck would follow. Beer was further said to drive away evil spirits when combined with certain spells and the drink was prescribed by physicians as a cure for stomach ailments. **See also** bread; food; Hathor.

Beit el-Wali

Located in Nubia south of Aswan on the west bank of the Nile, Beit el-Wali was once the site of a rock-cut temple built by Ramses II. On its walls were inscriptions providing details about the king's various military campaigns, as well as numerous reliefs and scenes related to the king's activities. The temple was dedicated to the god Amun-Re, among others. Between 1962 and 1965, a team of archaeologists worked to move the temple farther from the Nile River in anticipation of the flooding that building the Aswan High Dam would cause. The temple now stands at New Kalabsha, close to the dam. **See also** Amun; Nile River; Ramses II.

Belzoni, Giovanni Battista (1778–1823)

Giovanni Battista Belzoni was an Italian excavator of ancient Egyptian treasures. He was working as a salesman specializing in hydraulic engines when, after trying unsuccessfully to sell his wares to Egypt's Turkish viceroy, Ali Pasha, in 1815, he decided to become involved in the lucrative Egyptian antiquities market. By 1817 he was excavating several prominent tomb and temple archaeological sites at the request of the British consul general in Egypt, Henry Salt, among others. Belzoni's activities during this period include the removal of an obelisk from the island of Philae (within the Nile River near Aswan) and a colossal bust of Ramses II from the Ramesseum (a temple of Ramses II) in Thebes. Belzoni successfully transported this bust to London, England, but when he subsequently tried to transport the obelisk, it was taken from him by representatives of the French government before it could leave Egypt.

Belzoni also explored the ruins at Elephantine, the temple at Edfu, and the tomb of Seti I at the Valley of the Kings, and he discovered more than a dozen important statues at Karnak. He also excavated the tomb of Ramses II at Abu Simbel, became the first person since ancient times to enter King Khafre's pyramid at Giza, and found the ruins of the ancient city of Berenice on the coast of the Red Sea. In addition, Belzoni made detailed drawings and models of many of his discoveries. In 1825, two years after his death, some of these works were displayed at Egyptian exhibits in London and Paris. His drawings also appeared in a book he published about his experiences, the 1820 two-volume work *Narrative of the Operations and Recent Discoveries Within the Pyramids, Temples, Tombs, and Excavations in Egypt and Nubia.* **See also** Abu Simbel; archaeological expeditions; Edfu; Elephantine; Giza; Karnak; Philae; Valley of the Kings.

Beni Hasan (Beni Hassan; Menat-Khufu)

Located on the east bank of the Nile River north of Hermopolis, Beni Hasan served as the burial site for that city's prominent citizens. The site has approximately one thousand small tombs dating from the late Sixth

Dynasty to the First Intermediate Period as well as thirty-nine large rock-cut tombs dating from the Eleventh and Twelfth Dynasties. These large tombs were carved into limestone until bedrock was reached and then hollowed out to create elaborate chambers, columns, and chapels.

Eight of these rock-cut tombs belonged to overlords of the sixteenth nome of Upper Egypt, also known as the Oryx nome. Of these, the most elaborate was that of Amenemhet (not to be confused with several kings with the same name), a nomarch and military commander during the reign of Twelfth Dynasty king Senwosret I. Amenemhet's tomb contains scenes from three of the military expeditions he led for the king, as well as scenes of hunting, dancing, and grape pressing. In this and other nearby tombs, there are also carved and/or painted scenes related to Egypt's plants and animals and the daily life of its people. Among the other works contained in nearby tombs are a depiction of two wrestlers who apparently represent a god of light and a god of darkness; numerous illustrations of craftspeople, dancers, and businessmen such as barbers, chiropractors, and shopkeepers; hunting scenes; and depictions of foreign traders.

Just south of the Beni Hasan tombs is a shrine cut out of living rock. Its construction was begun by Eighteenth Dynasty queen-pharaoh Hatshepsut and continued by Nineteenth Dynasty king Seti I but never finished. Called the Speos Artimidos (Cave of Artemis) by the Greeks, this rock shrine was dedicated to the worship of Pakhet (She Who Claws), a lioness-headed Egyptian goddess who was a form of the goddess Hathor. **See also** Amenemhet; First Intermediate Period; Hatshepsut.

Berlin Papyrus

The Berlin Papyrus is a collection of papyri from various dynasties related primarily to literature and medicine but including other subjects as well. Most were written during the Middle Kingdom or Ramessid Period, but one medical papyrus appears to be from the Old Kingdom. Another, Papyrus Berlin 3027, is a Nineteenth Dynasty text dealing with illnesses of infants and mothers and includes magical spells for their protection. Papyrus B 304, from the Twenty-second Dynasty, features a marriage agreement and oath. Other papyri include popular stories, such as *The Tale of Sinuhe* and *The Tale of the Eloquent Peasant*. **See also** *Eloquent Peasant, The Tale of the;* marriage; medicine; papyrus; *Sinuhe, The Tale of.*

Bes

Bes was a household deity (i.e., a deity worshiped primarily at home, as opposed to temple ceremonies) connected to childbirth who was first worshiped in Egypt during the New Kingdom. Egyptologists disagree on where Bes might have originated, but Babylonia or Punt (a foreign land that might have been located in Sudan or Ethiopia) seem the most likely candidates. Egyptologists also disagree on how

Bes, a god often depicted as a bearded disfigured dwarf, was believed to protect babies and children from demons.

Bes came to be associated with childbirth, particularly since the deity was viewed as male. The two prevailing theories, however, relate to the deity's appearance. In many depictions, including Ptolemaic Period statues and birthing-room wall art, Bes was a disfigured, bearded dwarf with bowed legs. Some Egyptologists believe that these deformities made Bes a visible representation of a pregnant woman's worst fears for her child. Others believe that the deity's role was as a protector whose deformities would frighten demons away from the child about to be born. It does appear that women in labor called on Bes for good luck and that he was considered a kindly deity. He was also said to dance with a tambourine to keep evil spirits away, and many young children wore pendants with his likeness to have this same protection. In fact, entire families often worshiped Bes at household altars. However, Bes was also considered a patron of war and of hunters, and therefore typically dressed in animal skins to show his connection to the hunt and the kill. The deity's consort was Beset, appropriately a fertility figure. **See also** Babylonia and Chaldea; Birth House; Ptolemaic Period; Punt.

birds

Because the waters of the Nile created lush marshlands, lakes, and other areas attractive to wildlife, ancient Egypt was home to many different varieties of birds. These included quail, hawks, grouse, owls, swallows, sparrows, ravens, plovers, storks, cranes, egrets, herons, ibis, geese, and ducks. Some of these birds were considered sacred and therefore not eaten, whereas others were used routinely for food.

Birds acceptable as food, such as the quail and duck, were hunted by all classes of Egyptians. They used nets and traps to catch the birds or throwsticks to knock them from the sky. Throwsticks were one- to two-foot-long sticks of slightly curved

wood that were heavy enough to strike with considerable force when thrown. Entire families would sometimes go bird hunting together, perhaps gliding slowly and quietly along the Nile River in a boat or hiding in reeds.

Birds considered sacred were not only spared from being eaten but revered; in some cases, they were mummified after death as part of religious ceremonies. Particularly sacred were the hawk, which was associated with the gods Horus and Re; the falcon, associated with the gods Re-Horakhty, Horus, Mont, and Khons; the ibis, associated with Thoth; the goose, associated with Geb; and the swallow, associated with Isis. However, these associations were not consistent throughout Egypt. Some birds might be sacred in one location and not in another, or the degree of sacredness might vary from place to place. For example, the vulture was venerated in Upper Egypt and eventually came to be seen as the guardian of that region, but in some other places the bird apparently had no significance whatsoever. **See also** Geb; Horus; Isis; Re; Thoth.

Birth House

Also called a Mammisi, a Birth House was a small temple where a god or goddess had supposedly been born. Its walls were decorated with scenes of the gods giving birth to or witnessing the birth of kings, with the central figure usually being whichever king built the temple. Typically located within a larger temple dedicated to that deity, the Birth House primarily appears in temples built during the Late and Greco-Roman Periods. However, an early version of the Birth House appears in a section of the Temple of Karnak built by King Amenhotep III during the Eighteenth Dynasty. One of the scenes in this chamber shows the god Khnum fashioning the king and his *ka* (spirit) on a potter's wheel, while another shows the god Amun nursing the king. **See also** Amenhotep III; Amun; *ka;* Karnak; Khnum.

Black Land

The Black Land, or Kemet, was the ancient Egyptians' name for Egypt. The surrounding deserts were called the Red Land, or Deshret. Both of these terms came from the color of the ground. Whereas the desert glowed red in the morning sun, the soil of Egypt was rich and black, thanks to the silt brought by the annual flooding of the Nile River. **See also** Nile River.

Book of Aker, The

Found incomplete in the tombs of Ramses VI and Ramses IX, *The Book of Aker* is a funerary text that centers around Aker, a manifestation of the earth god Geb. Egyptologists have had difficulty understanding the meaning of this text because of its fragmentary nature, but they believe that its symbolism is related to the king's transition from an earthly being to a heavenly one. **See also** Geb.

Book of Caverns

A New Kingdom funerary text appearing on tomb walls, the *Book of Caverns* describes the sun god Re's passage through the Underworld. In this respect, it is similar to the *Book of What Is in the Duat* and *The Book of Gates.* However, the *Book of What Is in the Duat* mainly describes the journey and *The Book of Gates* mainly describes the gates impeding the progress of the journey and gives passwords to open them; the *Book of Caverns,* in contrast, is primarily concerned with the punishment—in the form of mutilation and obliteration—meted out to the enemies of Osiris in the caverns of the Underworld. In other words, the main emphasis in this text is punishment for bad deeds and rewards for good behavior. Moreover, the *Book of Caverns* has far more text and far fewer illustrations than other funerary texts of the period, and it does not always show the sun god in his solar bark as other texts do. Instead, the solar deity takes many different forms. The book's illustra-tions also include unusual images such as strange creatures whose symbolism is unclear. Because of these obscure allusions, Egyptologists concede that their understanding of the text is incomplete. **See also** barks of the gods; *Book of Gates, The; Book of What Is in the Duat;* Osiris; Re.

Book of Gates, The (*The Book of Portals*)

The Book of Gates (also known as *The Book of Portals*) is a New Kingdom funerary text that appears in fragments on the walls of several tombs, including that of Eighteenth Dynasty general-king Horemheb (which seems to be the oldest occurrence of the text), and in its entirety in the tomb of Ramses VI. Very similar to the *Book of What Is in the Duat,* the text and illustrations relate to the journey of the sun god Re through the Underworld. However, *The Book of Gates* adds material regarding the series of gates that block Re's path at locations reached hourly during this journey. In particular, it describes the guardian(s) at each gate, including serpents that spit fire and several dog- and cobra-headed monsters.

The gods Horus and Osiris figure prominently in the text, as they do in other funerary texts of the period, although other gods appear as well. In one section of the text, Horus is shown with four races of humankind said to have been created from the heart of Re: the Egyptians, the Asiatics, the Libyans, and the Blacks (which Egyptologists have identified as being from the interior of Africa). The Blacks were said to be under the special protection of Horus, the Asiatics and Libyans of the goddess Sekhmet, and the Egyptians of Re.

The Book of Gates is rich in symbolism. For example, knotted ropes, representing magic, appear frequently, and the donkey is shown at one point to symbolize the carrying of spiritual burdens. In addition, the book shows the solar deity in two other forms besides that of Re: the god Atum as the setting sun and Khepri, a winged scarab, as the sun poised to rise.

Many Egyptologists believe that the purpose of the text was not merely to portray the Underworld, whether directly or through symbolism, but also to act as a guidebook to the spirits of the deceased as they tried to reach the Afterlife. To this end, *The Book of Gates* provides the passwords required to make it through each of the gates on a journey through the Underworld. **See also** *Book of What Is in the Duat;* Horus; Ramses VI; Re; Sekhmet.

Book of the Day, The

One of several New Kingdom illustrated funerary texts, *The Book of the Day* concerns the passage of the sun during the day; a corresponding text, *The Book of the Night,* concerns the passage of the sun during the night. As with other New Kingdom funerary texts, both books were painted on tomb walls and/or ceilings and designed to resemble papyrus scrolls.

There are several known versions of *The Book of the Day.* In fact, the tomb of Ramses VI alone has two versions. Generally, however, the book begins with the solar disk emerging in the east from the womb of the goddess Nut, who is accompanied by other deities. The disk then travels west on a solar bark along a celestial river, past various gods and beautiful grain-filled fields. Upon reaching the farthest point west, where sunset would occur, the solar disk is swallowed by Nut. Throughout the book are cosmological and astrological images, such as that of the sun traveling along a heavenly river. **See also** barks of the gods; *Book of the Night, The;* Nut; Ramses VI.

Book of the Dead

A funerary text that first appeared at the end of the Second Intermediate Period, the *Book of the Dead* is an illustrated book of approximately two hundred spells whose purpose was to help a deceased person's spirit reach the Afterlife and therefore sur-

A scene from the Book of the Dead *depicts Anubis crouching under the scales, weighing the heart of the deceased.*

vive for eternity. These spells not only served as incantations that could be recited to guarantee smooth passage but also described various aspects of the Underworld and gave instructions regarding funerary rituals, including how to incorporate amulets into mummy wrappings. Passages from the *Book of the Dead,* accompanied by illustrations, would be written on rolls of papyrus to be left in the tomb and/or on scraps of papyrus tucked into mummy wrappings so that the deceased could take the material along on the trip to the Afterlife. Spells might also be inscribed on amulets and other funerary objects.

Whereas previous guidebooks to the Afterlife were intended for the upper classes (in particular, the Pyramid Texts for royalty and the Coffin Texts for the wealthy), the *Book of the Dead* promoted the idea that anyone from any social class could achieve an Afterlife, provided he or she was worthy of it. This worth was supposedly measured in the Judgment Hall of Osiris, where the heart of the deceased was weighed on a scale to see whether its owner could remain in the Afterlife. In the past, the Afterlife was supposed to be for the wealthy, but the *Book of the Dead* promoted the idea that a person of lesser means had just as good a chance of being judged worthy as a rich one did. However, since poor people could not afford to have temple scribes provide their tombs with a complete copy of the *Book of the Dead,* priests promoted the idea that a copy of only a portion of the text might be just as effective. As a result, people bought copies of certain spells depending on which ones they thought that they or their loved ones might need most. The most popular spells were those intended to ensure that the heart and spirit of the deceased would behave properly in the Judgment Hall of Osiris.

Because the *Book of the Dead* was selectively copied as a way to personalize the text for each tomb owner, archaeologists have found many versions of the book and refer to each one by the name of the person who commissioned it. Despite of finding many different copies of the *Book of the Dead,* archaeologists have never found a complete copy containing all known spells. **See also** Afterlife; Coffin Texts; Osiris; Pyramid Texts.

Book of the Divine Cow

The *Book of the Divine Cow* is a New Kingdom illustrated funerary text, although it appears to be based on material in Fifth and Sixth Dynasty Pyramid Texts. No complete version of the *Book of the Divine Cow* has been discovered, so Egyptologists are uncertain as to the purpose of this text. However, it appears to tell a story in which the Divine Cow, the goddess Hathor, is sent by the sun god Re to destroy humankind after he hears that people no longer support his rule over the earth. Midway into Hathor's attack, Re changes his mind and stops Hathor by tricking her into drinking too much beer. (He does this by coloring the beer red so that Hathor will think it is the blood of the enemies she has killed.) In other versions of the story, Hathor is replaced by Sekhmet, a lioness goddess more commonly associated with destruction. In either case, the story ends .with Re establishing a new order in his realm, creating the position of vizier, and appointing the god Thoth in this role. **See also** Hathor; Pyramid Texts; Sekhmet.

Book of the Night, The

One of several New Kingdom funerary texts, *The Book of the Night* concerns the passage of the sun during the night; a corresponding text, *The Book of the Day,* concerns the passage of the sun during the day. As with other New Kingdom funerary texts, this one was painted on tomb walls and/or ceilings to look like a papyrus with hieroglyphic writing and illustrations.

The Book of the Night shows the solar disk, upon a solar bark, in the company of other deities traveling through the darkness inside the body of the goddess Nut. Along the way, this group encounters other gods and strange beings, and they witness the god Horus punishing the enemies of Osiris. At the end of the book, the goddesses Isis and Nephthys take the solar disk from one bark and put it in another, because the solar god was believed to use one bark during the day and another at night. **See also** barks of the gods; *Book of the Day, The;* Horus; Isis; Nephthys; Osiris.

Book of Thoth, The

Said to have been dictated by the god Thoth himself, *The Book of Thoth* was a collection of papyri related to medicine and philosophy, with supplementary papyri that dealt with astronomy, astrology, religious rituals and festivals, the requirements and duties of priests, and magic. However, no copies of these papyri have yet been found; what Egyptologists know of them comes from references found in a few other papyri texts. **See also** astronomy; medicine; papyrus; religion.

Book of What Is in the Duat (Book of What Is in the Am Duat; Book of What Is in the Underworld; Book of He Who Is in the Underworld)

The earliest New Kingdom funerary text, the *Book of What Is in the Duat* concerns the nightly journey of the sun god Re through the Underworld in his solar bark (boat), ending with his resurrection at dawn. However, an introduction to the work essentially explains that the writings are a guidebook to the spirit's journey through the Underworld.

As with other New Kingdom funerary texts, this one was painted on tomb walls to look like a papyrus scroll with rows of hieroglyphic text and accompanying illustrations. Shown with Re in these illustrations is the king in whose tomb the funerary text appears. The first such king was apparently Tuthmosis I, although

some Egyptologists believe that the text on his tomb walls—which has been damaged, so only fragments remain—was copied from an earlier source. Complete versions of the *Book of What Is in the Duat* appear in the tombs of Tuthmosis III and Amenhotep II.

In its complete version, the text is divided into twelve sections, each of which represents one of the twelve hours between dusk and dawn. Each section describes the progress made and the challenges met by the king and sun god during that hour, incorporating a great deal of material related to magic and alchemy in the process. At the threshold of each new hour is a gate at which a guardian requires a password if the traveler is to proceed.

In the first hour of this journey, Re (shown with a ram's head topped by a solar disk) and the king set out to descend to the Underworld in Re's solar bark, preceded by a procession of deities that include Ma'at, Osiris, and Sekhmet. By the fourth hour their descent is complete, and as they begin to travel through the Underworld they pass monstrous serpents and see the birth of the scarab (a dung beetle symbolizing rebirth). Throughout the rest of the journey, other dangers and symbols (particularly related to rebirth and transformation) appear, as do other gods. For example, in the seventh hour the goddess Isis helps the bark move forward as the way grows more difficult. Also in this hour, Re's forces confront and defeat Apophis, a beast seeking to prevent Re's rebirth. The god Horus is prominent in the tenth hour, offering encouragement to lost souls swimming in the waters beside the bark, telling them to try harder for the shore. In the eleventh hour, Horus punishes wrongdoers by cutting them into pieces. In the final hour, the king's mummy is shown abandoned, and other imagery suggests that he has joined the other deities in the celestial realm. **See also** Afterlife; Horus; Osiris; Re; Underworld.

bread

Along with beer, bread was a staple of the ancient Egyptian diet, eaten at every meal by people of all social classes. Bread was baked daily in nearly every home. In fact, so central to life was this activity that models of servants engaged in bread making were often included in tombs, because it was believed that they would magically come alive in the Afterlife to continue making bread for the tomb's occupant. Without regular offerings of bread, Egyptians believed, the deceased's *ka* (one aspect of the spirit) was thought to risk dying of starvation.

Tomb and temple lists indicate that there were several types of bread in ancient Egypt, which were made with barley, emmer wheat or spelt wheat, and yeast. Some types of bread included ingredients such as eggs, milk, and perhaps butter, as well as sweeteners such as honey, fruit, and possibly various spices for flavoring. Egyptologists surmise that each type of bread had a uniquely shaped loaf so that people could tell one from another.

The process of making wheat bread began with crushing the grain in large mortars. The resulting material was then transferred to grinding stones or hand mills called querns to produce the finest flour. This flour was mixed with other ingredients, kneaded, and shaped into a loaf. To make barley bread, fine barley was mixed with water, aired, moistened again, pressed through a sieve, then crushed and kneaded into a loaf. Both wheat and barley loaves would then either be fried or, more commonly, placed on a clay platter and baked on an open coal-fueled fire or, during the New Kingdom, in a small clay oven. **See also** beer; food.

brick making

The ancient Egyptians used bricks made of Nile River mud as their building material for most structures. The mud was a mixture of clay and sand, with the proportions varying depending on where the mud was gathered. When the amount of clay in the mud was too little, the bricks were likely to crumble; in these cases, the ancient Egyptians trampled pieces of straw or animal dung into the mud with their feet so that the resulting bricks would hold together. Once the proper consistency had been achieved, the mud was pressed into wooden, rectangular molds to shape it into bricks. Once the bricks had been formed, they were carefully removed from their molds to dry in the sun. Sometimes during this process the brick was marked with the name of the king commissioning the building in which the brick was to be used.

The first brick molds appeared in Egypt in approximately 3400 B.C. and sun drying remained the most common method of hardening bricks until the latter part of the Greco-Roman Period, when bricks were baked in kilns. There is evidence that the ancient Egyptians knew how to produce kiln-baked and fired bricks earlier than this, but they probably rarely needed to employ this method given the intensity of the Egyptian sun. Therefore, it seems that the only reason kiln-baked bricks eventually became prevalent was because they were popular with the Romans. **See also** architecture; building materials; Nile River.

bronze

Although they knew how to make bronze, copper was the metal of choice for ancient Egyptians throughout their early history. From 3000 B.C. on, however, they slowly began using bronze for tools, razors, and, during the New Kingdom, armor. The reason for this slow adoption of bronze is that bronze is made by combining molten tin with molten copper, and ancient Egyptians had no nearby source of tin. Nonetheless, once the Egyptians learned that adding tin to copper created a harder metal, they were eager to acquire tin in trade with western

Asia, where it occurs naturally. Moreover, the Egyptians began to experiment with the manufacturing process to find the optimum proportions of the two metals, heating the ores over charcoal fires and blowing air on them using bellows made of goatskins and reed pipes. **See also** copper and copper molds; mining and metalworking.

Buchis (Bukhe) bull

Buchis was the sacred bull of Erment, south of Thebes, where there was a cult center dedicated to the god Mont. The Buchis bull was considered a physical manifestation of Mont, so it was kept in a special stall and was well cared for throughout its life. When the bull died, it was mummified, placed in a coffin, and entombed or buried in a Theban cemetery, whereupon a new Buchis was chosen from among the local population of bulls. However, only a bull with a black head and white body could be selected. Over time, the association between Buchis and Mont weakened, and eventually Buchis was associated with Amun-Re or Osiris instead. **See also** Amun; bulls, sacred; Mont; Osiris.

building materials

Prior to approximately 3400 B.C. ancient Egyptian homes, shrines, and other structures were made of bundles of reeds and other plant materials. Small buildings were occasionally made of wood, but since good timber was scarce, wood was rarely used. Then, sometime during the Predynastic Period, the Egyptians figured out how to turn their plentiful Nile River mud into bricks, and this became their main building material. Homes, tombs, palaces, shrines, and city walls were all made with mud bricks that had been shaped in molds and dried in the sun.

Mud bricks continued to be an important part of ancient Egyptian architecture throughout the country's history. However,

during the Second Dynasty stone began to be employed for doorways and other architectural details, and in the Third Dynasty the first all-stone buildings were constructed, including the first of many pyramids. By employing stone, pyramid builders made structures far grander than could have been achieved working in mud brick.

Nonetheless, in the Middle Kingdom some kings returned to using mud brick for their structures because the supply of easily attained and therefore less expensive stones had been depleted. However, even though the top half of a pyramid might be made of mud brick, the base and perhaps the central core was still limestone. Moreover, even the top-half mud brick might be encased in limestone to give the structure more strength.

Because of the expense of stone during this period, all buildings not intended to honor kings or deities were made entirely of mud brick, perhaps with various use of stone and wood in doorways and columns. Still, because of the difficulty and expense of obtaining good timber, the type of structures a king built during his reign would vary depending on his wealth and ability to trade with neighboring countries.

Those few Middle and New Kingdom kings who wanted to build all-stone structures either took stone from existing buildings, usually destroying them in the process, or launched massive quarrying expeditions to various sites. Except for white limestone, which could be quarried at Tura near Memphis, most stones came from places that required complicated transportation efforts and massive manpower. Red granite, for example, was brought down the Nile River from Aswan, and black granite was transported across land from an area near the Red Sea. Getting stone from such areas was so difficult and expensive that some stones were abandoned en route, or even before leaving the quarry. For example, an Aswan quarry still has a one-thousand-ton obelisk that was left there unfinished. Because of such difficulties, nobles increasingly had their tombs carved out of living rock, and as the New Kingdom progressed, an increasing number of shrines were constructed this way as well. **See also** architecture; pyramids.

bulls, sacred

There were three ancient Egyptian cult centers known to have sacred bulls within their temples. The city of Erment (Hermonthis) had the A'a Nefer bull and the Buchis bull, both considered to be manifestations of the god Mont. The city of Memphis had the Apis bull, thought to be a manifestation of the god Ptah. The city of Heliopolis had the Mnevis bull, thought to be a manifestation of the god Re. In each case, a bull with certain physical characteristics would be selected and then kept in the temple to participate in various ceremonies. Upon the animal's death, it was buried, much as a deceased person would be, and another animal with a nearly identical appearance was found to take its place. **See also** Apis bull; Buchis bull; Mnevis bull.

burial sites

Ancient Egyptians who were not kings or nobles were buried in shallow graves away from areas of human activity (unless this was impossible, which was the case with cemeteries within Egyptian frontier fortresses). The most common burial sites were along the edges of the desert or along the Nile River, the latter of which was believed to be linked to the Afterlife. The poor did not mummify their dead because the process was expensive, but mummification might occur naturally in some types of Egyptian soil. Coffins of the poor often consisted of only a bundle of reeds or an animal skin tied around the body, and their gravesites were either unmarked or topped with a simple pile of stones; occasionally, two people might be buried in one grave.

In sharp contrast, the wealthy in ancient Egypt received a much more elaborate burial, at first in underground tombs and later in tombs built of mud brick atop the earth or cut into the faces of cliffs and rocks. Some early kings chose to be entombed in pyramids, while later ones preferred to hide their burial sites to protect their tomb goods from robbers. At least sixty-two kings and nobles were entombed in the Valley of the Kings for this reason.

Archaeologists typically call a site with many tombs and other types of burials a necropolis (the Greek word for cemetery), reserving the word *cemetery* for smaller burial sites or for burial subdivisions within a necropolis. In addition to the Valley of the Kings, the most prominent necropolis sites include Giza, Tanis, Abusir, Saqqara, Dashur, el-Lisht, Meidum, Lahun, Hawara, Beni Hasan, Deir el-Bersha, Abydos, Thebes, and Deir el-Medina. **See also** funerals; mummification; necropolis; Valley of the Kings.

Butehamun (dates unknown)

Butehamun was a Twentieth/Twenty-first Dynasty tomb restorer whose name has been found in many of the structures of the Valley of the Kings, particularly in connection with work done around 1070 B.C. Together with his father, Djehutymose, Butehamun tried to repair damage wrought by tomb robbers on mummies as well as their tombs. The two men—who jointly held the title "the scribes of the necropolis"—also performed burial rituals for the mummies they reentombed. For this reason, the lid of Butehamun's own coffin shows him waving the smoke of incense over various kings. One of the kings depicted was most likely Ramses III, whose mummy wrappings indicate that Butehamun was responsible for replacing them after they had been damaged. Butehamun continued such work alone after his father died and by royal decree was rewarded with many titles, including "opener of the gates of the Underworld" and "overseer of works in the house of eternity." **See also** funerals; mummification; Ramses III; tombs; Valley of the Kings.

Buto

Located south of Tanis in the Delta region of Egypt, Buto was the capital of Lower Egypt prior to the Old Kingdom. At that time it was called Per-Wadjet, or "House of Wadjet," because it was considered the residence of the cobra goddess Wadjet. Per-Wadjet was a center of power for predynastic rulers, and Egyptologists credit an as-yet-unidentified First Dynasty king with erecting a temple there. The town eventually became part of the sixth nome of Lower Egypt, and it remained powerful at least until the Old Kingdom (ca. 2686–ca. 2125 B.C.). The latest remains found at the site, excavated by a German archaeological team during the late 1980s, date from this period.

In modern times, the town's name was changed from the Greek Buto to the current Tell el-Farain, or the "Mound of the Pharaohs," because the town's ancient remains are under three mounds of earth. The first two mounds have yielded town buildings, and in the third was found the First Dynasty temple. **See also** nomes and nomarchs; Tanis; Wadjet.

Byblos

In ancient times, Byblos (also known as Jubayl) was a town on the coast of Canaan or Lebanon whose people traded with the Egyptians from as early as the Second Dynasty. In fact, Byblos provided Egypt with most of its timber, particularly cedar. In exchange, the people of Byblos received many Egyptian goods, as evidenced by the fact that Egyptian objects—particularly from the Twelfth Dynasty—have been found in Byblos royal tombs. There is also evidence that Byblos relied on Egypt for military assistance; in a collection of correspondence known as the Amarna Letters is a letter from the ruler of Byblos, Rib-addi, asking Egypt to send troops to protect his city from invaders. Archaeologists have also found a Twenty-first Dynasty literary work called *The Tale of Wenamun* that refers to a Twentieth Dynasty Egyptian expedition to Byblos in which a king sends a government official, Wenamun, to acquire wood for a temple. From this and other material, scholars have concluded that Egypt and Byblos had a great deal of contact with each other in the Twelfth Dynasty and again between the Nineteenth and Twenty-third Dynasties, after which the bond between the two places apparently weakened. **See also** *Wenamun, The Tale of.*

caches, royal

Royal caches is the term used by Egyptologists to refer to groups of mummies that were hidden from tomb robbers by ancient Egyptian priests. During the New Kingdom, tomb robbery had become so common in Egypt that priests became concerned about the remains of their deceased kings and other members of royal families. In many cases, tomb robbers had defaced mummies in their quest to find jewelry and amulets within their wrappings. To protect them, in approximately 1000 B.C. Egypt's highest-ranking priests decided to collect these damaged mummies, repair their wrappings, and reentomb them together in two locations, one near Deir el-Bahariat in Thebes and the other in the tomb of Amenhotep II in the Valley of the Kings.

The reentombed mummies were discovered by archaeologists excavating the site near Thebes in 1881; although nineteenth-century tomb robbers had already stolen many of the tomb's funerary goods, forty royal mummies still lay undisturbed. The second site, in the Valley of the Kings, contained sixteen mummies and was found in 1898. Among the most prominent mummies at Deir el-Bahariat were those of kings Ahmose I, Amenhotep I, Ramses II, Ramses III, Ramses IX, Seti I, Tao II, Tuthmosis I, Tuthmosis II, and Tuthmosis III. The mummies of kings Amenhotep II, Amenhotep III, Ramses IV, Ramses VI, Seti II, Siptah, and Tuthmosis IV were found in the cache in the Valley of the Kings. There were mummies of many prominent queens and princes at both locations as well, along with those of some unidentified individuals who might have been royalty, valued members of the nobility, or servants sent to accompany the royal families to the Afterlife. **See also** *individual entries for the above-listed kings;* Valley of the Kings.

Caesar, Julius (Gaius Julius Caesar) (ca. 100–44 B.C.)

While fighting to become the sole emperor of Rome, general and statesman Julius Caesar pursued his chief rival, Pompey (also known as Gnaeus Pompeius), into Egypt. There, Caesar met Queen Cleopatra VII. Caesar aided the queen in her disputes with her corulers, first her elder brother Ptolemy XIII and then her younger brother Ptolemy XIV. Cleopatra soon became Caesar's lover, bearing him a son named Caesarion (also known as Ptolemy XV). Egypt enjoyed Rome's protection but was otherwise autonomous, until Caesar was assassinated and his heir Octavian took over as Rome's emperor in 31 B.C. **See also** Antony, Marc; Cleopatra VII; Greco-Roman Period.

calendars

In the Early Dynastic Period, the ancient Egyptians created a calendar to help them plan agricultural events and establish festival dates. The calendar they devised was divided into three seasons: the time of the Nile inundation, or flooding (*akhet*); the time of planting and growing (*proyer* or *perit*); and the time of harvesting (*shomu* or *shemu*). Each season had four months of thirty days each, giving the year a total of 360 days. However, since the true solar year is 365 ¼ days long, over time events that were scheduled to occur on certain dates would happen during the wrong season. A harvest festival, for example, might eventually be celebrated during flood times. In fact, after 120 years the ancient Egyptian calendar had fallen one full month behind the solar year.

To try to correct this problem, Third Dynasty vizier Imhotep added a five-day makeup period at the end of the year that was not part of any month. Now known as the Epagomenal Days, these five days were designated as the time to celebrate the birthdays of five deities in succession: Osiris on the first, Horus on the second, Seth on the third, Isis on the fourth, and Nephthys on the fifth. In ancient Egyptian mythology, these were the children of the deities Geb and Nut, believed to have been born to Nut on successive days. Moreover, the Epagomenal Days were said to be the only days that Nut, a goddess of the sky, was fertile. But even though the period was associated with fertility, it was also considered a time of great danger, when priests warned people not to take unnecessary risks. The third day, when the destroyer god Seth was said to have been born, was considered the most unlucky day of all.

Even though the concept of the Epagomenal Days integrated well with ancient Egyptian mythology, adding these days did not completely solve the problems with Egypt's calendar; because of the extra quarter of a day in the solar year, the 365-day calendar was still too short. To solve this problem, in approximately 2500 B.C. the Egyptians adopted a second calendar based on the lunar year (since the cycles of the moon do not vary, it provided them with a constant by which to establish certain events). Their original calendar was still used for agricultural purposes, when doing something on a set date was not as

important and the one day lost every four years was of little consequence, but they consulted the new calendar, which was reliable in regard to certain astronomical observations, to ensure that festivals, offerings, and other important events were always celebrated at precisely the right time in relation to the movements of the heavens.

In addition to celebrations, the lunar religious calendar dictated when people should engage in certain other behaviors. For example, on the nineteenth day of the second month of the season of *akhet,* people were supposed to drink wine instead of any other beverage in recognition of the day that the god Osiris was embalmed. (Ancient Egyptians washed the bodies of their dead with palm wine during embalming.) Many days had such mythological connections—in fact, each month and day had a god and goddess to which it was sacred—and these associations were used to predict what would become of a child born on any given day. Some days, such as a day associated with a god's success in some endeavor, were considered to be particularly lucky, and the ancient Egyptians believed that children born on such days would lead especially fortunate lives. Similarly, spells were worked on days that were thought to guarantee their effectiveness, and kings' coronations were never held on unlucky days.

One calendar in a New Kingdom papyrus discovered in Thebes has lucky days written in black and unlucky ones written in red. This calendar, known as the Cairo Calendar, dates from the reign of Nineteenth Dynasty king Ramses II (although many Egyptologists believe it was copied from an earlier document) and was used to help people determine which dates were best for certain undertakings. The beginning of this and other ancient Egyptian calendars was the time of the New Year (*Wep Renpet*), which was marked by the appearance of the star Sirius in the night sky—low on the eastern horizon—after a seventy-day hiatus. This event was a sign that the Nile River inundation was about to begin, so it held great significance for the ancient Egyptians. **See also** astronomy; mummification; Nile River; Osiris.

canopic jars and chests

Canopic jars were the four vessels used to store the body's internal organs—the liver, stomach, intestines, and lungs—which were removed during the embalming process. The canopic jars were then stored inside a wooden chest set within a stone chest for entombment in the deceased's burial chamber.

The first canopic jars appeared during the Old Kingdom as simple stone vessels. Soon these jars acquired decorations that became increasingly elaborate; by the Middle Kingdom, each had a lid carved with a human face. By the New Kingdom, the carved lids of the four canopic jars resembled the four sons of Horus: Imsety, who appeared human; Duamutef, who had the head of a jackal; Qebehsenuef, who had the head of a falcon; and Hapy, who appeared as a baboon. Each of these deities was believed to protect a specific organ; hence that organ was placed in that god's jar: Imsety housed the liver, Duamutef the stomach, Qebehsenuef the intestines, and Hapy the lungs. Meanwhile, four goddesses were said to protect the four canopic jars themselves: Isis watched over Imsety's jar, Neith watched over Duamutef's jar, Selket watched over Qebehsenuef's jar, and Nephthys watched over Hapy's jar.

Before being placed in their jars, the organs went through the mummification process—in other words, they were treated with various natural solutions and wrapped in linen just like a mummy. Eventually, the use of canopic jars for storage was abandoned, and from the Twenty-first Dynasty on, the embalmed organs were placed back into the body in-

Four canopic jars in a chest are topped with lids carved in the shape of human heads.

stead of into the canopic jars. But even though they were empty, the jars were still left in the tomb, because with them went the protection of the deities for the entombed individual. **See also** Horus; Isis; mummification; Neith; Nephthys; Osiris.

Carter, Howard (1873–1939)

British archaeologist Howard Carter became famous for his 1922 discovery of the tomb of Eighteenth Dynasty king Tutankhamun in the Valley of the Kings. Carter first went to Egypt as a young man to participate in a British expedition, sponsored by the Egypt Exploration Society, to excavate and study a temple built by Eighteenth Dynasty queen Hatshepsut in Thebes. At that time, Carter was a promising artist, and his job was to make sketches showing the sculptures, inscriptions, and other archaeological details at the site. After that assignment, which lasted from 1893 to 1899, Carter was hired to supervise Egyptian excavations as an inspector general for the Egyptian Antiquities Department. This brought him into contact with an American businessman, Theodore M. Davis, who was funding the search for antiquities in Egypt. Davis convinced Carter to help him find and excavate royal tombs, and their efforts soon led to the discovery of the Valley of the Kings tombs of King Tuthmosis IV, Queen-Pharaoh Hatshepsut, and royal courtiers Yuya and Tuya. Although the other tombs had already been raided by tomb robbers, the tomb of Yuya and Tuya was fully intact.

Eventually, Davis decided that there were no more tombs to be found or profit to be made in the Valley of the Kings, so he stopped supporting expeditions there. But Carter believed that King Tutankhamun's tomb was hidden somewhere in the area, and with a new sponsor, the fifth earl of Carnarvon, he received the required excavation permit from the Egyptian government so he could look for the tomb. However, the year was 1914, and the outbreak of World War I soon interrupted his

plans; it was 1917 before Carter could truly start his search. Carter chose to search a section of the Valley of the Kings near where embalming materials and the remains of a funerary feast had been found because Tutankhamun's name was on some of the items.

For the next five digging seasons, Carter had no luck in uncovering Tutankhamun's tomb. During the first of these digs he found the remains of a village for the men who had worked on the tomb of Ramses VI, and he assumed that Tutankhamun's tomb could not have been at this site. But in his sixth season of digging he decided on a hunch to look at this area again, this time excavating deeper and removing some of the huts. Once he did so, he found the entrance to King Tutankhamun's tomb.

Carter sent a telegram announcing his discovery to Lord Carnarvon, who was in England. When Carnarvon and his daughter arrived at the site several days later, they and Carter unsealed the tomb's doorway and entered its chambers. To their

English Egyptologist Howard Carter supervises carpenters working at Tutankhamun's tomb, which Carter discovered in 1922.

amazement, they found so many treasures that it would take ten years of painstaking effort to remove and catalog them all. The tomb also held Tutankhamun's mummy, inside a gold coffin placed in another gold coffin that was inside a gilded wood coffin decorated with precious stones. The mummy had a solid gold mask of the king over its face, wearing a royal headdress of glass that had been colored to resemble lapis lazuli. Its body was decorated with over 150 pieces of jewelry, most of them with symbols related to deities and/or kingship. These symbols included the uraeus, a spitting cobra representing the goddess Wadjet (the serpent goddess who was the protector of Lower Egypt), the winged scarab representing the solar deity Khepri, and the images of the gods Thoth and Re-Horakhty.

Also in the tomb were hieroglyphs warning that anyone who disturbed Tutankhamun's treasures would meet a terrible end. Although several persons connected with the discovery of the tomb, including Lord Carnarvon, died under mysterious circumstances, Carter lived another seventeen years after entering Tutankhamun's tomb, reaching the age of sixty-six before he died. **See also** Egypt Exploration Society; Hatshepsut; Tutankhamun; Tuthmosis IV; Valley of the Kings; Yuya and Tuya.

cartouche

Called the *shenu,* or the encircling, in ancient Egyptian, a cartouche is a rough oval drawn around certain names of ancient Egyptian kings from the Third or Fourth Dynasty on. Egyptologists generally believe that this shape, which emanates from a straight line to its right, symbolizes a knot of rope that appears to have no beginning and no end, thereby representing both eternity and security or protection. Two types of royal names appeared within this encircling, the king's birth name and a name he took upon assuming the throne to show his relationship to the god Re. For example, Montuhotep I was the birth name of an Eleventh Dynasty king whose throne name was Nebhetepre, or "Pleased Is the Lord Re," and the throne name of his successor, Montuhotep II, was Sankhkare, or "Giving Life to the Soul of Re." **See also** Montuhotep; Re.

cataracts

There are six major cataracts, or fast-water sections, in the Nile River, as well as several minor ones, and each serves as a natural impediment to boats navigating the river. These major cataracts are numbered from one to six, beginning with the First Cataract near Aswan and continuing south. Of these, the Second Cataract was the most restrictive to travel in ancient times; in fact, unless the river was at flood stage no boat could get through this segment.

The ancient Egyptians saw these cataracts as the logical places to establish a southern border. At various times the First, Second, Third, and Fourth Cataracts each served as the southernmost boundary for Egypt. The First Cataract, however, served as Egypt's border for the longest cumulative period of time. **See also** Aswan; fortresses; Nile River.

cemetery

Egyptologists and archaeologists use the word *cemetery* to refer to small burial areas in Egypt that were used for a relatively narrow period of history, such as a single dynasty or a single era like the Middle Kingdom. A large burial area containing the remains of many different historical eras is referred to as a necropolis. **See also** burial sites; necropolis.

cenotaph

A cenotaph is a false tomb built to mimic a mortuary structure but never intended to house a body. Egyptologists disagree on the symbolic purpose of cenotaphs. Some think that the kings who built these structures intended them to be temples to the chief god of the dead, Osiris, as a way of linking themselves with this god, or perhaps through him to other gods, in the Afterlife. Other experts believe cenotaphs were monuments celebrating the general importance of kings. Indeed, many cenotaphs, such as those of King Ramses II and King Seti I, bore lists displaying the names of all the kings who had ruled up until the time the cenotaph was built, along with an altar where people apparently left food offerings as a way of nourishing the spirits of the listed kings as well as various deities. **See also** king lists; Osiris; Ramses II; Seti I.

Champollion, Jean-François (1790–1832)

A French linguist and historian, Jean-François Champollion uncovered important clues that led to the deciphering of the system of ancient Egyptian hieroglyphic writing. As a youngster, Champollion was gifted with language, and by the age of sixteen he already knew Latin, Greek, Hebrew, Arabic, Aramaic, and several other languages. At nineteen he became professor of history at the Lycée de Grenoble (University of Grenoble) in south-central France, a position he held until he was forced to leave in 1816 because of his outspoken support of Napoléon (whom the French government at the time considered an enemy). Once away from university life, Champollion began to devote himself to deciphering the Rosetta Stone, a slab of black basalt that had been discovered in 1799 by a soldier during Napoléon's expedition to Egypt. The stone showed three different kinds of writing: hieroglyphic script, Greek script, and an unknown script later identified as demotic. Champollion compared the writings on this stone to copies of texts from the ancient temples of Tuthmosis III and Ramses II in Nubia, trying to find some common thread in the hieroglyphs.

At the time, the prevailing view among scholars was that hieroglyphic writing was symbolic, with each hieroglyph always standing for the same word or concept. Then one of Champollion's rivals in the translation effort, Dr. Thomas Young, determined that foreign proper names—for which the ancient Egyptians would have had no word of their own—were represented by symbols denoting spoken sounds, or phonemes. Using this idea, Champollion soon recognized that while some of the hieroglyphs did represent words or concepts, others could represent phonemes. Moreover, he saw that a single hieroglyphic might be used in different ways. For example, Champollion realized that a disk symbol could represent not only an object, the sun, and a concept, the sun god, but also a sound, *ra*. Aided by this insight, Champollion suddenly recognized that each type of writing on the Rosetta Stone was a translation of the same text, a 196 B.C. decree related to a celebration of the anniversary of King Ptolemy V's coronation.

This knowledge allowed Champollion to begin translating the Rosetta Stone's hieroglyphic writing and determining the structure of ancient Egyptian grammar. Soon he was publishing papers on his work with the Rosetta Stone, and in 1822 he gave a lecture on his discoveries at a meeting of the Paris Académie des Inscriptions et Belles Lettres. This lecture was subsequently published as *Lettre à M. Dacier.* Meanwhile, Champollion began applying his theories to numerous hieroglyphic texts, developing a list of hieroglyphic symbols and their Greek equivalents.

In 1826 Champollion was named curator of the Egyptian collection at the Louvre Museum in Paris, and two years later he embarked on a fifteen-month archaeological expedition to collect antiquities for the museum and to study additional ancient Egyptian texts. In 1831 the Collège de France created a chair of Egyptian antiquities especially for him. In addition to teaching there, Champollion wrote several books about ancient Egypt and its language, including *Précis du systeme hièroglyphique, etc.* (*Primer of the Hieroglyphic System, etc.,* published in 1824); *Panthéon égyptien, ou collection des personnages mythologiques de l'ancienne Égypte* (*Egyptian Pantheon, or Collection of the Mythological Figures of Ancient Egypt,* published in several volumes from 1823 to 1825 but left unfinished upon Champollion's death); a multivolume hieroglyphic grammar book published posthumously from 1836 to 1841; and a multivolume ancient Egyptian dictionary published from 1841 to 1843. **See also** Napoléon I; Rosetta Stone; writing, forms of.

chariots

The chariot was probably introduced into Egypt by the Hyksos, a group of foreigners from the east, when they invaded northeastern Egypt during the Middle Kingdom. During the subsequent Second Intermediate Period, the chariot's use spread throughout the Nile River Valley, and during the New Kingdom it was widely employed by royalty, nobility, and

In this Hittite depiction, a king in his chariot crushes his enemies.

the military (in a special division called the chariotry). The first Egyptian ruler known to have an army that made use of the chariot in warfare was King Kamose (ca. 1550 B.C.).

Ancient Egyptian warriors employed two-wheeled, unarmored chariots that generally went into battle as part of chariotry units with twenty-five chariots each. Each chariot was pulled by two horses, and each chariot held a driver and a warrior armed with bows and arrows, a sword, and perhaps a javelin. The chariots were made of a combination of wood, leather, and metal, and the metal was usually gilded. Leather straps were sometimes dyed purple, and feathers might adorn the horses' heads. **See also** animals; military; weapons and armor.

Chester Beatty Papyri

Originally associated with the Chester Beatty Library in Dublin, the Chester Beatty Papyri are a collection of ancient Egyptian texts dating from the Ramessid Period. One of the best known among scholars is the Chester Beatty Papyrus I, now in the Dublin Museum. A sixteen-page papyrus written in hieratic script dating from the Twentieth Dynasty reign of King Ramses V, its most significant section of text is a myth related to Horus and his brother Seth. In this myth, Seth is intent on killing the sun god Re and taking over his solar bark, while Horus is equally intent on defending Re. Horus and Seth have a series of confrontations, and eventually Horus destroys Seth. Scholars believe that the underlying message of this myth was that those who try to usurp the throne will meet a bad end.

A similar papyrus from the Nineteenth Dynasty, the Chester Beatty Papyrus IV (now in the British Museum in London), recounts a myth related to Re and Isis. Although a fragment of a longer work (the remains of which have been lost), the text tells how Isis got Re to reveal his secret name (never stated in the text) so that she could gain power over him. She passed this knowledge on to her son Horus, though she made him swear an oath not to use it. This myth is yet another example of the tie between Horus and Re, and it also expresses the ancient Egyptian belief that names had power. The Chester Beatty Papyrus IV is also one of ten known papyri to contain detailed medical information, offering treatments for various diseases and demonstrating that ancient Egyptians had a sophisticated knowledge of anatomy.

Another Beatty Papyrus written in hieratic script, the Chester Beatty Papyrus III (now in the British Museum in London), dates from the Ramessid Period but might be a copy of a Middle Kingdom text created during the Eleventh or Twelfth Dynasty. Archaeologists found the papyrus in the remains of the library of a scribe, Qenherkhepshef, at Deir el-Medina. The work is a Dream Book, or a guide to what various dreams prophesied. For example, dreaming of warm beer was considered to be a warning that something bad was going to happen. The book also offered recommendations regarding protective magical spells. **See also** Horus; Isis; magic; Ramessid Period; Re; Seth.

children

Children were highly valued in ancient Egyptian society, in large part because they traditionally helped support their parents later in life. A child's arrival was considered a blessing from the gods, and women who became pregnant gave thanks to Hathor and other deities. Mothers-to-be also recited various spells at different points during pregnancy and childbirth to confer protection on themselves and their unborn child.

Children were breastfed until age four and kept close to their mothers because it was believed that both practices helped prevent illness. Infant mortality was high throughout ancient Egypt, so parents often tied protective amulets around their children's necks or wrists to keep them safe. Various spells were routinely recited to protect a child as well. Sometimes a child's name reflected the parents' anxieties about health, or their gratefulness for their child's having survived birth. For example, a child's name might mean "This Child Is Wanted" or "Amun Is Good." Parents also sometimes chose names that reflected visits to the oracles of the gods, whom they might consult to find out whether their children would survive their first year of life. One such name would be "Thoth Says He Will Live."

Unless in poor health, children were considered able to leave the home without their mothers, although usually under the supervision of some adult. At some point, boys and sometimes girls also went to school—a village school, a temple school, or a private school held at the royal court—and boys began learning their father's trade. However, Egyptologists disagree on when a child might have been considered old enough to attend school and learn a trade. Apparently by the age of fourteen, though, every young man was either working in the fields alongside his father or working as an apprentice learning a trade or profession, and girls of this age were participating in household tasks such as cooking.

Whether learning, working, or playing games with friends, children who had not yet reached puberty wore no clothing. In addition, their shaved heads had a single lock of hair that was cut off at puberty, apparently as part of a ritual that Egyptologists know little about. Boys also underwent circumcision at the age of eleven or twelve, often with a group of boys undergoing the same procedure as part of a religious ritual. For girls, the first menstruation and every one thereafter was followed by a purification ritual. **See also** clothing; education; toys and games.

Christianity, spread of

Historians disagree as to exactly when and under what circumstances Christianity came to Egypt, but they generally agree that there were Christians in Alexandria in the second century among the Greek-speaking population (i.e., primarily the upper classes) and in the third century among those who did not speak Greek. To spread knowledge of the Bible to those who were not well versed in Greek, Christians developed Coptic, essentially the ancient Egyptian language written using Greek letters instead of hieroglyphs. They also instituted Christian schools in Egypt to teach converts to Christianity the intricacies of their new faith. Soon, cities with large Greek-speaking populations, specifically Alexandria, Panopolis, and Antinoopolis, had their own Christian churches as well.

However, the Romans, who then controlled Egypt, considered the monotheism (the acknowledgment of only one god) of Christianity and Judaism a threat to their own polytheism (the worship of multiple gods), and by extension a threat to their rule of Egypt. Therefore, in approximately A.D. 202 the Roman emperor Severus ordered that the spread of both Christianity and Judaism in Egypt be stopped. During the subsequent reign of Emperor Diocletian (284–305), Christian churches and texts were destroyed and Christian priests and their followers were tortured and/or executed.

Some Egyptian Christians escaped persecution by pretending not to practice their religion. And under Emperor Decius (249–251), any Christians who renounced their faith in a ceremony that involved worshiping the emperor received a certificate that would spare them from persecution. Meanwhile, those Christians unwilling to compromise their beliefs sometimes retreated to Wadi Natron, an oasis within the Western Desert with several walled and for-tified monasteries that were difficult if not impossible to invade. Following Roman emperor Constantine's decree in approximately 313 that all forms of worship would be allowed in the Roman Empire, Christian churches appeared in many parts of Egypt. **See also** Alexandria; Greco-Roman Period; Western Desert.

chronology

The study of the chronology of ancient Egypt has been problematic when it comes to determining the reigns of ancient Egyptian kings. There are few sources that list and date kings' rules, and even those that do exist are damaged and/or incomplete. Moreover, when ancient sources do provide dates, they can be based on either of two ancient Egyptian calendars, a civil one and an astronomical one, and the source might or might not indicate which calendar is being referenced. Adding to the confusion, the civil calendar was highly inaccurate because it was not based on the true solar year.

To surmount such difficulties, Egyptologists try to use references to the astronomical calendar, which was based on observations such as when the star Sirius was visible during a king's reign, to reconcile the two calendars and determine chronology. However, this method is inaccurate, and most Egyptologists estimate that the margin for error in New Kingdom dates is twenty years and in earlier dates fifty to two hundred years. Others believe not only that the margin of error is far higher but that because of the fragmentary nature of their sources some of the kings may be listed in the wrong order and/or misidentified.

The primary sources on which Egyptologists base their calculations are the Palermo Stone, the Royal List of Karnak, the Royal List of Abydos, the Royal List of Saqqara, and the Royal Canon of Turin. Of these, the Royal Canon of Turin (so named because it is in the Turin Museum in Italy) once offered the largest list of kings—over three hundred—complete with the precise length of each reign to the day (although the starting and ending dates are not given). However, the papyrus on which the Royal Canon of Turin was written has large gaps in information, having been mishandled by nineteenth-century antiquities collectors who damaged it to the point where many names were lost.

The Palermo Stone (so called because it is housed in the Palermo Museum in Sicily) also provides incomplete information. Considered the earliest king list, this piece of rock from a much larger slab that has been lost lists some of the kings who ruled prior to the Fifth Dynasty, including some from the Predynastic Period. The Royal List of Karnak (now in the Louvre Museum in Paris) provides the names of kings from the First to the mid–Eighteenth Dynasty, ending with the reign of Tuthmosis III. The Royal List of Abydos, on a wall in the temple of Seti I at Abydos, provides the names of seventy-six kings, from the First Dynasty to the mid–Nineteenth Dynasty, ending with the reign of Seti I. However, it omits all kings of the Second Intermediate Period (whose names Egyptologists have found in the Royal List of Karnak) and the kings in the Eighteenth Dynasty who worshiped the god Aten (specifically, Amenhotep IV—also known as Akhenaten—Smenkhkare, Tutankhamnun, and Ay). The Royal List of Abydos also appears on a damaged papyrus found in the tomb of Seti I's son, Ramses II, and now kept in the British Museum, where it is known as the Abydos King List. **See also** Abydos; king lists.

Cleopatra VII (69–30 B.C.)

Cleopatra VII was a queen of the Ptolemaic Period (part of the Greco-Roman Period) who ascended the throne of

Ptolemaic queen Cleopatra VII ruled Egypt from 51 to 30 B.C.

Egypt at age seventeen. Also known as *Netjeret mer-it-es* (Goddess, Beloved of Her Father), Cleopatra had been designated heir by her father, King Ptolemy XII Auletes, providing she marry her brother Ptolemy XIII, which she did. Cleopatra was an effective ruler, and holds the distinction of being the only ruler of Egypt during the Greco-Roman Period to learn the Egyptian language as opposed to just Greek and Latin (which she knew as well).

Cleopatra faced an unsuccessful attempt by her brother and consort, Ptolemy XIII, to usurp her power, but backed by Roman leader Julius Caesar, she was able to regain her throne. Through her liaisons, first with Caesar (with whom she had a son, Caesarion, or Ptolemy XV) and then with Roman general Marc Antony, Cleopatra was able to maintain much of Egypt's autonomy under the protection of Rome. Eventually, however, Rome elected to end Egypt's autonomy. Cleopatra's reign ended when, after forces under

Roman emperor Octavian laid siege to Alexandria, she committed suicide rather than allow herself to be captured. **See also** Alexandria; Antony, Marc; Greco-Roman Period.

Cleopatra's Needles

Cleopatra's Needles are two stone obelisks that were removed by nineteenth-century antiquities collectors from the city of Heliopolis, where they were erected by King Tuthmosis III around 1500 B.C. At that time, the pair of obelisks was thought to have a matching pair in heaven. The obelisks are called Cleopatra's Needles because of a reference to the Ptolemaic queen Cleopatra VII that was later inscribed on them. The obelisks are now separated; one is standing in Central Park in New York City, while the other is standing on the Thames Embankment in London, England. **See also** obelisk.

clocks

The ancient Egyptians recognized no unit of time measurement shorter than an hour. Nonetheless, they did keep track of time. In the Old and Middle Kingdoms, the prevailing timepiece was a sun clock similar to sundials. In the New Kingdom, they began using a water clock as well. This device consisted of a vase with a small hole at the bottom so that when it was filled with water its fluid level would drop at a set rate; markings on the side of the vase indicated the hour in accordance with the water level. Water clocks were typically shaped to look like a baboon because this was an animal manifestation of the god Thoth, who was associated with measurement. Another means of telling time was the star clock, first used in the Middle Kingdom. This clock was essentially a list of stars and their locations in the heavens depending on the hour of night and time of year. By studying the night sky and referring to such a list, ancient Egyptians were able to arrive at a rough estimate of the hour. **See also** Thoth.

clothing

Except for preadolescent children, who always went naked, the ancient Egyptians primarily wore clothing made of linen, usually plain white but sometimes dyed yellow, red, or blue using safflower, the root of the madder plant, and acacia, respectively. During the Old and Middle Kingdoms, women of all social classes wore simple knee-length linen dresses, while lower-class men wore loincloths and upper-class men wore knee-length skirts. By the New Kingdom, the clothing of upper-class men and women became more distinct. Men's skirts had pleats and women's dresses reached the floor, and both kinds of garments became more colorful and decorative. In addition, sometimes one garment was layered over another, with the outer one being shorter to create a tunic effect. Robes (long, loose garments tied at the neck) were also worn to distinguish the members of one profession from those of another. For example, only a high priest could wear a leopard skin fitted over his linen robes, which were pleated and often decorated with embroidery.

Men and women might also wear wool cloaks on occasion; archaeologists have found one man's cloak that was made with fourteen yards of wool. However, such cloaks were not allowed in a temple, because the ancient Egyptians believed that wool was ritually impure. Many Egyptologists believe that this attitude was held toward every product that came from an animal instead of a plant. However, leather sandals and slippers and fur-lined boots have been found at temple worksites, although there is no evidence that they were ever worn inside the temple buildings. The most common footwear was a reed or rush sandal. **See also** animals; children; linen; weaving.

coffins

In ancient Egypt, members of the lower classes were buried in plain coffins of wood or in some cases large woven baskets. Royalty and wealthy commoners were buried in stone sarcophagi. The middle classes also used wooden coffins, though theirs might be decorated with carvings and/or paintings. The most common decorations were eyes painted on the inside of the lid, theoretically so that the deceased could see through it, and texts known as Coffin Texts that functioned as guidebooks to the Afterlife, telling the deceased how to get past certain dangers along the way. Sometimes a painted map to the Afterlife was included as part of these interior coffin decorations. The wood used for coffins also varied according to the status of the individual. The poor used the cheapest wood, such as sycamore, while the rich used the most expensive, such as imported cedar.

During the Middle Kingdom, fashion dictated that middle- and upper-class people be buried in more than one coffin, one inside the other; if a person was wealthy or of royal lineage, this arrangement of double coffins then would be placed inside a sarcophagus. By the New Kingdom, more than two coffins per corpse might be used. Moreover, during the Middle and New Kingdoms, the innermost coffin might be an anthropoid coffin—that is, a coffin shaped like the body it held. Sometimes these were fashioned from linen coated with plaster rather than being carved from wood, and the more advanced versions included the image of not only a face but also arms crossed over the chest in the classic pose of death. Anthropoid coffins were usually decorated with religious imagery and funerary texts. **See also** Coffin Texts; funerals; sarcophagus.

Coffin Texts

Coffin Texts were spells and incantations painted on the inside of coffins beginning in the First Intermediate Period. Their purpose was to provide information that would help the deceased reach the Afterlife and succeed there. Previous texts of this nature, the Fifth and Sixth Dynasty Pyramid Texts, were for royalty only, whereas the Coffin Texts were for wealthy nonroyals as well. A subsequent collection of funerary texts, the *Book of the Dead*, for all classes, including the poor. **See also** Afterlife; *Book of the Dead*; coffins; Pyramid Texts.

colonization

In ancient times, Egypt established colonies for economic and strategic reasons. In particular, Egypt established colonies to ensure access to quarries and other natural resources and to gain a foothold in foreign territory to enhance military and political power. The first major push for colonization was in the Fourth Dynasty, during the reign of Snefru. At this time the king launched at least one major campaign south into Nubia to establish a settlement, Buhen. This Egyptian colony remained for at least the next 250 years, during which it was a base for mining expeditions and for trade with lands to the south. Another wave of Nubian colonization took place during the Twelfth Dynasty, when Egypt mounted several military campaigns to establish a series of huge fortresses there.

For the most part, the ancient Egyptians encountered little opposition to their colonization of Nubia. This was not the case, however, in Syria and Palestine, where during the Eighteenth Dynasty several military campaigns focused on establishing colonies. The people of this region resented Egyptian intrusions on their land and fought not only to keep the Egyptians out but also to take over Egyptian territory themselves. During such campaigns, not only there but even more so to the west in Libya, the Egyptians established military colonies where prisoners of war were forced to live as Egyptians even though they were still within their own lands. **See also** fortresses; mining and metalworking; Nubia; Syria.

colors

To the ancient Egyptians, colors carried meaning. For example, black (*kem*) symbolized the Nile mud and therefore fertility; as a result, it might be used in paintings as the color for ripe emmer wheat or for cattle. Black also symbolized death and rebirth, the gods Osiris and Anubis, and the Underworld, and was therefore featured prominently in scenes related to these concepts. Black could be used in a more literal sense as well to color hair, eyes, and people with dark skin. Similarly, white (*hedj*) was used symbolically to paint crowns, honey, luxurious items, and other good things, or to portray realistically such everyday items as milk, teeth, bones, and white bread. Red (*desher*) symbolized negative ideas and emotions (although for reasons unclear today, red sometimes symbolized positive emotions as well). Blue (*khesbedj*) was often used to color images of the gods. Green (*wadj*) was associated with health and was typically used to paint any representations of protective amulets depicted in a scene. Yellow (*ketj*) was associated with many kinds of food and with the sun. Yellow and red were also used to paint skin colors, yellow for Egyptian women and red for Egyptian men.

To make pigments, the ancient Egyptians used various minerals. White was created with crushed limestone, black with carbonized materials such as burnt wood. Red was made from an anhydritic iron oxide, yellow from a hydrated iron oxide. Blue came from crushed azurite, lapis, or copper carbonate, green from malachite and similar ores. The ancient Egyptians were not afraid to experiment with various minerals to get the precise color they wanted, and occasionally they mixed two colors to produce a third. Alternatively, they might paint one color over another in artwork, either blending the two or allowing one to show through the other. **See also** painting.

construction rituals, temple

Ancient Egyptians performed various rituals at different points during the construction of a temple. The first rituals were performed as part of the laying of the foundation. The night before this was to take place (or earlier, according to some Egyptologists), the king performed a ritual whereby he consulted the stars to determine the best location and orientation for the temple. Certain gods were said to help the king in this endeavor—usually Ptah and Khnum, who were gods of creation, and Seshat, a goddess of builders and measurement, although others might be invoked as well or instead. Additional rituals were conducted as the foundation was laid. Egyptologists disagree on the nature of these rituals, which were first conducted in the Predynastic Period. However, they know that priests knotted cords in a ritualistic way prior to using them for measurement and hammered stakes in a ritually meaningful pattern as part of laying out the foundation.

As the foundation of the walls was established, small-scale models of the tools that would be used during construction were placed at various points under the first row of bricks. The king himself participated in this ritual, along with priests representing certain gods. Once the walls were up, the king dusted them with a substance called *besen*—probably chalk—in order to symbolically purify the temple. Probably during this ritual but perhaps later, the head of a bull might be buried nearby, perhaps along with the head of a goose (both animals were associated with creator gods).

Upon the building's completion, a consecration ceremony was performed that involved naming the building for a particular god and calling upon that god to accept the building as his or hers. At the end of this ceremony, the god was thought to enter the building. The consecration ceremony was repeated annually to maintain the connection between god and temple. Afterward, there was a feast for all who had worked on the temple. **See also** architecture; Khnum; Ptah; Seshat.

copper and copper molds

Copper was first used in Egypt shortly before the First Dynasty. The earliest attempts at metalworking involved hammering the copper into various shapes, and only small objects such as beads were formed from copper. The Egyptians eventually began experimenting with methods of heating and cooling the metal so that it could be more easily shaped into large objects, using hammers or simple molds. Within a short time, most cooking pots were being made from copper, as were a variety of other items.

By the New Kingdom, copper molds were much more sophisticated. First, beeswax was sculpted in the shape of the object or statue intended to be made in copper. Then this beeswax replica was covered with clay, leaving a few small holes, and buried in the ground, where it was subjected to enough heat to make the beeswax melt and run out of the holes. Molten copper was then poured into the holes to create the final product, which when cool was broken free from the clay.

Egypt got its copper ore from various sources. One was its own Eastern Desert, but the rest were in foreign lands. From the Third Dynasty to the Middle Kingdom, the main source was the Sinai, where Egypt sent military expeditions to obtain the ore, but subsequently the main sources were farther to the east, particularly Syria. **See also** bronze; mining and metalworking; Syria.

Coptos

Located south of Dendera (near Luxor), Coptos was a common rest stop for traders traveling between the Nile River and the port of Kuser on the Red Sea. This territory was wild and frequented by bandits, so Egyptian kings stationed soldiers there to protect merchants. Because of its importance to travelers, Coptos was a cult center for Min, a god of travel, and as such it had several temples. Most are from the Sixth Dynasty, but one was built by the Eighteenth Dynasty king Tuthmosis III. In these temples, archaeologists have found documents, now known as the Coptos Decrees, relating to various temple matters from the Eighth Dynasty on. These documents have provided insights into the kind of political and legal power that such temples had. For example, a document from the Eighth Dynasty decreed that property belonging to the temples of Min would not be taxed. Another, from the Seventeenth Dynasty, decreed that a nobleman who stole items from a temple should lose all his property and possessions. **See also** Min; Tuthmosis III.

coregency

Coregency was the practice whereby a king shared his rule with his heir apparent, usually his oldest son. The founder of the Twelfth Dynasty, King Amenemhet I, introduced the concept of coregency to ensure that his rule would pass without dispute to his eldest son, Senwosret I. In the twentieth year of his reign, fearing that a rival would usurp the throne after his death, Amenemhet I decreed that Senwosret I would share his rule of Egypt; this arrangement lasted until the king died twenty years later. Subsequent kings of the Twelfth Dynasty also followed this practice, as did some rulers in other dynasties. However, the heir brought on as a coruler apparently did not have the same level of power as the original king, even though the original king sometimes claimed he did. **See also** Amenemhet I; Senwosret I.

coronations

The ancient Egyptians held coronation ceremonies whenever a new king assumed the throne or an existing king allowed a coruler to share his throne. Coronation rituals varied, but generally they involved the king donning the white crown of Upper

Egypt followed by the red crown of Lower Egypt to create the Double Crown of a united Egypt. (Egyptologists believe that during the New Kingdom a purification ritual might have preceded this event.) The king then took up the crook and the flail (two sticks, one curved at the end), two symbols of Egyptian kingship. During this process, the statues of certain deities were present so the gods they represented were deemed present as well. These deities were acknowledged and honored throughout the coronation, as well as during associated processions and festivals.

One scene found on a wall at Medinet Habu shows the royal family, scribes, soldiers, priests, musicians, incense bearers, emblem bearers, and many other people all taking part in a king's coronation procession, while the king is carried along in a canopied shrine. His throne is decorated with figures of a lion and a sphinx; the figure of a hawk is carried in front of the shrine, while figures representing Truth and Justice are carried behind. Another scene in Memphis, dating from the Old Kingdom, shows a coronation ceremony in which the king was required to run around the Palace of White Walls in a solitary race to display his vitality and symbolically reunite the two lands. This ceremony was repeated periodically to reassure the Egyptian people that their country was in good hands. **See also** crowns; Medinet Habu; Memphis.

cosmetics and perfumes

Ancient Egyptian men and women both used a variety of cosmetics and perfumes, with their quantity and nature dependent on whether a person was rich or poor. Most common among all classes were oils, ointments, and creams intended to moisturize and soothe the skin, which often became dry or burned in the intense Egyptian sun. Most of these substances were made from plant extracts using cat, hippopotamus, or crocodile fat as a base. Faces were also cleaned with oils, some-

times along with lime juice as an astringent; carob was also used, either alone or in combination with oils, for cleaning. Ointments were used to protect the skin of eyelids, and women typically added powders to them for coloring.

Egyptians commonly added color to their faces. The two most popular colorings were malachite, a green ore, for the lower lids and galena, a bluish-gray ore, for the upper lids. To make this eye makeup, the minerals were ground very fine and then mixed with animal fat (usually from a cat, hippopotamus, or crocodile) or vegetable oil. The mixture was then applied with a wooden or ivory stick. First, though, the eye was typically outlined with kohl (the Arabic term for ancient Egyptian eye makeup made from a black sulfide powder). Henna might be used to color nails, and a powdered red ocher called hematite, mixed with oil, was used to color lips or give a blush effect.

Creams and ointments intended for use on the body were usually perfumed by the addition of flower petals, spices, or other fragrant substances. One cream said to eliminate wrinkles was made from moringa oil (made from seeds taken from the pods of moringa trees) and fruit wine scented with frankincense. A popular skin-softening ointment was perfumed with a type of lily grown especially for this use. Egyptians of all classes were fastidious when it came to body odor, so perfumes were also used specifically to eliminate the smell of sweat. In fact, this purpose was considered so vital that when tomb builders at Deir el-Medina did not receive their government shipment of perfume they went on strike.

Still other perfumes were intended to scent the air. For example, some temple priests created Kyphi, a mixture of wine, raisins, and fragrant herbs, to scent and therefore purify the air, probably either prior to or during rituals. For secular gatherings, the ancient Egyptians mixed herbs and spices with wax and shaped the wax into cones. They then placed these cones atop the wigs on their heads, and over the course of the evening the cones would gradually melt and release their scent into a room while making the wig shiny. **See also** Deir el-Medina; hair.

Creation myths

The ancient Egyptians had various myths of how their world began. Which myths held sway depended on location, and Egyptologists disagree on whether any one of these myths became more widespread than the others. However, there were similarities among them. For example, in all Egyptian Creation myths, one god created himself and then created all others. In addition, natural elements that sustain life—sunlight, water, air—had to appear before Creation could begin, and it was the creator god's purpose to bring order out of chaos.

The four main Creation myths came out of the cult centers of Heliopolis, Memphis, Elephantine, and Hermopolis, respectively. Heliopolis mythology says that in the beginning there was water, the essence of the goddess Nun, and that from this water arose a primordial mound of mud. (Such imagery is understandable given that as the annual floodwaters of the Nile River receded such mounds often appeared, and during the Nile's inundation everything was underwater except for the highest ground.) On the primordial mound, the god Atum created himself and then created the god of air, Shu, and the goddess of moisture, Tefnut. These two deities soon conceived the god of the earth, Geb, and the goddess of the sky, Nut. Geb and Nut immediately became lovers, creating the deities Osiris, Isis, Seth, and Nephthys, but shortly thereafter their father separated them, pushing Nut into the sky to create the heavens.

In the Creation myth of Memphis, the creator god was not Atum but Ptah, and whereas Atum made two deities who then made the others, Ptah directly made all life. All other deities, towns, people, animals, and everything else in existence formed first within his heart, whereupon he spoke their names to call them into being. This myth was undoubtedly connected to the ancient Egyptian belief that the heart was the center of all human thought and emotion.

In the Creation myth of Elephantine, the ram-headed creator god Khnum also made all beings, but instead of creating them within his heart, he fashioned them on a potter's wheel using Nile River clay. One of the first goddesses he created, Heket, similarly fashioned children within their mothers' wombs. Heket had the head of a frog because the animal was associated with fertility, due to the abundance of frogs when the Nile flooded.

The frog is also featured in the Creation myth of Hermopolis, which held that four frog-headed gods (Nun, Amun, Kuk, and Huh) and four snake-headed goddesses (Naunet, Amaunet, Kauket, and Hauhet) had to unite for Creation to take place. Paired together, these couples represented water, air, darkness, and infinity, respectively. Once they joined, one of two things happened (because the myth had at least two versions): Either a mound formed within the primordial waters or a lotus flower formed on the surface of the primordial waters. In the myth with the lotus flower, the petals opened to release the sun, in the form of the solar deity Horus. In the myth without the lotus flower, an ibis appeared on the mound as a manifestation of the god Thoth, laid an egg, and hatched out the sun. Because the sun was the focus of both versions of the myth, illustrations of both sometimes depicted the eight deities as baboons; these animals were strongly associated with the sun because of the way their screeches and antics seemed to greet the dawn. **See also** cult centers; deities; religion.

crocodiles

Crocodiles were common along the Nile River, and ancient Egyptian writings indicate that many people were killed by the animals. Nonetheless, in some places these animals were revered as the physical manifestation of the god Sobek. In the Faiyum (an oasis west of the Nile near the Delta), for example, they were kept in sacred pools, where priests not only fed them but also sometimes bedecked them with jewels. Crocodiles kept in this manner were mummified and perhaps also entombed after death. The largest number of entombed crocodiles has been found in the Faiyum's capital city, Crocodilopolis, and Kom Ombo near Aswan, both of which were cult centers dedicated to the god Sobek. However, in some other cities the crocodile was associated with the destroyer god Seth rather than with Sobek, and in such places the animal was typically hated and slaughtered in large numbers. **See also** Faiyum; Kom Ombo; Seth; Sobek.

crowns

There were six main ancient Egyptian crowns worn by the rulers of Egypt, each with its own symbolism and/or ceremonial association. One was the *deshret;* made of red wicker, it represented Lower Egypt. The *hedjet* was a white war crown representing Upper Egypt. The *pschent* or *wereret* was a double crown created by putting the *deshret* and the *hedjet* together to represent both Upper and Lower Egypt. The *khepresh* was a blue crown worn during military campaigns and processions.

The *atef* or *hemhemet* was a ram's-horn crown worn during rituals connected to the gods Osiris or Re. The *seshed* was a beribboned crown with symbols of the cobra and the papyrus that was apparently used during various festivals. **See also** coronations; festivals.

cult centers

Cult centers were towns or cities that over time developed into administrative and religious centers where people worshiped one deity more than the rest. There were forty-two cult centers in Egypt, one in each nome (administrative district), with twenty-two in Upper Egypt and twenty in Lower Egypt. These cult centers had temple complexes dedicated to a particular deity, and each cult center had its own population of priests dedicated to serving and honoring this deity, whether through daily temple rituals or large public festivals.

Some deities were adopted by more than one cult center. For example, Horus was the focus of the cult centers of Edfu, Hierakonpolis, and Letopolis. Moreover, in many cult centers, not only the main deity but certain associates were worshiped, usually in the form of a triad of gods. For example, even though Abydos was the cult center of Osiris, Isis and Horus were worshiped there as well. In Memphis, the triad was Ptah, Sekhmet, and Nefertem. In other cases, neighboring cult centers would combine their efforts and their gods during certain festivals to honor multiple deities. **See also** deities; Horus; nomes and nomarchs; religion.

Dakhla Oasis

Located approximately 185 miles west of Luxor, the Dakhla Oasis is the site of an important archaeological discovery. Near the modern town of Arnhada, Canadian archaeologists uncovered a fifteen-room, two-story building featuring Greco-Roman art on its walls. The purpose of this building is currently unknown. The Arnhada area also has a cemetery that was used during the First Intermediate Period. Another important site was a region near the modern town of Balat where Sixth Dynasty officials built numerous mastaba tombs. There were temples scattered throughout the area as well, dating from various periods and dedicated to various deities (but particularly Mut). In ancient times the Dakhla Oasis had many towns, largely because it had many rich fields that provided ample food for its inhabitants. **See also** oases.

dancing

In ancient Egypt, dancing was practiced at every level of society, including royalty. Who actually participated in a dance depended on the dance's purpose. Most dances were performed for religious and ritualistic reasons; the remainder were performed for entertainment or personal enjoyment at secular festivals, banquets, and parties or in streets and harems.

There were apparently dozens of standardized religious dances. However, Egyptologists are uncertain about their steps because there are no detailed descriptions of them. Moreover, some dances were held in secret, performed by priests within restricted areas of temples. One such dance was the "dance of the stars," in which priests somehow mimicked the movements of the stars in the heavens. Egyptologists disagree on the purpose of this dance, though they know it was tied to ancient Egyptian beliefs regarding the connection between astrology and the gods.

Most religious dances were performed to honor deities, and during these dances the performers often wore masks representing the deities being honored. Some deities were more strongly associated with dancing than others. During the Old and Middle Kingdoms, the goddess Hathor seems to have been connected to such performances more than any other deity, although the goddess Bastet was often honored in this way as well. During the New Kingdom, the gods Amun and Osiris and the goddess Isis were most often the focus of festival dances, particularly those relating to the Nile's flooding and the idea of rebirth. During the harvest season, however, dances were held to honor the god Min, who was associated with the land's fertility. The royal family—including the king or, if he was unwell, his representative—participated in one such dance annually.

Royal princesses sometimes became part of dance companies that were associated with certain temples. Each cult center had its own dance company, which was dedicated to dancing in certain established religious rituals. Professional dancers also performed funeral dances intended to represent the grief of the mourners. Depictions of New Kingdom funerals show that both men and women danced at such events.

Professional dancers participated in secular events as well, performing for the crowd's pleasure. At festivals, banquets, or other events, their dances could be slow or fast, and they might include gymnastics, juggling, and other spectacles. They might dance in large groups, although trios and pairs seem to have been more popular, or a single performer might dance alone. When in pairs, dancers apparently mirrored one another's movements, symbolizing the Egyptians' belief that every action and object on earth had a counterpart in the heavens.

Although they might adorn themselves with jewelry and paint, to allow freedom of movement dancers at public events, as well as in harems, typically wore little or no clothing. If they did wear clothes, the common choice was a loincloth for men and a skirt (with no top) for women. During the New Kingdom, it became fashionable for women dancers to wear dresses in a fabric so thin that the dancer appeared to be naked. At no time did dancers wear shoes.

Artwork also shows that soldiers sometimes danced to celebrate a military victory. In addition, men and women from all classes of society might dance to entertain themselves, either at home or in the street. Professional dancers might put on street performances as well.

Although Egyptologists believe that dances were accompanied by music, they are unsure of its nature since no ancient Egyptian musical scores have been found. They do know, however, that Egyptians used a variety of percussion instruments, including clappers and cymbals, as well as rudimentary trumpets, flutes, pipes, lyres, and harps. **See also** music.

Dashur (Dahshur)

Dashur served as a burial site for the nearby city of Memphis, and its necropolis area includes several pyramids. The most unusual is one that archaeologists call the Bent or False Pyramid, which was built by Fourth Dynasty king Snefru. Midway to its peak, the slope of its sides decreases; thus the upper half of the pyramid is not as steep as the bottom half. There are various theories regarding why this is so. The most prevalent theory is that the angle was lessened as

Some Egyptologists believe that the ancient builders changed the slope of the sides of the Bent Pyramid at Dashur during construction to prevent the structure's collapse. Others believe that the changing slope was a symbol of duality.

the pyramid was built from the bottom up because as its workers neared the top they began to fear that their structure would collapse. One Egyptologist, a physicist named Kurt Mendelssohn, believes that this fear stemmed from the fact that, during the construction of the Bent Pyramid, another pyramid at the town of Meidum collapsed. However, other Egyptologists do not believe that the Meidum pyramid collapsed during its construction but sometime later, and therefore did not influence the building of the Bent Pyramid. Some of these Egyptologists believe that the shape of the Bent Pyramid was changed not for architectural reasons but for religious ones. The pyramid, they note, has many elements that represent duality, including two entrances and duplicate chambers and halls. Therefore it is possible that the difference between the pyramid's top half and its bottom was yet another way of expressing this duality.

Another unusual Dashur pyramid, also built by Snefru, is known as the Red or Pink Pyramid, named for the color of limestone used to build the structure. This pyramid has the second largest base of any pyramid, measuring 712 feet by 712 feet (the Great Pyramid at Giza is slightly larger), and one of its many chambers has a ceiling 50 feet high.

Dashur has three Twelfth Dynasty pyramids: the White Pyramid, built by King Amenemhet II; the Black Pyramid, built by King Amenemhet III; and a nondescript pyramid built by King Senwosret III. The latter has a burial chamber made of red granite, and nearby the Egyptians buried at least six wooden funerary boats. A great deal of jewelry was also found nearby, and more jewelry was found in some Dashur mastaba tombs built for Twelfth Dynasty princesses. There were many tombs and tomb chapels in the area; the Dashur pyramids make up only the southern edge of a large necropolis. **See also** Amenemhet II; Amenemhet III; mastaba tomb; pyramids; Senwosret III; Snefru.

deification of mortals

Kings—and, more rarely, prominent nobles or commoners—were sometimes deified (made into gods) after death. These newly created gods were worshiped with festivals, shrines, and cult statues identical to the type employed in the worship of other deities. Such deity worship differed in magnitude from that of each deceased king's official funerary cult, which involved temple rituals and cult statues as well. Whereas most deceased kings were considered an aspect of an existing god, such as Osiris, very few were considered independent gods.

The most significant deified king was the Eighteenth Dynasty ruler Amenhotep I. He and his mother, Queen Ahmose-Nefertiry, were the main deities worshiped in Deir el-Medina, a workers' village near Thebes, and perhaps elsewhere as well. Among the better-known nonroyals who were deified are a Third Dynasty vizier, Imhotep, and an Eighteenth Dynasty official, Amenhotep, Son of Hapu. **See also** Ahmose-Nefertiry; Amenhotep I; Amenhotep, Son of Hapu; deities; Imhotep; kings.

Deir el-Bahri (Djeseru)

Deir el-Bahri is the Arabic name for the ancient Egyptian town of Djeseru, which was directly across the Nile River from the religious center of Thebes. There were four major building complexes in Deir el-Bahri: the Eleventh Dynasty mortuary temple of Montuhotep I (Nebhetepre), the Eighteenth Dynasty temples of Queen Hatshepsut and King Tuthmosis III, and the Nineteenth Dynasty temple of Ramses II. The temple of Montuhotep II was carved from a cliff and had two levels; the burial chamber was under the terraced temple, which had 140 columns. The structure also featured wall art with scenes from Montuhotep II's life, including his foreign campaigns and hunting trips. The

The rock-cut tomb and mortuary temple of Queen Hatshepsut, built at Deir el-Bahri around 1478 B.C., consists of three colonnaded terraces connected by ramps.

mortuary complex of Queen Hatshepsut featured scenes from her life as well. They included such events as her coronation, a sea voyage to Punt, and the transportation of obelisks down the Nile River from quarries near Aswan to Karnak in Thebes. The style of her temple was modeled after Montuhotep II's, but her complex also included two chapels and two shrines honoring, respectively, the goddess Hathor, a solar cult, the god Anubis, and a royal cult. King Tuthmosis III also built a chapel dedicated to Hathor, as well as a temple complex dedicated to Amun. The stone mortuary temple of Ramses II, also known as the Ramesseum, concentrated on honoring the king; it included scenes showing his military battles, among other events in his life, and two colossal statues made in his likeness. All that remains of these statues is a single head. **See also** Anubis; Hathor; Hatshepsut; Karnak; Montuhotep; Ramses II; Thebes; Tuthmosis III.

Deir el-Gebrawi

Located near the town of Asyut, Deir el-Gebrawi was the site of the necropolis for the twelfth nome of Upper Egypt. Approximately one-hundred rock-cut tombs have been found there, some of them still containing their tomb goods. Many of them are the tombs of Sixth Dynasty nomarchs from not only the twelfth nome but others. **See also** Asyut; nomes and nomarchs.

Deir el-Medina

Located west of the Nile River opposite Thebes, Deir el-Medina was a walled settlement with approximately seventy houses built for workers constructing royal tombs in the Valley of the Kings and tombs at a nearby necropolis called Qurnet Murai. The settlement was first established during the reign of Tuthmosis I, although most of the ruins there date from the Ramessid Period, and the settlement was abandoned after the last tombs were built in the area during the Twentieth Dynasty.

Deir el-Medina has provided archaeologists from the nineteenth century onward with valuable information about how work proceeded on major construction projects in the area. For example, work records found in the village show that there were two work crews, each with more than sixty men overseen by a foreman and his assistant. Occasionally, the king's vizier would visit construction sites to check on their progress, and two or more royal scribes kept track of details related to various building projects, including the number of days each man worked so that pay could be determined.

Pay was primarily in the form of grain distributed monthly, although wine, salt, sesame oil, and other goods might be included as well. A typical laborer's ration fed ten people; a foreman received one-third more than that amount. Archaeologists estimate that the workers in Deir el-Medina had a much higher standard of living than people living in agricultural villages along the Nile River. Nonetheless, whenever their pay was late, the workers at Deir el-Medina went on strike.

Workmen actually lived in Deir el-Medina only when they had a day off; otherwise, they slept at the construction site while their wives and children remained in the village. Workers would typically labor for eight days straight, followed by two days of rest. In addition to these days off, there were numerous religious holidays when work was suspended. Interestingly, because the village was well removed from the Nile River and there was no other source of water nearby, the government provided construction workers and their families with a laundry service and brought fresh drinking water in by donkey on a regular basis. **See also** Amarna; architecture; villages, workers.'

deities

The ancient Egyptians worshiped numerous deities, many with multiple manifestations and complex relationships to one another. A single deity might be associated with many different characteristics, roles, people, objects, and geographical locations. For example, the jackal-headed god Duamutef was associated with the east, canopic jars, and the protection of the stomach and upper intestines. Two or three gods might also merge with one another to produce a manifestation with characteristics of each. For example, the creator god Ptah sometimes merged with Sokar, a god who guarded Memphis tombs, to become Ptah-Sokar in Memphis. In addition, some deities that revealed themselves as distinct individuals were apparently manifestations of another deity. For example, Bastet (who typically appeared as a cat) and Sekhmet (who typically appeared as a lioness) seem to have been two manifestations of the female energy that was associated with Hathor.

It was very common for deities to manifest as a particular animal or combination of animals. Many Egyptologists surmise that gods were believed to do this in order to look frightening to combat evil forces. For example, the goddess Taweret, associated with childbirth, had the physical attributes of a hippopotamus, lion, and sometimes crocodile as well, and her job was apparently to keep evil spirits away from women during labor.

Such beliefs about gods varied according to location. For example, in some places the god Horus was considered the son of the goddess Hathor, in others of the goddess Isis. Moreover, some gods were specific to certain regions while others were worshiped nationally; when a king from a particular region came to the throne, he often elevated his local god to national status. When kings from Heliopolis were on the throne, for example, their local sun god Re gained prominence across Egypt.

Many deities had their own cult centers, cities that were home to both a priesthood serving a particular deity and a temple with a shrine believed to be the residence of that and related deities. Every nome (administrative district) in ancient Egypt had its own cult center; there were twenty-two nomes in Upper Egypt and twenty in Lower Egypt, making forty-two nomes and forty-two cult centers. Some gods appeared in the family groupings of more than one cult center. Amun, for instance, shared a residence with two other gods in Thebes and seven other gods in Hermopolis. Sometimes a political alliance between cult centers would result in one god merging with another to create a new manifestation, as with Ptah-Sokar or Amun-Re.

Wherever they were worshiped, deities were the focus of a wide variety of ceremonies intended to honor and sustain the gods and to benefit the mortals who relied upon them. The ancient Egyptians believed that the realm of the deities and the realm of mortals were linked, so chaos in one place created chaos in the other. Consequently, they considered their worship of the gods to be vital to harmony and prosperity in Egypt. **See also** cult centers; magic; priests; religion; *individual entries for dieties.*

Delta

North of the modern city of Cairo, Egypt, the Delta is a triangular area of lowlands where the Nile River divides into several branches just before reaching the Mediterranean Sea. (At various times in history, the number and precise courses of these branches have changed.) There are numerous lakes, marshes, and other watery regions in the Delta, and the land is extremely fertile. Therefore, throughout Egypt's history the Delta has been a particularly productive area for crops. With food so readily available, several important cities grew up in the region, including Tanis, Bubastis, and later Alexandria. The city of Memphis, at the southern end of the Delta where the river splits, also benefited from the area's fertility. **See also** Alexandria; Memphis; Nile River; Tanis.

Den (Udimu) (dates unknown)

The fourth king of the First Dynasty, Den was most active around 2950 B.C. Some Egyptologists believe that he ruled for at least fifty years, probably ascending the throne as a boy. Others say that his reign was far shorter, perhaps only fourteen years. In either case, during his time as king, Den established a military presence in the Sinai, east of Egypt, in order to acquire its natural resources. He also became involved in medicine and magic, writing medical treatises and creating spells. In fact, many of the spells in the *Book of the Dead* are said to be his, and his medical work is mentioned in the Berlin Papyrus.

For many years, a tomb found at Saqqara in 1935 was thought to be Den's. More recently, though, Egyptologists have come to believe that this tomb is that of Den's chancellor, Hemaka; Den's tomb is now thought to be at Abydos. The Abydos tomb is particularly significant to Egyptologists because of its granite floor, which is believed to be the first instance of the use of that stone in Egyptian architecture. **See also** Berlin Papyrus; *Book of the Dead*; Saqqara.

Dendera (Denderah; Dendara; Iunet; Tantere; Tentyris)

Located south of Abydos and north of Luxor on the edge of the desert, the modern city of Dendera (Iunet or Tantere in ancient Egyptian, Tentyris in Greek) was once the capital of the sixth nome of Upper Egypt and the main cult center of the goddess Hathor. Some Egyptologists believe that Dendera was also a major destination for Egyptians hoping for cures for various ailments, because the goddess Hathor was, among other things, a goddess of healing.

A series of temples dedicated to Hathor was erected at Dendera over the course of many years, from predynastic times to the Greco-Roman Period. The first was a Predynastic Period shrine, which was rebuilt in the Fourth Dynasty by King Khufu. In Khufu's version, the shrine was dedicated not only to Hathor but also to her son Ihy, who was shown in temple art playing an ancient Egyptian rattle called a sistrum that belonged to his mother. In the Sixth Dynasty, King Pepy I added a gold statue of Ihy to the temple. Subsequent kings—including Montuhotep III, Amenemhet I, Tuthmosis III, Amenhotep III, and Ramses II—added other features to the temple or rebuilt parts of it. During the Greco-Roman Period, a Ptolemaic king—probably Ptolemy XII—began construction on a temple complex, and this series of structures has survived to modern times. The temple complex was still under construction when Rome took control of Egypt, and wall reliefs in the temple offer depictions of five Roman emperors: Augustus, Tiberius, Caligula, Claudius, and Nero.

The temple features a great deal of other artwork as well. The main hall has wall carvings that depict temple offerings and tell mythological stories. The ceiling shows images related to astronomy and astrology, including deities representing the signs of the zodiac. Another hall, the Hall of Appearances, depicts a ritual that was traditionally conducted whenever the foundation of a temple was about to be laid. The Hall of Offerings shows various items associated with Hathor, including musical instruments and milk (since Hathor's main physical manifestation was as a cow).

Outside the temple is a false door, a stela carved to resemble a door that was said to allow spirits of the dead to enter the realm of the living so that they could receive offerings left for them there. False doors typically appear inside of temples, but at the Temple of Hathor it was outside so the public could use it as a shrine to the goddess (since only kings and priests were allowed inside the temple). Another important exterior feature of the temple is a wall relief of Queen Cleopatra VII with her son Caesarion, who is shown making offerings to the gods.

There are several other buildings in the temple complex, including a small temple dedicated to Isis, a Birth House depicting the birth of King Nectanebo II with the deities Hathor and Amun as his parents, a Roman-era healing center whose pool of water was believed to cure bathers of various ailments, and a Coptic Christian church from the fifth century A.D. **See also** Birth House; Greco-Roman Period; Hathor.

Denon, Dominique-Vivant (1747–1825)

Baron Dominique-Vivant Denon was a French artist and archaeologist who was hired to sketch monuments for Napoléon Bonaparte on his 1798 expedition to Egypt. After Denon returned from Egypt, Napoléon made him the director general of museums in France, a position Denon held from 1804 to 1815. During this time he accompanied the emperor on several foreign expeditions, helping him to decide which works of art to bring home. This collection formed the basis of the Louvre Museum in Paris. Denon also published a book of his sketches of and observations on various sites in Egypt, *Voyages dans la Basse et la Haute Égypte* (*Travels in Lower and Upper Egypt*), published in 1802. Four volumes of an unfinished illustrated history of art called *Monuments des arts du dessin chez les peuples tant anciens que modernes* (*Monuments of the Arts of Design Among People as Much Ancient as Modern*) were published posthumously in 1829. **See also** Napoléon I.

Dialogue Between a Man Tired of Life and His "Ba"

A Middle Kingdom literary text, *Dialogue Between a Man Tired of Life and His "Ba"* is considered to be perhaps the earliest written work to address the topic of suicide. In the text, a man debates with his *ba,* the part of the spirit that the Egyptians believed gave a person his or her individuality, over whether life is worth living. **See also** *ba.*

Diodorus Siculus (ca. first century B.C.)

Greek historian Diodorus Siculus traveled through Egypt during the years 60 to 57 B.C. and included his observations on the country's ancient sites in his history, *Bibliotheca Historica.* This work contains one of the first descriptions of the Colossi of Memnon, two massive statues of a seated King Amenhotep III that were constructed together near Thebes, and a description of a nearby temple of Ramses II. A contemporary of Diodorus Siculus, Strabo, also wrote about these sites, and together the two men helped spread interest in ancient Egypt among travelers in classical times. **See also** Amenhotep III; Ramses II; Strabo; Thebes.

Divine Wife of Amun (Divine Adoratrice of Amun; God's Wife of Amun)

King Ahmose I of the Eighteenth Dynasty established the title "Divine Wife of Amun" or "God's Wife of Amun" for principal royal wives, beginning with his queens Ahhotep I and Ahmose-Nefertiry. The holder of the title participated in various rituals and festivals associated with the god Amun at Luxor and Karnak.

In the Twenty-first Dynasty, the position was changed so that not the king's wife but his daughter was the God's Wife during rituals, and she was now called the Divine Adoratrice of Amun. This title came with vast estates in Thebes, where the Divine Adoratrice was required to live because it was the cult center of Amun, and along with these estates came wealth and the power that that wealth could buy. Out of concern that a consort of the Divine Adoratrice might use her wealth and power to challenge the king's rule, the king decreed that she had to remain unmarried and celibate. (All members of her court, considered to be members of Amun's harem, were required to be virgins as well to prevent a man from gaining access to the adoratrice.) By the Twenty-fifth Dynasty, the position had become so powerful that kings were using it to their political advantage, influencing the Divine Adoratrice to strengthen their own power in Thebes. **See also** Ahhotep I; Ahmose I; Ahmose-Nefertiry; Amun.

djed

The *djed* is an ancient Egyptian symbol resembling the trunk of a palm tree or a column or pillar with three horizontal logs or bars cutting across its upper end. The *djed* stood for strength, stability, and the god Osiris, and was therefore believed to aid the body's transition to its Afterlife form. For this reason, it was used on amulets related to mortuary rituals and magic. The *djed* was also featured in an annual *djed* festival. During this festival, sometimes referred to as the Djed Pillar Festival, a pillar resembling the *djed* was erected to mark the first day of harvest season. Various rituals were then conducted at the pillar's base, including a symbolic fight between the forces of good and the forces of evil. **See also** amulets; magic; Osiris.

Djedefre (Radjedef; Redjedef) (?–ca. 2558 B.C.)

The younger son of King Khufu, Fourth Dynasty king Djedefre ("Enduring Like

Re") assumed the throne under suspicious circumstances. Around the same time that his father died, Djedefre's brother Kewab—the first in line for the throne—also died, and Djedefre subsequently married Kewab's widow, Hetepheres II, to solidify his claim to the throne. Egyptologists have long speculated that Djedefre murdered Kewab, and it appears that Egyptians at the time questioned his right to rule. In fact, a few Egyptologists believe that this opposition was so strong that it ultimately led to the king's death, because there is evidence that Djedefre's rule ended suddenly. In particular, several building projects were stopped shortly after they were begun, including Djedefre's pyramid and temple complex at Abu Roash just north of Giza. The most likely candidates for the king's murderers, if he was indeed killed, were his uncles Princes Ankhaf and Minkhaf, who were supporters of Djedefre's eventual successor, his brother Khafre. **See also** Abu Roash; Kewab; Khafre.

Djehutihotep (Djehutyhotep) (ca. 1922–ca. 1855 B.C.)

A Twelfth Dynasty nomarch, Djehutihotep is best known today for his tomb at el-Bersheh, once the capital city of his nome, Hare. His career spanned the reigns of Kings Amenemhet II, Senwosret II, and Senwosret III. Egyptologists consider the wall paintings in Djehutihotep's tomb to be among the best of the Middle Kingdom, both in quality and in subject matter. Of particular significance is a painting showing how a colossal alabaster statue weighing nearly sixty tons was transported to the tomb from a quarry at Hatnub. According to an inscription by a scribe named Sipa, the statue—which no longer exists—was dragged on a sledge by 172 workers. Additional inscriptions indicate that the tomb was decorated by an artist named Amenaankhu and built under the super-

vision of a director of works named Sep. Djehutihotep's tomb was particularly grand, as were his coffin and his wife's coffin, because of the great power he held as the hereditary governor of his nome. **See also** Amenemhet II; nomes and nomarchs; Senwosret II; Senwosret III.

Djer (Zer; Ity) (dates unknown)

Djer, the second king of the First Dynasty, ruled Egypt for fifty to sixty years. Sometime around 3000 B.C., he led at least one military campaign against the people of a land called Setjet, which Egyptologists hypothesize was Sinai. (Lending credence to this idea is the fact that archaeologists have found numerous objects from Djer's reign that are made of copper and turquoise from Sinai.) Records from the period also indicate that Djer traveled at least once from his palace at Memphis to the Delta town of Buto, but little else is known of his reign. Egyptologists are uncertain whether Djer was the son of his predecessor, King Aha (also known as Hor-Aha); if he was, then his mother would have most likely been Queen Khenthap.

Djer appears to have been entombed at Abydos, along with three hundred of his servants and craftsmen. There is evidence that human sacrifice was practiced during Djer's reign, so most Egyptologists believe that these people were killed so that they could accompany the king to the Afterlife. **See also** Abydos; Buto; Manetho.

Djoser (Zoser; Netjerykhet) (ca. 2684–ca. 2648 B.C.)

The son of King Khasekhemwy and Queen Hapnyma'at, Djoser (also known as Netjerykhet) was the second king of the Third Dynasty. His reign lasted approximately twenty years, during which time he strengthened his hold on the throne by threatening to use force against unruly no-

This statue of the Third Dynasty king Djoser was created about 2620 B.C.

marchs and by launching military campaigns to prevent incursions by nomads on Egypt's eastern border and Libyans on its western one. Egyptologists disagree on the extent of Djoser's realm, but it appears to have included the First Cataract of the Nile River, making this the first time that Egypt's border had extended so far south.

Djoser's reign was also marked by advances in agriculture, trade, and the arts. Urbanization increased, with many more people living in cities than before. Among the innovations Djoser sponsored was the Step Pyramid, the first all-stone monument not only in Egypt but perhaps in the world.

Djoser also built a temple to the god Khnum at Elephantine, and according to ancient texts he did so after having a

dream that building the temple would end a drought and famine. According to the writings of the priests of this temple, when the drought and famine did indeed end, Djoser gave them a gift of land, an area near Aswan that encompassed approximately eighty-five square miles. However, writings of the priests who served the goddess Isis at the nearby island of Philae mention the same territory as being theirs, so Egyptologists suspect that there was either a dispute over the land or one or both of the parties was bragging about a benefit that was not really theirs. **See also** Elephantine; Imhotep; Khnum; Philae; pyramids.

drama

Plays as a form of entertainment were unknown in ancient Egypt. The only drama performed by ancient Egyptians appears to have had sacred purposes. Temple dramas featured people reenacting various events in the gods' lives, and since these plays were typically part of temple ceremonies, Egyptologists have speculated that their purpose was to draw the attention of the gods and perhaps create magic.

One of the most prominent examples of religious drama was a series of plays performed as part of a pageant at Abydos to honor the god Osiris. Known as Osiris's Mysteries, the plays reenacted the life of Osiris as a mortal king, his death at the hands of his evil brother Seth, and his resurrection as a god through the intervention of his sister Isis. Principal players in the drama were temple priests or high-ranking government officials, and the cast possibly changed as performances were repeated over the course of several days. At the end of the performances, a symbolic battle between the forces of the god Horus, known as the Followers of Horus, and those of the god Seth was staged. **See also** Abydos; Followers of Horus and Seth; Osiris.

Drovetti, Bernardino (1776–1852)

One of the most successful nineteenth-century antiquities dealers was Bernardino Drovetti, the consul general of Egypt from 1810 to 1829. Because of his position as consul general, he supervised excavations and had ample opportunity to grab the best finds for himself. In making his selections he was aided by his assistant, French sculptor Jean-Jacques Rifaud. Together these two men collected and sold many important works. A great percentage of them went to a single private collector, the king of Sardinia, who donated them to the Turin Museum in 1824. Other of Drovetti's finds went to the Louvre Museum in Paris and the Berlin Museum. **See also** archaeological expeditions; Egyptomania.

dynastic race

The term *dynastic race* refers to a theory developed by British archaeologist Sir William Matthew Flinders Petrie that foreigners brought new practices, such as funerary rituals, into Egypt early in the dynastic period of the country's history. These foreigners, the theory held, possessed more advanced technology and architectural skills and employed more sophisticated burial practices than the native Egyptians did. Petrie further speculated that this "dynastic race" of foreigners eventually comprised Egypt's original kings and nobility. Various origins for the dynastic race have been proposed, both by Petrie and others, with Mesopotamia being the most frequently mentioned, in part because Mesopotamian culture predated Egyptian civilization.

However, Petrie's theory has had many critics who believe that the ancient Egyptians developed their culture without outside intervention. These critics have argued that when one culture develops at a later time than another it does not necessarily mean that the second culture had to have been inspired by the first, even if there are similarities between the two cultures. Moreover, Petrie's critics do not believe that there is sufficient evidence to prove that any foreigners came into contact with Egypt during the formation of its ancient culture. **See also** Mesopotamia; Petrie, William Matthew Flinders.

dynasties

Historians generally define dynasties in terms of family lineages. In the case of ancient Egyptian history, however, dynastic divisions are based not on family ties but on seemingly arbitrary divisions that were created by a third-century-B.C. Greco-Egyptian priest named Manetho. In writing a chronicle of Egyptian history that spanned from approximately 3100 B.C. to 343 B.C., Manetho decided (for unknown reasons) to group Egypt's kings into thirty dynasties. To do this, he sometimes created a new dynasty when a new family seized power or when a king chose a successor who was not related to him by blood; in other cases, however, kings from the same family were put in successive dynasties. Historians still use these divisions today but have added as many as three dynasties: a Zero Dynasty, a Thirty-first, and a Thirty-second. **See also** Manetho.

Early Dynastic Period (ca. 3000–ca. 2686 B.C.)

Also called the Archaic Period, the Early Dynastic Period was an era of Egyptian history lasting from approximately 3000 to 2686 B.C. It incorporated two dynasties, the First (ca. 3000–2890 B.C.) and the Second (ca. 2890–2686 B.C.), and at least twelve kings ruling in sequence: Aha (Hor-Aha), Djer, Djet, Den, Anedjib, Semerkhet, and Qa'a, all of the First Dynasty, and Hotepsekhemwy, Raneb, Nynetjer, Peribsen, and Khasekhemwy, all of the Second Dynasty. On the basis of the writings of the third-century-B.C. Greco-Egyptian historian Manetho, who established the demarcations of ancient Egyptian dynasties still used today, some historians believe that there were several additional kings in the Second Dynasty, bringing the total to nine. However, hard evidence of the existence of these kings has yet to be found.

The kings of the Early Dynastic period ruled from around Memphis but controlled both Upper and Lower Egypt from the First Cataract of the Nile River at Aswan north to the Delta. In fact, according to Manetho, this unification of the two lands under one king is what marked the beginning of Egyptian civilization. Many Egyptologists believe that this took place just before the First Dynasty, during the reign of a Predynastic Period king called Narmer. Aha, the first king of the First Dynasty, was apparently Narmer's son.

The Early Dynastic Period was one of rapid cultural development in Egypt. Writing, calendars, and astronomy all developed during this period. At the same time, art, architecture, and burial practices became more sophisticated, particularly in association with royal tombs. Stone monuments were constructed to glorify kings after their death, and temples were constructed to honor the gods. In addition, a belief system predicated on the idea of an eternity existing after death was established. Advances in technical know-how were similarly dramatic. For example, it was during this time that a system for irrigating dry land was developed, increasing the amount of arable land and thereby increasing the food supply. **See also** agriculture; Aha; Narmer; Predynastic Period.

Eastern Desert

During ancient times, the Eastern Desert was considered to be all lands east of the Nile River. This region was the source of many minerals and building stones and was therefore a main focus of ancient Egypt's mining and quarrying expeditions. The Eastern Desert site of Gebel Ahmar yielded quartzite; Hatnub, alabaster or calcite; and the Wadi Hammamat, graywacke (a hard, blackish stone also known as siltstone because it consisted of compacted dry silt). Gold was mined in the Eastern Desert as well, along with jasper, limestone, lead ore, emerald, amethyst, diorite, granite, feldspar, and other stones. Because of the position of the Eastern Desert, Egyptians on their way to the coast of the Red

Sea had to cross this wasteland. There were three main routes across the desert to towns along the sea, each following a dry riverbed or gully, known as a wadi; one route went through the Wadi Gasus to Safaga, another through the Wadi Hammamat to Quseir, and the third through the Wadi Abbad to Berenice. **See also** Hammamat, Wadi; mining and metalworking; quarrying; Sinai.

Ebers Papyrus

Now at the Berlin Museum, the Ebers Papyrus is an Eighteenth Dynasty papyrus featuring a medical text listing over nine hundred treatments for various diseases (particularly of the digestive tract), injuries, and other medical conditions. The papyrus is quite lengthy, with 108 separate pages. Archaeologists believe that, like similar medical papyri of which ten are currently known, the Ebers Papyrus is probably a copy of an earlier work that has yet to be discovered. **See also** medicine; papyrus.

economic system

The ancient Egyptian economic system was based on bartering, trading for items rather than paying for them in coin. Even taxes and tributes to the king were paid in goods rather than money. In fact, coins were not used in Egypt until after approximately 252 B.C. However, even though currency was not used in earlier times, sometime around 1580 B.C. every item was assigned a value in terms of precious metals such as gold or silver in an attempt to make trade more uniform and equitable. In earlier times, grain was used as a way to even out the relative value of items being exchanged, so in this sense grain served as a form of money. Grain was also the standard form of payment for workers building royal tombs.

Since food was the main type of bartered good, when farmers had a bad year the economy suffered. Eventually the government instituted a policy for cushioning the impact of a low crop yield by storing food from productive years to stave off shortages. However, during reigns by weaker kings, Egypt's centralized government was less able to fulfill this role, so the system did not always work.

The government, in the person of the king, was also involved in the redistribution of wealth. The king—who was considered to own everything and everyone in Egypt—granted lands and other economic benefits to people he favored or removed such benefits from those he disliked. Such a system of patronage and favoritism meant that Egyptian society was firmly divided into the rich and the poor, although there was a middle class of craftsmen and artisans. However, there was no true merchant class, for two primary reasons: First, people did their bartering themselves without using intermediaries, and second, trading with foreign lands was strictly handled by government officials. **See also** food; kings; taxation; trade.

Edfu

Located midway between Luxor and Aswan, Edfu (called Behdet by the ancient Egyptians) was once the capital of the second nome of Upper Egypt. It was also a cult center dedicated to the worship of Horus the Elder or Horus the Falcon; as such, its main building complex was the Temple of Horus. The temple was begun in 237 B.C. by Ptolemy III Euergetes I and features various decorations contributed by the king's successors, Ptolemy IV Philopator and Ptolemy VIII Euergetes II. However, it suffered from many interruptions in construction before finally being completed in 57 B.C. Nonetheless, the temple is one of the best preserved ancient temples in the world, as well as one of the few Egyptian temples to contain construction from only the Ptolemaic Period.

Inside the temple at Edfu are several wall reliefs, including one showing a battle between Horus and Seth, the latter of whom manifested himself as a hippopotamus. The temple is also unusual in that its entrance faces south rather than the traditional east or west. Some Egyptologists believe that this orientation was chosen so that the temple would face toward another temple at nearby Dendera, while others believe that the orientation was dictated by the terrain at the building site.

Other structures in Edfu include several Sixth Dynasty tombs and Twentieth Dynasty tombs with wall reliefs. During the Second Intermediate Period, the city had various fortifications, including an inner and outer wall. These structures were erected by kings of Upper Egypt who had come to Edfu from Thebes to protect themselves from Hyksos kings who had taken over the Delta area of Lower Egypt. **See also** Greco-Roman Period; Horus; Ptolemaic Period; Seth.

education

Egyptologists disagree on some of the details related to the education system of ancient Egypt, in particular the age at which a child began school and whether or not children of all levels of society and both genders had access to a formal education. Generally, however, most believe that all boys were allowed to attend school provided that their fathers paid the cost of their education in the form of grain or other goods, but even though schools were open to all qualified candidates, it is believed that few peasants took advantage of them. Therefore, it appears that most of the population remained illiterate, because peasants made up roughly 80 percent of the ancient Egyptian population.

In small rural communities, boys went to village schools or to trade schools to learn particular crafts. Those who intended to go into the priesthood or any other profession related to religion or into government administration of any kind went to schools located within temples or government centers. The children of royalty and those nobility favored at court were tutored privately in palaces, sometimes along with the children of royal servants.

All types of schools taught not only academics but sports, morals, good manners, and self-discipline. Sports included swimming, wrestling, and archery. To learn what constituted good behavior, students studied various didactic texts known as admonitions and instructions, copying them over and over again to learn their moral content. Extensive copying of texts was also involved in the teaching of writing, and many works of literature, including moral compositions and letters, were produced specifically to teach reading and writing to students. The earliest works were directed at an audience of royal and noble children, who were admonished to treat those of lower birth with kindness but firmness. Gradually, however, such works were addressed to the lower middle classes as well, promoting the idea that wealth and social position were not as important as moral character in general and humility in particular. This changing message leads some Egyptologists to believe that by the New Kingdom the lower classes were attending schools in greater numbers than in earlier ages.

In addition to copying pages and pages of text—with their teachers correcting their handwriting mistakes in the margins—schoolboys learned other subjects depending on their intended career. For example, future architects concentrated on mathematics, while future diplomats learned foreign languages. Students who learned in temple schools got the broadest education, with a variety of priests teaching multiple subjects. After several years of study, educated young men went on to take apprenticeships as scribes or other prominent positions in society. **See also** admonitions and instructions; children.

Edwin Smith Papyrus

One of ten known ancient Egyptian medical papyri, the Edwin Smith Papyrus contains forty-eight discussions of various diseases and their treatments. It dates from the Eighteenth Dynasty but is probably a copy of a Third Dynasty text. **See also** medicine; papyrus.

Egypt Exploration Society

Founded in 1882 as the Egypt Exploration Fund, the Egypt Exploration Society has long been at the forefront of the study of ancient Egyptian archaeological sites, funding numerous expeditions and supporting the work of such noted Egyptologists as Sir William Matthew Flinders Petrie and Howard Carter. The foundation was created by British author Amelia Edwards, who visited Egypt in 1873–1874 and two years later published a book, *A Thousand Miles Up the Nile,* describing the ancient Egyptian monuments she observed. Many of these monuments had been damaged over time, whether by the elements or by humans, and Edwards rallied support for her foundation by warning people that knowledge of ancient Egypt soon would be lost forever unless archaeologists rushed to study its ruins. As a result, she and her cofounder, Reginald Stuart Poole of the Department of Coins and Medals at the British Museum, were able to garner enough funds to support numerous archaeological expeditions to Egypt, as well as efforts to record the condition of ancient sites throughout Egypt.

The first expeditions, directed by Swiss scholar Edouard Naville, were in the Delta, where it was then believed that several cities mentioned in the Bible had been located. (Tanis, for example, was thought to be the biblical city of Zoan.) Soon, however, many other ancient cities were being excavated regardless of whether scholars believed that they were associated with the Bible. In fact, the Egypt Exploration Society has sponsored archaeological studies at some of the most important sites in Egypt, including Deir el-Bahri, Amarna, Saqqara, Memphis, and Abydos, as well as the Nubian fortress of Qasr Ibrim. Work sponsored by the society continues up to the present day, with a continuing emphasis on preserving artifacts threatened by modern civilization. **See also** archaeological expeditions.

Egypt, geographical features of

Located in northern Africa, with the Nile River cutting through its center, ancient Egypt consisted of five main geographical regions. The first was the Nile Valley, a fertile strip of land on either side of the Nile River. In the south, this long river valley was flanked by steep granite and sandstone cliffs on either side, with desert lands beyond. In the north, it broadened to become the second geographical region, the Delta. This was a marshy area where the river split into several tributaries on its way to the Mediterranean Sea; it was rich in both agricultural lands and settlements. The third geographical region was the Faiyum, a large natural depression of wetlands, marshes, swamps, and agricultural lands on the west side of the Nile River near the Delta. The other two regions were the Eastern Desert and the Western Desert, rocky desert landscapes located on the east and west sides of the Nile River, respectively. At various times, however, Egypt's border on the west shifted to exclude the Western Desert. **See also** Delta; Faiyum; Nile River.

Egyptology

Egyptology is the study and/or scientific investigation of all aspects of ancient Egypt, including its antiquities, society, and language; anyone who specializes in such study is called an Egyptologist. Some of the most prominent Egyptologists have also been archaeologists, meaning that they excavate ancient Egyptian sites as well as study the results of such excavations. This was the case with a man considered to be one of the founders of modern Egyptology, Sir William Matthew Flinders Petrie. Other notable Egyptologists include Giovanni Battista Belzoni, Howard Carter, Karl Richard Lepsius, Auguste Mariette, and Jean-François Champollion. **See also** archaeological expeditions; Belzoni, Giovanni Battista; Carter, Howard; Champollion, Jean-François; Lepsius, Karl Richard; Mariette, Auguste; Petrie, William Matthew Flinders.

Egyptomania

Egyptomania is a term used by Egyptologists to describe a drive to acquire Egyptian antiquities that took hold of both scholars and nonscholars, particularly in Europe, during the nineteenth century. At this time, private art collectors, public institutions, tourists, and others raced to collect Egyptian artwork, artifacts, mummies, and other items, often paying exorbitant prices for them. Because of the high demand for their wares, antiquities dealers became unscrupulous in selling objects that had obviously been looted from tombs, and workers at excavation sites often fought with one another to gain the best pieces either for themselves or for their employers. These sites sometimes were scenes of violence when several employers sent work crews to the same place at the same time.

Gradually, however, Egyptomania died out, partly because serious scholars spoke out against the looting of ancient Egyptian treasures and partly because the Egyptian government made it more difficult for such treasures to be taken from the country. For example, archaeologists were required to get a permit allowing them to dig at a specific site for a specific period of time, and a portion of the artifacts they found during an excavation had to be handed over to the Egyptian government. Another factor in the dying out of Egyptomania was a new public concern about supposed mummies' curses. Shortly after the discovery of King Tutankhamun's tomb in 1922, for example, some of the people who had entered the tomb died, and rumors began that the ancient Egyptians had put a curse on anyone who might disturb the king's remains. This rumor spread and changed, and eventually many people in England and Europe began to believe that all items removed from any tomb might be cursed. Such people stopped buying Egyptian artifacts and disposed of ones they already owned. **See also** archaeological expeditions; Drovetti, Bernardino; Egyptology; Tutankhamun.

Elephantine

Called Abu or Yebu by the ancient Egyptians, Elephantine is an island approximately one mile long and one-half mile wide lying in the Nile River at the north end of the First Cataract. The island was first inhabited during the Predynastic Period and was probably the site of a fortress during the Early Dynastic Period. Elephantine was important militarily because it was at a point in the river where navigation was impeded by the rocks of the cataract. This often forced travelers to pull their boats from the river and drag them along the shore past the rocks, making them vulnerable to attack.

Together with the nearby town of Aswan, Elephantine was the capital of the first nome of Upper Egypt, as well as an administrative center overseen by Egypt's viceroy of Nubia. It was also a cult center dedicated to the creator god Khnum and, to a lesser extent, the deities Satis and Anukis.

Thanks to its strategic and administrative importance, Elephantine is home to temples built by several of Egypt's rulers, including Amenhotep III, Tuthmosis III, Hatshepsut, and Alexander III. It also contains a shrine built by the Sixth Dynasty official Heqaib that held numerous stelae and statues. In addition, the nearby west bank of the Nile River has several Old Kingdom, Middle Kingdom, and New Kingdom rock-cut tombs of various prominent officials.

Excavations in the last three decades of the twentieth century uncovered several burials of sacred rams on the island. Such burials lend credence to the theory that Elephantine was a cult center for the god Khnum, since the ram was believed to be a manifestation of that god. The rams found on Elephantine had been mummified, fitted with gilt headpieces, and set inside stone sarcophagi before burial.

Elephantine is also known for two artifacts found there, the Elephantine Papyrus and the Elephantine Calendar. The papyrus is a Thirteenth Dynasty text recounting various events of the period, the calendar was inscribed on stone during the reign of Eighteenth Dynasty king Tuthmosis III, although only fragments of it remain. **See also** Aswan; calendars; Khnum; Nile River.

el-Kab

Called Nekheb in ancient Egyptian, el-Kab was one of the earliest Egyptian settlements. The town was located in Upper Egypt just north of Edfu, and by the Eighteenth Dynasty (if not before), it was the capital of Upper Egypt's third nome. El-Kab was first occupied in prehistoric times, probably as early as 6000 B.C., and grew in importance during the Predynastic and Early Dynastic Periods, along with its sister city across the Nile River to the west, Nekhen (Hierakonpolis under the Greeks, now Kom el-Ahmar). From early on, el-Kab was a cult center for the vulture goddess Nekhbet, patroness of Upper Egypt.

Surrounded by a mud-brick wall, the town included a temple complex dedicated to Nekhbet, which included a sacred lake, a predynastic cemetery, and a Birth House (a small temple where a god or goddess had supposedly been born). Markings within the complex indicate that some of its smaller buildings date from the Second Dynasty. However, most are from the Eighteenth Dynasty, particularly the reigns of Tuthmosis III and Amenhotep II. The Ramessid kings of the Nineteenth and Twentieth Dynasties also added to the temple complex, as did kings from the Twenty-fifth, Twenty-sixth, Twenty-seventh, Twenty-ninth, and Thirtieth Dynasties. Some of these kings also added chapels outside the temple complex. Nearby are a temple dedicated to both Nekhbet and Hathor, built by Tuthmosis IV and Amenhotep III, and a few small chapels and a sanctuary dedicated to Hathor and other deities. In addition, north of the town are several rock-cut tombs dating from various periods. Two are particularly significant because inscriptions provide biographical information about their owners, Ahmose Pen-Nekhebet and Ahmose Son of Abana, as well as details about their lives as military leaders. **See also** Ahmose Pen-Nekhebet; Ahmose Son of Abana; Amenhotep III; deities; Edfu; Hathor; Hierakonpolis; Tuthmosis IV.

Eloquent Peasant, The Tale of the

Featured in several papyri dating from the New Kingdom, *The Tale of the Eloquent Peasant* was a popular ancient Egyptian story about a peasant, Khunianupu, in Heracleopolis who was unjustly treated by government officials. Going before the king in an attempt to obtain relief, he gave a speech on justice so eloquent that the king subsequently had him repeat it at various public gatherings. This story was first discovered in a papyrus (now in the Berlin Museum) found at the Ramesseum, the mortuary temple of Ramses II at Thebes. **See also** Ramses II; tales.

Ennead

A Greek word meaning "group of nine," Ennead (or *pesedjet* in ancient Egyptian) refers to the nine deities that form the basis of the Creation myth of Heliopolis. The names of these nine deities vary according to the version of the myth, but generally they are Atum (or Atum-Re or Re-Atum), Shu, Tefnut, Geb, Nut, Isis, Nephthys, Osiris, and Seth. **See also** Atum; Geb; Heliopolis; Isis; Nephthys; Nut; Osiris; Seth; Shu; Tefnut.

entertaining guests

When entertaining guests, ancient Egyptians followed certain rituals. Upon arriving at a home, a guest would remove his sandals, whereupon the host would offer him water and a pan to wash his feet. The host would then give the guest, whether a man or woman, a flower or a necklace or garland of flowers, usually lotus blossoms. (Containers of flowers were kept in entrance halls for this purpose.) During certain historical periods, ceremonies involving anointment with scented oils were also part of the greeting. Next came the serving of wine, which almost always preceded festivities and banquets. Hands were washed right before eating, again using water pans, and the dinner that followed typically featured the best foods the host could afford. The wealthy would also provide professional dancers and musicians as dinner entertainment. **See also** dancing; food; music; plants and flowers; songs.

Esna

Called Iunyt by the ancient Egyptians and Latropolis by the Greeks, the city of Esna today contains in its midst the remains of a Greco-Roman temple dedicated to the god Khnum. Because the temple was built close to the Nile River, with each flood it became more and more buried in mud and silt. By the time Napoléon visited Esna in the eighteenth century, all but the temple's roof was underground. Meanwhile, the town buildings had been constructed at the new height of the ground, which means that the temple was many feet lower than the surrounding streets and structures. Only after several modern excavations were people once again able to enter the temple.

One of the most interesting features of the temple's interior is a ceiling depicting scenes whose meaning is unclear. Among these scenes are a forty-legged serpent and a slug with two human heads and a tree rooted into its body. Another interesting feature appears above two small doorways. Each has a relief with a riddle involving the hieroglyph for a crocodile and a ram, respectively, but nobody has yet been able to fully understand them or solve them. Some Egyptologists say that these reliefs are cryptographic hymns to the god Khnum, while others call them cryptographic puns. The temple interior also has several scenes, including one of Roman emperor Commodus (reigned A.D. 180–192) netting birds and fishing. On the exterior walls are military scenes, including one showing a ritual massacre of prisoners.

The last inscriptions in the temple date from A.D. 250, but most of its construction and decorations were completed under Emperor Domitian (81–96) and Antoninus Pius (138–161). Texts within the temple mention four other temples near Esna, but archaeologists have found evidence of only one, which is buried in the Nile silt under the nearby village of Kom Mer. **See also** Greco-Roman Period; Khnum.

Exodus

The Exodus is the story of the flight of enslaved Hebrews from bondage in Egypt.

Scholars have long argued over which ancient Egyptian king might have been the pharaoh referred to in this story. However, the general consensus is that if the story has any basis in fact, the king would have been Ramses II or Merneptah. Scholars also say, however, that the foreigners living in Egypt at this time would not have been Hebrews but Sea Peoples, a group of tribes from elsewhere in the eastern Mediterranean who tried to invade Egypt during the reigns of these two kings. As with the Hebrews in the Bible, the Sea Peoples were in search of new lands that they could call home and traveled with their families and all of their possessions; therefore the Exodus story could well have been based on their experiences. However, a few scholars have suggested that it was the Hyksos, another group of foreigners from the east, who are the true people of the Exodus, since the Hyksos took over northern Egypt and were later expelled. Most scholars reject this notion since the people in the Exodus are portrayed as peaceful and downtrodden, whereas the Hyksos were accomplished warriors. Meanwhile, religious scholars contend that the Exodus is literally the story of the Hebrews' flight from Egypt. **See also** Hyksos; Merneptah; Ramses II; Sea Peoples.

Faiyum (Fayoum)

The Faiyum is a large oasis in the Libyan desert, west of the Nile River and south of modern-day Cairo. In ancient times a huge saltwater lake, the Birket Qarun (renamed Lake Moeris by the Greeks), covered much of its northwest; consequently the original ancient Egyptian names for the region were She-resy, "Southern Lake," or Ta-she, "Land of the Lakes." The area received water from a branch of the Nile River called the Bahr Yusef (Arabic for "River of Joseph"). However, the Faiyum had no natural outlet, so water entered it easily but then had nowhere to go. This created great marshlands, many of which were plagued with stagnant water and crocodiles. In fact, there were so many crocodiles in the Faiyum that the primary god worshiped in the region was Sobek, who took the form of a crocodile. To honor this god, many crocodiles were buried— sometimes with elaborate decorations—at various cities in the Faiyum.

The waters of the Faiyum also had many fish and aquatic birds during ancient times, so it was a popular place for kings to fish and hunt. In addition, the region provided a variety of produce, including lemons, oranges, mangoes, olives, and honey, although not all of this was cultivated in the early periods of ancient Egyptian history. Palms and papyrus plants, however, were plentiful in the Faiyum from the earliest times, and linen was made from flax that had been grown there since the earliest periods of history. Cotton was grown there much later, during the Roman Period. Agricultural production, however, was relatively low until the reign of the Twelfth Dynasty king Amenemhet III, who began a series of engineering projects to reclaim the land of the Faiyum from its waters. These projects involved building dams, retaining walls, sluices, canals, and other structures so that the size of the Birket Qarun was reduced and the flow of the Bahr Yusef was regulated not only to increase the amount of land but also to create reservoirs where flood water could be directed and stored for use during times of drought. Amenemhet III's interest in the region was spurred in part by the fact that his capital, Itj-tawy, was located nearby. (Archaeologists are unsure where Itj-tawy was located, but generally believe that it was at or near the modern town of el-Lisht, south of Memphis.)

Because of its proximity to a city that was prominent during the Middle Kingdom, the Faiyum is the site of several pyramids built by Middle Kingdom kings. One of these was the mud-brick pyramid of Amenemhet III, located at the town of Hawara beside the king's mortuary temple. According to later accounts by Greek historians, this temple was a confusing maze of passageways through more than three thousand rooms. Another Middle Kingdom pyramid, that of King Senwosret II, is located in the Faiyum town of Lahun, but of greater interest to Egyptologists is the nearby town of Kahun, which was a village built to house workers constructing Senwosret II's pyramid. First excavated by archaeologist Sir William Matthew Flinders Petrie in 1894, Kahun has provided many details about Twelfth Dynasty life.

Much later, during the Greco-Roman Period, the Faiyum's lake was made still smaller, more canals were built, and new cities were founded. Among the new cities was Karanis, where many military veterans settled during the early Greco-Roman Period. The reason for this influx of Greek settlers was a policy, beginning with King Ptolemy II Philadelphus, of rewarding valorous veterans with plots of land in the region. Archaeologists excavating Karanis have discovered many Greco-Roman houses, temples, and other buildings, along with documents related to taxation, finance, and the sale of grain, leading them to believe that the city was an agricultural and trading center. Elsewhere in the Faiyum, archaeologists have discovered few structures predating the Greco-Roman Period, because the Greeks and Romans demolished the ancient Egyptian structures there to build new ones. **See also** Amenemhet III; Greco-Roman Period; Hawara; Middle Kingdom; Senwosret II; Sobek.

false door

Usually located in an offering chapel of a tomb or temple, a false door is a stela (a slab of stone decorated with texts and pictures) that was said to allow the spirits of the dead to enter the realm of the living in order to receive offerings. The stela was typically made from red granite in royal tombs and limestone in others; sometimes limestone was painted red to look like the more costly granite. Many false doors had carved, painted reliefs featuring scenes from the life of the deceased (if in a tomb) or a deity (if in a temple). **See also** Dendera; *ka;* stelae.

fertility

Fertility was important to most women in ancient Egypt, and barrenness was considered a curse to the individual and a sign of disorder in society. Consequently, the ancient Egyptians had numerous fertility rituals, figurines, and amulets. Figuring most prominently in rituals to assure or restore fertility were the deities Hathor and Min, and many of the amulets were representations of the deities Bes, Taweret, and Hathor, all associated with pregnancy and female sexual organs.

In cases where efforts to assure fertility failed, sometimes a female slave would be enlisted to produce a child by the woman's husband, and the barren woman would be considered the child's mother. However, the ancient Egyptians also tried to limit the number of children they had, as evidenced by the many medical papyri with information on various forms of contraception. **See also** children.

festivals

Festivals were an important part of ancient Egyptian life. Prior to each new year, a group of priests known as Hour priests, associated with the House of Life (an institution where sacred texts were written and stored), used astronomical observations to determine the festival calendar for the upcoming year. According to one of these religious calendars, found in the Medinet Habu mortuary temple of Ramses III, there were sixty festivals, but Egyptologists estimate that during other reigns there might have been as many as seventy-five.

Festivals featured a great deal of eating, drinking, offerings and perhaps sacrifices to the gods, dancing, music, and various forms of entertainment, such as performances by acrobats. In many cases, a statue of the deity being honored by the festival was paraded through the streets hidden within a small portable shrine. Some Egyptologists believe that the crowds were not allowed to see the statue itself but might be allowed to approach the shrine to speak to the god. Others believe that festivals were the one time that people from all walks of life were allowed to see cult statues, which were normally viewed only by priests.

In some festivals, the cult-statue procession provided the opportunity to bring one deity to visit another. For example, once a year, a cult statue of the goddess Hathor was taken from her temple at Dendera, her main cult center, by boat to Edfu to visit a cult statue of the god Horus there. Similarly, a statue of the god Amun was taken down the Nile River on a ceremonial boat, or bark of the god, from Karnak to Luxor. Sometimes, coffined mummies were taken on visits as well, particularly during the Beautiful Festival of the Valley. As part of this twelve-day festival, people honored the dead and shared meals with their spirits by eating at burial sites.

The most important ancient Egyptian festivals often attracted pilgrims from throughout the country. For example, according to the writings of fifth-century-B.C. historian Herodotus, more than seven hundred thousand people attended a festival in Bubastis dedicated to the goddess Bastet. Thousands more attended a festival in Abydos each year that was dedicated to the god Osiris, with some participants marking their annual attendance by adding an inscription to a family stela at the site.

Other festivals were held monthly or biannually rather than annually. For example, beginning in the Old Kingdom, the appearance of each new moon marked a festival day, and twice a year the Nile River was honored with its own festival, during which flowers were floated on its surface. However, other festivals were held at intervals much longer than a year. For example, the *sed* festival, which was a ceremony of renewal related to the king's power, was held every three years of a king's reign, beginning in Year 30. **See also** Amun; barks of the gods; Horus; *sed* festival.

First Intermediate Period (ca. 2181–ca. 2040 B.C. or ca. 2160–ca. 2055 B.C.)

A term coined by modern historians, the *First Intermediate Period* is the era of ancient Egyptian history that followed the collapse of the Old Kingdom, but historians disagree on when it began and what dynasties it incorporated. Some date the First Intermediate Period as being from approximately 2181 to 2040 B.C. and including the Seventh, Eighth, Ninth, and Tenth Dynasties. Others identify the First Intermediate Period as being from approximately 2160 to 2055 B.C. and including the Ninth, Tenth, and Eleventh Dynasties. This disparity comes from the fact that historians disagree on when the central government collapsed, ending the unity of the Old Kingdom.

The First Intermediate Period was fraught with disorder as the leaders of various provinces vied for power against weak kings who, beginning in the Ninth Dynasty, ruled from the city of Heracleopolis. These provincial leaders, called nomarchs, functioned as warlords, and it was roughly 140 years before they were brought under control by a series of three forceful kings—Intef I, Intef II, and Intef III—who used Thebes as their capital. All three kings were warriors who had forced their way north toward Heracleopolis to challenge the weak kings there, taking various nomes along the way and establishing a rival throne. By the time of Intef III, the northern boundary of the Theban kingdom was near Asyut, far north of Thebes though not yet to Heracleopolis. Nonetheless, Intef III's successor, Montuhotep I or II, was able to mount sustained attacks on Heracleopolis, and eventually he took the city. He subsequently united Egypt under his rule, thereby ushering in the prosperity of the Middle Kingdom. **See also** Heracleopolis; Intef I, II, and III; Middle Kingdom; Thebes.

flagstaffs

Flagstaffs, or *senut* in ancient Egyptian, were wooden staffs that displayed pennants with symbols of gods, temples, or nomes. They were typically displayed at the entrance to major shrines and temples. **See also** symbols; temples.

flail

Believed to resemble a stick used to herd goats and sheep, a flail was one of the symbols of a king's rule. It often appears in depictions of Osiris, who carried a flail to signify his position as chief god of the dead, and it was often shown in depictions of deceased kings as well. **See also** Osiris.

Followers of Horus and Seth

The Followers of Horus and the Followers of Seth were two groups of performers who participated in festival reenactments of events related to the gods Horus and Seth. Specifically, these two companies of performers conducted mock battles with each other. The Followers of Seth were defeated in every performance, just as in ancient Egyptian mythology the god Seth was defeated by Horus. In mythology, the Followers of Horus were said to be a group of creatures—mainly hippopotamuses and crocodiles—that accompanied the god Horus as his warriors. Mortuary texts, however, tell of an alternate role for these individuals. There, the Followers of Horus were said to purify the newly deceased during their journey to the Afterlife, while the Followers of Seth were said to be predynastic rulers who dwelled in the Afterlife, sometimes welcoming new arrivals. **See also** Afterlife; crocodiles; festivals; hippopotamuses; Horus; Seth.

food

Archaeologists have discovered menus from ancient times that show what Egyptians of the period ate. The main staples of people from all social classes were bread (of several varieties), onions, and beer. Most households regardless of wealth made their own beer and bread, both most commonly from barley. The wealthy also drank wine, although this beverage was primarily used for temple rituals and festivals. Beef, mutton, and goat meat were also served as part of festivals, rituals, and offerings, but Egyptologists disagree on whether anyone but the wealthy ate meat—particularly beef—on a regular basis. They also disagree on whether eating pork was a taboo for all Egyptians, just some religious groups, or no one. Clearly, though, birds were eaten by all social classes, and fish was particularly popular with the lower classes. In addition, milk and honey were consumed regularly, the latter most often as a sweetener in drinks, along with a wide variety of fruits and vegetables. These included dates, figs, melons, pomegranates, lettuce, cucumbers, radishes, and garlic. Herbs included dill and mint. The Egyptians also had a variety of cakes that they served at religious festivals and other celebratory events. These cakes were probably firm rather than crumbly, because the ancient Egyptians ate with their fingers, not with utensils.

During the New Kingdom, the Egyptians also enjoyed spices and delicacies from the Near East. During the Greco-Roman Period, they ate oranges, lemons, peaches, mangoes, almonds, and other produce introduced into the country by foreigners.

Egyptologists generally know what ancient Egyptians ate and when, but they are uncertain as to how foods were prepared. It seems as though vegetables were eaten raw while meats were roasted or cooked in pots but, from the size of some ancient Egyptian cooking pots, Egyptologists speculate that meats and vegetables might have been stewed together. The amount and type of seasonings used in cooking various dishes are also unknown. **See also** agriculture; animals; Greco-Roman Period; New Kingdom.

foreign relations

The focus of ancient Egypt's relations with other countries was obtaining through trade needed resources that were unavailable at home. Trade was, moreover, conducted by Egypt's government as part of its overall foreign policy. Most of Egypt's foreign interactions were with Lebanon, Syria, Nubia, Punt, Libya, and, from the New Kingdom on, Greece. Lebanon and Syria supplied Egypt with much of its high-quality timber; from Nubia came ivory, ebony, semiprecious stones, building and sculpting stones, gold, and various minerals; Punt (if it was indeed a real place, and not a mythical one as some Egyptologists suppose) supplied Egypt with spices; Libya supplied olive oil; and Greece was a source of a variety of fruits and other products.

Besides trade, Egypt formed political alliances with some neighboring countries, often cemented by some sort of exchange of people. For example, weaker nations, particularly Mitanni, might send princesses to be wives to Egypt's kings. Such women were usually considered tribute—payments to Egypt in return for being allowed to live in peace. Underlying Egypt's relations with other countries was the belief that their own country was so superior to all others that they deserved to control all the world's people and places. Given this belief, Egyptians were always prepared to use military force when diplomacy failed. **See also** Afrocentrism; Libya; Mitanni; Nubia; Punt; Syria; trade.

fortresses

The ancient Egyptians built fortresses at militarily strategic locations to protect Egypt's borders or its foreign mining and quarrying sites. They also built fortresses to house prisoners; in fact, the ancient Egyptian word for fortress, *mennu*, meant "prison" as well as "fortress." In addition, small forts were constructed as desert way stations and surveillance posts for use by travelers and the military.

Although the cities of Abydos, Hierakonpolis, and perhaps elsewhere were fortified during the Old Kingdom, the first fortresses were constructed during the Twelfth Dynasty at several points overlooking the Nile River or on islands within the river from Elephantine south to the Second Cataract, which was then Egypt's southern border. At this time, Egypt had an official policy that no one from Nubia, which lay just south of the border, was allowed to travel north into Egypt along the Nile River. Any Nubian attempting to do so would be confronted by guards stationed at the southern fortresses. Another location with numerous forts was the region east of the Nile River Delta, which was constantly subject to foreign invasion.

Fortresses were constructed using sun-dried bricks. The earliest fortresses were oval in shape, while some later ones were rectangular. In either case, they were encircled by as many as three walls supported by buttresses, one wall inside the next. Sometimes, ditches were used as well to make it difficult—if not impossible—for the enemy's ladders to reach the top of the exterior wall. At least one fortress, at Semna in Nubia, had two-tiered enclosure walls and buildings within the fortress with walls sixteen to twenty feet high. Beginning in the Middle Kingdom, fortresses also had balconies and parapets for defensive purposes. In the New Kingdom they might have keeps (fortified rooms) and turrets as well. In most eras as many as three thousand soldiers may have lived inside just one fortress. **See also** Abydos; Aswan; Elephantine; Hierakonpolis; military; Nubia.

funerals

For those who could afford one, funerals were conducted after the mummification process was complete. The funeral began with the mummy being conveyed to the burial chamber in a procession that might be lavish or simple, depending on the status of the deceased. In the most extravagant funerals, professional mourners headed the procession; these were women paid to scream, cry, tear out their hair, and otherwise engage in behaviors to show distress over the death. Next in the procession came the servants and/or poorer relatives of the deceased, carrying tomb goods and offerings and perhaps also animals for sacrifice. The amount and type of goods and offerings depended on the wealth of the family of the deceased.

After the people carrying the funerary goods in the funeral procession came a line of priests. First in line was the *sem,* or mortuary priest, and after him the *ka* (spirit) priests and other priests and embalmers. The main job of the priests, not only during the procession but also before (during embalming) and after (during funeral rituals at the tomb), was to recite spells that would ensure that the deceased would have a successful journey to and existence in the Afterlife. Priests also made offerings of food and drink to the spirit of the deceased to nourish it for this journey and sustain it in the Afterlife. Such offerings were also carried in the funeral procession.

Following the priests in the procession was the mummy, which was atop an oxen-pulled sled for land processions or in a special mortuary boat if the journey to the tomb required a trip along the Nile River. In early eras, the mummy appears to have been carried in an open or closed coffin or wrapped in a bundle of reeds or other plant materials; in later eras, it was inside a closed coffin or a nest of several coffins placed one inside the other. Sometimes a *tekenu,* a body-shaped bundle of reeds and other plants, preceded the mummy. Like the mummy, it too was carried in the procession on an oxen-pulled sled, but once it reached the tomb, it was ceremoniously burned. Some Egyptologists think the *tekenu's* purpose was to act as a stand-in for a human sacrifice; such sacrifices were once conducted to supply a king with servants in the Afterlife. Other Egyptologists, however, believe that the burning was part of a purification ritual.

Once the procession reached the entrance to the tomb, the priests began performing a series of rituals, with their number and complexity depending on the status of the deceased. In general, the number of rituals depended on what the deceased's family could afford to pay the priests who performed them. One of the most critical rituals, however, appears to have been the Opening of the Mouth Ceremony. This involved seventy-five different movements and gestures as various parts of the body were ritually touched with various implements, including the leg of a freshly butchered ox and an assortment of knives, rods, wands, and tools. When mummies were inside a nest of coffins, a statue of the deceased was used for this ceremony instead of the mummy itself.

Additional rituals involved purification ceremonies and offerings. During these ceremonies, there might be professional dancers performing in front of the tomb to celebrate the fact that the deceased would be going to the Afterlife. At some point, the mummy would be taken inside its burial chamber, along with the canopic jars bearing most of its internal organs. Other funerary goods were also taken inside at this time. Archaeologists have found that some of these were carefully arranged around the deceased; others seem to have been stacked with careless abandon.

In the New Kingdom, two new items appeared within many tombs. First, priests might put a box inside the burial chamber that was filled with silt from the Nile

River, within which they had planted and watered seeds of grain. Called an Osiris box because it was made in the likeness of Osiris (chief god of the dead), this box was a symbolic representation of rebirth. The second new item in the tomb was a set of four bricks made of unbaked Nile River mud. These bricks were ritualistically placed at the four directional points—west, east, north, and south—along the interior walls of the tomb. Each brick contained within its mud a specific amulet with a symbol or image associated with the particular direction: west, the *djed;* east, the god Anubis; north, a mummified man; and south, a reed torch. Also inscribed with magic spells, each brick was believed to prevent evil forces from entering the tomb from each of those directions. Other amulets were placed in the tomb as well, in addition to the ones that had been wrapped within the mummy's linens during the embalming process.

Once all of the funerary goods and offerings were in their proper places in the tomb, it was sealed, and the seals were often marked according to whose tomb it was. In addition, clay cones approximately five inches tall were placed around the tomb as markers, detailing the deceased's titles and lineage. After sealing and marking the tomb, any embalming materials not considered worthy of the tomb were buried nearby, and the friends and family of the deceased had a feast beside the tomb.

After the funeral, the deceased continued to be honored with daily offerings and rituals intended to ensure his or her continued enjoyment of the Afterlife. These ceremonies included the Opening of the Mouth Ceremony, performed every day to magically allow each of the body's parts to work as they had when they were living, and a series of 114 different rituals designed to make daily food and drink offerings to sustain the *ka,* an element of the spirit that had to be nourished to survive eternity. Beginning in the New Kingdom, however, these practices became fewer and less complex as newer beliefs about the Afterlife made such devotions less critical. **See also** coffins; mummification; tombs.

furniture

Ancient Egyptian furniture consisted of various types of stools, chairs, armchairs, couches, tables, and beds, though the poor did not possess as many of these items as the rich. Stools had seats roughly eight to fourteen inches from the floor; these seats were typically made of wood, woven reeds, or interlaced thongs. Their designs varied, with some having two legs, some three, and some four. The least expensive were of carved wood with no ornamentation; the most expensive were inlaid with ivory.

Chairs were similarly varied. Some were relatively plain, with straight backs and no arms, while armchairs—found only in wealthier homes—were constructed of

This chair was among the funerary goods found in the tomb of Fourth Dynasty queen Hetepheres I.

imported woods (most often ebony), usually inlaid with ivory, and typically had arms and legs carved to resemble animals or animal heads. Chairs and armchairs both had seats made of wood, interlaced thongs, or more commonly wide pieces of leather. When the seat was leather, it was often painted; the chairs of kings usually featured painted scenes illustrating a king's military prowess or painted symbols of power. Pillows, cushions, and throws were frequently used to make chair seats and backs more comfortable.

Couches were similarly covered, and their legs might be carved to look like an animal's legs. Unlike modern couches, though, ancient Egyptian couches had no back. Instead the user reclined on its base, which was curved so that one end was higher than the other. Tables were of various shapes but primarily square or round and mounted on a pedestal or three or four legs.

Beds were much like tables and were either simple or ornate depending on the owner's social class. The poor usually slept either on earthen cots (beds shaped from earth) or, in hot weather, on the flat reed roofs of their houses, while the middle classes might use wood-framed beds with platforms of plaited strings covered with large woolen cushions. In the summer, people covered themselves with linen sheets; in the winter, they might use woolen blankets, which were actually woven more like thick, shaggy rugs.

One of the best-preserved examples of an ornate bed is that of Queen Hetepheres I, who was the wife of King Snefru and the mother of King Khufu. Found in 1925 in a shaft tomb near Khufu's pyramid, the bed has carved legs, gilded wood, a portable canopy, and a box for its curtains. The canopy was portable because Queen Hetepheres took the bed with her when she traveled. In addition, there was a curved headrest to support the head during sleep instead of a pillow. Hetepheres' headrest was made of gilded wood (others might be made of alabaster, pottery, or stone). Hetepheres' tomb also contained two gilded wooden chairs and a gilded wooden sedan chair with carrying poles. Used to carry the seated queen in processions, this sedan chair is particularly ornate; its backrest has ebony panels decorated with golden hieroglyphs that identify the chair as hers and list her titles. **See also** Hetepheres I; Khufu.

gardens

All ancient Egyptian houses had gardens, in which they grew vegetables, herbs, and fruits for their own consumption. The most common types of garden produce were onions, leeks, lentils, chickpeas, beans, radishes, cucumbers, garlic, and castor-oil plants. Many gardens also had trees and vines that produced figs, dates, grapes, and, during the New Kingdom, apples and olives (which were introduced to Egypt by the Hyksos). Flowers were grown as well, even among the lower classes, because upon entering a home, a guest was customarily greeted with a garland of blossoms. The most common flowers in ancient Egyptian gardens were the lotus, chrysanthemum, and cornflower.

The upper classes usually arranged their gardens for beauty as well as practicality. Moreover, the rich often gardened as a hobby, as evidenced by the many scenes on royal and noble tomb walls that show the tomb owner enjoying his garden. According to such scenes, in gardens of the wealthy, canals were used to redirect water to ponds or reservoirs, where the water was stored until it could be carried in pots, buckets, or skins to whatever plants needed it. Most gardens of the wealthy had walkways shaded by rows of trees, such as sycamore, fig, date, palm, and pomegranate. Such walkways helped to divide the garden into sections, with each dedicated to a different purpose. The garden was usually separated into a vineyard, an orchard, a flower garden, and a kitchen garden; in some cases, there was an area for beehives as well. Herbs might also be grown in earthen pots beside the walkway. There might also be areas where poultry and domesticated animals were housed. In addition, homes of royalty or the highest-ranking nobility might have very large areas called paradises, intended as places to relax and/or hunt. Paradises usually had ponds stocked with fish and functioned as game preserves. **See also** entertaining guests; food; plants and flowers.

Geb

As an ancient Egyptian god of the earth, Geb was one of the key deities of the Ennead, a family of nine deities worshiped in the city of Heliopolis beginning in the Early Dynastic Period. According to the Creation myth of this city, Geb's father, Shu, parted Geb from Geb's lover and sister, Nut, the goddess of the sky, and raised her up from his reclining body to form the heavens. In some versions of the myth, Geb's anguish over this separation caused him to fall on his face and weep copiously, thereby creating the oceans; the flat of his back as he lay prone became land. Prior to their separation, though, Geb and Nut produced two sons and two daughters, all of whom were deities: Osiris, Seth, Nephthys, and Isis.

As the father of Osiris, the Egyptian god of the dead, Geb was eventually recognized throughout Egypt as a major deity and became the subject of other myths, one of which provided the model for royal succession. Geb was said to have held the throne in the divine realm for a time and then passed his rule on to his son Osiris, just as human kings passed their crowns on to their sons. Because of his position, many kings of Egypt strongly identified with Geb, and in some times and places Egypt's kings were said to be Geb's heirs. Perhaps for this reason, Geb was almost always depicted as having a human form, although in a few works of art he is shown with a goose atop his head. The goose was a reference to a myth in which Geb— called the Great Cackler—produced a cosmic egg that held the sun. **See also** Isis; Nephthys; Nut; Osiris; Re; Seth; Shu.

Gebel el-Silsila

A site just north of Aswan on the western banks of the Nile, Gebel el-Silsila was once named Kheny (or Khenu), the "Place of Rowing," because it is a site where the river narrows and travel by boat upstream is hard work. Here the river is bordered by sandstone cliffs that were cut and carved to create shrines, chapels, and other structures, primarily during the Eighteenth and Nineteenth Dynasties. Quarries nearby produced the materials for buildings elsewhere from the Eighteenth Dynasty on.

One of the most significant structures in the area is the Great Speos. (*Speos* is the Greek word for a rock-cut chapel.) Built by Eighteenth Dynasty king Horemheb, it includes statues of the king, the crocodile god Sobek, and other deities. Reliefs in the chapel depict the king's military campaigns, particularly against the Nubians. Other structures honor Nineteenth Dynasty kings Seti I, Ramses II, and Merneptah and their most powerful administrators. **See also** Horemheb; Merneptah; Nubia; Ramses II; Seti I.

Giza

Just southwest of modern-day Cairo near what was once the ancient city of Memphis, Giza was the necropolis site for royal families and court officials who lived in Memphis during the Old Kingdom. As such, it contains several important pyramids, tombs, and temples. The most famous of these structures is the Great Pyramid, also known as Khufu's Pyramid. Built by Fourth Dynasty king Khufu, the structure has a base that is 417 feet on a side and is 450 feet high. (The Great Pyramid was even larger when it was finished, but damage over time reduced its dimensions slightly.)

How the Egyptians managed to build such an enormous structure remains a mystery. There were approximately 2.5 million blocks used in the construction of the pyramid's core and another one hundred thousand stones used as its casing. The area covered by these casing stones was twenty-two acres. The stone blocks used in the construction of the pyramid weighed an average of 2.5 tons, and archaeologists estimate that to complete the pyramid during Khufu's twenty-three-year reign its builders had to quarry, transport, and place one hundred thousand stone blocks a day. Egyptologists disagree over whether Khufu would have had a large enough workforce to accomplish this task given known methods of construction; those who believe he did not have enough workers suggest that ancient Egyptian pyramid builders employed construction techniques that remain unknown to archaeologists.

Inside the Great Pyramid are the Subterranean Chamber, the Grotto, the Grand Gallery, the King's Chamber, and the Queen's Chamber. These rooms were named by the ninth-century-A.D. governor, or caliph, of Cairo, Al Mamun, when he entered the tomb after it had been sealed for centuries. Mamun's names for the pyramid's chambers were purely speculative. This means, for example, that

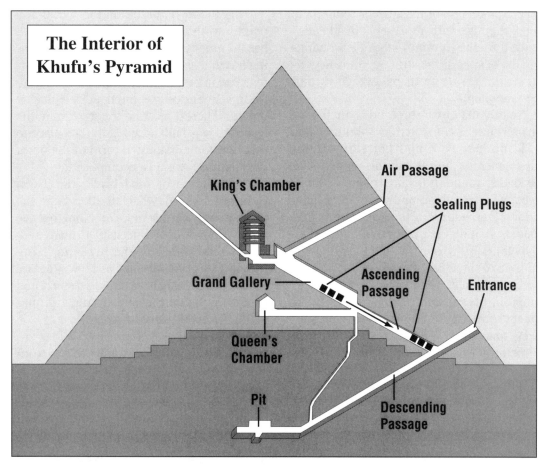

The Interior of Khufu's Pyramid

King's Chamber

Air Passage

Sealing Plugs

Grand Gallery

Ascending Passage

Entrance

Queen's Chamber

Pit

Descending Passage

there is no evidence that a queen was ever buried in the Queen's Chamber. In fact, archaeologists even disagree on whether the king was buried in the pyramid. The King's Chamber has a sarcophagus, but it is too large to have passed through the doorway and therefore must have been built while the pyramid was under construction. Moreover, it has no lid and does not seem to have ever had one. Therefore, some archaeologists believe that the pyramid was not a tomb but a false tomb, a sort of monument.

Perhaps the most impressive part of the pyramid is the Grand Gallery. It is 157 feet long and has a ceiling that gradually rises to 28 feet. The slope of its floor is at a 26-degree ascending angle, so walking from one end of the gallery to the other involves a steep climb. In addition, there is an equally steep passageway running

from this gallery down to the original entrance of the tomb. Egyptologists disagree on the purpose of the Grand Gallery, which unlike most other gallery chambers has no religious imagery of any kind on its walls. Some believe that it was meant as a storage area for building stones that were used to seal the pyramid from inside; others say the chamber had another, as-yet-undiscovered purpose.

Egyptologists also disagree on whether all of the pyramid's chambers have been found. There are several vertical shafts that were once thought to be air vents but are now suspected to have had some other purpose. Some archaeologists have sent remote-controlled video cameras into these narrow passageways trying to discover where they might lead, and they have found several walled-off areas. Some archaeologists believe that chambers lie on the other side of these walls, but others think that the walls represent "dead ends" caused by the pyramid's builders changing the design of the structure during construction, resulting in passageways that lead nowhere.

Nearby the Great Pyramid is another—actually a series of structures—built by one of Khufu's sons, King Khafre. Egyptologists generally simply call this pyramid the Second Pyramid. It is fairly plain, with undecorated smooth granite walls and calcite floors. One oddity of the structure is that tourists visiting the pyramid often feel that something is "wrong" with the air in comparison to the Great Pyramid, but despite several studies, nobody has been able to pinpoint the reason for this sense of disquiet. Some Egyptologists, however, suspect that this uneasiness might have something to do with the way that sound echoes in the pyramid; perhaps the interior of the structure produces a slight discord that upsets visitors in some subtle manner.

This theory is based on the fact that a neighboring pyramid, the Third Pyramid, has an inner chamber whose vaulted ceiling has unusual acoustic properties. Sounds resonate in the chamber in a way that Egyptologists believe was intended to enhance music. Therefore they theorize that the chamber was built specifically as a place to practice some unknown form of magic of which music was a key component.

Constructed of mud brick, the Third Pyramid is somewhat smaller than the other two pyramids in Giza. Nonetheless, it has yielded many fine statues, many featuring the builder of the pyramid, King Menkaure (or Mycerinus, as he was called by the Greeks). This pyramid was restored at some point during ancient times, probably in the Twenty-sixth Dynasty.

Together these three pyramids are among Egypt's most famous relics from ancient times, but there are other pyramids in the area as well. These include one for Khufu's mother, Queen Hetepheres I, lo-

The three largest Giza pyramids are those of (left to right) Menkaure, Khafre, and Khufu.

cated near Khufu's pyramid, and other queens' tombs and surrounding structures, which were converted into a Temple of Isis during the Twenty-first and Twenty-sixth Dynasties.

Dominating the landscape near the three large Giza pyramids is the Great Sphinx, a huge depiction of a lion's body with a man's head and face. Egyptologists have disagreed over whether the face of the Sphinx is supposed to be that of King Khufu, King Khafre, or a solar deity who has taken human form. By the New Kingdom, most Egyptians associated the Sphinx with Harmakhis, or Horus on the Horizon, a manifestation of the god Horus. Consequently, Eighteenth Dynasty king Amenhotep II built a brick temple dedicated to Harmakhis very near the Sphinx. King Seti I later added to this temple, which became a major destination of religious pilgrims.

The kings who built the pyramids of Giza often rewarded priests and esteemed administrators by building tombs for them nearby. These tombs dot the surrounding fields of the Giza plateau. Most are in the mastaba style common to the Old Kingdom. The word *mastaba* comes from the Arabic for "bench," because these rectangular tombs were shaped much like benches. The burial chamber of the tomb was subterranean, as were storerooms of goods that the deceased planned to use in the Afterlife. A shaft led to an aboveground offering chapel; the aboveground structure was shaped like a mound, probably as a symbol of the primordial mound from which all life was said to have arisen. Over time, the mounds of royal tombs were slightly terraced to look like steps to suggest that the deceased king would be ascending to join the solar deity in the heavens.

Because of the number of impressive structures at Giza, the area has long attracted the attention of both archaeologists and treasure hunters. The first serious archaeological excavations of the site began during the nineteenth century, with various expeditions led by such people as Giovanni Battista Belzoni, Karl Richard Lepsius, Auguste Mariette, Sir William Matthew Flinders Petrie, and others. In the twentieth century, archaeologists George Andrew Reisner, Hermann Junker, and Selim Hassan excavated the site, and archaeological excavations continue in the area. **See also** Amenhotep II; Khafre; Khufu; pyramids; Seti I; Sphinx, Great; tombs.

glassware and glazed ware

The ancient Egyptians used glassware and glazed pottery throughout their history. Monuments from the Old Kingdom depict transparent bottles containing wine, and artwork from later periods shows glassblowers at work. In addition, archaeologists have found colored bottles, beads, and mosaics and jewelry containing glass imitations of emeralds and other precious stones. As for glazed ware, excavations have yielded numerous examples of faience, a glazed ceramic material made from crushed quartz or quartz sand that has been combined with substances to color it blue, green, or blue-green.

Glass was colored using various types of earth and minerals in the glassblowing process. Sometimes in manufacturing a bottle, the Egyptians would place bands of gold between two layers of glass so that the bottles had thin gold stripes, sometimes with different colors of glass between each pair of stripes. Some glass bottles were covered with woven strips of leather or other materials to make them easier to hold.

Although the ancient Egyptians were apparently expert in making glass, they never used it for windows. Since the sun in Egypt was always bright and hot, glass windows would have trapped the heat inside, resulting in building interiors that would have been unbearably warm. **See also** jewelry; pottery.

These gold figures representing (left to right) Horus, Osiris, and Isis were created during the New Kingdom.

gold and silver

Gold was found in many parts of the Eastern Desert and along sections of the Nile River, either as loose nuggets or as veins within rocks. Consequently, the ancient Egyptians mined and used gold from very early times and became highly skilled in fashioning it into jewelry, statues, funerary objects, and other decorative items. Because Egypt had no silver mines, however, this metal had to be imported from Asia at a great price and was therefore rarely used. **See also** mining and metalworking.

government

Originally, the basic unit of ancient Egyptian government was the nome (a name coined by the Greeks), an adminis-

trative district controlled by a local governor, or nomarch. There were forty-two nomes, twenty-two in Upper Egypt and twenty in Lower Egypt, each with its own capital city and an administrative system for collecting taxes (in the form of grain and other goods), which were passed along to the central government. The central government in turn supported works that benefited the nomes, such as building projects and the construction and maintenance of irrigation systems.

The nomarch system originated during predynastic times, as communities with tribal chiefs joined to create small kingdoms. Eventually one king, probably Narmer, united these kingdoms under one rule. His successor, Aha (or Hor-Aha), established the first national government administration and the first dynasty; the first official nomarchs were chosen from among his followers, both as a reward for their loyalty and as a way to ensure that they continued to be loyal. From that point until the Fourth Dynasty, nomarchs rotated their assignments so that they ended up having governed many different nomes during their careers. Beginning in the Fifth Dynasty, however, most nomarchs served in only one nome during their lifetime; and by the end of the Old Kingdom, the position of nomarch—and many other government jobs as well—had become hereditary, no longer assigned by the king or his agents but passed down from father to son. From this point on, nomarchs established their own dynasties, the power of which rivaled that of the kings; in fact, at times, nomarchs proved to be a threat to the kings.

During the Twelfth Dynasty, King Senwosret III tried to end this threat by reorganizing the government so that his administration, rather than the administrations of the nomes, controlled most aspects of people's lives. Egyptologists are unsure how he managed this without a fight, but they do know that he succeeded in reducing the power of the nomarchs. However, around the same time, the power and influence of Egypt's largest priestly cults grew, so some priests became more powerful than any nomarch ever had been.

In the process of taking power away from the nomarchs, Egypt's central government became much more complex, with an extensive bureaucracy that involved a large hierarchy of officials, all working directly for the state. These officials were responsible for equally complex administrative divisions such as Departments of Granaries, Agriculture, the Army, the Frontiers, Trade, Justice, Prisons, Foreign Diplomacy, and Architectural Works. These agencies were typically directed from offices that were within the royal residence, usually a palace complex within the capital city. Originally there was only one such residence but eventually kings had several residences, which meant that there were administrative centers in more than one city. Therefore some official positions were duplicated, further complicating the ancient Egyptian government. In addition, a king might designate a new capital city upon assuming the throne, so the king's administration might be in one place during one dynasty and in another the next.

The people who worked for the king's administration were well rewarded for their efforts. Government employees often received a share of temple revenues or land rents as well as royal gifts such as a tomb near the king's own. They were also paid a salary in the form of goods. (However, in effect, all ancient Egyptians, regardless of whether they were part of government, worked for the king because he was considered to own everything in Egypt—land, goods, animals, even people—and could force anyone to labor on his behalf, usually on massive building projects. In return, he was expected to make decisions based on the principles represented by the goddess Ma'at: balance and order.)

Outside of the king, the most powerful person in the country was the vizier, or *tjaty,* the king's chief minister. Vizier was an appointed position, with selections usually made from among the best of the temple scribes; in a few reigns there were two viziers, one for Upper Egypt and one for Lower Egypt. The vizier's main job was to act as a liaison between the king and his people, telling the people what the king wanted and the king what the people thought of him. The vizier also supervised the king's building projects, and he was the head of the judiciary and the keeper of the state archives. Over time, the vizier was involved in almost every aspect of the administration. Other important positions in ancient Egypt were scribes, priests, artisans, and police. Farm laborers, however, were the most prevalent, because peasants made up over 80 percent of the ancient Egyptian population. **See also** kings; Ma'at; nomes and nomarchs; taxation.

graffiti

Graffiti are writings left in public places, particularly on walls, where their appearance has not been sanctioned by the government or the owner of the property. Construction workers in ancient Egypt often left such writings at building sites. For example, the ancient Egyptian builders of the Red Pyramid of King Snefru left inscriptions on certain pyramid stones while they were working at a particular location, in effect saying "I was here!" Because the inscriptions sometimes refer to known events, archaeologists have been able to estimate how long it took for builders to finish a pyramid. For example, from inscriptions experts conclude that the Red Pyramid probably took twenty years to build.

Archaeologists have also learned important information from graffiti left by New Kingdom visitors to the pyramid complex of King Djoser, which was built at the beginning of the Old Kingdom. The intent of this graffiti was to praise the complex and the king who built it; in doing so, however, one graffiti writer used the name Djoser to refer to the king. Official inscriptions at the site had used the name Netjerykhet for the king instead, so this graffiti not only told Egyptologists that Djoser and Netjerykhet were the same person but also confirmed their theory that ancient Egyptian kings used more than one name even during the early Old Kingdom. **See also** Djoser; Snefru.

Greco-Roman Period (332 B.C.–A.D. 395)

The Greco-Roman Period is an era of ancient Egyptian history that lasted from 332 B.C. to A.D. 395. Some historians divide it into two periods, the Greek Period (332–30 B.C.) and the Roman Period (30 B.C.–A.D. 395). The Greco-Roman Period began when the Macedonian ruler of Greece, Alexander III (also known as Alexander the Great), took control of Egypt in 332 B.C. After Alexander's death, a succession of would-be heirs assumed Egypt's throne until one of his former generals, Ptolemy, seized control and established a dynasty of fifteen Greek kings of Egypt, all with the name Ptolemy (Ptolemy I, II, III, and so on). For this reason, some people call this period of Egyptian history the Ptolemaic Period or Ptolemaic dynasty. In addition, some people call the brief period when Alexander and his heirs ruled the Macedonian dynasty, because even though the Greek Period is said to have begun with Alexander's conquest of Egypt, he was actually Macedonian rather than Greek.

Understandably, the early centuries of the Greco-Roman Period were a time when Greek traditions increasingly became intertwined with Egyptian ones, each culture influencing the other within Egypt's borders. When in 30 B.C. Rome seized control of Egypt and subsequently incorporated it into the Roman Empire, Egypt quickly became important to the Romans because of the grain it produced. Rome, however, placed little value on Egyptian culture. Therefore, although Egypt prospered under Roman control the country's artistic and religious traditions languished, and knowledge of ancient Egyptian ways gradually disappeared, replaced by Roman cultural traditions. **See also** Alexander the Great; Ptolemaic kings.

Hadrian (A.D. 76–138)

Hadrian was a Roman emperor who collected Egyptian antiquities of all kinds and took them to Italy for his own enjoyment. He also built a city in Egypt called Antinopolis to honor a friend, Antinous, who had drowned in the Nile River. Hadrian's interest in Egypt began during his first trip there in A.D. 130. One member of his traveling party, the poetess Julia Balbilla, carved grafitti on a colossal statue at the funerary temple of Amenhotep III. This grafitti was a tribute not only to Hadrian but also to a mythical Ethiopian king named Memnon, so the colossal statue and a twin at the same site are now called the Colossi of Memnon. **See also** Amenhotep III; graffiti; Greco-Roman Period.

hair

Using copper or bronze razors, many ancient Egyptians of both sexes routinely shaved their heads bald. An individual's first head shave took place during childhood, although at this time a lock or braid of hair was left growing on the left side of the scalp to signify immaturity. As soon as a boy or girl reached puberty, this lock was shaved off as well.

People of the middle and upper classes usually covered their bare scalps with black wigs. (Egyptians in the lower classes who did hard physical labor and/or could not afford wigs usually did not shave their heads but instead wore their hair very short as a protection from the hot Egyptian sun.) Wig hair, which was either natural or a mixture of natural hair and dyed vegetable fibers, was typically fashioned in various combinations of tiny braids and curls. Sometimes the hair was coated with oil to make it shiny. A more common practice, however, was to place a cone of perfumed tallow atop the wig while it was being worn so that the hot desert sun would melt the tallow and perfume and oil the wig. So important were wigs to many Egyptians that some people were entombed with boxes of wigs for use in the Afterlife. In the Greco-Roman Period, however, the practice of wearing wigs was gradually abandoned as short haircuts in Greek and

Roman emperor Hadrian, shown in this bust from around A.D. 135, collected Egyptian antiquities of all kinds.

Roman styles apparently became popular among members of the upper classes.

Egyptologists have various theories regarding why the ancient Egyptians preferred to have bald scalps covered with wigs. Some believe that the practice of shaving began because of chronic problems with head lice and that wigs were necessary in turn to keep scalps from being sunburned. Others believe that the Egyptians chose to wear wigs because they considered them more beautiful and/or easier to care for than natural hair and that scalps were shaved to keep heads cooler under wigs. In any case, the ancient Egyptians clearly thought that graying and/or thinning hair was unappealing, as evidenced by the fact that their medical papyri had recipes for various treatments to prevent both conditions. Among the treatments were a variety of spells and potions with ingredients such as blood from a black cat. **See also** cosmetics and perfumes.

Hammamat, Wadi

Located in Egypt's Eastern Desert near Coptos, the Wadi Hammamat had gold mines and quarries of graywacke (a hard, blackish stone also known as siltstone because it consisted of compacted dry silt) as early as the Eleventh Dynasty. Later the Wadi Hammamat also became part of one of three main routes to the Red Sea; people traveled through this wadi, or dry riverbed, on their way from Coptos to the port of Quseir. **See also** mining and metalworking.

Hapi

Hapi was the god of the Nile River inundation, the annual flooding that enriched the soil of Egypt. As such, he was the focus of several rituals and festivals connected to the flood, fertility, and agriculture. Because of these associations with fertility, Hapi was typically portrayed with large breasts and a slightly swollen belly although he was a man, because this visual image was a symbol of human fertility. However, even though the Nile inundation was vital to the survival of Egypt's people, Hapi was never considered a major god like Amun, Osiris, Ptah, or Thoth. **See also** Nile River.

Hapy

The son of the god Horus and the goddess Isis, Hapy was a deity associated with embalming and the dead. Specifically, he was said to protect the lungs of those who had died. Hapy's physical manifestation was as a baboon or a man with a baboon's head. It is unclear how this association developed. However, some Egyptologists believe it is related to the baboons' screeches, which require great lung capacity, and the fact that the ancient Egyptians sometimes connected baboons to rebirth because they always screech at dawn, the beginning of a new day. **See also** Horus; Isis.

harem

Called *per-khenret* by the ancient Egyptians, a harem was a king's collection of secondary, or lesser, wives. The harem was typically housed away from the royal court in a separate palace that was under the control of the king's principal wife even though she did not live there. The harem's members normally had vast estates and a large number of servants at their disposal, as well as scribes, entertainers, and others to make their lives more comfortable and enjoyable. Children of the harem's women also lived on this estate, as did former principal wives who had either fallen out of favor and left the court or had become too old to bear children.

Having a large harem could be risky for a king. On at least three occasions, for example, this separate community of women plotted to assassinate the king. The first such plot—which most Egyptologists think succeeded—was against Sixth Dynasty king Pepy I, led by a lesser wife named Weretyamtes who wanted to put her own son on the throne. The second—also widely believed to have succeeded—was against Twelfth Dynasty king Amenemhet I; this time, several members of the harem were involved in plans to kill the king before he had a chance to name Senwosret I, the son of an apparently unpopular secondary wife, his coruler and heir. The third plot, generally known as the Harem Conspiracy, was against Twentieth Dynasty king Ramses III. Led by a lesser wife named Tiye who wanted to see her son on the throne, the conspiracy involved most of the king's harem as well as nearly thirty high-ranking court officials and members of the military (a military and police coup was to coincide with the king's assassination). However, someone told Ramses III about the plot before the appointed day, and the conspirators were arrested and put on trial. Twelve officials were drawn from the government and military to oversee the trial (the king excused himself from the proceedings), but five of these judges were replaced before the trial ended, after the accused harem women tried to influence their decision, apparently through sexual favors.

Several papyri of the period, including the Judicial Papyrus of Turin, comment on the Harem Conspiracy trial, providing Egyptologists with information about what happened to some of the participants. The harem women involved in the plot were found guilty, as were twenty-eight government and military officials and Queen Tiye's son. He was given the option of committing suicide or being executed, and he chose suicide. Several of the condemned officials made the same decision. One of the misbehaving judges committed suicide as well; three others had their ears and noses amputated as punishment. (The fifth judge was merely removed from his duties.) However, the fate of Queen Tiye does not appear in any of the records, leaving some Egyptologists to speculate that the king might have quietly pardoned her. **See also** Amenemhet I; Pepy I; Ramses III; Weni.

Harkhuf (Harkhaf) (dates unknown)

Harkhuf was the governor of Elephantine during the Sixth Dynasty, as well as a powerful nomarch. However, he is best known for the autobiographical inscriptions (made around 2278 B.C.) on the wall of his rock-cut tomb in Aswan, which report that he led several foreign trade expeditions. Harkhuf led at least four of these expeditions into Nubia during the reigns of Merenre I and Pepy II, probably traveling by boat along the Nile and by donkey on land. His purpose was to establish trade routes and bring such items as ivory, ebony, oil, incense, and panther skins back to Egypt. On one of his trips, which were otherwise fairly routine, Harkhuf acquired a pygmy, or possibly a dwarf, for a young King Pepy II in keeping with the common practice of housing unusual people and animals at court. The inscriptions at Harkhuf's tomb also tell of an attempt by the chieftain of Yam in Nubia to take over a Nubian oasis controlled by Egypt. Harkhuf stopped the chieftain with the help of the Egyptian soldiers accompanying his trade expedition; from this information, scholars know that during the Sixth Dynasty the Egyptian military provided support for trading expeditions. **See also** Aswan; Merenre I; Nubia; Pepy II.

Harris Papyrus

Discovered with three other papyri in a Twentieth Dynasty nonroyal tomb at Deir el-Medina, the Harris Papyrus (named for Mr. A.C. Harris of Alexandria, Egypt, who first bought it on the antiquities market) is a papyrus related to the reign of Ramses III. Scholars believe that it was written upon the king's death at the behest of his son and successor, Ramses IV. Measuring 133 feet long with 117 columns of text, the papyrus has provided Egyptologists with many valuable details about Ramses III's decades-long rule, particularly in regard to temple activities. For example, the Harris Papyrus reports that the Karnak Temple of Amun employed 81,322 workers in various jobs and its priests controlled 65 villages, 83 ships, 46 workshops, 924 square miles of agricultural land, 433 orchards, and 421,362 head of cattle, goats, and sheep. The Harris Papyrus further reports that the king allowed the temple to control its own finances, a decision probably based in part on the temple complex's large staff and the power that such resources gave the priests.

The Harris Papyrus is also one of only four texts to contain ancient Egyptian love poetry. (The other texts are the Chester Beatty Papyrus I, the Turin Papyrus, and an inscription on a vase at the Cairo Museum.) Egyptologists do not know how the Harris Papyrus came to reside in a nonroyal tomb, but they suspect that it was once part of the archives of King Ramses III's mortuary temple at Medinet Habu. The Harris Papyrus is now housed in the British Museum. **See also** Chester Beatty Papyri; Karnak; Ramses III; Ramses IV.

Hathor

Hathor was one of the most important ancient Egyptian mother goddesses, with many associations and manifestations. In particular, she was connected to female sexuality and fertility, music and dancing, and the consumption of beer and wine. She was also a sky goddess, in some places called the daughter of the solar deity Re and the mother of his son Horus, in others the wife of Horus (with Isis being Horus's mother). As a sky goddess, Hathor was typically depicted as the cow of the heavens, her feet marking true

Hathor was a sky goddess and was also connected to female sexuality and fertility, as well as to the drinking of beer and wine.

north, south, east, and west. In addition, she was said to manifest herself as a cow on earth. Alternatively, she might appear as a woman wearing a headdress with a cow's horns or the image of a solar disk or falcon, the symbols of Re and Horus, respectively. As the celestial cow, Hathor was featured in a myth in which Horus slept within her womb each night and left through her mouth each morning to rise as the sun. Probably for this reason, Hathor's name means "Temple of Horus."

Because of her position as the mother of Horus and the fact that Horus was associated with the living king, Hathor was often said to be the mother of the king. In this role she was typically depicted in temple and tomb art nursing the king at her breast. But Hathor had many other roles as well. Her titles included Queen of the West, in reference to the location of the realm of the dead, and in this capacity she was charged with protecting royal tombs. She was also the Queen of Byblos, a port town on the coast of Lebanon, and the Queen of Turquoise, which was mined in the Sinai. In fact, Hathor is the goddess most often associated with foreign lands and desert mining and quarrying regions. Shrines to Hathor appear in such places as Nubia at Abu Simbel and the Sinai at Serabit el-Khadim.

The first temples dedicated to Hathor appeared in Dendera (the location of her main cult center) and a few other locations during the Fourth Dynasty. Besides Dendera, among the most prominent sites of Hathor worship were Deir el-Bahri, Philae, and Deir el-Medina. At all of these sites, which still have the remains of temples once dedicated to the goddess, worship was most likely conducted by priestesses who were the wives of the highest-ranking local officials. **See also** Deir el-Bahri; Deir el-Medina; Dendera; Horus.

Hatshepsut (ca. 1493– ca. 1458 B.C.)

Daughter of Queen Ahmose Meryt-Amon and King Tuthmosis I and the principal wife and half-sister of Tuthmosis II, Hatshepsut was an Eighteenth Dynasty queen who eventually declared herself pharaoh. Her path to becoming queen-pharaoh began upon the death of King Tuthmosis II when the throne went to Tuthmosis III, the young son of another of the king's wives, Isis, because Hatshepsut had no son. Because she had been the king's principal wife, Queen Hatshepsut was declared the boy's regent; within a very short time, she usurped the throne. Hatshepsut's closest adviser was her royal steward and architect, Senenmut, whom some Egyptologists believe was also her lover and might have been the father of Hatshepsut's daughter Neferure, who was born when Hatshepsut was still married to Tuthmosis II.

After declaring herself queen-pharaoh, Hatshepsut apparently adopted all of the titles and trappings of any male king, including masculine attire and perhaps a false beard used by very young kings to make themselves appear more mature. She also engaged in a traditional activity for an Egyptian king: launching numerous building projects. Hatshepsut oversaw the building, rebuilding, or enlargement of several temples and shrines and constructed her tomb at Deir el-Bahri. One of the reliefs there shows the spirit of her father, King Tuthmosis I, making her his coruler, and there is evidence that she claimed this sponsorship in arguing her right to rule.

By most accounts, Hatshepsut was an effective ruler, but there is also evidence that the public disapproved of her kingship

A granite figure of Hatshepsut, who adopted male attire and ruled as pharaoh.

and her association with Senenmut. Meanwhile, the child whose throne she had usurped grew into a man. At some point during this time, Hatshepsut apparently made him marry her daughter, but the girl died in the eleventh year of the queen's reign. Over the next few years, Tuthmosis III became a powerful military commander, fighting for Egypt in foreign campaigns. During the twentieth year of Hatshepsut's reign he suddenly took over the throne, probably because the queen died; the year before, Senenmut also appears to have died. Some Egyptologists suspect foul play in one or both deaths, particularly since supporters of Tuthmosis III defaced or destroyed many of Hatshepsut's monuments, reliefs, and statues after her death. She was subsequently omitted from king lists as well, so for many Egyptians it was as though her rule had never existed. Moreover, some Egyptologists believe that Tuthmosis III's supporters also destroyed Hatshepsut's body, since it has never been found. Others, however, suspect that an unidentified mummy found in a royal cache in the tomb of Amenhotep II is that of Hatshepsut, because the body, even though female, is poised in the traditional manner of the king, with arms crossed over the chest to hold the symbols of kingship known as the crook and the flail. **See also** caches, royal; Deir el-Bahri; flail; king lists; kings; Neferure; Senenmut; Tuthmosis III.

Hawara

Located in the Faiyum near Lahun, Hawara is primarily known as the site of the Labyrinth of Amenemhet III. Made of mud brick cased in limestone, this two-level structure once had twelve separate courts, numerous shafts, and three thousand chambers joined by a maze of corridors, as reported by classical authors like Herodotus and Strabo. Herodotus also reported that crocodiles were entombed in certain rooms in honor of the crocodile god Sobek. Archaeological investigations have confirmed that the Labyrinth was once as large as 1,000 by 800 feet in dimension or larger, and the mummified remains of crocodiles were found at the site. Consequently, some archaeologists have labeled the Labyrinth a temple complex or cult center. Others, however, believe it was a mortuary complex, a palace, or an administrative center. **See also** Amenemhet III; Lahun and Kahun.

headrests

From at least the Third Dynasty on, the ancient Egyptians used headrests to support their heads during sleep instead of pillows or cushions, perhaps because headrests did not provide a place for head lice to hide. Made of wood, pottery, alabaster, granite, or some other type of stone, a headrest was essentially a rectangular base with a short pedestal supporting a curved platform. Sometimes this platform was padded for more comfort. **See also** furniture.

This Eighteenth Dynasty wooden headrest bears the face of the god Bes.

Hearst Papyrus

The Hearst Papyrus is a Seventeenth or Eighteenth Dynasty papyrus that was discovered at Deir el-Ballas (near Dendera on the Nile River north of Luxor), where the palace complex of King Tao I was located. Its text relates solely to medicine, including information on various diseases and injuries and their treatment. The Hearst Papyrus is currently housed at the University of California at Berkeley. **See also** medicine; Tao I.

Heliopolis

Called Iunu (the "Pillar") in ancient Egyptian but renamed by the Greeks (with Helios meaning "Sun"), Heliopolis (now part of modern-day Cairo) was once the capital of the thirteenth nome of Lower Egypt. It was also a main cult center for the god Re, combined with Atum to take the form of Re-Atum or with Horakhty to take the form Re-Horakhty. Consequently, the city once had numerous temples dedicated to Re, Atum, Re-Atum, and Re-Horakhty. The largest was apparently the Temple of Atum the Complete One, whose name referred to the ancient Egyptian belief that the god was capable of self-generation, creating himself without the need of parents. By the New Kingdom, at least ten smaller temples surrounded this structure, but in modern times these were dismantled and their stones reused for other construction. The remains of a few New Kingdom secular buildings, however, still exist, including a fort and an obelisk erected in the Twelfth Dynasty by King Senwosret I.

In excavating the area, archaeologists have also found scores of Sixth Dynasty tombs of high priests and shrines dedicated to the worship of the benu bird, or phoenix, representing rebirth. In addition, Heliopolis was the site of worship dedicated to the god Mnevis and the goddesses Hathor and Isis. The city had a sacred Mnevis bull that was cared for in one of the city's temples as a living manifestation of the god Mnevis. **See also** Atum; bulls, sacred; Re; Senwosret I.

Henutsen (ca. 2589–2566 B.C.)

Fourth Dynasty queen Henutsen was one of the wives of King Khufu (also known as Cheops) and the mother of several government officials, as well as Prince Khafre, who became ruler after King Khufu's death. She might also have been the half-sister or daughter of King Khufu. A pyramid honoring her is located at Giza next to the Great Pyramid, which was built by her husband. **See also** Giza; Khafre; Khufu.

Hepzefa (Hapidjefa) (ca. 1965–1920 B.C.)

Hepzefa was a nomarch of the Twelfth Dynasty who served as governor of Asyut during the reign of Senwosret I. His tomb is also in Asyut, located in Middle Egypt, but his mummy has not yet been found. Inscribed on the tomb walls is a contract listing the rituals and offerings that priests were to perform to honor Hepzefa after his death, providing Egyptologists with valuable information about ancient Egyptian mortuary practices and contractual agreements. Hepzefa also placed a large statue of himself and his wife, Princess Sennuwy, at Kerma in Nubia, but Egyptologists do not know why he chose this location for his likeness given that his tomb was elsewhere. At one time, Egyptologists thought that the statues indicated that a nearby, unidentified tomb was that of Hepzefa and his wife instead of the one labeled as his in Asyut, but this theory has been abandoned for lack of other evidence supporting it. **See also** Asyut; nomes and nomarchs; Nubia.

Heracleopolis (Herakleopolis; Herakleopolis Magna)

Located beside the Bahr Yusef, a tributary of the Nile River that feeds the Faiyum, Heracleopolis (also known as

Herakleopolis Magna) was named by the Greeks, who associated its main god Harsaphes with their god Heracles. (The city was called Henen-nesut by the ancient Egyptians and Ihnasya el-Medina in modern times.) The town had a Twelfth Dynasty temple (modified in subsequent dynasties) dedicated to Harsaphes; it was first excavated by archaeologist Edouard Naville in 1891–1892 and was further studied by Sir William Matthew Flinders Petrie in 1904. During the 1970s and 1980s, several other archaeologists excavated other areas of the city, where numerous cemeteries and tombs have been found dating from the New Kingdom. During the Ninth and Tenth Dynasties, Heracleopolis was the capital of Egypt; consequently, these dynasties are often jointly called the Heracleopolitan dynasty. Heracleopolis was also the capital of the twentieth nome of Upper Egypt for much of the country's history. **See also** First Intermediate Period.

Herihor (?–1070 B.C.)

Herihor was a powerful general of the Twentieth Dynasty, as well as a vizier and a high priest of Amun. Many Egyptologists believe he also usurped the throne of Egypt around 1080 B.C., but others think that his ancestors, not Herihor, had done this. According to one of the most prevalent theories of what took place, Herihor was a general who was sent to Thebes to deal with a rebellion. In some scenarios, this roughly nine-month rebellion was led by the high priest of Amun at Thebes; in others, the high priest, Amenophis, disappeared, perhaps killed by assassins. In either case, once Herihor had put down the rebellion, he either took command of the city or was placed in charge of it by a superior, Panehsi, or perhaps by King Ramses XI. Herihor then strengthened his hold on the region by restructuring the government of Upper Egypt so that its military was under the control of the high priest of Amun. A short time later, Herihor apparently set himself up as a king, adopting various symbols and titles traditionally reserved for royalty. For example, he often had his name inscribed within a royal cartouche, and reliefs in a temple he constructed, the Temple of Khons (a Theban god of the moon and the son of the sun god Amun), show him beside Ramses XI in a position and size that indicates he was the king's equal.

King Ramses XI appears to have been unable to challenge Herihor's power, and many Egyptologists believe that, during the last six years of Ramses XI's reign, he controlled only the north while Herihor ruled the south. At some point during this time, Herihor began to insist that the god Amun was advising him on matters of the state and that as a priest of Amun he was favored by the god as the ruler of both Upper and Lower Egypt. Nonetheless, when Ramses XI died, rule of Egypt was officially divided between two dynasties, a secular one ruling in the north at Tanis and a priestly one ruling in the south at Thebes. Egyptologists agree that King Smendes I was the ruler in Tanis, but they disagree as to whether Herihor was in Thebes at this time. Some say that Herihor died before Ramses XI and that Herihor's immediate successor began this newly separated dynasty. Egyptologists also disagree on whether this successor was Piankh or Pinedjem I, although both were kings of Upper Egypt at some point.

No one knows where Herihor's mummy is. However, the mummy of Herihor's wife Nodjmet, whom archaeologists suspect was also the sister of Ramses XI, was found in 1881 in a cache of royal mummies hidden from tomb robbers by ancient Egyptian priests. Prior to this discovery, an illustrated *Book of the Dead* prepared for Herihor and his wife surfaced at an antiquities sale, but no one knows where this funerary papyrus was found. **See also** Amun; Ramses XI; Tanis; Thebes.

Hermopolis (Khmun; el-Ashmunein)

The ancient Egyptians called the city of Hermopolis, located in the Nile Valley, Per-Djehuty, or House of Thoth, because it was the main cult center of the god Thoth. Alternatively, they called it Khmun, meaning "Eight Town," in reference to a group of eight deities (known as the Ogdoad) who were believed to constitute all aspects of the essence of Thoth. The Greeks, however, associated the city with their god Hermes Trismegistas (Thrice-Great Hermes), and so they renamed it Hermopolis. Today it is the modern city of el-Ashmunein.

In the center of town was a temple enclosed by walls that created a sacred district. These walls date from the Ramessid Period but were modified during the Thirtieth Dynasty. The temple also shows evidence of having been remodeled on several occasions and serves as an excellent example of how the ancient Egyptians continually recycled building materials. Its foundation stones clearly were salvaged from another temple, one located in the nearby city of Akhetaten (also known as Amarna), following the end of the reign of King Akhenaten (also known as Amenhotep IV). **See also** Amarna; Amenhotep IV; cult centers; Thoth.

Herodotus (ca. 490–420 B.C.)

A Greek historian noted for his travels throughout the ancient world, Herodotus visited Egypt in the mid–fifth century B.C. and subsequently wrote about his experiences in his *Histories*. This work consisted of nine volumes, all of which still exist; the material on Egypt is in Book Two. Its context is a discussion of the Persian Empire, of which Egypt was a part when Herodotus visited.

Herodotus's writings on Egypt include his descriptions of the landscape, ancient structures, statues, and the like, as well as information about Egypt's myths, his-tory, and cultural features such as crocodile hunting, fishing, agriculture, burial practices, and religious traditions and ceremonies. Regarding the descriptive passages, Herodotus provided perhaps the earliest detailed account of the sights along the Nile River. He claimed to have traveled south on the river by boat as far as Elephantine; however, some historians believe that he did not actually go that far but relied on the stories of earlier travelers, such as a Greek known as Herataeus of Miletus, for some of his work. Nonetheless, Herodotus's descriptions of the Nile River Valley appear to be accurate.

His work, however, appears to have some serious flaws. Herodotus relied on people he met on his journey for information about Egyptian history and early culture, and in his writings he reported their

The fifth-century B.C. Greek historian Herodotus was noted for his travels throughout the ancient world, including Egypt.

stories as fact. Much of what he was told, however, has proven to be incorrect, although his recitation of the historical events of the Twenty-sixth Dynasty appears to be fairly accurate. Also accurate was one of the few facts that he reported as myth: that the annual flooding of the Nile River was caused by changes in weather conditions somewhere far south of Egypt.

Egyptologists consider Herodotus's descriptions of religious ceremonies particularly valuable in providing insights into more ancient practices, because these descriptions came from Herodotus's discussions with and observations of priests who were then practicing a religion that was relatively unchanged from far earlier times. However, most modern scholars do not accept Herodotus's theory, derived from his observation that ancient Egyptian gods were similar to Greek ones, that the Greeks had derived their beliefs from those of the Egyptians. **See also** Nile River.

Hetepheres I (dates unknown)

Fourth Dynasty queen Hetepheres I was probably the daughter of King Huni and the sister and wife of King Snefru. She was also the mother of Khufu, Snefru's heir. Egyptologists suspect that Queen Hetepheres died sometime during Khufu's reign, and it appears that shortly after her burial her tomb was robbed. She was then reburied by the king's vizier, Hemiunu, in a shaft tomb near her son's pyramid; her large alabaster sarcophagus was placed within a small chamber ninety-nine feet below an entrance camouflaged with plaster. This tomb was discovered by accident in 1925 by a photographer surveying the Giza area. Archaeologists believe that when found it was in the same state as when it was first sealed. However, the queen's sarcophagus was empty, suggesting that Vizier Hemiunu never checked inside to see whether Het-

epheres' tomb robbers had taken her mummy. Fortunately, though, her canopic chest was still intact, providing Egyptologists with the oldest known embalmed internal organs. The tomb also included the queen's canopy bed; several chairs; various containers of gold, copper, and alabaster; twenty silver bracelets; and numerous toilet articles, including a gold manicure set. Many of these items are now in the Egyptian Museum in Cairo or in the Museum of Fine Arts in Boston, Massachusetts. **See also** canopic jars and chests; Khufu; mummification; Snefru.

Hierakonpolis (Hieraconpolis; Nekhen; Keken; Kom el-Ahmar)

Located in southern Upper Egypt, Hierakonpolis received its name from the Greeks but was called Nekhen by the ancient Egyptians; today it is known by its Arabic name, Kom el-Ahmar (the "Red Mound"). Prior to the New Kingdom, the city was the capital of the third nome of Upper Egypt. During the New Kingdom, the capital was changed to el-Kab (also known as Nekheb), which was Hierakonpolis's sister city across the Nile River. The ancient Egyptians considered these two cities to be two parts of a whole, both under the protection of the vulture goddess Nekhbet.

Archaeologists excavating Hierakonpolis have found the remains of many structures, some dating from as early as the Predynastic Period. These include a predynastic mud-brick tomb decorated with wall scenes (among the earliest such works) and a temple complex dating from the reign of King Narmer but showing signs that subsequent dynastic kings added to it. In fact, Hierakonpolis has been one of the most important sources of late Predynastic Period artifacts, which include stone palettes and ivory figurines. **See also** Narmer; palettes; Predynastic Period.

hieratic script

Developed by priests of the First Dynasty (ca. 3000 B.C.), hieratic script, or hieratics, was a cursive form of hieroglyphic writing that enabled scribes to write more quickly and easily with ink on either papyrus or ostraka (small, thin pieces of stone or pottery). While religious documents were traditionally written in hieroglyphs, hieratic script was the writing form of choice for administrative and legal documents until the Twenty-sixth Dynasty, when it was replaced by an even easier form of writing, demotic script. **See also** hieroglyphs; writing, forms of.

hieroglyphs

Hieroglyphs are pictographic markings that the ancient Egyptians used as written language. Hieroglyphs were typically arranged in vertical columns and horizontal rows that are usually read from right to left. Interpreting hieroglyphs proved impossible for modern archaeologists until nineteenth-century French linguist and historian Jean-François Champollion realized that, in addition to representing the object pictured, a hieroglyph could represent a sound made while naming such an object. Complicating matters, one hieroglyph might be used in more than one way. For example, a disk symbol might represent not only an object, the sun, but a concept, the sun god, and a sound, *ra.*

The first hieroglyphs appeared on clay seals used to mark First Dynasty tombs with their owners' names, but soon hieroglyphs were appearing elsewhere as well. Hieroglyphic texts could be painted on rock, stucco, wood, metal, or other surfaces, but they were most often inscribed on stelae and tomb and temple walls. In fact, they were so strongly associated with these religious structures that the Greeks called them *hieros glypho,* or "sacred carved," from which the modern word *hieroglyph* is derived. (The ancient Egyptian phrase for hieroglyphs was *medw netjer,* or "the gods' words.") Hieroglyphs might also be marked on papyri, but more typically a cursive form of hieroglyphics, known as hieratic script or hieratics, was used for such documents. **See also** Champollion, Jean-François; writing, forms of.

hippopotamuses

The marshes along the Nile River provided food and shelter for numerous hippopotamuses, which because of their large numbers understandably became a part of ancient Egyptian religious beliefs. In many cases, these associations were with gods representing powerful but negative forces, because hippopotamuses were known to kill people with little provocation. For example, the hippopotamus was said to be one manifestation of the destroyer god Seth.

However, because of these animals' fierceness, the Egyptians also viewed them as an attacker of evil spirits and therefore, ironically, as protectors of humans. So, some of the religious associations connected to hippopotamuses were positive. For example, one of the deities said to manifest as a hippopotamus was Taweret, who watched over pregnant women during labor.

Because of such positive associations, hippopotamus tusks were often inscribed with protective symbols and carried as amulets (i.e., magic charms intended to protect the wearer). Similarly, hippopotamus figurines were either carried or featured in religious rituals, and tables were occasionally carved with hippopotamus legs or other features of the animal. In addition, live hippopotamuses were sometimes kept in temple pools. In fact, there were so many hippopotamuses in such pools during the Seventeenth Theban Dynasty that a Fifteenth Hyksos Dynasty king, Apophis, supposedly claimed that he could hear the animals living in Thebes from his capital of Avaris four hundred miles away. **See also** Seth; Taweret.

historical sources

In studying ancient Egyptian history, Egyptologists have had to rely on a limited number of sources. For the most part, these historical sources are tomb, temple, pyramid, and stelae inscriptions and papyri written by ancient Egyptians; however, Egyptologists also rely on writings by classical authors who visited Egypt not long after the last of its kings ruled. Egyptologists compare the material in each source, using one to validate the information in another and making educated guesses to fill in any gaps in information.

The most important sources for Egyptologists developing a chronology of ancient Egyptian history are five ancient Egyptian king lists, each of which provides a list of Egypt's kings prior to the time it was written and perhaps the number of years of each reign. These five lists are the Palermo Stone, the Royal List of Karnak, the Royal List of Abydos, the Royal List of Saqqara, and the Royal Canon of Turin. Of these, the Royal Canon of Turin once offered the largest list of Egypt's kings—over three hundred—complete with the precise length of each reign to the day (although the starting and ending dates are not given), but it has been severely damaged, so Egyptologists have had to use other sources to try to fill in its missing information. The Palermo Stone, a fragment of a larger stone slab, lists some of the kings who ruled prior to the Fifth Dynasty, including some Predynastic Period ones. The Royal List of Karnak provides the names of kings from the First to the mid–Eighteenth Dynasty, ending with the reign of Tuthmosis III. The Royal List of Abydos, on a wall in the temple of Seti I at Abydos, provides the names of seventy-six kings, from the First Dynasty to the mid–Nineteenth Dynasty, ending with the reign of Seti I, but it omits all kings of the Second Intermediate Period and the kings in the Eighteenth Dynasty who worshiped the god Aten.

In addition to these lists, Egyptologists have based much of their knowledge of Egypt's kings on the writings of third-century-B.C. Greco-Roman Period historian Manetho, who established the ancient Egyptian dynasty divisions still used today. However, some of his work is believed to be unreliable. This is true as well of other important classical sources of information about ancient Egyptian history and culture, including the writings of Herodotus (specifically *The Histories,* Book II), Diodorus Siculus (*Bibliotheca Historica*), Strabo (*Geography,* Book XVII), Pliny the Elder (*Historia Naturalis*), and Plutarch (*Moralia*). For example, Herodotus received much of his information about ancient Egypt from people he met on a journey up the Nile River, and he seemed to accept even the most distorted material as the truth and report it in his writings as fact. Such distortions have made it difficult for modern historians to get an accurate picture of what ancient Egyptian life was really like, and there are many disagreements about a variety of historical events. **See also** chronology; Diodorus Siculus; Herodotus; king lists; Strabo.

history, periods of ancient Egyptian

Egyptologists divide ancient Egyptian history into ten periods, although they often disagree on the dates and duration of the periods and occasionally on which kings belong in which period. The ten periods and their approximate dates are:

Predynastic Period (ca. 700,000–ca. 3000 B.C.) Egypt moves from being a divided land, with one king in the north and one in the south, to being a unified kingdom.

Early Dynastic Period (ca. 3000–ca. 2686 B.C.) The first evidence of Egyptian religious beliefs emerges. The king is identified with the god Horus, the first royal tombs are built, and Egypt begins to send expeditions to exploit the natural resources of foreign lands. Egypt's capital is established in Memphis.

Old Kingdom (ca. 2686–ca. 2125 B.C.) Religion becomes more complex; the first pyramids are built, containing detailed drawings and carvings; and art and architecture make great strides. The country prospers under a series of strong kings. However, the final king of the period, Pepy II, is weak, and under his long rule, the power of the king diminishes while the power of local governors, or nomarchs, increases. (Egyptologists disagree on exactly when the Old Kingdom ended and the First Intermediate Period began, resulting in overlapping dates.)

First Intermediate Period (ca. 2160–ca. 2055 B.C.) The Old Kingdom ends due to political disunity brought about by King Pepy II's policies. Midway through the period, a new line of kings establishes a new capital in Heracleopolis to rival the one in Memphis. At the end of the period, Theban princes sharing the birth name Montuhotep reunite the country under one rule. One of these king's viziers, Amenemhet I, then usurps the throne, thereby (according to most Egyptologists) founding the Middle Kingdom.

Middle Kingdom (ca. 2055–ca. 1650 B.C.) Amenemhet I moves the capital of Egypt north to Itj-tawy. He and his successors expand Egypt's influence abroad, colonize Nubia to the south, embark on major building and irrigation projects, and encourage art and architecture. Under their reigns, the country prospers. By the middle of the period, however, a weak king (Amenemhet IV) is once again on the throne, and Egypt declines. His throne is soon usurped by his sister Sobeknefru (also known as Nefru-Sobek), who cannot maintain the unity of the crown.

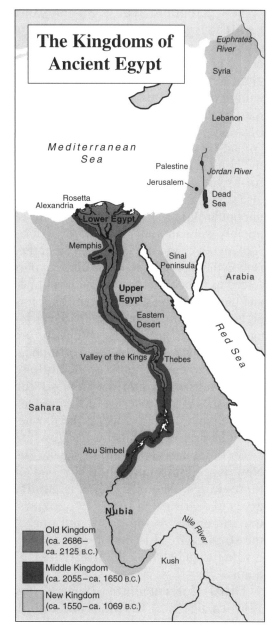

The Kingdoms of Ancient Egypt

Old Kingdom (ca. 2686– ca. 2125 B.C.)

Middle Kingdom (ca. 2055–ca. 1650 B.C.)

New Kingdom (ca. 1550–ca. 1069 B.C.)

Second Intermediate Period (ca. 1650–ca. 1550 B.C.) Two lines of Egyptian kings rule the country, one from Thebes and the other in a small part of the Delta. Meanwhile, foreign invaders known as the Hyksos take over the eastern Delta and set up their own rival dynasty. War breaks out between the Hyksos kings and the Theban kings, and the period ends with the Theban kings triumphant.

New Kingdom (ca. 1550–ca. 1069 B.C.) The Hyksos are driven out of Egypt altogether, and the country enters a new era of prosperity. Art, architecture, religion, and many other aspects of Egyptian culture flourish. Building projects are numerous, as are military, mining, quarrying, and trading expeditions designed to spread Egypt's influence and to exploit the natural resources of other countries for Egypt's benefit. However, there are also signs of trouble in the kingdom. A few unpopular kings sit on the throne—most notably Amenhotep IV (also known as Akhenaten), who tries to force monotheism on the Egyptian people—and Egypt is forced to fight off invasions by the Hittites and the Sea Peoples. Moreover, other foreigners enter the country as mercenaries and tradesmen, and the Egyptian culture begins to show signs of their influence. Toward the end of the New Kingdom, during a time sometimes called the Ramessid Period, a series of kings sharing the name Ramses sits on the throne; the first rule well, but the last few are either cruel and unpopular or weak. The New Kingdom ends when the last of these kings, Ramses XI, essentially gives over his reign to his two viziers, one in control of the north and one of the south. After his death, these kings divide Egypt between them as two kingdoms.

Third Intermediate Period (ca. 1069–ca. 664 B.C.) The kings of the north rule from the Delta city of Tanis, while those of the south—who are also priests—rule from Thebes. Eventually, the Tanis kings unite the country and continue ruling all of Egypt from Tanis. Meanwhile, princes in the city of Sais establish their own independent rule there. Near the end of the period, a line of Nubian kings establishes a new dynasty at Thebes. They are defeated by invading Assyrians, who then install a prince of Sais as the king of a united Egypt. Eventually, however, the Persians invade and conquer Egypt and make it a part of the Persian dynasty, thus ending the Third Intermediate Period.

Late Period (ca. 664–332 B.C.) During this period, the Persians and the Egyptians both vie for control of Egypt. This struggle finally ends when the Persians are defeated by Alexander the Great (Alexander III) and the Greeks take control of Egypt.

Greco-Roman Period (332 B.C.–A.D. 395) A string of Greek kings rules Egypt until 30 B.C., when Rome takes over the country. Egypt then becomes part of the Roman Empire. **See also** *individual entries for the periods.*

Hittites

The Hittites were a warrior people who probably originated from somewhere around the Black Sea. Beginning in approximately 1650 B.C., they gradually conquered much of Anatolia (modern-day Turkey) and northern Syria, and then moved into Babylonia to take over that country by approximately 1590 B.C. From approximately 1400 B.C. to 1200 B.C., the Hittite empire was at its most powerful—so powerful, in fact, that the widow of Eighteenth Dynasty king Tutankhamun tried to marry a Hittite prince to keep Egypt's throne away from those who had conspired to kill her husband. The prince was murdered before he could reach her; nonetheless, Egypt was able to convince the Hittites not to retaliate.

Under the reign of Hittite king Muwatallis (ca. 1320–1294 B.C.), however, the animosity that the Hittites felt toward the Egyptians led them to encroach on Egypt's eastern border. Consequently the Hittites and the Egyptians, first under Seti I and then under Ramses II, fought several major battles, the largest of which was the Battle of Kadesh, which took place in 1299 B.C. During this battle, King Ramses II, then in the third year of his reign, marched into the valley of the Orontes River, near the city-state of Kadesh (an ally of the Hittites), with more than twenty thousand men. There he was ambushed by the Hittite king, and after a complex series of military maneuvers the battle came to an end. Various versions of what happened during this battle exist, featuring the death of King Muwatallis's brother and the drowning of most of the Hittite army. But although King Ramses II later claimed he won the battle and boasted about its outcome, he clearly did not take the city, and modern historians believe that the battle was actually a draw.

Sixteen years after the Battle of Kadesh, after several minor skirmishes, the Hittites and the Egyptians made a permanent peace pact. Relations between the two peoples continued on good terms until approximately 1193 B.C., when the Hittite empire abruptly collapsed. Historians disagree on why the empire fell, but many suspect it was due to massive migrations of the Sea Peoples into Hittite territories, which weakened the Hittite culture, economy, and social systems. **See also** Ankhesenamun; Babylonia and Chaldea; Ramses II; Sea Peoples.

Hor (Awibre; Awibre Hor) (dates unknown)

Hor was a Thirteenth Dynasty king who reigned for only a few months in approximately 1750 B.C. and was most likely a weak ruler. There are few details available about Hor's life, although his shaft tomb was found by archaeologist Jacque de Morgan in Dashur, the city Hor used as his capital. There archaeologists discovered a life-size wooden statue that they have determined represents the king. The figure is stepping from a shrine with its arms outstretched, and the hieroglyphic symbol of the *ka,* an aspect of the spirit, is on its head. The statue is naked, which is unusual since kings are generally depicted as clothed. Archaeologists

suspect that the figure once wore an Egyptian loincloth made of gold or linen that was either stolen or destroyed. The inlaid eyes of the statue, however, are still in place; they are made of white quartz and crystal surrounded by a rim of copper. Hor's tomb lacks decoration, as does the nearby shaft tomb of his wife, both located near the mortuary complex of Amenemhet III. Archaeologists have found numerous inscriptions left by King Hor on monuments at sites as far north as Tanis and as far south as Elephantine. **See also** Dashur; Elephantine; *ka;* Tanis.

Horemheb (Horemhab) (?–1295 B.C.)

During the Eighteenth Dynasty, Horemheb ("Horus in Festival") was a powerful military general who became king of Egypt. Some Egyptologists believe that his rise to the throne involved not only shrewd political maneuvers but also the murder of at least one of his predecessors. Born in Heracleopolis, Horemheb was apparently a commoner, although he later claimed to be an aristocrat. He joined the military during the reign of Amenhotep III, rising through the ranks to acquire the honorific great Commander of the Army under King Amenhotep IV. Upon the king's death, Horemheb continued to serve under his successors Smenkhkare and then Tutankhamun, who was still a young boy.

Together with another powerful courtier, Ay, Horemheb controlled every aspect of Tutankhamun's life. Officially, however, Horemheb was the general of Tutankhamun's armies, and when Tutankhamun became a young man, Horemheb accompanied the king on military campaigns in Nubia and Libya. Egyptologists suspect that by this time Tutankhamun was beginning to resist Horemheb and Ay and that at some point the two had the young man murdered, apparently by a blow to the back of the head. Horemheb is the prime suspect as the

Horemheb, shown in this bas-relief, was an Eighteenth Dynasty military general who later became king.

murderer because when Tutankhamun's widow sent for a foreign king to marry her and assume the throne, Horemheb sent military forces to kill him at Egypt's border. In this, Horemheb was probably a conspirator with Ay, who by then was a very old man. Ay ruled Egypt for a brief time before his death, whereupon Horemheb became king as Ay's heir.

Horemheb was a strong ruler, ending government corruption and imposing greater order on the country. One of his first acts was to issue an edict declaring that nomarchs and other officials would be held responsible for any cheating or corruption that took place within their administrations. Moreover, the king decreed that any official involved in corruption would be executed. Another

of Horemheb's acts was to divide the army into two completely separate forces, one for Lower Egypt and one for Upper Egypt, so that no one general could control the entire military and perhaps threaten the king's rule. Horemheb also intimidated foreign rulers into paying him tributes in large amounts and took aggressive measures to eradicate all records of kings between Seti I and himself. Horemheb's actions in this regard were so effective that subsequent king lists produced by the Ramessid Period rulers show Horemheb's reign coming immediately after Seti I's.

Part of Horemheb's motive in such historical revision was to return Egypt to religious practices that had been banned under Amenhotep IV (Akhenaten), who had tried to create a monotheistic faith based on the worship of Aten. While he was destroying all vestiges of Aten worship, Horemheb took steps to restore the worship of other gods. He supported various priesthoods, particularly that of the god Amun, built a temple dedicated to the god Ptah, and remodeled or repaired numerous temples and shrines. He built two tombs for himself as well, one at Saqqara and the other at the Valley of the Kings. The former has many fine reliefs, primarily with military scenes. The latter was unfinished at the time of Horemheb's death but nonetheless once held his funerary goods. When archaeologist Theodore Davis found this tomb in 1908, he saw evidence of tomb robbery, including smashed statues and damaged furniture. A team of archaeologists found the Saqqara tomb in the nineteenth century and removed its sculptures and reliefs, sending them to the Leiden Museum and elsewhere. Memory of the tomb's location was then lost until an expedition of the Egyptian Exploration Society rediscovered it in 1975.

Horemheb's body has never been found. However, his Valley of the Kings tomb held his red granite sarcophagus, along with four mummies. Two of them were of a mother and newborn that Egyptologists suspect are the remains of Horemheb's wife Queen Mutnodjmet and her child, both of whom died either during or shortly after labor. Egyptologists suspect that Horemheb's mummy was taken to another, as-yet-undiscovered location after the robbery of his tomb. **See also** Ay; Smenkhkare; Tutankhamun; Valley of the Kings.

Horus

A solar deity, Horus was one of the oldest ancient Egyptian gods, although until the Greek Period he was called Hor. In fact, beliefs about Horus and the names by which he was known varied widely depending on local traditions. Sometimes the deity was known as Horus the Elder, or Hor-Wer in ancient Egyptian, a force of good battling evil. He was also Horus of Gold, or Hor-Nubti, destroyer of the evil god Seth; Horus of the Horizon, or Har-akhtes, a sun god who became part of the solar deity Re as Re-Horakhty; or Harsiesis, or Hor-sa-iset, featured in mythology as the young son of the goddess Isis. In some myths he was considered the son of the goddess Hathor instead. Worshiped as Horus the Behdetite at a shrine in Edfu, he was a falcon god who transformed into a winged sun disk. Elsewhere he was Horus, the Uniter of the Two Lands, or Horu-Sema-Tawy, who after vanquishing the evil god Seth united Egypt within himself as king on earth and the god Osiris as king of the celestial realm. Thus Egypt's kings were sometimes called the physical manifestation of Horus while they were living and of Osiris after they died.

From at least as early as the First Dynasty, Horus was associated with Egypt's kings. At that time they began using his name as one of their royal titles and his main symbol, the falcon, as the symbol for kingship. Therefore Horus was often called the protector of the king even though he was also said to be the king in physical form. Because of this connection, the king played the part of Horus in certain festivals and rituals.

As a major god in the Egyptian pantheon, Horus is the subject of numerous myths. One of these myths—found in the Chester Beatty Papyrus I and dating from the Twentieth Dynasty reign of Ramses V—tells of a dispute between Horus and his uncle, Seth. The two go before the court of the gods, presided over by the god Re, and each argues that he deserves to succeed Osiris as the living king of Egypt. Seth claims this right as the brother of Osiris, even though he was also his murderer, while Horus claims it as Osiris's son and heir. (In other myths, Horus is Osiris's brother.) The gods consider both arguments and begin arguing among themselves, some saying that Seth would make a better king because of his more advanced age and strength and his fierceness; others favor Horus for his goodness and honor and his position as Osiris's son. After much debate, the gods adjourn without making a decision.

Then Horus's mother Isis goes to Seth disguised as a widow whose son has been cheated out of his inheritance (a herd of cattle). When she tells the god her plight, he condemns all those who would steal a son's position, and upon hearing this the gods sitting in judgment of the case between Horus and Seth award the throne to Horus. Angry over this development, Seth challenges Horus to a contest to determine who will rule, and it quickly turns into a battle. The myth goes on to tell of a series of violent and/or strange contests and battles that ensue before Osiris finally calls out from the Underworld that Horus is his choice for successor.

In another version of this myth, shown on the walls of a temple at Edfu, Seth and Horus battle over the throne of Re, each in the company of a group of followers. At some ancient Egyptian festivals, this battle or similar ones were reenacted by two companies of performers, the Followers of Horus and the Followers of Seth. The Followers of Horus always won these mock battles, because in the myth Horus defeated Seth.

During other versions of this battle, Horus lost an eye, though he soon recovered it. Consequently one of his symbols was an eye, the Eye of Horus, and because it was associated with the recovery of sight the symbol was often placed on amulets intended for healing. The Eye of Horus was also sometimes associated with the moon, most typically with its cycles of waning and waxing (death and re-

birth). In some places where this association was made, Horus's other eye symbolized the sun, and mythology concerning his battle with Seth involved imagery relating to a battle between light (goodness) and dark (evil). **See also** Chester Beatty Papyri; Creation myths; Isis; Re; Seth.

Hotepsekhemwy (Hetepsekhemwy; Bedjau) (dates unknown)

The first king of the Second Dynasty, Hotepsekhemwy ruled for over thirty years sometime around 2890 B.C., but modern scholars know very little about him, including whether he was related to his predecessor. They suspect, however, that this king brought peace to Egypt after a period of civil unrest, since his name means the "Two Mighty Ones [i.e., Horus and Seth, gods of Upper and Lower Egypt, respectively] at Rest."

Hotepsekhemwy's tomb has never been found. However, archaeologists suspect that it lies somewhere near the pyramid complex of Fifth Dynasty king Unas at Saqqara, because tomb seals (seals on tomb entrances imprinted with the occupant's name) with Hotepsekhemwy's name have been found in the area. Archaeologists have also found a Third Dynasty statue of a public official, Hotepdief, that has King Hotepsekhemwy's name inscribed on it. **See also** Saqqara.

houses

Archaeologists have few examples of ancient Egyptian houses, for two main reasons. First, houses were not built to last, the way tombs were, and second, new homes were typically built on the sites of old homes, so over time most earlier structures were obliterated. However, three villages that were abandoned in ancient times offer some insights into early Egyptian architecture: Kahun and Deir el-Medina, which were villages intended to provide temporary housing for workers on nearby sites, and Amarna, built by King Akhenaten (also known as Amenhotep IV) to honor the god Aten. From such sites, archaeologists generally know that there were three basic types of dwelling: simple homes for the poor and working classes, villas for the middle classes and nobility, and palaces for royalty.

Made of mud brick, simple homes might have four to seven rooms within a boxlike one-story structure of four walls and a flat roof. The primary rooms were an entrance hall, which usually had an offering table and shrine area; a kitchen; a living room; and a bedroom. Additional rooms were for sleeping and storage. The only entrance into the house was through a doorway into the entrance hall. This doorway usually faced the street and had a wooden door. Windows had no glass because glass would have trapped the sun's heat; if there were any windows at all, they were typically high off the ground and small to let in air but keep the sun out. Although some roofs were made of mud brick, most were made of date-tree beams, palm branches, and reed mats, sometimes sealed with dried mud except for a few small holes that were left to provide light to the rooms below. These types of roofs were strong enough to support considerable weight, so people would sleep there on hot nights; therefore, most houses had steps leading up to the roof. In workers' villages, houses were often arranged in terraces so that more houses could fit in a confined cliffside area.

In contrast, villas were sprawling, with numerous rooms, corridors, and at least one courtyard. Made of mud brick but possibly including stone trim, villas might have two stories plus a basement that was usually used for storage. Sometimes the structures were terraced to provide an upper-level patio for sitting outside. A villa's many rooms included reception areas, bedrooms, and living,

eating, bathing, and storage rooms. The kitchen might be part of the main house or it might be in a separate structure, typically within a central garden that provided herbs, fruits, and vegetables as well as flowers. Other buildings on the property might include granaries and servant quarters. The wealthier the owner, the more vast the villa.

Palaces were even larger than villas, because they served as not only the king's residence but also a government building where matters of administration were carried out. In fact, the palace—or *per-a'a* (Great House), as it was called during ancient times—was divided into two sections, one for each purpose. Rooms related to government work were around the perimeter of the palace, surrounding an inner area of rooms for the private use of the king, his family, and his harem. Above the private rooms was a balcony that could be seen from the street, where the king stepped outside to make public appearances. Government rooms included a large hall for public meetings and audiences and a smaller room where the king might meet with individuals on a one-to-one basis for political purposes. Palaces had wall decorations—especially paintings on stuccoed walls—but most villas and some workers' homes had them as well. Decorative columns, however, were only in upper-class homes and palaces. **See also** architecture.

Huni (Nysuteh; possibly also Horus Qahedjet) (?–2613 B.C.)

The last king of the Third Dynasty, Huni reigned for approximately twenty-four years. However, Egyptologists know little about his life, except that his principal queen was Meresankh I (the mother of Huni's heir, Snefru) and that his vizier was a famous sage named Kagemni. Egyptologists disagree on whether King Huni built a structure known as the Meidum pyramid or whether his son Snefru built or completed it. Located at Meidum on the edge of the Faiyum, approximately fifty miles south of modern-day Cairo, this was a very tall, very steep pyramid (approximately 214 feet tall, with a 74-degree slope) that collapsed sometime prior to the Nineteenth Dynasty. Some archaeologists believe the collapse occurred during the Fourth Dynasty, when another pyramid (that of King Snefru) was built nearby. Others think it collapsed sometime during the Eighteenth Dynasty, because graffiti from that era has been found inside the collapsed structure.

Where Huni was entombed is also unknown. Egyptologists doubt that he was entombed in the Meidum pyramid because no sarcophagus was found in its underground burial chamber. However, a nearby tomb holds what appears to be a royal sarcophagus, empty and badly damaged by tomb robbers. **See also** Kagemni; Meidum; Snefru.

hunting and fishing

Many ancient Egyptian tombs contain depictions of people hunting and fishing. Therefore Egyptologists have concluded that they were popular pastimes among those wealthy enough to afford tomb art. However, scholars disagree on the extent to which the lower classes engaged in such activities.

In the most common scenes related to hunting and fishing, the deceased is shown in a boat or on the shore around marshlands, in the act of using a throwing stick to strike and stun birds for capture. People are also depicted trapping birds in nets, stringing nets to catch fish, stampeding game animals into nets, harpooning fish, and throwing spears and shooting arrows at wild animals. One unique scene in the tomb of Eighteenth Dynasty architect Ineni shows a hyena being hunted by dogs; dogs appear as hunting companions in other scenes as well. **See also** animals; birds; food; Ineni.

Hyksos

The Hyksos were a people from somewhere east of Egypt, probably Palestine or Syria, who took over Egypt's eastern Delta during the Second Intermediate Period and established two dynasties of kings, the Fifteenth, or "Great Hyksos," Dynasty covering most of their territory and the Sixteenth, or "Minor Hyksos," Dynasty controlling the remainder. Both coincided with the Seventeenth Dynasty of Egypt's native rulers in Thebes.

The ancient Egyptians considered the Hyksos to be a group of Asiatics, which was the name they used in reference to people from lands to the east. The name Hyksos, meaning "rulers of foreign lands," was coined by third-century-B.C. Greco-Roman historian Manetho, who derived it from two ancient Egyptian words originally applied to Bedouin tribal chiefs who gradually moved into Egypt during the Middle Kingdom.

Manetho made it sound as though the Hyksos stormed into Egypt suddenly and unexpectedly to take the Delta. In actuality, the Hyksos had lived in Egypt for years before establishing their own kingship; they had settled in the country gradually and worked and lived as Egyptians. Consequently their rule was not dramatically different from the rules of the Theban kings they rivaled, with Egyptian art, culture, and religion all being respected. In fact, there is some evidence that the Hyksos worshiped ancient Egyptian gods, especially Seth (probably because his cult center had long been established in the city they took as their capital, Avaris).

Nonetheless, the Theban kings were determined to drive the Hyksos from Egypt. Three Theban kings in particular—Tao II, Kamose, and Ahmose I—engaged in a series of military campaigns during the Second Intermediate Period to expel the Hyksos. Tao II and Kamose were both killed during such battles. Eventually, Ahmose I took the Hyksos capital of Avaris after a long siege and the Hyksos fled to Palestine, thereby ending their control of Egypt. Afterward, the Egyptians built up their military hoping to prevent a foreign occupation from happening again. **See also** Ahmose I; Asiatics; Kamose; Second Intermediate Period; Tao II.

hymns

Hymns were a part of religious ceremonies and rituals and public events to honor and praise deities and/or kings, and the texts of these hymns have been found on temple and tomb walls, on stelae, and in papyri. Some of these texts make reference to the temple musician, so most Egyptologists assume that the hymns were set to music and sung, although no written ancient Egyptian musical scores have ever been found. The most common hymns were in praise of the god Osiris, but other gods had hymns dedicated to them as well. For example, the *Litany of the Sun,* a hymn dedicated to the solar deity Re, was inscribed on many Nineteenth and Twentieth Dynasty tombs. Hymns were also sometimes dedicated to kings. For example, six hymns dedicated to Twelfth Dynasty king Senwosret II were discovered at Kahun, a town near the location of the king's pyramid complex. Written on a forty-five-inch-wide sheet of papyrus, the hymns were probably sung during at least one of the king's visits to the pyramid building site. **See also** Lahun and Kahun; music; Osiris; Senwosret II.

Ibi (ca. 2320–ca. 2220 B.C.)

The son of a powerful Sixth Dynasty vizier named Djau, Ibi was a prominent figure during the reigns of Pepy I, Merenre I, and Pepy II. He held various administrative positions, including governor of the south (a position that later became known as the viceroy of Nubia), and gained control of the Cerastes Mountain nome by marrying a member of its ruling family. Ibi was also the nephew of Queens Ankhnesmery-Re I and Ankhnesmery-Re II and the cousin of Pepy II. Although his base of power was in the city of Hierakonpolis, his family was from Thinis and he built his tomb near Asyut, at Deir el-Gebrawi. An inscription in this tomb curses anyone who might disturb it; nonetheless, it was violated by tomb robbers. **See also** Ankhnesmery-Re I; Ankhnesmery-Re II; Asyut; Merenre I; Nubia; Pepy I; Pepy II.

Ihy (Ni-Tawi-Izezi) (dates unknown)

Ihy was an official during the reign of Fifth Dynasty king Unas and held three different titles: instructor of gardeners, overseer of gardeners, and inspector of gardeners of the (king's) great house. These titles appear to have been merely honorary since there is no evidence that he actually had any knowledge of gardening or any duties related to gardening. In fact, inscriptions at his tomb, which has been located at Saqqara, indicate that Ihy was the king's vizier.

Interestingly, Ihy's tomb was discovered in the 1920s but at that time was thought to have been built for Princess Idut, a daughter of King Teti, who died as a girl in approximately 2300 B.C. But in 2002, archaeologists noted that some of the reliefs in the tomb had been chiseled over older ones, with the princess's image replacing that of an unidentified man. These researchers then studied ancient writings and determined that Ihy was the original owner of the tomb, so they concluded the defaced images must have been his. Some Egyptologists now surmise that Ihy opposed Teti's succession to the throne after Unas died and was therefore punished by having his tomb taken from him. Others suggest that Ihy was involved in a subsequent plot to assassinate the king since there is evidence that several members of Teti's royal court successfully conspired to kill him. **See also** Saqqara; Teti; Unas.

Ikhernofret (Ikernofert) (?–ca. 1855 B.C.)

Egyptologists know about the life of Twelfth Dynasty government official Ikhernofret from a mortuary stela that he left at Abydos, where as chief artisan he was responsible for restoring temple complexes. He also oversaw new construction on temples and monuments, constructed a portable shrine dedicated to Osiris, and supervised mining operations to obtain building materials, all during the reign of King Senwosret III. The king placed Ikhernofret in charge of several important religious events, including festivals dedicated to the gods Osiris and Wepwawet and a series of plays dedicated to various gods. In addition, Ikhernofret stood in for the king in certain ceremonies requiring Senwosret III to pose as the god Horus, although it is unclear why. At some point during his career, Ikhernofret also served as a nome treasurer. In his writing, he claimed that he was raised in the royal palace, but his connection to the royal family is unclear. **See also** Abydos; Horus; Osiris; Senwosret III; Wepwawet.

Imhotep (?–ca. 2648 B.C.)

Imhotep was a Third Dynasty vizier and architect who served King Djoser. As such, he was responsible for the design and construction of the first stone pyramid, the Step Pyramid, which was also part of the first complex of monumental buildings in the world made entirely of stones. Reputed to be a master carpenter and sculptor (and by some accounts a priest as well), Imhotep was probably the son of Kanofer, who himself had worked at the royal court as the royal superintendent of works either for Djoser or his predecessor, Sanakhte. It is unclear where Imhotep's family originated, although it was most likely in Upper Egypt. Also unknown is the location of Imhotep's tomb, and thus any inscriptions that might have shed further information on this important individual's life. However, Egyptologists do know that Imhotep was deified as a god of wisdom and medicine approximately two hundred years after his death. **See also** architecture; deification of mortals; Djoser; pyramids.

Inaros (?–ca. 454 B.C.)

A prince of the Twenty-sixth Dynasty, Inaros declared himself king of Egypt during a time of Persian occupation sometime after his father, King Psamtik III, was killed by the invaders. However, he probably controlled only a part of northern Egypt near his capital at Heliopolis. Eventually, Inaros amassed an army of Egyptian rebels and killed Prince Achaemenes, the son of the Persian king Xerxes, in a battle at Papremis. He then gained the support of another Egyptian prince, Amyrtaeus, and his forces; although Amyrtaeus would later become king of Egypt himself, Inaros was no match for the Persians, who captured, imprisoned, and killed him in 454 B.C. After his death, Inaros became the hero in a number of tales that historians collectively call the Pedubastis Cycle. **See also** Persia and Persian Periods; Psamtik III.

incense

Called *senetier* in ancient Egyptian, incense was a part of religious rituals, ceremonies, and celebrations. Temple priests often burned incense to purify places where they were going to conduct rituals. Incense was also offered to the cult statues of deities or to living or dead kings or other dignitaries as a way to honor them. Embalmers burned incense both as a part of rituals connected to mummification and to cover the smell of the body being mummified.

The most common types of incense were myrrh and frankincense, both of which were fragrant resins from trees. The Egyptians initially acquired myrrh from a small country known as Punt, which was probably located on the coast of the Red Sea in modern-day Ethiopia, and eventually planted their own myrrh trees in temple gardens to ensure an ample supply of incense. It is unclear whether they did the same with frankincense, which grew naturally elsewhere in northern Africa and the Arabian Peninsula and was apparently acquired through trade with Punt and Nubia. **See also** mummification; Nubia; Punt; trade.

Ineni (ca. 1510–ca. 1470 B.C.)

Ineni was one of the most prominent architects of the New Kingdom, supervising building projects for Eighteenth Dynasty king Amenhotep I and four of his successors (Tuthmosis I, II, III, and Hatshepsut). It is therefore likely that Ineni built the Great Hall at Karnak for King Tuthmosis I and the king's tomb in the Valley of the Kings—the first of many tombs to be located there. Ineni also built a wall around an existing shrine dedicated to the god Amun at Thebes, adding additional features to the shrine as well. For his work he was honored many times during his lifetime, and in addition to his architectural duties he was given the prestigious honorific title of Steward of the Granaries of Amun during the reigns of Amenhotep I and Tuthmosis I, II, and III. The walls of Ineni's tomb at Qurna within the Theban necropolis tell of his honors. Scenes in the tomb also show that he designed numerous gardens as well as buildings. The walls have pictures of his trees and gardens, including a scene of him in his own orchard receiving offerings from his servants. There is also an illustrated list of the hundreds of fruit and shade trees that Ineni planted. **See also** Amenhotep I; Hatshepsut; Karnak; Tuthmosis I; Tuthmosis II; Tuthmosis III.

inscriptions

The most common ancient Egyptian inscriptions were names engraved on objects to identify their owners. Numerous tomb goods, including coffins, furniture, amulets, and figurines, have such inscriptions, as do household shrines and statues. Longer passages might also be inscribed on the interior and/or exterior walls of pyramids, tombs, and temples. These include magical and/or religious texts, autobiographies composed by tomb owners, and lists of kings. For example, at Aswan, autobiographical inscriptions in the rock-cut tomb of Harkhuf, Sixth Dynasty governor of Elephantine, tell of his acquiring a pygmy for a young King Pepy II while on a trade expedition. Inscriptions of a religious and magical nature have been found in Fifth and Sixth Dynasty pyramids. Known collectively as the Pyramid Texts, they consist of spells, incantations, and prayers that were probably recited during mortuary rituals, as well as myths, information, and instructions intended to help the spirit of the deceased make the transition to the Afterlife. **See also** amulets; Coffin Texts; graffiti; Harkhuf; magic; Pyramid Texts; writing, forms of.

Intef (dates unknown)

Beginning about 1450 B.C., Intef served as the official herald for the Eighteenth Dynasty king Amenhotep III. He held the titles of minister of communications, master of ceremonies, and chief of protocol, among others. He also supervised several expeditions for the king, overseeing the transport of natural resources such as building stones from desert regions beyond the eastern banks of the Nile to various locations. Egyptologists believe that Intef's most important role, though, was as the king's connection to his people, passing information both to and from the king. In other words, Intef told Amenhotep III what his subjects were saying about him and told the king's subjects what their ruler wanted them to do. There is also evidence that Intef acted as a priest for a temple devoted to the god Min. Intef's tomb is located at Thebes. **See also** Amenhotep III; Thebes.

Intef I, II, and III (Inyotef I, II, and III) (?–ca. 2117 B.C., ?–ca. 2069 B.C., ?–ca. 2060 B.C.)

During the Tenth and Eleventh Dynasties, three Theban kings with the name Intef (or Inyotef) ruled in succession. They were apparently from a family of nomarchs, or local governors, and used their power to usurp the throne from the reigning line of kings in Heracleopolis. The founder of their dynasty, Intef I, united several nomes in the south to fight against the Heracleopolitan kings of the north, and Intef II (probably his younger brother) continued this fight. Intef I's control never went much farther north than Thebes, but Intef II pushed his border to include the nomes of Abydos and then Antaeopolis, moving closer and closer to Heracleopolis. Intef III (the son of Intef II) pushed this border still farther north, nearly to Asyut.

In spite of the ongoing rebellion, there was apparently some friendly contact between the Heracleopolitan kings and the Intefs during this time; records indicate that Intef II traded with the Heracleopolitan Tenth Dynasty king, Khety III. During the reign of Intef III, the Heracleopolis kings tried to regain some of their lands, but the Thebans held their ground. Intef III's son Montuhotep II finally took control of all of the country and reunited Upper and Lower Egypt.

The tombs of Intef I, II, and III are all in Dra Abu el-Naga, near Thebes. Although they have been stripped of ornamentation, they were once quite ornate, with numerous reliefs, stelae, and other features. All three tombs also share the same style, known as *saff* (Arabic for "row") because they feature rows of doorways. **See also** Heracleopolis; Khety III; Thebes.

Intef VII (Inyotef VII; Nebkheperre) (ca. 1650– ca. 1550 B.C.)

Intef VII (also known as Inyotef VII or Nebkheperre) was a king of the Seventeenth Theban Dynasty who reigned during a time when foreign invaders called Hyksos had established a rival dynasty in the eastern Delta. Attempting to oust the Hyksos, Intef VII fought in many military campaigns, leaving behind information about his exploits in temple inscriptions at Abydos, Thebes, Coptos, and elsewhere. Archaeologists have also found one of his edicts, now called the Coptos Decree, ordering the punishment of a thief named Teti, who had stolen goods from the temple.

Intef VII's tomb has never been found, though ancient records indicate that it was at Thebes. However, archaeologists do have a scribe's copy of mortuary texts from the tomb's walls, including a text called the Song of the Harper. This text is unusual in that it questions whether there really is an Afterlife. **See also** Coptos; Hyksos.

Ipy (Ipuy) (ca. 1279– ca. 1213 B.C.)

Ipy was a sculptor of the Nineteenth Dynasty during the reign of Ramses II. The walls of his tomb, which is located at Deir el-Medina (near Thebes), feature numerous scenes taken from Ipy's daily life and provide a glimpse into the personal activities of an artisan. Among the scenes are depictions of Ipy gardening, making furniture, and traveling by boat across a garden pool. **See also** Deir el-Medina; Ramses II.

iron

There is evidence that in predynastic times the ancient Egyptians in the Eastern Desert and the Sinai fashioned iron ores into amulets. Otherwise, ancient Egyptian archaeological sites have yielded few artifacts made with iron, and those that have been found date from after the New Kingdom, when Greek and Roman metalworking techniques had been widely adopted. Egyptologists are uncertain as to why ironworking developed so late in Egypt, especially since most other civilizations in the region—particularly the Hittites—had already been using iron for some time. **See also** mining and metalworking.

irrigation

Because water was vital for crops and Nile River silt enhanced soil fertility, the Egyptians created an irrigation system to redirect water from the Nile, especially during the annual flooding. In the Nile Delta area known as the Faiyum, beginning at least as early as the Old Kingdom, the Egyptians dug ditches and canals anywhere from one inch to two feet deep and created dikes to channel water from a Nile tributary, the Bahr Yusef, to new locations. During the Twelfth Dynasty, Amenemhet II ordered that this system of artificial waterways be expanded and that more creative means be used to manipulate the supply of water. Consequently, various gully reservoirs were cut into the land to store water, and reed mats and wooden slats were placed in sluices and raised or lowered to control the distribution of water from these reservoirs. In addition, earth dikes were constructed to compartmentalize the fields so that water could be directed to particular areas depending on the need of the crops being grown there. Using natural depressions in the land, the Egyptians structured many of these compartments so that they formed a series of basins, with each one slightly lower than the next so that water would move from one field to another. The Egyptians also built a retaining wall nearly thirty miles long to contain a body of water, now called Lake Moeris, that would double in size during the annual inundation. All of the digging for these projects was done by hand, and baskets were used to transport soil. As a result of their efforts, the Egyptians were able to reclaim nearly thirty thousand acres of farmland that was otherwise either too wet or too dry for crops.

During the annual flooding, or inundation, of the Nile River, armies of workers redirected floodwaters into channels leading to various fields and reservoirs. This enormous effort ensured that the crops would be properly irrigated even during the period each year when the floodwaters had greatly receded. From the Second Intermediate Period on, areas not reached by these redirected floodwaters might be watered with a device called a *shaduf*. Introduced by Hittite invaders, a *shaduf* consisted of a pole with a bucket on one end and a counterweight on the other. The pole was typically mounted on a wooden post and the bucket dipped down to draw water from a river or other source. The pole could then be swung around and the bucket emptied into a canal or ditch a pole's reach away.

Anyone whose land was moistened by the floodwaters worked a *shaduf* or used some other means to direct water to his crops. However, he also had to contribute some amount of labor to maintaining the irrigation system for the entire Faiyum. Throughout the region, people coordinated their efforts, which were overseen by local government officials who strictly regulated the use of irrigation water to ensure that there would be enough to last throughout the growing season. **See also** agriculture; Faiyum.

Isis

Isis was the name the Greeks assigned to a goddess variously called Eset (the "Seat"), Weret-Hekau ("Great of Magic"), and Mut-Netjer ("Mother of the Gods") by the ancient Egyptians. Isis was featured in the Creation mythology of Heliopolis as the daughter of the deities Geb and Nut; the sister of the deities Osiris, Seth, and Nephthys; the wife of Osiris; and the mother of Horus. Mythology about Isis and depictions of her varied depending on location. In Abydos she was worshiped as part of a triad with husband Osiris and son Horus. In Memphis she was said to have given birth to the sacred Apis bull and therefore was depicted as a cow. More commonly, however, the an-

The goddess Isis was associated with magic, agriculture, fertility, marriage, and motherhood.

cient Egyptians depicted Isis as a woman perhaps with a cow's horns, which was similar to depictions of the mother goddess Hathor.

Because in most myths Isis was the mother of Horus, whom the living king of Egypt was said to personify, she was sometimes referred to as the throne of Egypt. In fact, her name in hieroglyphics is a drawing of a throne. Isis was also associated with agriculture, healing and medicine, and marriage. At her cult center on the island of Philae (within the Nile River at Aswan) and at many other sites, she was worshiped as a goddess of magic, and many of the myths featuring Isis show her in this capacity. In particular, she often transforms herself in some way to accomplish good. For example, in one myth she turns herself into a woman whose son has been cheated out of his inheritance in order to trick Seth, who tried to cheat Horus out of his inheritance, into saying such behavior is wrong.

One of the most important Isis myths concerns the death of Osiris at the hands of his brother, Seth. In this myth, Seth casts the dead king's coffin into the Nile River, where it is carried to a foreign land. Isis goes there in search of her husband's body so that she can give it proper funerary rites, knowing that without these Osiris will not be reborn in the Afterlife. Although she is successful in bringing the body back to Egypt, when she leaves it unattended before performing its rites, Seth discovers it and hacks it into pieces, which he then scatters across the land. Nonetheless, Isis finds the pieces and fulfills her obligation to the dead, thereby enabling Osiris to become the king of the celestial realm.

Isis shows her dedication to kingship and honor again in another myth when she learns the true name of Re, a solar deity associated with kingship. With her magic skills, Isis could easily use this knowledge to destroy the god, but instead she keeps it to herself. In another version of this myth, however, she uses the secret name to increase her own magical power.

During the Late and Greco-Roman Periods, the magical aspects of Isis were downplayed and her role as a mother figure emphasized. In this capacity, she was worshiped not only in Egypt but also in Greece, Syria, Palestine, and eventually the Roman Empire, and some early Christians equated her with the Virgin Mary. **See also** Creation myths; Geb; Greco-Roman Period; Hathor; Horus; Late Period; Nephthys; Nut; Osiris; Re; Seth.

Isis, Temple of

There were several temples in ancient Egypt dedicated to the worship of the goddess Isis, but perhaps the most significant archaeologically is the Temple of Isis on the island of Philae (within the Nile River near the First Cataract). Archaeologists believe that this temple was one of the most beautiful complexes of buildings in ancient Egypt, further enhanced by its island setting. The building complex includes a great court with thirty-two columns on one side (thirty-one of which remain standing) and six on the other (archaeologists believe that another ten colums were originally planned for this side but not completed). Beyond the great court is a forecourt with reliefs featuring King Ptolemy XII, who was responsible for numerous building projects on Philae and elsewhere throughout Egypt. Beside the forecourt is a Birth House with reliefs showing the birth of Horus as well as other scenes from Horus-related myths. Across from the Birth House is a building that archaeologists believe might have been dedicated to medical and/or scientific activities. Other areas of the temple complex have rooms that apparently served as libraries, with wall niches to hold papyri. There is also a room that seems to have been related to the manufacture of an aromatic substance, Kyphi, used for purification rituals. Its recipe, including wine and herbs, was inscribed on the wall.

The main building of the complex, which archaeologists call the temple proper, has a sanctuary and inner chambers, both containing wall scenes showing King Ptolemy XII honoring the goddess Isis. On the roof of the building, which is reached via a staircase outside the sanctuary, are additional chambers with scenes featuring the death and rebirth of Osiris. Such scenes were common on Ptolemaic temple rooftops.

At the front of the temple are pylons with reliefs depicting various subjects, but most of these have been seriously and intentionally damaged. Who damaged these works is uncertain, but the vandalism appears highly selective: The only surviving reliefs are those with images such as the sunrise that symbolize the future; all reliefs related to the past or the present at the time have been defaced. Such selectivity means that whoever attacked the reliefs must have known how to read Egyptian hieroglyphs and been familiar with Egyptian religious symbolism, making it unlikely that early Christians or invading Muslims, who probably would not have had such knowledge, damaged the reliefs. The prevailing theory is that Temple of Isis priests did the damage just before early Christians forced them off the island as a way of expressing their faith that their religion would some day be reborn.

In approximately A.D. 540, the Roman emperor Justinian permanently closed all temples on the island. It appears, however, that Philae was already less important by this time. No new hieroglyphs had been inscribed on monuments on the island since A.D. 394, and all of the priests of Isis were gone by 495. **See also** Isis; Philae.

J

jewelry

The most common types of jewelry in ancient Egypt were bracelets, anklets, necklaces, rings, and belts, as well as head and chest pieces. Egyptians did not wear earrings until the New Kingdom, when the first ones were imported from Asia. Beginning in the Predynastic Period and continuing throughout Egypt's history, jewelry might be given as an award to worthy individuals or given as an offering to the gods or to the deceased in religious rituals.

Gold was the most popular material for jewelry among the upper classes, while wood, plant fibers, and other easily available materials were used by the poor.

This gold ring is inscribed with the cartouche of Tutankhamun.

Gold jewelry was commonly decorated with precious and semiprecious stones often selected on the basis of their color, since different colors had different symbolic meanings. In addition, many items of jewelry had religious symbols etched on them. For example, images of the scarab beetle (a symbol of the sun and of rebirth), the cobra (a symbol of kingship), and the solar disk (a symbol of the sun god) all appear among the more than 150 pieces of jewelry found in the tomb of King Tutankhamun.

In addition to being decorative, jewelry was worn by the living to indicate status; the more ornate the piece of jewelry, the wealthier and more powerful the person wearing it. Not surprisingly, then, the most lavish jewelry has been found in the tombs of kings and their family members. Among the most important finds in this regard were a series of Twelfth Dynasty tombs of princesses. One was that of Princess Sithathoriunet, a daughter of King Senwosret II, whose tomb contained five large boxes of jewelry as well as cosmetics and other personal items. Another of the king's daughters, Princess Sathathor, had a great deal of ornate jewelry as well, including a belt with two shell halves that acted as a buckle when fit together. **See also** amulets; scarab; symbols.

Joppa, The Capture of

The Capture of Joppa is a New Kingdom text within the Harris Papyrus concerning the taking of the walled Palestinian city of Joppa by Egyptian forces during a military campaign of King Tuthmosis III. In the story, an Egyptian general named Djehuty places his men in large baskets and then delivers them to the people of Joppa as a gift. Assuming the baskets hold food, the men of Joppa carry them inside their walls. Once inside, Egyptian soldiers jump out and kill the Joppan men. Because of its similarity to the Greek story of the Trojan horse, as well as to an ancient Persian story later incorporated into *Tales of the Arabian Nights,* some Egyptologists believe that *The Capture of Joppa* is a myth rather than a factual account. However, because the story is reported as fact in the tomb of General Djehuty in Thebes, other Egyptologists believe that it reflects a real historical event. **See also** papyrus.

ka

According to ancient Egyptian beliefs regarding the Afterlife, the *ka* is one of three elements or forms of the spirit that survive after death, along with the *ba* and the *akh*. Scholars disagree on how the word *ka* should be translated and on this element's nature in the Afterlife. Generally, however, they define the *ka* as the spirit, the conscience, and the essence of what animates a human being.

The ancient Egyptians believed that the *ka* remained linked with the physical body after death and required nourishment if it was to survive. For this reason, offerings of food and water were left at the tomb daily for the *ka*'s benefit. Family members might bring these offerings, but usually they paid a priest, called a *ka* priest, to oversee the tomb. The *ka* priest not only set the food out for the *ka* but also performed complicated rituals to make the food nourishing for the *ka*. In fact, according to an Old Kingdom list found on a temple wall, the priests performed 114 separate rituals during ceremonies to make food edible for the *ka*.

In some eras, a false door—a stela carved to look like a door—was created on the exterior wall of a tomb or temple in the belief that the *ka* could come through the door to receive offerings placed on the other side. However, in general the *ka* did not leave the mummy, depending on it to be its vessel in the Afterlife. The *ka* depended not only on the mummy, but also on the *ba;* although the

ba had mobility, ancient Egyptians believed that if the *ba* stayed away from the *ka* too long, both would cease to exist. The traditional symbol of the *ka* was widespread arms, open as if to receive offerings. **See also** Afterlife; *akh; ba;* mummification; religion.

Kagemni (dates unknown)

Egyptologists disagree over the identity of Kagemni, who was the central figure in a work called *Instructions of Kagemni.* In this work, which is set in the Third Dynasty, the author offers advice to a young Kagemni who is poised to inherit his father's position as vizier. Consequently, some Egyptologists believe that Kagemni was a vizier under Third Dynasty king Huni and his successor, Snefru. Others believe that Kagemni was a vizier in an earlier reign, perhaps that of Third Dynasty king Khaba. However, there is no corroborating evidence of a Third Dynasty vizier named Kagemni, but at Saqqara there is a tomb of a Kagemni who was a court official under the late Fifth Dynasty king Unas and a vizier under Sixth Dynasty king Teti, around 2350 B.C. Therefore, many Egyptologists believe that this is the Kagemni mentioned in *Instructions of Kagemni* and that the text was written no earlier than the Sixth Dynasty and merely set in an earlier age as a literary device.

According to inscriptions in Kagemni's tomb, Kagemni was also a high priest and a judge, and Egyptologists have viewed the scenes in his tomb as representative of the lifestyle of people in these positions. Kagemni's tomb reliefs include depictions of him being carried in a sedan chair and watching five dancers performing what appears to be part ballet and part acrobatics. There are also several scenes of animals being force-fed, perhaps as a way to fatten them for slaughter. **See also** admonitions and instructions; Huni; Khaba; Snefru; Teti; Unas.

Kakai (Neferirkare) (?–ca. 2455 B.C.)

A king of the Fifth Dynasty, Kakai ascended to the throne after the death of his brother King Sahure. Kakai took part in several military campaigns, yet according to writings of the period, he was said to be a man who cared about his subjects' well-being. In one account, for example, Kakai arranged medical care for a man who became ill in his presence.

Kakai holds particular significance for archaeologists because he began the practice of a king using his birth name as well as his throne name in public inscriptions. Kakai's mortuary temple at Abusir has also provided archaeologists with several important papyri, including one that appears to be the oldest existing example of a papyrus with hieroglyphs on it. This document offers details about temple finances, employees, and work duties, providing insights into temple management. The full collection of papyri, commonly called the Abusir Papyri Cache, covers the reigns of Djedkare to Pepy II. **See also** Abusir; papyrus; Pepy II; Sahure.

Kamose (?–ca. 1570 B.C.)

The son of Seventeenth Theban Dynasty king Tao II and Queen Ahhotep, King Kamose took up his family's crusade against the invading Hyksos upon the death of his father, who had been killed in battle. Upon assuming the throne, Kamose launched his own military expedition to fight the Hyksos, employing a Nubian military force called the Medjay to supplement his forces. Kamose reigned less than three years before he was killed in a battle just as he was about to take the Hyksos capital city of Avaris in the eastern Delta, and he was succeeded by his brother, Ahmose I. At Karnak, there are two stelae relating the details of Kamose's military campaigns. **See also** Ahhotep I; Ahmose I; Tao II.

Karnak (el-Karnak)

Called Ipet-isut (the "Best of Places") in ancient Egyptian, Karnak was a 250-acre region within Thebes containing numerous structures related to the worship of the god Amun. Among these structures were several temples and chapels representing more than two thousand years of continued construction, restoration, and remodeling at the site, as well as many statues, columns, and obelisks. In fact, beginning in the Middle Kingdom, the date of the earliest structures at the site, nearly every ancient Egyptian king added something to Karnak.

Mud-brick walls once divided Karnak into three temple precincts, one in the center of town, one in the north, and one in the south. The central precinct held the Temple of Amun, several smaller temples, and a sacred lake. In fact, all three precincts had sacred lakes, which were primarily used for purification ceremonies in which people were ritually bathed in or anointed by the waters. The northern precinct also had a large temple dedicated to the god Mont, a solar deity worshiped in the Theban area since the Predynastic Period. The southern precinct held a large temple dedicated to the goddess Mut, considered Amun's wife, as well as some smaller temples dedicated to other gods. The Temple of Mut was connected to the Temple of Amun by an avenue of sphinxes, statues of lions with human heads that probably symbolized the sun god. Sphinxes also lined an avenue linking the Temple of Amun at Karnak with a similar temple at nearby Luxor. In addition, a canal connected the Temple of Amun and the Temple of Mont with the Nile River. These waterways and avenues were used for various festival processions in which a cult statue of Amun was carried from one temple to another. **See also** Amun; Luxor; Mut; priests; Sphinx, Great.

Kenamon (Kenamun; Quenamun) (ca. 1427– ca. 1400 B.C.)

Kenamon, the son of a royal nursemaid, held several important positions during the Eighteenth Dynasty reign of Amenhotep II, serving as both a government official and a temple priest. He was in charge of purifying statues of the gods and caring for the king's northern estates. A stela near his tomb in Thebes depicts Kenamon making offerings to two deified kings, Amenhotep I and Senwosret I. **See also** Amenhotep II; Senwosret I.

Kewab (Kawab) (?–2566 B.C.)

A prince of the Fourth Dynasty, Kewab was supposed to succeed his father, King Khufu, to the throne but died before this could happen. Some Egyptologists think that the prince was murdered by the person who succeeded in his place, his brother Djedefre. Kewab's widow, Queen Hetepheres II, married Djedefre shortly after her husband's death. Before this, however, she and Kewab produced a child, a girl who became Queen Meresankh III, the wife of King Khafre. Kewab's tomb is located beside the Great Pyramid of Giza. **See also** Djedefre; Giza; Khafre; Khufu; Meresankh III.

Khaba (dates unknown)

Khaba may have reigned as king during the Third Dynasty, but so little evidence of his rule exists that some Egyptologists question whether he was ever king, although he is believed to have been most active from ca. 2650 B.C. to ca. 2637 B.C. His name is mentioned only on a couple of stone bowls and in an inscription found within the tomb of another king, Sahure. Even if they accept that Khaba was a king, Egyptologists disagree over the timing of his reign, sometimes placing it right before King Huni and sometimes right before King Djoser. There are also disagreements over whether Khaba was the builder of the Layer Pyramid located just south of Giza at Zawiyet el-Aryan. **See also** Djoser; Giza; Huni; Sahure.

Khabausoker (dates unknown)

Thought by Egyptologists to have been most active around 2630 B.C., Khabausoker was a high priest of the Third Dynasty who apparently served three gods during his lifetime: Anubis, Ptah, and Seth. He also had some connection to Seshat, a goddess of architecture, which made him responsible for directing the king's carpenters. Eventually, he oversaw other professionals as well, such as craftsmen, brewers, and dancers. Some Egyptologists further believe that Khabausoker helped establish many of the royal religious rituals that were subsequently practiced for most of ancient Egypt's history. Khabausoker and his wife Hathorneferhetepes were entombed at Saqqara in a structure that archaeologists have deemed especially significant because it blends elements of the traditional Third Dynasty mastaba style with new elements that would come to the fore in later dynasties. **See also** Anubis; mastaba tomb; Ptah; Seth.

Khaemwaset (Khaemweset) (dates unknown)

A Nineteenth Dynasty prince apparently popular among his peers, Khaemwaset was the son of King Ramses II by one of his chief queens, Istnofret. Khaemwaset is thought to have been most active around 1270 B.C. As the crown prince, Khaemwaset served as high priest of Ptah in Memphis and was also governor of Memphis. In addition, he oversaw the restoration of the Temple of Ptah as well as various pyramids and tombs, including those of Kings Shepseskhaf, Sahure, Neuserre, and Unas. He also supported a study of the history of Saqqara, and he instituted a project to catalog all of the manuscripts in palace and temple libraries. Khaemwaset was so committed to his research that Egyptologists have dubbed him the Egyptologist Prince, although he was said to be a magician as well as a scholar. There is some evidence that he had military experience too, campaigning in Nubia on behalf of his father. Khaemwaset died in the fifty-fifth year of King Ramses II's reign. **See also** Neuserre; Nubia; Ramses II; Sahure; Shepseskhaf; Unas.

Khafre (Khephren; Chephren; Ra'Kha'ef) (ca. 2580–ca. 2532 B.C.)

Fourth Dynasty king Khafre reigned for approximately twenty-four years, during which he built the Second Pyramid at Giza and possibly the Great Sphinx there as well. However, his ascension to the throne was marked by conflict. Khafre's father, King Khufu, had designated another of his sons, Prince Kewab, as his heir. However, before the crown prince could assume the throne, he died, leaving the succession to fall to Khafre. However, another prince, Djedefre, married Kewab's widow and through her claimed the right to rule after King Khufu died. Khafre therefore had to wait until Djedefre died, eight years later, to become king.

During his reign, Khafre had three powerful princes as his closest advisers: Minkhaf, Ankhaf, and Neferma'at. (Some Egyptologists think that these men might

have been Khafre's brothers, since they appear to have had great influence over him.) Khafre had several wives; a principal wife was Queen Khamernebty I, but she apparently provided him with no male heir. Another principal wife, Meresankh III, had Prince Nebmakhet by him, and two of his lesser wives each gave him a son. Yet another wife, Queen Persenti, gave him two sons—Nekaure and Menkaure. Menkaure became his successor. **See also** Djedefre; Kewab; Menkaure.

Kharga Oasis

Because it was quite large, the Kharga Oasis, about one hundred miles east of Luxor, was an important agricultural area. During the New Kingdom, its inhabitants paid taxes to Egypt's kings in the form of dates, grapes, wine, and various minerals. In fact, heavy taxes were probably one of the reasons why the people of the oasis tried—unsuccessfully— to free themselves of Egyptian control during the Twenty-second Dynasty reign of King Sheshonq I. During the reign of King Darius I, when the Persians controlled Egypt, two temples dedicated to the god Amun-Re were built in the area, one at Hibis and the other at Qasr el-Ghueida. Qasr el-Ghueida was also the site of a sandstone temple, the Fortress of the Beautiful Garden, dedicated to the gods Amun, Mut, and Khons. Built during the Roman Period, it was one of a series of temples that were constructed in those times like fortresses. Genuine fortresses were also constructed during this period, along with numerous wells and roads, throughout the oasis. **See also** oases.

Khasekhemwy (Khasekhem) (dates unknown)

The last king of the Second Dynasty, Khasekhemwy apparently quelled rebellions to create the first truly unified Upper and Lower Egypt, as opposed to a country unified in name only. For this reason, according to some Egyptologists, the king changed his name from Khasekhem to Khasekhemwy, which means "In Him the Two Powers Are at Peace." Other Egyptologists dispute this version of events, arguing that Khasekhem and Khasekhemwy were two different kings, neither of whom were responsible for Egypt's unity.

Egyptologists disagree on many other aspects of Khasekhemwy's reign as well. Much of Khasekhemwy's life was the subject of ancient Egyptian legend, and, as a result, researchers have difficulty separating fact from fiction. The majority opinion, however, is that Khasekhemwy reigned for approximately thirty years, during which he had to fight some major battles before he could achieve a long-lasting peace. Inscriptions on a victory statue of the king record that the king's armies killed more than forty-seven thousand enemies from the north after they attacked the southern city of Hierakonpolis, the king's capital; the king's carved figure shows him wearing the White Crown of Upper Egypt.

Khasekhemwy built a number of monuments, including a temple at Hierakonpolis, a mortuary complex at Abydos, and possibly a mortuary complex at Saqqara as well. Khasekhemwy's trapezoid-shaped tomb at Abydos was huge; its two nonparallel sides were 230 feet in length. Near the Abydos complex, twelve boats were buried just beneath the sand for use by the king in the Afterlife.

When he died, Khasekhemwy was probably succeeded by Sanakhte, who might have been his son-in-law, who in turn was followed by Djoser Netjerykhet, the son of Khasekhemwy's daughter Nema'athap. It is also probable that Nema'athap was Khasekhemwy's wife and that Djoser was therefore his son, although Egyptologists disagree on this point, with some believing that Sanakhte and Djoser were brothers. A few Egyptologists further suggest that Nema'athap was not Khasekhemwy's daughter but the daughter of a king from the northern enemies who once attacked Hierakonpolis, and she married Khasekhemwy as part of a peace agreement. **See also** Abydos; Djoser; Hierakonpolis.

Khentkawes I (possibly also Reweddjedet) (ca. 2560–2490 B.C.)

Khentkawes I was the principal wife of the last king of the Fourth Dynasty, King Shepseskhaf, and the mother of two Fifth Dynasty kings, Sahure and Kakai. She was revered during and after their reigns as the ancestress of their dynasty.

Egyptologists disagree regarding Khentkawes I's parentage. Some say that she was the daughter of King Djedefre, others of King Menkaure, who was the father of Khentkawes I's husband, King Shepseskhaf. If Menkaure was Khentkawes I's father, then she would have been her husband's half-sister—a common practice among royalty in ancient Egypt. A further controversy is over whether after her husband's death, Khentkawes I married King Userkaf, the founder of the Fifth Dynasty. This seems likely, however, given the queen's designation as the Fifth Dynasty ancestress. Perhaps because of her honored position, Khentkawes I's mortuary complex at Giza is quite large for that of a queen. However, this structure—which was a combination of a pyramid and a sarcophagus-shaped tomb—was never finished. **See also** Djedefre; Menkaure; Sahure; Shepseskhaf.

Khety I (Akhtoy I) (dates unknown)

Khety I was a king of the Ninth Dynasty who ruled much of Upper Egypt at a time when a dynasty of Theban kings (the Eleventh Dynasty) established by Intef I controlled Lower Egypt and some Upper Egypt lands. Although his birth and death dates are unknown, he is thought to have been most active from ca. 2160 B.C. to ca. 2130 B.C. Khety I began his political career in the city of Heracleopolis as governor of the twentieth nome of Upper Egypt. When the stability of Egypt's Old Kingdom gave way to the chaos of the First Intermediate Period, Khety I took advantage of the confusion by declaring himself king and taking the throne name of Meryibre, thereby establishing a line of Heracleopolis kings that would last over one hundred years.

To solidify his claim to the throne, Khety I used military force gradually to bring together competing nomarchs, who had established their own independent states in the years following the Old Kingdom, and then subjugate them. Modern scholars do not know what became of Khety I in his final years. However, the third-century-B.C. Greco-Egyptian historian Manetho reported that a king named Achthoes, whom scholars believe might have been Khety I, went insane and was subsequently attacked and eaten by a crocodile. **See also** First Intermediate Period; nomes and nomarchs; Old Kingdom.

Khety II (Akhtoy II; Akhtoy II Nebkaure) (dates unknown)

Also called Akhtoy II Nebkaure, Khety II was a Ninth Dynasty king who left behind little evidence of his reign. On the basis of scant archaeological evidence, however, Egyptologists generally believe that he was the king from Heracleopolis featured in a popular story of the period called *The Tale of the Eloquent Peasant.* **See also** *Eloquent Peasant, The Tale of the.*

Khety III (Akhtoy III; Wahkare) (dates unknown)

Tenth Dynasty king Khety III was one of a series of rulers who tried to control Egypt from the city of Heracleopolis. Known as

the Heracleopolitan line, these kings had rivals in the city of Thebes, and the adversaries fought an ongoing war for the country's throne during Egypt's First Intermediate Period. Historians believe that this conflict began during Khety III's reign after some of the king's soldiers plundered some tombs in the cemeteries of Thinis near Thebes during an invasion of southern Egypt. This event is mentioned in a manuscript known as *Instructions for Merikare,* which purports to be Khety III's instructions on kingship to his son and heir, Merikare. Egyptologists disagree on whether Khety III actually wrote this material or whether it was written by someone else. In either case, *Instructions for Merikare* expresses Khety III's regret over the plundered Thinis tombs. In spite of his troubles with the Thebans, Khety III ruled for approximately fifty years, during which he extended his lands into the northeast by establishing colonies there. **See also** admonitions and instructions; First Intermediate Period; Heracleopolis; Merikare.

Khnum

According to beliefs initially held by ancient residents of Elephantine Island and subsequently by the Nubians as well, Khnum was a god of creation often depicted with a ram's head. His name means Molder, appropriate since he was thought to have created the world by molding various beings and realms on a potter's wheel. Specifically, Khnum was often depicted using Nile River mud to shape items such as a cosmic egg that contained the earth, all people, plants and animals, various gods (particularly Osiris), and the *ka* (one aspect of the spirit) of royal children. Khnum was sometimes shown in tomb art with his consorts, water goddesses Satis and Anukis. A goddess of hunters, Satis was often depicted pouring water on Nile mud to bring life, either on her own or assisting Khnum at his wheel. Anukis was a fertility goddess of the First

Cataract of the Nile River, a location believed to be linked via an underground stream to the celestial waters. **See also** *ka;* Nile River; Osiris.

Khnumhotep I (dates unknown)

A Twelfth Dynasty nomarch from a prominent Beni Hasan family, Khnumhotep ("The God Khnum Is Content") I held many titles during his lifetime. Because of his family's power, he became ruler (or great lord) of their nome, Oryx, in approximately 1985 B.C. and used his position to help Amnenemhet I achieve the throne. The king rewarded him by naming him the count of Menet-Khufu and then hereditary prince. Later, he was called seal-bearer and sole companion for the king. As the king's confidant, Khnumhotep I accompanied Amenemhet I on military campaigns and launched military expeditions to quell rebellions against Amenemhet I's rule.

Khnumhotep I had at least three children who further strengthened his family's position. His sons Nakht and Amenemhet became prominent officials serving the royal court, and his daughter Beket was the mother of Khnumhotep II, who became another important nomarch. **See also** Amenemhet I; Khnum; Khnumhotep II.

Khnumhotep II (dates unknown)

Khnumhotep II was a Twelfth Dynasty nomarch from a powerful family who furthered his family's fortunes by marrying into the family of a neighboring nomarch. Many nineteenth- and early-twentieth-century Egyptologists cited scenes on the walls of his tomb as proof that the biblical account of Abraham of Israel visiting Egypt is accurate, contending that these scenes show Khnumhotep II receiving gifts from Hebrews. Most modern scholars, however, do not share this view. **See also** nomes and nomarchs.

Khufu (Cheops) (?–ca. 2566 B.C.)

The son of King Snefru and Queen Hetepheres I, Fourth Dynasty king Khufu (Cheops) ruled for approximately twenty-three years. However, Egyptologists know little about his rule, except that he was the

Fourth Dynasty king Khufu's pyramid, also known as the Great Pyramid, was built around 2589 to 2566 B.C.

first king to identify himself with the god Re as well as Horus. Apparently, he launched military and mining expeditions to the Sinai to acquire building stones for his pyramid at Giza, now known as the Great Pyramid. According to an inscription left at the pyramid, it took nearly thirty years to build, at a cost of sixteen hundred silver talents, which scholars estimate would have been over $7 million today at the modern-day value of silver. However, given that silver was extremely rare in ancient Egypt, the actual value would have been far greater.

In 1954, near the south side of the pyramid, archaeologists found a 101-foot-long pit in which the king's wooden funerary boat had been sealed using forty-one large stones. Because the boat, at 141 feet, was too large to fit in its pit, the vessel had been divided into 650 sections, with a total of 1,224 pieces, but archaeologists have now restored it and placed it in a special museum, the Boat Museum at Giza. But despite the presence of a funerary boat, experts disagree on whether Khufu was ever actually entombed in his pyramid or even ever intended to be entombed there.

This is just one of several mysteries related to the pyramid. Among the other mysteries are questions concerning exactly how the pyramid was constructed, given the size and number of building stones involved. Egyptologists disagree on whether the king had access to a workforce large enough to build the structure, even over thirty years, using known construction techniques. Therefore, some theorize that unknown techniques were used. In addition, Egyptologists historically disagreed about whether all of the pyramid's chambers have been found, but in September 2002, using a remote-controlled camera, researchers discovered two sealed doors off impassable corridors. This suggests that much of the pyramid's interior is yet to be explored. Another mystery is why Khufu's name has been scratched off some monuments and records, an action typically taken when a ruler later fell out of favor. This is particularly strange in Khufu's case because a cult honoring the king was established after his death and remained viable for over one thousand years.

During his lifetime, Khufu produced many children, including Kewab, Khafre, and Djedefre. His principal wife was Queen Meritites, but he apparently had several others. **See also** Djedefre; Giza; Hetepheres I; Kewab; Khafre; Snefru.

king lists

King lists are ancient Egyptian writings that provide the names of kings who ruled within a selected period of time, sometimes but not necessarily in the order of their succession. Because many of these lists have cartouches with various kings' titles and the number of years of their reigns, they have enabled Egyptologists to roughly approximate when a king sat on the throne. However, the purpose of such lists in ancient times was not historical. Instead, they were an important part of certain rituals; the names of deceased kings were read off as a way to honor them and bring blessings upon Egypt. The five known king lists are as follows:

Palermo Stone. The earliest king list, the Palermo Stone was inscribed on both sides of a large freestanding temple stela, only a fragment of which remains today. Egyptologists believe that the intact stone would have provided a record of every king who ruled prior to the Fifth Dynasty, including some Predynastic Period ones, as well as a complete record of the events of their reign (such as expeditions of various kinds, military victories, and building projects).

Royal List of Karnak. Now in the Louvre Museum in Paris, France, the Royal List of Karnak originally appeared as a wall relief inscribed within the Temple of Amun complex at Karnak. The list originally provided the names of sixty-one or sixty-two kings from the First to the mid–Eighteenth Dynasty, ending with the reign of Tuthmosis III, but when it was discovered in A.D. 1825, only forty-eight of these names could still be read.

Royal List of Abydos. Found inscribed on a wall in the temple of Seti I at Abydos, this list originally provided the names of as many as eighty kings from the First Dynasty to the mid–Nineteenth Dynasty. Today, seventy-six names are still visible. The list also appears on a damaged papyrus known as the Abydos King List, which was found in the tomb of Seti I's son, Ramses II.

Saqqara List. Found inscribed in a tomb at Saqqara, this list originally had fifty-seven or fifty-eight names given in reverse order—that is, with the most recent ruler listed first.

Turin Canon. Now in the Egyptian Museum in Turin, Italy, this list was written in hieratic script on a papyrus that, over time, became seriously damaged. It once provided the names of every king from Egypt's first to Ramses II, in order and with the total number of years each one ruled. However, fewer than ninety names are legible today. **See also** Abydos; Ramses II.

kings

From at least the time that Egypt first became a unified country in approximately 3000 B.C. the country's kings were considered the center of every aspect of Egyptian society. They controlled not only institutions such as the bureaucracy, judiciary, and military but also religion. In fact, upon coronation, Egypt's kings were considered the earthly embodiment of a god (usually Horus or Re), bringing order out of chaos within Egypt just as the gods of creation did by bringing life to earth. (A prince did not become a living god until he went through the coronation ceremony to become king.) After death, kings were considered an aspect of a god (usually Osiris), and therefore deserving of worship. As a result, an official funerary cult was usually established in honor of a deceased king, with rituals routinely held at his cult center. However, a few kings, most notably Amenhotep I, were deified after death as unique gods rather than as aspects of an existing god; in this case, the scope and intensity of religious observances held in their honor were much greater.

While on the throne, kings were said to have the three qualities of the creator god: Sia, or divine wisdom; Hu, or divine speech; and Heka, or divine magic. Their primary function was to use these godly attributes to maintain Ma'at—roughly translated as Truth, Justice, Order, and Balance—in Egypt and therefore in the celestial realm. It was believed that any chaos on earth would be mirrored in the heavens, causing such disasters as droughts and famine; therefore it was important for the king to rule with a strong, wise, and balanced hand, and he was blamed for any evidence of the gods' displeasure.

Because kings were associated with the gods and their influence over all elements of earthly existence, the main symbols of the king's status were the crook and the flail, which were also symbols of life and death, respectively. Kings were often depicted holding these items as a way of showing that they had the power of life and death in their hands. Moreover, kings were considered the intermediary between gods and humankind, and as such they were deemed the highest-ranking priest of every temple in the land. In this role, they officiated at all major rituals, or at least oversaw the actions of the priests who performed such ceremonies in their stead. Rituals were considered vital to appeasing the gods and assuring the king's success, as well as the world's order and the land's fertility.

To attract the gods' favor, many kings built or restored existing temples to the gods and maintained or restored the mortuary complexes and monuments of deceased kings (who, after all, were considered aspects of gods). Living kings particularly honored gods from their hometowns, meaning that a local god might come to be worshiped throughout Egypt when a new king ascended the throne. Kings also built their own tombs, mortuary complexes, and monuments, although some rulers were much more active builders than others.

During the Old Kingdom, ancient Egyptians believed the king's tomb to be particularly important, because only those entombed near the king would accompany him to the Afterlife, and only if his tomb was properly prepared and his funerary rites properly conducted would the king be able to transform into his true godly form and bring others to the Afterlife. Therefore, people were willing to work hard to provide the king with a grand tomb or pyramid, the latter of which might have steps to help him ascend to the solar deity's realm.

Since proximity to the physical remains of the deceased king was considered vital to a person's ability to follow him to the Afterlife, powerful nobles typically built their tombs in the area of the king's, and the king might build and maintain tombs near his own for his relatives and others close to him. The number of people in a king's inner circle could be considerable, since he might have several wives (among them, in many cases, the king's sisters, half-sisters, and/or daughters), children, and advisers.

Since kings were thought to be able to enjoy their worldly goods in the Afterlife, their tombs were often filled with such items. These artifacts have given modern archaeologists an idea of the great wealth most kings commanded. Archaeologists suspect that the king's palaces were just as lavishly outfitted as their tombs. However, because these structures were not built to last for eternity, little evidence of them remains today.

The king amassed enormous wealth easily, because everything in Egypt was considered his property—not only all land and goods but people and animals as well. Therefore, he had the right to give or take whatever he wanted, from the land or from his people. In fact, he could even call on people to leave their homes and serve him elsewhere as builders, miners, laborers, or soldiers (although by the New Kingdom, the Egyptians had developed a professional military). However, few kings abused their rights, because an unpopular king had difficulty keeping his throne despite his perceived divinity. In fact, in ancient Egyptian mythology, a bad king (Seth) was portrayed as deserving destruction.

Because the king's continued power depended on the loyalty of his subjects, the king rewarded certain key individuals with grants of land and gifts of various goods. However, over time, this outflow of wealth strengthened the nobility, who gradually came to believe that they no longer needed the king to help them enter the Afterlife. Furthermore, as the Afterlife was increasingly thought to be accessible to all honorable men, the king's rule was increasingly challenged as various powerful nobles aspired to power themselves.

As the commander-in-chief of Egypt's military, however, many kings were skilled warriors, and they used their abilities to maintain Ma'at in their lands. They also led their own forces into battle in foreign lands, either to deal with threats of invasion or to acquire new lands whose natural resources they could exploit. In fact, for some Egyptian kings, their military activities took precedence over all other aspects of governance, whether because the political climate demanded it or because a particular king simply enjoyed battle. This was particularly the case when a military general became king, by inheritance or by circumstance. However, a few kings (such as Kamose) jeopardized Egypt's stability when they were killed in battle.

Most ancient Egyptian kings were men. However, sometimes a woman would step forward to take command of the country, functioning just as a king would. For example, Queen Ahhotep I, mother of King Ahmose I, acted as her son's regent after he assumed the throne as a boy under age ten, and as part of her rule she personally led an army from Thebes into battle against the Hyksos. Other queens, such as Hatshepsut, took command of the throne in their own right, independent of any male.

There were more than 170 Egyptian kings in all, followed by a series of Persian and then Greek ones. Modern archaeologists group all of Egypt's rulers according to a system devised by a third-century-B.C. priest of the city of Heliopolis, Manetho, who organized the kings into thirty dynasties, with the first king of the First Dynasty being the ruler who first united Egypt. During three periods of history, the First, Second, and Third Intermediate Periods, Egypt was not unified; instead, it had more than one king, each one claiming the right to rule.

Throughout ancient times, the Egyptians had many different words to designate their ruler, each one dependent on the role he was filling at a particular time. For example, the word *nyswt* referred to the king when he was acting in his official capacity as leader of the government, judicial system, and military. The king might also be called *netjer* (god), *nefer netjer* (good god), or *a'a netjer* (great god) in inscriptions. (A common word now used for ancient Egyptian kings, *pharaoh,* was coined by the Greeks.) **See also** deification of mortals; government; pharaoh.

Kiya (dates unknown)

A queen of the Eighteenth Dynasty, Kiya was one of the wives of King Amenhotep IV (also known as Akhenaten). Egyptologists disagree on Kiya's heritage. Some believe that she was a foreign princess, perhaps from the land of Mitanni, who came to Egypt around 1350 B.C. It is also unclear who her children were. However, many Egyptologists believe that she was the mother of Tutankhamun, who became king after Amenhotep IV's successor, King Smenkhkare, died.

Queen Kiya's mummy has never been found. For unknown reasons, her coffin was used for King Smenkhkare's burial even though she likely died before him. The prevailing theory regarding why this occurred is that Kiya somehow angered Amenhotep IV and was sent into exile. **See also** Amarna; Amenhotep IV; Smenkhkare; Tutankhamun.

Kom Ombo

Located on a bend in the Nile River north of Aswan, Kom Ombo was an agricultural town whose most prominent architectural features were an Eighteenth Dynasty gateway (which was destroyed sometime in the nineteenth century) that marked an entrance to the town and a Ptolemaic Period temple dedicated to Sobek, a crocodile god, and Haroeris, a falcon-headed form of the god Horus, along with other deities associated with them.

The Temple of Sobek and Haroeris is made up of a great court, a vestibule, a large hall, an antechamber, and various sanctuaries. Its right side is dedicated to Sobek and his associates and the left to Haroeris and his. Most of the scenes in the temple feature various deities, not only those to whom the temple is dedicated but others as well, particularly Isis, Nut, and Thoth. One of the scenes in the antechamber, however, shows King Ptolemy VI Philometor and his wife. He is the earliest Ptolemaic king featured in the temple, although the building was probably begun prior to his reign. Most of the temple's decorations, including reliefs in which the eyes of the figures were decorated with inlaid stone, were created or completed by Ptolemy XII Auletes.

The temple was apparently still under construction by the time the Romans conquered Egypt, because there are inscriptions acknowledging Roman emperors Tiberius (reigned A.D. 14–37), Domitian (81–96), Trajan (98–117), and Macrinus (217–218). A Roman relief shows Emperor Trajan with the Egyptian vizier Imhotep, who lived centuries earlier in the Third Dynasty and was deified after his death as a god of healing and medicine. Near the two figures are depictions of what appear to be medical instruments, including forceps, surgical saws and drills, and a birthing stool; these have provided archaeologists with visual evidence of what ancient Egyptian physicians used in practicing their trade.

Another interesting feature of the temple is a small Roman Period shrine to Hathor where mummified crocodiles have been stored ever since it was constructed. Apparently from this time forward, whenever townspeople found such a crocodile buried around Kom Ombo's necropolis area, they would take it to the shrine. Archaeologists suspect that the temple might have had other interesting features as well, but damage to the temple's forecourt leads them to believe that a flood of the Nile River carried them away. **See also** Hathor; Horus; Imhotep; Isis; Nut; Sobek; Thoth.

Lahun and Kahun
(el-Lahun; Kahun)

Located approximately where the Bahr Yusef (a tributary of the Nile) feeds into the Faiyum, Lahun is the site of the pyramid complex of Twelfth Dynasty king Senwosret II and Kahun was a nearby walled settlement built to house the complex's builders and their families. The king called this city Hotep-Senwosret, or "Senwosret Is Satisfied." Kahun has proved invaluable to archaeologists because, after the completion of the pyramid complex, its workers abandoned the town and left many artifacts behind, including hundreds of papyri with texts on such subjects as medicine, animal husbandry, legal matters, and temple matters.

Since the entire town of Kahun was built all at once by Egypt's central government, it was more carefully planned than most. As a result, unlike in most cities at the time, people of different social classes and occupations were segregated from one another within separate walled areas, as opposed to most ancient Egyptian cities, where houses of the poor were scattered among those of the rich. One area contained a large structure that might have been a palace to be used by the king and other prominent administrative or temple officials whenever they visited the construction site. Another area had several large villas for the wealthy, some with over seventy rooms and large courtyards. These rooms included reception chambers; rooms for washing, bathing, and cooking; granaries; and servants' quarters. A third area had terraced townhomes intended for workmen. These structures usually had between four and seven rooms, and their flat roofs provided a place for people to sleep on hot nights. In addition to the ruins of such structures, Kahun has yielded numerous Twelfth Dynasty artifacts, including basketry, pottery, footwear, games and toys, other household and personal items, and various objects of magical and religious significance.

The nearby pyramid complex of King Senwosret II and four nearby shaft tombs belonging to royal princesses have also yielded some interesting artifacts. The king's pyramid complex once featured a stone core, mud-brick chambers, and a stone exterior but is now very badly damaged, largely because Ramses II took many of its stones for his own building projects. Nonetheless, in 1889, the first archaeologist to fully explore the pyramid, British archaeologist Sir William Matthew Flinders Petrie, found a flooded burial chamber in the pyramid that contained a gold and inlaid uraeus (insignia for a crown) that was probably once on Senwosret II's mummy. This uraeus was all that was left of the king's funerary goods after tomb robbers had gotten to them. In 1913, Petrie excavated the nearby shaft tombs and in one found a large collection of jewelry in a niche that tomb robbers apparently had missed. **See also** architecture; houses; Petrie, William Matthew Flinders; Senwosret II.

Lamentations of Isis and Nephthys

The *Lamentations of Isis and Nephthys* is a Late Period religious text that describes certain aspects of a myth related to the death of the god Osiris. According to the text, which had several variations, after his evil brother Seth had him killed, Osiris's sisters, Isis (who was also his wife) and Nephthys (who was Seth's wife), wailed over his body as they mourned his death and then performed all rites necessary so that Osiris could be reborn in the Afterlife. In some versions of the *Lamentations,* Seth hacked the body into over a dozen pieces and scattered them, so Isis had to find them and put them together before mummification could begin. In another variation, she buried each piece where she found it, forgoing mummification. In telling of the sisters' sorrow and their efforts to resurrect their brother, *Lamentations* stresses the god's immortality. As a result, the text was recited at certain religious festivals devoted to Osiris. Egyptologists believe that at least one version of *Lamentations* was meant to be sung, perhaps accompanied by music. **See also** Isis; music; Nephthys; Osiris; Seth.

Late Period (664–332 B.C.)

Lasting from 664 B.C. until 332 B.C., the Late Period began when King Shabaka of Nubia ended the chaos of the Third Intermediate Period by reuniting Egypt and establishing a strong central government that kept it united for several years. During this time, the country prospered, and art and architecture flourished. The most powerful cities were Tanis and Sais, the latter of which gave its name to an era within the Late Period known as the Saite Period or Saite dynasty.

Prosperity ended abruptly in 525 B.C. when a Persian conqueror, Cambyses III, invaded Egypt and declared himself king. He ruled for three years before dying in a desert sandstorm, and his heir to the throne, Darius, drained the Egyptian economy until the Egyptian king Amyrtaeus expelled his forces from the Delta in 404 B.C. and from all of Egypt in 400 B.C. Prosperity then returned to Egypt, until the Persians again took the country in 343 B.C. Persian kings remained in control of Egypt until Alexander III (also known as Alexander the Great) conquered the country in 332 B.C. ushering in the Greco-Roman Period. **See also** Alexander the Great; Greco-Roman Period; Saite Period.

leather goods

The ancient Egyptians tanned the skins of oxen, gazelles, and other animals to produce leather, although they never used spotted or otherwise patterned, unusual, or highly beautiful skins for this purpose. (Such hides were instead used to decorate shields, furniture, and other items.) Leather was made into a variety of items, including bags, bracelets, belts, aprons, sandals and slip-on shoes, chair cushions and seats, wrist protectors for archers, coverings for glass bottles and other objects, and vellum for writing and painting.

Egyptologists know that, although the Egyptians probably used several methods to make leather, one was the most prevalent. The animal skin was placed in a sequence of solutions. The first was intended to remove the hair, the next was to clean the hide, and the next to soften it. If tanning was desired, the hide was soaked in a final jar with tanning solution. To create the tanning solution, the Egyptians probably used the pods of a tree called *Acacia arabica,* which have tannin in them. Then the skin was washed again, and in some cases it was dyed. Egyptologists do not know what types of dyes were used for coloring leather, but they do know that red, yellow, and green were the colors of choice. Finally, the skin was stretched on a table or frame, where it was softened with oils and then cut into various shapes depending on its intended use. **See also** clothing; colors; furniture; glassware and glazed ware.

legal system

The ancient Egyptian legal system was directly connected to both the royal court and the priesthood. By divine right, the king was the ultimate authority on all matters within ancient Egyptian society, and he was considered the head of the judiciary system. His deputy, or vizier, was the chief justice of the courts. Together these two men upheld balance and order in all legal matters in accordance with a concept represented by Ma'at, the goddess embodying Truth, Justice, Order, and Balance.

The vizier personally handled the most important legal cases, particularly those involving crimes that would result in the death penalty. These were tried in the High Court of Egypt's capital city, with not only the vizier present but other judges (perhaps as many as twelve) there as well. Lesser matters were handled in local courts, or *kenbet*, run by a panel of local high-ranking officials. Lesser court trials typically involved disputes over contracts and business transactions. Such matters were decided on a case-by-case basis, but judges often considered earlier, similar cases in making their decisions and often followed precedent. There appears to have been no gender bias in the courts; men and women were treated equally and had equal rights under the law.

Archaeologists have found many legal documents at ancient Egyptian sites, and these generally relate to four areas of the law: property, marriage, inheritance, and matters related to tomb management and goods. Papyri transferring property were usually marked by three witnesses and sealed with the insignia of a high-ranking official. Marriage contracts might also transfer property from husband to wife, but their main purpose was usually to spell out the rights of each person within the marriage. For example, a marriage contract might state that a particular woman would remain in control of all of the possessions and money with which she entered the marriage, both during the marriage and, should the couple divorce or the woman's husband die, afterward as well. Inheritances were usually handled by means of a transfer document passing on ownership of specific items, rather than by means of a will, although one of the earliest wills, that of Fourth Dynasty prince Nekaure (a son of King Khafre), included instructions that left fourteen towns to five heirs. More typically, however, a will was a document in which a type of priest known as a *ka* priest or *ka* servant agreed to conduct rituals and leave offerings on a daily basis at a particular tomb in exchange for a portion of the profits produced by that tomb owner's estate. (Relatives of the deceased would traditionally set aside part of the estate they inherited from the deceased in order to fund the tomb, theoretically for eternity.)

From the many legal documents found, archaeologists believe that the ancient Egyptian legal system was highly sophisticated and well established by the time of the Old Kingdom. However, in the Nineteenth Dynasty, the impartiality of the system was weakened by a new practice: A cult statue of a god was sometimes placed in the courtroom to decide cases. The verdict was inferred from signs in the environment, such as a sound or subtle movement, that were supposedly offered by the deity while ceremonies were conducted in front of its statue. The interpretation of such signs was highly subjective, and defendants found themselves largely at the mercy of the whims of judges.

In administering the death penalty, the High Court sometimes gave the guilty party the option of committing suicide. Otherwise those sentenced to death were typically fed to crocodiles or executed in other brutal ways, and children who murdered their parents were usually tortured before death. Other punishments for various crimes included beatings, the amputation of body parts (particularly the ear, nose, or hand), forced labor in mines or quarries, or some form of torture. The prevailing beliefs were that a punishment had to be extremely harsh in order to prevent a recurrence of the behavior and that almost every criminal could be rehabilitated. **See also** government; Ma'at; marriage; tombs.

Leiden Papyrus

The Leiden Papyrus is a papyrus that was written by Nineteenth Dynasty scribes primarily using material copied from earlier documents. For example, the best-known section of the papyrus, *The Admonitions of Ipuwer* (also known as *The Admonitions of a Prophet*), was written during the Old Kingdom to offer advice on how to deal with Egypt's problems at that time, providing a pessimistic view of the country's future if its advice was not heeded. Other sections of the Leiden Papyrus deal with magic spells. For example, one spell was supposed to cure burns as long as the wound was covered with honey. Another spell was said to cure a stomachache provided that it was recited while the sufferer was drinking beer. Yet another spell required the figurine of a dwarf, probably the deity Bes, that had to be set on the forehead of a woman giving birth. With the figurine in place, the spell was recited four times to relieve the woman's pain. **See also** admonitions and instructions; Bes; medicine.

Lepsius, Karl Richard (1810–1884)

German archaeologist Karl Richard Lepsius was a major figure in nineteenth-century Egyptology who, unlike many of his era, was seemingly more concerned with creating a scholarly record of Egypt's history and artifacts than with profiting from the sale of antiquities. For this reason, many modern scholars consider him the founder of scientific archaeology. As part of his work, Lepsius cataloged numerous archaeological sites and established a chronology of Egyptian history.

After studying comparative languages and archaeology and examining Egyptian artifacts and texts in a variety of European museums, Lepsius led an expedition to Egypt and the Sudan from 1842 to 1845 at the behest of Prussia's King Friedrich Wilhelm IV, who wanted Lepsius to report on the monuments of these lands and acquire antiquities for Prussia. During his investigations, Lepsius discovered the first evidence that pyramids were built as early as 3000 B.C., studied over 130 mastaba tombs, and found the first material concerning King Amenhotep IV (Akhenaten) in Tell el-Amarna. In addition, he collected more than fifteen hundred casts of tomb and temple reliefs and inscriptions; oversaw the creation of hundreds of drawings depicting Egyptian sites, structures, art, and artifacts; collected papyri and antiquities for his sponsor; and was the first person to determine the exact dimensions of the Valley of the Kings.

Lepsius's descriptions of various ruins were so thorough that they enabled late-twentieth-century archaeologists to rediscover sites that had been buried by sand and forgotten since Lepsius's time. One of these sites was the tomb of Horemheb, the general who might have played a role in King Tutankhamun's demise, which had been covered by sand at Saqqara.

Lepsius published his findings, along with illustrations contributed by artist Joseph Bonomi and architect James Wild, in a major work titled *Denkmäler aus Ägypten und Äthiopian* (*Monuments of Egypt and Ethiopia,* published in 1849–1858). He also published an 1849 work titled *Chronologie der Ägypter*

(*Egyptian Chronology*) and an 1858 work titled *Königsbuch der Alten Ägypter* (*Book of Egyptian Kings*). In addition, he was the editor of an important journal on Egyptology, the German publication *Zeitschrift für ägyptische Sprache und Altertumskunde.*

After returning to Prussia, Lepsius became a professor at the University of Berlin. He went on a second expedition to Egypt in 1866, this time concentrating on the Delta region. There in the city of Tanis he discovered the Canopus Decree, which because it was written in both demotic script and Greek helped scholars translate Egyptian texts. Back once again in Prussia, Lepsius worked as the keeper of Egyptian antiquities for the Berlin Museum, overseeing its entire Egyptian collection. In 1873 he became the director of Berlin's Royal Library as well. **See also** Amarna; Amenhotep IV; Horemheb; Rosetta Stone; Tanis; Tutankhamun; Valley of the Kings.

libraries

Ancient Egyptian priests maintained and added to a library within the *Per-ankh,* or House of Life, which was a part of most large temples. These libraries were huge archives of papyri, which came from many different eras and dealt with a wide variety of scientific, religious, and practical subjects, including astronomy, temple rituals, and annual census figures. New texts were continually added to these libraries, and old ones were copied and recopied as a way to preserve them and ensure that new generations of scholars would learn from the wisdom they contained. **See also** astronomy; education; writing, forms of.

Libya

From the Early Dynastic period on, ancient Egyptians considered all the lands to their west to be part of Libya. The Egyptians periodically attacked the Libyans as a means of defending their western border,

to push their border farther into Libya, or simply to acquire cattle and other goods from Libyan settlements. Several Old Kingdom kings, most notably Snefru and Sahure, launched military campaigns to invade Libya, and by the Middle Kingdom such campaigns were routine. During the chaos of the Second Intermediate Period, some Libyans managed to invade Egypt's Delta region, but by the Eighteenth Dynasty they had been repelled. In the Nineteenth Dynasty, a group of Libyans again invaded the Delta, and in the ensuing battle led by Egypt's King Merneptah, more than six thousand Libyans were killed. Still another group of Libyans unsuccessfully fought the forces of Ramses III twice in the same region. These Libyans succeeded in gaining a foothold in Egypt during the chaos of the Third Intermediate Period and eventually acquired enough power to take the throne as the Twenty-second Dynasty, sometimes called the Libyan dynasty. **See also** Merneptah; Ramses III; Sahure; Second Intermediate Period; Snefru; Third Intermediate Period.

linen

Usually bleached but sometimes colored with vegetable dyes, linen was the primary fabric in ancient Egypt, beginning in predynastic times. Its source was flax, a plant with fibers that could be spun and woven after some preparation. This preparation involved soaking, beating, and combing the flax to separate its fibers from other parts of the plant. The fibers were then spun on spindles, a process that involved pulling apart the fibers and twisting them to form threads. Weaving was done on one of two kinds of wooden handloom, one horizontal and one vertical. Mummy wrappings were linen as well because, for reasons unclear to Egyptologists, the ancient Egyptians considered wool impure and forbade its use in any religious rituals. **See also** clothing; weaving.

el-Lisht (Lisht)

Located in Middle Egypt, el-Lisht is the site of the pyramids of Twelfth Dynasty king Amenemhet I and his son Senwosret I, both of which display serious damage from the elements. Also damaged but still in evidence are the remains of several smaller pyramids and tombs at el-Lisht that were built by the two kings for relatives and high-ranking officials. From markings on various structures in the area, archaeologists know that royal architects used stones taken from other tombs in the Memphis area to build the el-Lisht pyramids.

Because of the large number of burials at el-Lisht related to King Amenemhet I's reign, archaeologists suspect that the site lies near what was once Itj-tawy, the place where the king had his capital, administrative center, and royal residence. However, the remains of this royal city have never been found, despite several excavations in the area by French and American archaeologists. **See also** Amenemhet I; pyramids; Senwosret I.

Litany of Re, The (*The Litany of the Sun; The Great Litany*)

Also known as *The Great Litany* or *The Litany of the Sun, The Litany of Re* is an illustrated text that was often placed on the wall at the entrance to a royal tomb and was meant to be spoken or perhaps sung aloud. Many Egyptologists believe that it was an incantation intended to magically transform the speaker—the deceased king whose tomb it was—from an ordinary spirit into an aspect of the god Re. In the text, the king is paying homage to Re, and in doing so provides over seventy different names for the god, including Supreme Power, the Becoming One Who Folds His Wings, and He Who Goes to Rest in the Underworld. The text was first found on the walls of the tomb of Nineteenth Dynasty king Seti I, but was subsequently discovered in many other Nineteenth and Twentieth Dynasty royal tombs in the Valley of the Kings. **See also** Re.

literature

The ancient Egyptians had both secular and religious literature. Secular literature included legal and scientific texts, the latter of which include discussions of mathematics, astronomy, agricultural techniques, and medicine. Most secular literature, however, appears to have been intended to provide information about Egypt's kings and their military exploits, appearing as inscribed texts on tomb and temple walls. Autobiographical texts appeared in this context as well.

The ancient Egyptians also had popular stories, or tales, which were usually spread with the intent of changing public opinion on some political or moral issue. Sometimes they were presented as someone's autobiography, even though they were fictional, or as a prophecy of some disaster, even though they were apparently written after the prophesied events had already taken place. During the New Kingdom, popular stories increasingly had foreign settings and incorporated mythological elements. Historians believe that by this time stories were written down prior to being told, whereas before the New Kingdom popular stories were probably shared orally by traveling storytellers before being recorded. The New Kingdom also saw the introduction of the love poem, sometimes presented as song lyrics. Love poems often featured birds, particularly swans, in the role of lovers. Three papyri feature love poems, the Chester Beatty Papyrus I, the Harris Papyrus 500, and the Turin Canon.

Ancient Egyptian religious literature included texts intended to help a person reach the Afterlife, such as the Pyramid Texts, Coffin Texts, and the *Book of the Dead*, which were either inscribed on tomb walls or coffin interiors or written on papyri. Other texts in temples and tombs dealt with religious rites, magic, and mythology or were apparently intended as hymns to the gods. **See also** *Book of the Dead*; Coffin Texts; love poems; Pyramid Texts.

lotus

Two types of water lily commonly known as the lotus or lotus flower, the white *Nymphaea* lotus and the blue *Nymphaea caerulea,* grew along the Nile River during ancient times; the Egyptians considered the second of these two flowers to be sacred. One reason for this association was the nature of the flower itself. The lotus is submerged in the water at night, its flower petals closed, but with the morning sun it rises up above the water's surface and opens its petals. For this reason, it was a symbol of rebirth and creation to Egyptians and was linked with gods who were similarly allied, such as the sun god Re, sometimes called the Great Lotus and featured in Creation myths, and another sun god, Nefertem, who was sometimes said to be the son of the creator god Ptah. Nefertem was typically shown in human form wearing a crown of lotus flowers or with a lotus emerging from the top of his head. Similarly, kings were sometimes depicted as emerging from a giant lotus flower. For example, a painted wooden sculpture of King Tutankhamun shows his head emerging from a lotus flower.

The lotus also appeared in some myths related to the creation of the world, particularly in the city of Hermopolis. These myths typically feature the lotus rising out of the primordial waters to open its petals and give birth to the sun. In addition, the scent of the lotus was said to soothe the gods. For this reason, the lotus was often presented as an offering to various gods. It was also the traditional welcome in a home; upon entering a residence, each guest would be given a single lotus flower. Sometimes necklaces and/or wreaths of lotus flowers were given as well. This custom led to the

practice of homeowners keeping vases of lotus flowers and stands of lotus wreaths and necklaces about the home in preparation for guests. **See also** Creation myths; Nefertem; plants and flowers; symbols.

love poems

The ancient Egyptians wrote many love poems, usually as monologues in which the speaker professes undying affection for an unnamed individual. Many of these texts were apparently meant to be sung, or at least spoken to musical accompaniment. Certain images are prevalent throughout the genre, particularly those associated with natural beauty (e.g., flowers or colorful birds). Three papyri feature love poems, the Chester Beatty Papyrus I, Harris Papyrus 500, and the Turin Papyrus. **See also** Chester Beatty Papyri; Harris Papyrus; literature; Turin Canon.

Lower Egypt

Called Ta-Meht in ancient Egyptian, Lower Egypt is a triangle-shaped region that encompasses a broad stretch of coastline along the Mediterranean Sea, where the Nile River ends, south to somewhere around the town of el-Lisht. Lower Egypt therefore encompasses all of the Delta, a region where the river splits into many different tributaries (perhaps seven in ancient times) on its way to the sea. With ample water and good soil, Lower Egypt was perfect for agriculture.

As a political entity, it was divided into twenty nomes, although Egyptologists disagree on when these political subdivisions were established. The only records listing all twenty nomes date from the Greco-Roman Period. However, the nomes of Upper Egypt to the south of Lower Egypt clearly existed during the Early Dynastic Period, so some Egyptologists have suggested that Lower Egypt might have been similarly divided during this early period even though the nomes did not act as a unified entity until much

The Temple of Amun at Luxor, on the east bank of the Nile, was connected to a similar temple at Karnak by an avenue lined with statues of sphinxes.

later. **See also** Delta; government; Upper Egypt.

Luxor

Coming from the Arabic name "el-Askur," translated as the Castles or the Palaces because of the many temples in the area, Luxor is the modern name for the southern part of Opet, a section of ancient Thebes that was dedicated to the god Amun or Amun-Re. Its Temple of Amun was constructed by Amenhotep III and then enlarged by Ramses II. Seven subsequent rulers added to it as well, including Alexander III (also known as Alexander the Great). Wall reliefs within the temple include scenes of ceremonies honoring Amun. In approximately 300 B.C. the Roman emperor Diocletian took over part of the temple for a cult dedicated to worshiping Rome's emperor.

Luxor also has many statues and columns, including two colossal statues of Ramses II and a large pylon with reliefs and text related to Ramses II's military victory against the Hittites. At one time, an avenue lined with statues of sphinxes (creatures with the body of a lion and the head of a ram) linked the Temple of Amun at Luxor with a similar temple at nearby Karnak, and during certain festivals, a cult statue of Amun was carried from one temple to the other. **See also** Amenhotep III; Amun; Karnak; Ramses II.

Ma'at

Ma'at was both an ancient Egyptian goddess and an ancient Egyptian concept, but both were connected to Order, Truth, Justice, and Harmony. A king's job was to maintain Ma'at, a balance between the earth and the heavens in which every entity behaves as it should; Egypt's legal system was also charged with this duty. Maintaining Ma'at in Egypt was vital to ensuring that the gods would remain benevolent, because the level of order and

This painted Nineteenth Dynasty bas-relief depicts Ma'at, the goddess connected to Order, Truth, Justice, and Harmony.

harmony on earth was believed to be mirrored in the heavens. Consequently, priests admonished people to behave in ways that would promote harmony, cooperation, and peacefulness. Meanwhile, the goddess Ma'at was said to operate the scales in the Judgment Hall of Osiris, weighing the hearts of the deceased to determine whether they and their owners were worthy of entering the Afterlife. **See also** Afterlife; kings; legal system.

Macedonia

In ancient times, Macedonia was a kingdom located to the north of Greece that was linguistically and culturally linked to Greece. During the beginning of the Greco-Roman Period of ancient Egyptian history, a succession of three Macedonians ruled Egypt; some archaeologists call their collective reigns the Macedonian dynasty. Spanning from approximately 332 B.C. to 305 B.C., this dynasty included the reigns of Alexander III (also known as Alexander the Great), who ruled Egypt from approximately 332 B.C. to 323 B.C., Philip Arrhidaeus (ca. 323–316 B.C.), and Alexander IV (ca. 316–305 B.C.). **See also** Alexander the Great; Greco-Roman Period.

magic

In general, the ancient Egyptians viewed magic as a force that could bring about either positive or negative changes. As such, magic was deeply intertwined with medicine and involved complex rituals, spells, and symbols. The recitation of magic spells was seen as a way to obtain a desired result, such as improved health and fertility. Magic amulets marked with symbols and spells might also be used to repel evil, thereby conferring protection against dangers such as a scorpion bite.

The ancient Egyptians further believed that they could use magic to call on a particular deity to gain certain attributes of that deity. The deity most often called on was dedicated to magic: Heka, a god typically worshiped at home rather than at a cult center (although Heka was sometimes worshiped in city temples as one of a group of deities). Some rituals involved calling out a name of another human being instead of a deity, because the ancient Egyptians believed that names had the power to influence reality. For this reason, many spells of destruction sometimes involved writing an enemy's name.

Most magic rituals were the domain of a certain class of priests known as *hekau* (magicians). A man particularly skilled in magical arts might be called a *Hery Seshta,* or "chief of mysteries." Each priest practiced a form of magic that was his specialty. For example, a *hekau* who specialized in spells to protect against poisonous bites was called a *Kherep Selket,* or "commander of the scorpion goddess." A person—perhaps a priest or craftsman—who made amulets and/or perhaps charged them with magic through a ritual was called a *Sau* (from *sa,* meaning "amulet"). A man or woman specializing in contacting spirits was called a *Rekhet,* or "wise person." **See also** amulets; medicine.

Mahu (?–ca. 1336 B.C.)

During the Eighteenth Dynasty, Mahu was the chief of police in Akhetaten (now known as Amarna or Tell el-Amarna), the city built by King Akhenaten (also known as Amenhotep IV) to honor the god Aten. Mahu also might have been a member of a division of the national police force known as the Medjay, which consisted solely of men from Nubia. Mahu died before the city of Akhetaten was abandoned,

so the pictures on his tomb walls are considered by Egyptologists to be representations of events that took place in the city during its peak. They show Mahu going about his duties, which included interrogating suspects and escorting prisoners to trial, and depict scenes such as King Akhenaten and his principal wife, Queen Nefertiti, traveling by chariot. **See also** Amarna; Amenhotep IV; Aten; Medjay; Nefertiti; Nubia.

Manetho (dates unknown)

A third-century-B.C. Greco-Egyptian priest from the town of Sebennytus in the Delta, Manetho was hired by King Ptolemy II to write a history of Egypt. In doing so, he divided Egypt's history into thirty dynasties (essentially, ruling houses), divisions that are still used by historians today (although sometimes they add Zero, Thirty-first, and Thirty-second Dynasties as well). Moreover, Manetho listed the kings of each dynasty, beginning with the first king of Egypt. He called this first king Menes, who historians now believe was probably King Aha.

Manetho's work, *Aegyptiaca* (*Egyptian History,* also known as *Notes About Egypt*), was apparently written in Greek on papyrus, but it has never been found. Historians know about Manetho's work only from other ancient writers who quoted from it in their own manuscripts. These writers include late first-century-A.D. author Josephus in his *Jewish Antiquities* and *Contra Apionem,* third-century Christian scholar Sextus Julius Africanus in his *Chronicle,* and fourth-century Palestinian bishop and historian Eusebius of Caesarea (also known as Eusebius Pamphili) in his book *Ecclesiastical History* and others. Using these and additional sources, modern scholars have been able to reconstruct Manetho's list of kings, and by combining it with other ancient records and inscriptions they have developed the most accurate list of Egyptian kings possible. According to Egyptologists, however, Manetho's sources were probably not entirely reliable. As a priest in the temple at Heliopolis, he undoubtedly used temple records—which included both secular histories and religious books—as well as wall inscriptions and scenes, but he also seems to have relied on legends and stories. **See also** king lists; Ptolemaic kings.

maps

The oldest known land maps in the world are two maps, written on papyrus, of parts of ancient Egypt. One map shows a gold-mining region near Coptos during the Nineteenth Dynasty reign of Ramses II. The other charts an unidentified gold-mining region, depicting the location of workers' homes, a shrine, and travel routes out of the area. Although no other ancient Egyptian geographical maps have been found, archaeologists have discovered ancient Egyptian maps of the heavens and the Underworld (also known as the Duat), an otherworldly realm that the solar deity was believed to pass through each night. Maps of the heavens, which most typically appear on temple and tomb ceilings, were intended to help priests chart the movements of the stars so that they could establish a calendar for keeping track of festival dates. These maps also offered representations of the deities and their relationship to Egypt and its nomes. Maps of the Underworld, usually found on tomb walls or in funerary papyri, were usually intended to help guide the deceased to the Judgment Hall of Osiris in the Afterlife, showing various monsters and other challenges to be surmounted. **See also** Afterlife; astronomy; calendars; mining and metalworking; Underworld.

Mariette, Auguste (1821–1881)

Frenchman Auguste Mariette was one of the most important Egyptologists of the nineteenth century. His cousin Nestor L'Hôte had been part of Napoléon Bonaparte's 1798 expedition to Egypt and had drawn some reproductions of ancient Egyptian writing. When Mariette saw this material in 1842, he became fascinated with it. Consequently, he studied ancient Egyptian writing himself and eventually got a job with the Louvre Museum in Paris. Mariette was initially charged with cataloging the Louvre's Egyptian papyri, but in 1850 he was sent to Egypt to collect them as well. Once in Egypt, however, he decided to launch an excavation at Saqqara in Memphis instead because part of a sphinx could be seen there in the sand and he was curious about what lay beneath. His excavation soon uncovered a line of sphinxes now known as the Avenue of the Sphinxes, leading up to a temple called the Serapeum. Inside this temple were tombs containing mummified bulls that the ancient Egyptians believed were the physical manifestation of the god Hapi (Apis in Greek), who was associated with the Ptah-Sokar-Osiris cult. (The Apis bull was associated with all these deities, but Ptah most of all.)

Mariette's excavations of the Avenue of the Sphinxes and the Serapeum took four years. During this time, he sent most of the antiquities he found to the Louvre, becoming famous in the process. However, he was criticized initially for his decision to excavate and subsequently for his methods, which involved using dynamite and therefore severely damaged some structures. Furthermore, his poor treatment of some of his workers was controversial. He also neglected to document much of his work, making it difficult for scholars to interpret what he uncovered. Nevertheless, when Mariette was finished, the Serapeum's underground passages were so well cleared of rubble that tourists could walk through them.

In 1853, Mariette began working at another site, Giza. There he found a pyramid built in the Fourth Dynasty by King

Khafre. While its excavation continued, Mariette returned home to become curator of the Louvre, but in 1858 he left the position to become conservator of monuments for the Egyptian government. Later his title was director of the Egyptian Antiquities Service.

Mariette remained in Egypt until his death in 1881. During that time, he made it impossible for anyone to excavate a site without a government permit, which gave him control over all archaeological activities in the country. Meanwhile, Mariette excavated the most promising sites, including the burial grounds at Meidum, Abydos, and Thebes; the pyramids at Saqqara; the temple of Nineteenth Dynasty king Seti I at Abydos; and various structures at Edfu, Dendera, Karnak, Tanis, and elsewhere. He also made sure that the best antiquities remained in the country, even if a foreign archaeologist found them, by severely limiting the export of such items. In 1859 he convinced the government to build a museum near Cairo to display all of the antiquities he had found or acquired from others. Today the Egyptian Museum at Cairo is one of the primary places to view ancient Egyptian art. Mariette left behind several publications about his work, including *Abydos* (1869) and *Les Mastabas de l'Ancien Empire* (*The Mastabas of the Old Kingdom,* 1889). **See also** Apis bull; Giza; Khafre; Saqqara.

marriage

Marriage for ancient Egyptians was marked with a ceremony, but it was a civil one rather than a religious one. The families of the bride and groom drew up a marriage contract, telling what each individual was bringing to the household. If the two people later divorced (an option that held no stigma among the ancient Egyptians), the woman would keep whatever she had contributed to the marriage (i.e., her dowry) and receive some

form of payment from her husband for the work she had contributed to the household. Marriage contracts also stated all matters related to the disposition of goods and property. For example, a contract sometimes stated that the man was giving all his property to the woman with the provision that their children would receive all of it after her death. Without such a statement, under Egyptian law, all property was held jointly by a husband and wife, and at least one-third of the estate traditionally remained hers after his death, with the rest going to their children. However, even when the wife held all property, the man typically managed the household's business affairs—although women were considered equal to men and had great input on such matters.

Even though marriage contracts emphasized business matters, marriages were largely undertaken for emotional reasons. A man could have more than one wife, but outside the royal family, polygamy was uncommon. Parents rarely arranged marriages for their children, allowing young people to choose whomever they wanted as partners. The exception to this was the royal family; in this case, almost every marriage was arranged for political purposes. However, in no case was an Egyptian princess given in marriage to a foreigner. There were two major reasons for this practice. For one thing, Egyptians believed they were superior to all other people and did not want a member of their royal family subjugated to a foreigner. In addition, the Egyptians believed that unless the princess was buried in her native land under the proper rituals she would not be able to reach the Afterlife.

Young men were encouraged to choose a mate by the age of twenty, young women as soon after puberty as possible. The woman's primary goal was to start producing children immediately after the marriage was established. The creation of a new household was usually marked with a party, where friends and family celebrated the couple's signing of the marriage contract. Gifts might be given to the couple as part of this celebration, and the couple exchanged gifts with each other both then and upon agreeing to marry. **See also** children; queens; women, role of.

Maspero, Gaston (1846–1916)

From 1881 to 1886, French Egyptologist Sir Gaston Maspero worked for the Egyptian government as the director general of excavations and antiquities, following the death of another noted French Egyptologist, Auguste Mariette. Maspero took over Mariette's excavations of the pyramids at Saqqara and visited many important tombs to make copies of their wall inscriptions and scenes. He also followed up on clues to the locations of lost tombs and artifacts and launched expeditions that might lead to their discovery. Maspero had many successes in this regard. For example, in 1881 he entered the pyramid of King Unas and found a burial chamber holding a sarcophagus with a royal mummy inside. The chamber and its antechamber were covered with hieroglyphic inscriptions that, along with other inscriptions, became known as the Pyramid Texts, a collection of spells intended to help the deceased king reach the Afterlife. Other Fifth and Sixth Dynasty pyramids also had these texts, but those in King Unas's pyramid are the oldest ever found.

Maspero was also involved in the discovery of the tomb of Sennedjem, a worker in the village of Deir el-Medina. (Egyptologists suspect that this worker was a master artist or sculptor, but the only title provided at his tomb is "servant.") In 1886, someone living in the area told Maspero about a tomb filled with artifacts, and other than this man, Maspero was the first at the site. There-

fore, Maspero had access to all of its treasures: the funerary goods of several generations of Sennedjem's family, as well as the mummies of Sennedjem, his wife Iineferti, their son and daughter-in-law, and an unidentified woman. The tomb walls had paintings of Sennedjem and his family in various scenes; in some they were enjoying the Afterlife while in others Sennedjem was a mummy in the company of deities. The ceiling of this tomb featured a funerary text called *The Book of Gates,* a spellbook providing the magic passwords that would enable Sennedjem and his family to go through the gates of the Afterlife.

Yet another important discovery often credited to Maspero (although credit actually belongs to his assistant, Emile Brugsch) was a cache of royal mummies found near Deir el-Bahri in 1881 after a robber confessed that his family had been plundering the cliff tomb over the course of ten years. Although the family had already sold many of its artifacts, the tomb still held the remains of forty kings, queens, and high priests that had been damaged by tomb robbers but subsequently restored and entombed together by ancient Egyptian priests. Maspero identified many of these remains, including the mummies of Seti I, Amenhotep I, Tuthmosis III, and Ramses III, and in 1889 he published a book about this discovery titled *Les Momies royales de Deir-el-Bahari* (*The Royal Mummies of Deir el-Bahri*).

Shortly after the book's publication, Maspero began cataloging the artifacts that he and his predecessor Mariette had amassed for Egypt, and in 1902 this work helped lead to the founding of the Egyptian Museum at Cairo. From 1899 on, Maspero focused his attention on preserving and protecting Egypt's ancient treasure. To this end, he strongly enforced laws against antiquities trading and limited access to excavation sites.

During this period, Maspero also wrote several books on ancient Egypt and Egyptian archaeology. He retired in 1914, two years before he died in Paris. **See also** *Book of Gates, The;* Mariette, Auguste; Pyramid Texts.

mastaba tomb

A mastaba tomb is an oblong burial structure whose style developed during the Early Dynastic Period. The burial chamber of the tomb was subterranean, as were storerooms of goods that the deceased planned to use in the Afterlife. A shaft led to an aboveground offering chapel. The aboveground structure was shaped like a mound, probably as a symbol of the primordial mound from which all life was said to have arisen, but because later Egyptians thought these mounds looked like mud benches, they called them *mastaba,* from the Arabic for "*bench.*" Over time, the mounds of mastaba tombs housing kings were slightly terraced to look like steps to suggest that the deceased king would be ascending to the heavens to join the solar deity.

The first ancient Egyptian pyramid, the Step Pyramid of Third Dynasty king Djoser, was based on the mastaba style. The designer of this pyramid, the king's vizier and architect Imhotep, changed the mastaba design to give his structure more pronounced steps and made it much taller. Imhotep also copied the roof style of mastabas, imitating those structures' palm tree logs in stone. The Step Pyramid also had stone doors carved to look like they were made of wood. Therefore it appears that Imhotep's goal was not to change the prevailing mastaba architectural style but to make a more lasting, grander version of it. **See also** pyramids; tombs.

mathematics

Most ancient Egyptian mathematics was related to measurement, primarily in regard to building architectural monuments.

Egyptians used addition and subtraction as well as complex methods of multiplying and dividing, but apparently did not use algebraic formulas. However, archaeologists have found ancient Egyptian discussions of fractions, proportions, and basic calculus in a Seventeenth Dynasty papyrus called the Rhind Papyrus. Written by a Theban scribe, this papyrus is one of very few documents to address the subject of mathematics. Consequently, Egyptologists have concluded that the ancient Egyptians were not interested in advanced mathematics, but their awareness of calculus suggests that they at least had a grasp of mathematical theory.

The basic method of counting in ancient Egypt was a base-10 decimal system. Vertical lines represented the numbers 1 through 10, while various signs and symbols represented numbers in the tens place, hundreds place, thousands place, and so on. For example, the image of a tadpole stood for 100,000, so 600,005 would be written with six tadpoles followed by five vertical lines.

Despite the limitations imposed by a lack of algebraic concepts, Egyptians could calculate—although slowly and clumsily—angles, areas, diameters, and similar measures necessary for building construction. The Egyptians also could perform calculations to determine taxes, such as calculating the areas of irregularly shaped tracts of land. They based their measurement of area on the cubit, which was approximately twenty inches (a measurement based on the average length of a man's arm). The basic units for measuring area were the setat (100 square cubits) and the land mile (1,000 square cubits). **See also** architecture; economic system; weights and measures.

medicine

Most of what Egyptologists know about ancient Egyptian medicine comes from ten papyri dealing with diseases, cures, anatomy, surgeries, gynecology and obstetrics, and eye and dental problems. From these, they know that ancient Egyptian doctors, called *sunu,* practiced medicine in conjunction with magic, using spells and rituals to heal a variety of illnesses. They also used ointments and other cures that might be rendered potent through magic prior to use. Although they relied on magic to some extent, these priest-physicians thoroughly examined patients and consulted medical texts before attempting a cure. For example, Egyptian physicians would take a patient's pulse. Moreover, doctors chose treatments based on carefully noted symptoms, such as those of a heart attack. Physicians prescribed specific treatments for problems they found, but if they did not know of a remedy that would address a problem, they would usually turn the patient away without treatment.

Doctors knew how to disinfect and cauterize wounds, although they had no knowledge of microbes. In fact, many cures involved vile ingredients like animal feces because foul substances were believed to drive illness from the body. They believed that demons caused many illnesses, such as fever and headaches, and in such cases magic was their primary treatment. There were also herbal and holistic cures, such as treating skin burns and wounds with honey and bee extracts and using garlic to cure digestive and other problems. Physicians in ancient Egypt were quite skilled in treating broken bones through splinting, bandaging, and other means. In dentistry, they might replace a bad tooth with a gold one.

The most common complaints among ancient Egyptian patients seem to have been headaches, ear infections, hernias, gallstones, indigestion, pneumonia, tuberculosis, and polio. Tapeworms, hookworms, roundworms, and other parasites were other common problems. In addition, a viral illness that today is called river blindness was rampant because poor hygiene encouraged the breeding of Nile River flies, which spread the disease. Due in large measure to the lack of effective treatments for certain diseases, the average life span of an Egyptian in ancient times was thirty-five years for men and thirty for women, who often died in childbirth. Infant mortality was extremely high as well, also in large part because of complications during birth. **See also** Leiden Papyrus; magic.

Medinet Habu

Located on the western shore of the Nile River across from Luxor, Medinet Habu (called Tjamet in ancient Egyptian and Djeme in Coptic) was a religious center associated with the sun god Amun in his role as creator. For this reason, the main structure at the site is a temple dedicated to Amun. It was begun in the Eighteenth Dynasty by King Amenhotep I and then finished by Queen-Pharaoh Hatshepsut, and several subsequent kings later added to it. One of these kings, Twentieth Dynasty ruler Ramses III, built a nearly five-hundred-foot-long mortuary temple beside the structure with numerous reliefs and hieroglyphics cut deep into the stone. In fact, it is the depth of many of the hieroglyphics, over eight inches, that sets these carvings apart. Egyptologists have several theories regarding why this material was cut so much deeper than was customary. One is that it was a stylistic choice; another theory is that it was a way to keep subsequent rulers from covering Ramses III's inscriptions with their own.

Another unusual feature of Ramses III's temple was its entrance, which was through a gatehouse built like a Syrian fortress. When the members of French emperor Napoléon's eighteenth-century expedition saw it, they named it the Pavilion, a name that has continued in use despite uncertainty regarding its purpose. At

The mortuary temple of Ramses III at Medinet Habu is unique because of its fortresslike entrance.

one time, the Pavilion apparently linked the temple to a palace where Ramses III stayed during visits to the area. The palace had two upper stories with apartments for the king's harem; wall reliefs show his women attending him. Other walls in the palace depict military scenes and the king making offerings to gods. The palace-temple complex also once had a canal connecting it to the Nile River, as well as massive pylons with carved reliefs showing military scenes and scenes from daily life. Sanctuaries in the complex showed scenes of the riches in the king's treasury, which included musical instruments as well as jewels and other items.

The Temple of Hatshepsut at Medinet Habu also has an interesting feature, an inscription that identifies the site as the Primeval Hill, where matter was supposedly formed from chaos. In addition, the hill was said to be the site where eight primordial deities were buried, the male-female pairs of Nu and Nut (or Nun and Naunet), Heh and Hehut (Huh and Hauhet), Kekui and Kekuit (Kuk and Kauket), and Kerh and Kerhet (Amun and Amaunet). **See also** Amenhotep I; Amun; Hatshepsut; Luxor; Ogdoad; Ramses III.

Medjay

Although they were known to the ancient Egyptians as early as the Old Kingdom, Nubian desert nomads called the Medjay worked for Egyptian kings as mercenaries during battles with the Hyksos in the Seventeenth Dynasty. As such, they were involved in some of the most important military actions of the period. Because of the skill and loyalty that the Medjay displayed, once the Hyksos had been expelled, Egypt established a separate branch of law enforcement employing only Medjay, and the name became associated with the national police force.

The Medjay's job was to protect various towns and building sites, particularly in Thebes and the surrounding area. In this regard, they were so effective that the Medjay became valued members of Egyptian society. Some even acquired upper-level government positions with political power, which helped to erode prejudice against foreigners holding such positions. After their mercenary days were over, however, some Medjay returned to their nomadic life in the Eastern Desert in an attempt to maintain their cultural identity. **See also** Eastern Desert; Hyksos; police.

Mehy

There were two important individuals in ancient Egypt with the name Mehy: a Fifth Dynasty vizier and a Nineteenth Dynasty military official. Vizier Mehy (ca. 2375–ca. 2345 B.C.) served King Unas and held the title "overseer of all the king's works," supervising various important building projects. The role of the Nineteenth Dynasty Mehy (dates unknown) is far less clear. He was apparently a military officer, perhaps a general, for King Seti I during the late fourteenth century B.C. There is also evidence that the king elevated Mehy to the position of prince: Wall scenes depict Mehy dressed like a prince, and Nineteenth Dynasty stories identify him as a commoner who rose to greatness. Egyptologists suggest that if Mehy did become prince, this explains why Seti I's successor, Ramses II, obliterated Mehy's name and image wherever he found them. Ramses II, they theorize, perhaps viewed Mehy as his rival. **See also** Ramses II; Seti I; Unas.

Meidum (Maidum)

Meidum is the site of one of Egypt's oldest pyramids, built by either Third Dynasty king Huni or Fourth Dynasty king Snefru or both. At some point after it was built, the bottom portion of the pyramid's outer walls collapsed, causing the top portion to tumble to the ground. Only the pyramid's vertical core remains standing, so the structure appears to be a tower.

What caused the pyramid's collapse is unclear. Some Egyptologists believe that it occurred when later builders removed its lower stones for use in other construction projects. Other Egyptologists believe that the damage was caused by ground tremors, perhaps from work on another building project nearby or from an earthquake. Still others believe that the collapse occurred during the construction of the pyramid, shortly before it was finished. According to this theory, a design flaw caused the collapse, suggesting that this is why the builders of the next pyramid completed in Egypt—the so-called Bent Pyramid at Dashur—apparently changed its design in midconstruction. **See also** architecture; Dashur; Huni; pyramids; Snefru.

Meir

West of the ancient village of Meir, which lies in Upper Egypt north of Asyut, are several rock-cut tombs from the Twelfth and Sixteenth Dynasties. Many of their owners were officials from the nearby town of Qis (also known as Kusai), then the center of the fourteenth nome of Upper Egypt. Most of the tombs have wall reliefs or paintings depicting scenes from daily life. For example, the Middle Kingdom tomb of Ouk-hotep has scenes showing papyrus harvesters reaping, gathering, and carrying away papyrus stalks, as well as scenes of people boating and jousting. These scenes are particularly interesting to Egyptologists because, unlike most artwork from the period, they depict a few people with recognizable deformities, including a boatman with an abdominal protrusion. Why artists strayed from the convention of depicting only idealized forms of the human body is unknown. **See also** medicine; papyrus.

Memphis

Called Ankh-tawy ("That Which Joins the Two Lands") or Men-nefer (after the name of a nearby pyramid) in ancient times, Memphis was the capital of Egypt and therefore the residence of kings during the Predynastic Period and Old Kingdom. Its location was just south of the place where the Nile spreads to form the Delta, approximately fifteen miles south of what is now Cairo. Its founder, either King Narmer or King Aha, chose this site for its location between Upper and Lower Egypt. According to legend, the king established the city by building a dam to reroute a branch of the Nile and form a flat plain where he could build, and this dam was reinforced by subsequent kings. Indeed, scientists from the Egypt Exploration Society, a British organization that supports scientific research in Egypt, recently discovered that the course of the Nile River near Memphis is significantly east of its original location, and from geological evidence they suspect that this redirection was artificial rather than natural.

To the west of Memphis lies a necropolis with a large number of tombs and pyramids. Today this necropolis area is referred to in terms of its various regions, each one named for a nearby village: Dashur, Saqqara, Abusir, Zawiyet el-Aryan, Giza, and Abu Roash. All of these are important archaeological sites that continue to be scenes of ongoing research.

Even after Twelfth Dynasty king Amenemhet I moved Egypt's capital to nearby Itj-tawy (probably in the area of el-Lisht, though it has never been found), Memphis remained a major administrative and religious center. In fact, throughout its history Memphis was a cult center for the god Ptah, and therefore has a Temple of Ptah. The city also has a palace, the Palace of White Walls, built by either Narmer or Aha. **See also** Abu Roash; Abusir; Amenemhet I; Dashur; Giza; Narmer; Saqqara.

Menkauhor (Menkauhor-Akauhor) (?–ca. 2414 B.C.)

The son of King Neuserre, Menkauhor was a Fifth Dynasty king who reigned for approximately eight years. During this time, according to some ancient Egyptian records, he built a pyramid and a sun temple; however, archaeologists disagree on the identity of these structures. The prevailing theory is that the Headless Pyramid at Saqqara, named for its missing top, is Menkauhor's pyramid and that a temple located at Dashur is his sun temple. Following Menkauhor's death, a cult dedicated to him formed at Saqqara and lasted until the New Kingdom. There is not much else known about Menkauhor's reign except that the material for his tomb came from the Sinai, where his administrators conducted mining operations. A small alabaster statue of Menkauhor is displayed in the Cairo Museum. **See also** Dashur; Neuserre; Saqqara.

Menkaure (Mycerinos) (ca. 2548–ca. 2503 B.C.)

The son of Fourth Dynasty king Khafre, Menkaure (called Mycerinus by the Greeks) was a king who is best known for the small pyramid he built near his father's pyramid at Giza. The lower portion of the pyramid's outer casing was made of Aswan red granite, the upper portion Tura white limestone. The entire structure was originally intended to be approximately 100 feet tall but was 228 feet tall upon its completion because of several changes in its design during its construction. When Egyptologist Colonel Howard Vyse entered and explored the pyramid in 1837–1838, he discovered a sarcophagus later determined to be from approximately the fifth century B.C.; it was probably placed in the king's burial chamber as part of a restoration project undertaken during the Greco-Roman Period. Another major archaeological expedition, led by George A. Reisner of Harvard University, explored the pyramid and its surroundings from 1905 to 1927. This expedition uncovered several sculptures of the king, usually depicted with his wife or deities. Menkaure's principal wife, also his sister, was Queen Khamerernebty II, who gave birth to his heir, Shepseskhaf. **See also** Giza; Shepseskhaf.

Menkheperre (ca. 1080– ca. 992 B.C.)

Some Egyptologists refer to Menkheperre as an Eighteenth Dynasty high priest serving King Tuthmosis III, but the majority believe that Menkheperre was the high priest of Amun during the Twenty-first Dynasty reign of King Pseusennes I. If the latter are correct, then Menkheperre apparently rose to prominence because he was the son of a powerful high priest, Pinudjem I, and because he was King Pseusennes I's son-in-law. Menkheperre is distinguished by the fact that his name sometimes appears in the cartouche format (i.e., contained within an oval) usually reserved for kings. One explanation for this is that Menkheperre lived in southern Egypt at a time when the high priests there saw themselves as rival rulers to the kings of the secular north, so it is likely that Menkheperre thought of himself as the king's equal. Certainly Menkheperre behaved in royal fashion, going into battle as his army's commander just as kings did during this period and fortifying the town of el-Hibeh as a military base. His victories in various battles seem to have resulted in a peaceful and apparently unified south.

In 1891, archaeologists found a tomb that they concluded was Menkheperre's, based on the number of artifacts they could identify as once belonging to Menkheperre or his family members. The tomb's wall scenes show various foreigners paying tribute to a generic king, supporting the idea that Menkheperre thought of himself as a king, or at least acted like one during his military con-

quests. Ancient records indicate that Menkheperre lived to be nearly ninety years old. **See also** priests; Tuthmosis III.

Menna (dates unknown)

During the Eighteenth Dynasty, Menna served King Tuthmosis IV as a royal scribe who held the title "scribe of the fields," which made him responsible for supervising the tallies of herd sizes and crop yields for government and temple estates. Menna's tomb in Thebes contains wall scenes dating from around 1390 B.C. that have provided archaeologists with valuable information about harvests, feasts, and other activities related to Eighteenth Dynasty agriculture. These scenes also have small details related to ancient Egyptian life, such as a depiction of a girl getting a friend to remove a thorn from her foot. In a mortuary stela left beside the tomb, Menna tells of his friendship with the farmers he regularly encountered as part of his work. **See also** scribes; Thebes; Tuthmosis IV.

mercenaries

Ancient Egyptian rulers employed mercenaries at least as early as the Second Intermediate Period, when military men from neighboring Nubia fought for Egypt against the Hyksos. During the Eighteenth Dynasty, when the Hyksos were finally expelled, Nubians also began serving as a special police force. Known as the Medjay, their job was to protect certain Egyptian towns, particularly Thebes. In addition, Nubian, Syrian, and Libyan mercenaries served as private guards for Eighteenth Dynasty king Akhenaten (also known as Amenhotep IV).

By the New Kingdom, Nubians, Libyans, Syrians, and other mercenaries had become a vital part of the Egyptian army. In fact, some historians believe that by the end of this period most Egyptian soldiers were foreign born. Some of these mercenaries had originally entered Egypt as captives of foreign wars and then joined the military upon being set free. Consequently, on some occasions a mercenary might be found fighting for Egypt against his own countrymen.

Mercenaries were valued in Egypt partly because of their superior fighting skills. However, mercenaries were useful for another reason as well. Native Egyptians who died in foreign lands were customarily brought back home for entombment, because the Egyptians believed that otherwise they might not reach the Afterlife. Foreign mercenaries, on the other hand, had no such requirement, thereby sparing the king great expense and inconvenience.

Soldiers who returned from foreign wars having proven themselves in battle, whether they were native or foreign-born men, were typically rewarded with land. Libyan mercenaries were particularly successful in acquiring such rewards. As a result, a number of Libyans rose to political power during the Twenty-first Dynasty as wealthy landowners. By this time they had adopted Egyptian clothing, burial customs, and other attributes, so their practices eventually became almost indistinguishable from those of native Egyptians. Consequently, Libyan military commanders and their family members had the same opportunities as native Egyptians to acquire prominent administrative positions, and during the Third Intermediate Period, the first Egyptian kings of Libyan descent sat on the throne at Tanis, beginning with Osorkon I. These kings continued to control parts or all of Egypt for approximately the next four hundred years. **See also** Libya; Medjay; military; Nubia.

Mereneith (Merneith; Meryetnit) (dates unknown)

A queen of the First Dynasty, Mereneith acted as regent for King Den and apparently ruled for a brief time around 2950 B.C. until he was old enough to serve as king. She was probably also Den's mother and the wife of his predecessor, King Djet.

Mereneith is primarily known today for her mortuary complexes at Saqqara and Abydos. The tomb in Abydos held more than twenty of the queen's retainers and craftsmen, who were expected to serve her in the Afterlife; one of the mummies was that of her shipmaster, because her tomb also contained a solar bark to carry the deceased queen across the sky. Egyptologists disagree on whether these people were killed and mummified upon the queen's death or were added to her tomb later, after dying of natural causes. **See also** Abydos; Den; Saqqara.

Merenre I (Merenra; Nemtyemsaf) (?–ca. 2278 B.C.)

The third king of the Sixth Dynasty, Merenre I ("Beloved of Re") is also known by his birth name, Nemtyemsaf ("Nemty Is His Protector"). He reigned only five years, although some Egyptologists believe that he coruled with his father prior to assuming the throne in approximately 2283 B.C. In either case, Merenre I was apparently still in his teens when he became king and was under the influence of his uncle and vizier, Djau, and a powerful noble, Harkhuf, who was the governor of Elephantine. Archaeologists have also found an inscription in the tomb of Merenre's aunt, Ankhnesmery-Re II, stating that she married Merenre after her husband, King Pepy I, died; she then gave birth to Merenre's heir, Pepy II. Since inscriptions in Ankhnesmery-Re's tomb suggest that she was very powerful, some Egyptologists believe that Merenre I was greatly influenced by her as well.

Egyptologists know little about Merenre's accomplishments other than that he built a canal at Aswan and added fortifications to cities there. Researchers also know he built a pyramid at Saqqara. A sarcophagus was found within this structure, but Egyptologists disagree on whether the mummy it contained was that of a man young enough to have been King Merenre. **See also** Ankhnesmery-Re II; Harkhuf; Saqqara.

Mereruka (ca. 2365–ca. 2323 B.C.)

During the Sixth Dynasty reign of King Teti, Mereruka served as a vizier, the governor of Memphis, and an architect of the king's mortuary complex. He was also the king's son-in-law, having married either Princess Shesheshet or Princess Hertwatet-khet. Mereruka's tomb, located at Saqqara, is a well-preserved structure, and is actually a joint tomb for Mereruka, his wife, and their son Meriteti. The tomb has numerous wall reliefs, beginning with one at its entrance featuring Mereruka at an easel painting scenes that apparently represent each of Egypt's seasons. On a cham-

ber wall, Mereruka is shown inspecting various craftsmen at their work; on the opposite wall, he and his wife are shown hunting. In other rooms, they are depicted playing board games and musical instruments or are engaged in other leisure activities. There are religious symbols in the tomb scenes as well. For example, Mereruka's wife is shown sniffing a lotus flower, a powerful ancient Egyptian symbol related to creation and rebirth.

The tomb also contains many statues of Mereruka, including one of him as his *ka,* or spirit, going through a false door to receive offerings. All of the statues in the tomb were originally placed so that they faced west (the direction associated with the realm of the dead), which was true of all Sixth Dynasty tomb statues. (In Fifth Dynasty tombs, all statues face east, the direction associated with rebirth.) **See also** art; *ka;* lotus; tombs; toys and games; viziers.

A relief, created about 2345 B.C., from Sixth Dynasty vizier Mereruka's tomb at Saqqara depicts farm accounts being settled.

Meresankh III (ca. 2558–ca. 2500 B.C.)

Fourth Dynasty queen Meresankh III was a principal wife of King Khafre and the mother of Prince Nebmakhet. However, she is best known for her rock-cut mortuary complex at Giza. It was prepared by her mother, Queen Hetepheres II, whose own tomb was atop her daughter's. Egyptologists disagree on when Queen Meresankh III died, but most believe it was during the reign of King Shepseskhaf. From records found in the tomb and elsewhere, Egyptologists know that Queen Meresankh III had numerous connections to the royal family; she was the daughter of Crown Prince Kewab (who died before succeeding to the throne), the granddaughter of King Khufu, and the great-granddaughter of Queen Meresankh I. **See also** Kewab; Khafre; Khufu.

Meresger (Mertsager)

An ancient Egyptian snake goddess, Meresger was considered a form of the goddess Hathor, who was usually depicted as a cow. Consequently, Meresger became popular in places where Hathor was worshiped, particularly the village of Deir el-Medina, which housed the people who worked on tombs in the Valley of the Kings and the Valley of the Queens. The temple of this village was decorated with snakes representing Meresger. This association between Meresger and tomb workers probably stemmed from an earlier association between the goddess and tombs; indeed, her name means "She Who Loves Silence" in reference to the quietness of tombs. Eventually the goddess was considered the patroness of a west Theban peak that could be seen from the tomb workers' village, and she was sometimes called the Goddess of the Peak. The villagers also believed that Meresger could inflict poisonous bites, stings, and blindness on humans to punish wrongdoers. Some Theban religious texts portray Meresger as a goddess of punishment who wreaked havoc on wrongdoers until they begged her for mercy. **See also** Deir el-Medina; Hathor; Thebes.

Merikare (ca. 2160–ca. 2125 B.C.)

Probably the son of King Khety III, Merikare ("Beloved Is the Soul of Re") was a king of the Tenth Dynasty, which had been established in the city of Heracleopolis at the beginning of the First Intermediate Period. This period was a time of great political instability in Egypt, and during Merikare's reign, a rival dynasty existed in Thebes. The kings there threatened to encroach on the territory of the Heracleopolitan king. Because he was distracted by such threats, Merikare was unable to accomplish much during his reign. However, he did manage to build a mortuary temple near Memphis. **See also** First Intermediate Period; Heracleopolis; Khety III.

merkabot

The *merkabot* was a type of carriage used during the New Kingdom, probably first brought to Egypt from Palestine. It had two wood and metal wheels with four to six spokes each and was pulled by two horses sharing a leather harness. The carriage was relatively lightweight and was therefore popular with desert hunters, although it could also be used in warfare. However, it was fairly small, so it was not practical for use on long trips that required much in the way of supplies. **See also** animals; military.

Merneptah (Merenptah) (ca. 1275–ca. 1203 B.C.)

Nineteenth Dynasty king Merneptah was elderly when he assumed the throne and apparently ruled for only ten years before dying of old age. Moreover, part of this reign seems to have been a corule with his father, Ramses II. Merneptah was Ramses II's thirteenth or fourteenth son, but all the others died before their father did.

Merneptah left behind three inscriptions telling about his reign, one on a wall within the Temple of Amun in Karnak, one on a stela at the town of Athribis (now called Tell Arib) in the Delta, and one at his mortuary temple in Thebes. From these and other sources, archaeologists know that Merneptah gave grain to the Hittites (a warrior people probably from somewhere around the Black Sea) when they were suffering from a famine. At the same time, he was fighting a military campaign against invading Libyans and Sea Peoples in the Delta. His records indicate that he took more than six thousand men and their families prisoner during this conflict. Archaeologists have also found Merneptah's mummy in a tomb carved into cliffs at the Valley of the Kings. From these remains, they know that Merneptah had arthritis and bad teeth when he died at the age of seventy-two. **See also** Delta; Karnak; Ramses II; Thebes.

Meshkent

Sometimes associated with the goddess Hathor, Meshkent was an ancient Egyptian goddess connected to childbirth. Specifi-

cally, she was the goddess of the birthing bricks, a brick chair that supported women as they crouched to give birth. Because of this association, Meshkent was typically depicted as a woman wearing a brick headdress or as a brick with a woman's head. However, in some depictions, her brick elements were replaced with a symbol that some Egyptologists believe represented the knife used to cut a baby's umbilical cord. Many ancient Egyptians thought that Meshkent was present at each birth to decide each child's fate. In some myths, she was also said to participate in the judging of people's character in the Afterlife, speaking to Osiris and his forty-two judges on behalf of those who deserved absolution rather than condemnation for their misdeeds during life. **See also** Hathor; Osiris; women, role of.

Mesopotamia

Ancient Mesopotamia ("Land Between Two Rivers") was located between the Tigris and Euphrates Rivers in what today is Iraq. The land is significant in terms of ancient Egypt because some modern scholars theorize that ancient Egyptian culture came from people who entered Egypt from Mesopotamia in approximately 3400 B.C.

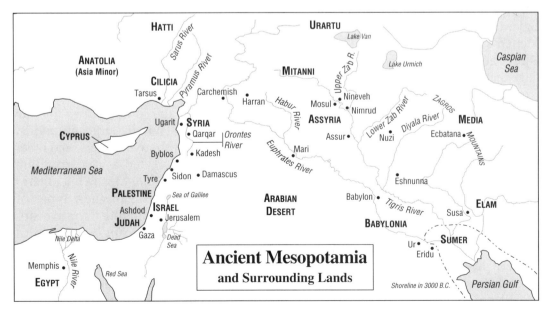

Ancient Mesopotamia
and Surrounding Lands

At that time, Mesopotamia had an advanced culture that included brick architecture with decorated facades, cuneiform writing inscribed on clay tablets, and other elements similar to what would later be found in Egypt. However, other scholars note that although these elements were similar they were not identical. They argue that since the Mesopotamians developed their culture without outside influence (an idea that is in dispute), the Egyptians could well have done so too.

Metjen (Methen) (dates unknown)

The son of a scribe and judge named Anubisemonkeh, Metjen was an important nomarch and public official during the Third Dynasty reign of Djoser. His first government position was as a scribe, but eventually he became governor of the Delta region and later oversaw Egypt's lands in the Faiyum and elsewhere in the east. For Egyptologists, of greatest significance are his writings about his life, which are in the form of reliefs and inscriptions in his mastaba tomb at Saqqara. This material, the oldest surviving autobiography of an Egyptian official, has provided Egyptologists with a great deal of information not only about Metjen but also about ancient Egyptian society, politics, and religion. Metjen's tomb is beside that of King Djoser at Saqqara, but Egyptologists believe that Metjen died during the reign of King Snefru. **See also** Djoser; Faiyum; Saqqara; Snefru.

Middle Kingdom (ca. 2055– ca. 1650 B.C.)

The term *Middle Kingdom* was coined by nineteenth-century historians to identify a period of stability and prosperity in ancient Egyptian history that followed the chaos of the First Intermediate Period. Modern historians disagree on exactly when this period began, but it is generally considered to have lasted from approximately 2055 B.C. to 1650 B.C. and encompassed all or part of the Eleventh Dynasty as well as the Twelfth. Some historians also place the Thirteenth and Fourteenth Dynasties (which existed in the city of Avaris in the Delta during the same period as a rival dynasty in Thebes) in the Middle Kingdom, but most historians consider those two dynasties as being part of the turbulent Second Intermediate Period.

Moreover, while many scholars consider Intef I to be the first Middle Kingdom ruler, the period's stability did not really become established until Upper and Lower Egypt were unified with a strong central government under King Montuhotep II. A king of Thebes who defeated a group of rival kings in the city of Heracleopolis, Montuhotep II crushed a rebellion in a nome (Abydos) that he had taken from the Heracleopolitan kings. His success intimidated the other nomes into bowing to his rule, and by the thirty-ninth year of his fiftieth-year reign, he had conquered all of Egypt.

Subsequent rulers strengthened the newly reunited country through changes in government and military policies. For example, Amenemhet I, who established his capital at Itj-tawy (as yet undiscovered, but probably near el-Lisht) just south of Giza and Saqqara, built fortresses to strengthen Egypt's borders and began invading neighboring territories, both to take over new lands and to acquire building material for numerous construction projects. He and other kings of the Twelfth Dynasty built large pyramids, temples, administrative centers, and other structures and created a vast irrigation system in the Faiyum. Meanwhile, literature flourished and many new types of works appeared, including narrative stories like *The Tale of Sinuhe* and philosophical dialogues like *Dialogue Between a Man Tired of Life and His "Ba."*

In fact, during the Middle Kingdom, art, architecture, engineering, and religion all flourished; mummification became widespread, tomb decorations became lavish, and beliefs related to the Afterlife became more complex. The cult of Osiris, chief god of the dead, grew dramatically, and with it came the conviction that people from all classes of society would have a chance to enjoy eternity. Consequently, the Middle Kingdom was a time of hope as well as prosperity. Toward the end of the Twelfth Dynasty, however, foreign invaders known as Asiatics began to establish themselves in parts of the Delta, and eventually some of them, the Hyksos, took over Egypt, bringing about a definitive end to the Middle Kingdom. **See also** Amenemhet I; Faiyum; First Intermediate Period; Montuhotep; Second Intermediate Period.

military

Most of what Egyptologists know about the ancient Egyptian military comes from the New Kingdom, when Egypt developed a national standing army. Egyptologists have gathered information about this army from wall scenes and inscriptions in various tombs, as well as from chariots that were placed in their owners' tombs. For example, King Tuthmosis IV, soldier Yuya, and scribe Userhet were all entombed with chariots, and the tomb of the king featured reliefs related to his military exploits. Temples at Abydos, Karnak, Abu Simbel, and elsewhere have also provided reliefs related to the military, as have walls in the city of Amarna (Akhetaten). A few papyri also offer such information.

A wall painting from the tomb of the Eighteenth Dynasty scribe Userhet shows military recruits being addressed by an officer (top), biding time (center), and having their hair cut (bottom).

One of the most complete sources of information about the military in terms of the ordinary soldier, as opposed to a king or general, is the tomb of Ahmose Son of Abana, an Eighteenth Dynasty professional soldier who fought in wars against the Hyksos. His autobiographical wall inscriptions tell how he was trained in the use of the bow and arrow and several bronze-tipped weapons and blades. He also describes his body armor, made of overlapping metal pieces stitched to a linen or leather sleeveless jacket, which he wore over a short kilt and breechcloth complemented by a leather helmet.

In charge of the professional army was the king, who often led troops into battle himself. However, the king's vizier actually took on most of the responsibility for a military campaign as minister of war. Also important were princes and generals, who would take charge of military action on the battlefield whenever the king was not present. There was also a hierarchy of lesser commanders, grouped under a lieutenant commander who reported directly to the general, who took charge of various divisions and special forces of soldiers; the titles of these commanders were usually based on how many men were under their control. For example, the honorific Greatest of Fifty denoted the commander of the smallest unit of men, numbering fifty.

Some of these divisions saw action on the battlefield, while others were assigned to a variety of permanent duties. For example, the 'w'yt was a force placed in charge of army garrisons and fortresses and perhaps the king's household as well. The chariotry was an elite fighting group that fought from within chariots, while all other soldiers were on foot. Soldiers also manned the ships of the Egyptian navy, which was considered a part of the army because its main purpose was to transport troops and supplies.

As with the army, there was a hierarchy of naval officers, including the admiral, the captain, the captain's mates, and the sailors (or w'w). By all accounts, life on an ancient Egyptian warship was difficult, particularly since they were powered by oars as well as wind. Nonetheless, many men wanted to be in the professional navy—and in the army as well—because it offered them an opportunity to gain great wealth. Soldiers and sailors typically received a share of the spoils of war as well as their regular pay and exemptions from taxes.

Whenever the Egyptian military won a foreign war, it usually allowed the conquered leaders to remain in control of their own land in return for payment of tribute to Egypt's king. These conquered leaders could and did mount rebellions, so it was not unusual for the Egyptian military to have to retake the same lands on several occasions. **See also** Ahmose Son of Abana; chariots; fortresses; mercenaries; weapons and armor.

Min (Menu)

Called Menu by the ancient Egyptians but renamed by the Greeks, Min was a god of desert travel. However, he was thought to protect not only travelers but also crops; harvests; the fertility of plants, animals, and people; and the productivity of the Eastern Desert mines. He was often depicted as a man partially wrapped in linens for mummification. In a few locations, Min was said to have fathered the god Horus with the goddess Isis.

The main center of Min worship was at Coptos (north of Luxor), where many festivals and rituals were held in his honor, but Min festivals were held elsewhere as well. During the New Kingdom, after the people of Thebes promoted the idea that Min was an aspect of the popular sun god Amun, Min worship became more widespread. For example, Ramses III built a mortuary temple at Medinet

Habu dedicated to Amun that has wall scenes depicting a festival of Min. In addition, the mortuary temple of Ramses II at Thebes shows the king watching a festival procession in which two poles topped by Min's traditional headdress, a plumed crown decorated with a streamer, are carried by priests, followed by statues of the king's ancestors. **See also** Amun; Coptos; Medinet Habu; Thebes.

mining and metalworking

Egyptians had relatively few domestic sources for the metals they used in making weapons, tools, jewelry, and other items. For example, the best sources of gold were the Eastern Desert and Nubia. Copper was mined in the Eastern Desert and Nubia as well, and in the Sinai. The Sinai was also an important source of turquoise. Galena (lead sulfide), used in cosmetics, came from Gebel Zet on the Red Sea.

Mining operations in these regions were supervised by the military and were extremely complex, since they involved the transportation of hundreds—if not thousands—of workers along with their food, tools, and other supplies to distant sites. In some parts of Nubia, colonies were established to house workers near particularly productive mining sites. However, in most cases, miners were transported to a site and left there only as long as it took to acquire the amount of ore specified in a government work order. Archaeologists have found examples of these work orders, either inscribed on rock walls at the mining site or written on ancient papyri, giving precise details about how much stone or ore was needed and/or how long the expedition was given to achieve its objectives.

Once a mining order had been filled, the expedition returned the ore to the state and temple workshops, where it would be refined so that the metal could be worked. The craftsmen used a variety of techniques to melt the metal, shape it, cool it, and hammer it into desired forms. The ancient Egyptians were not particularly skilled in working with copper and bronze because they rarely chose to work with these metals, but with gold they became experts in producing fine jewelry and other items. To convert gold into such items, they first placed it within a crucible and heated it on an open fire, blowing onto the flames through reeds or, in later periods, using foot- or hand-pumped bellows made from goatskin and reeds. Once the gold had melted, they used metal tongs to lift its container and pour the molten substance into molds of various shapes, then waited for it to cool enough for the shape to be refined using hammers and other tools and polishers. They might then set various semi-precious stones within the gold. For this reason, the workshops of goldsmiths were typically combined with the workshops of stonecutters and jewel and bead makers. **See also** building materials; Eastern Desert; Nubia; stoneworking.

Mitanni

Mitanni was a militaristic kingdom located between the Tigris and Euphrates Rivers in a region called Naharin (River Country), which is now the border region between modern-day Syria and Iraq. The Mitanni were at first Egypt's enemy but later their ally against the Hurrians, another people in the region.

At the beginning of the Eighteenth Dynasty, the Mitanni began pushing their border south, where they collided with a newly established Egyptian border at the Euphrates River. Soon, northern Syria became a site of skirmishes between the two forces, each side aided by various Palestinian and Syrian princes. Then King Tuthmosis I led a major military expedition to the region and succeeded in capturing and killing many Mitanni and driving back their forces. Tuthmosis I returned home triumphant, but his success failed to end the Mitanni threat. His son Tuthmosis II would also fight in Syria and Palestine, yet by the subsequent reign of Tuthmosis III, the Mitanni had gained much of the region and had crossed the Euphrates River, pushing back Egypt's border. Inconclusive fighting between Mitanni and Egypt continued for the remainder of Tuthmosis III's reign. After his death, however, his son Amenhotep II decided to leave the Mitanni in peace in exchange for payment of tribute to Egypt, and did not encroach on lands previously established as his to rule. From this point on, Egypt and Mitanni became allies, and Amenhotep II further cemented this relationship by marrying several Mitanni princesses. **See also** Amenhotep II; Tuthmosis I; Tuthmosis II; Tuthmosis III.

Mnevis bull

Sacred to the city of Heliopolis, the Mnevis bull was thought to be a manifestation of the god Re. Therefore, the animal was cared for in the god's temple and included in various rituals there. To be considered a manifestation of Re, a bull had to have an all-black body with tufts of white hair scattered throughout its coat. Once the Mnevis bull died, it was mummified much as a human body would be, and another bull of similar appearance was found to take its place. **See also** bulls, sacred.

models, tomb

Tomb models were statues of servants and replicas of boats and other items that were placed in tombs. The ancient Egyptians believed that, through certain rituals performed at the tomb owner's funeral, such items would magically be transformed into real, full-sized servants and items that could be employed in the Afterlife. Such models were typically carved out of wood and painted to look as real as possible.

Ancient Egyptians believed that tomb models, such as this boat and its crew, would transform to full size and serve the deceased in the Afterlife.

The earliest tomb models date from the Old Kingdom and were simply figures of servants. By the Middle Kingdom, however, servant models had become complex, featuring groups of servants engaged in activities using models of tools, equipment, and buildings. For example, Middle Kingdom models might represent servants using beer-making equipment, plowing a field, working in a granary, or taking care of various other elements of the tomb owner's estate.

Sometimes, the tomb owner's house was modeled in complete detail. The wealthiest tomb owners might have models of soldiers as well, complete with weapons with which they could protect the tomb owner throughout eternity; models of concubines to serve male tomb owners as sexual partners were also in some tombs. Model boats were even more important to many tomb owners. They might have several ships of various sizes and shapes—sometimes enough to be considered a fleet—always reproduced in complete and exact detail. Some of these model boats were for fishing, some for pleasure boating, some for short- or long-distance travel, and some for the transportation of food and supplies. The most ornate model boats were intended to carry the deceased tomb owner on pilgrimages to religious ceremonies and festivals. **See also** funerals; *shabti;* tomb goods; tombs.

Mont

Mont was an ancient Egyptian deity first worshiped as a warrior god. By the time of the Old Kingdom, however, he had become a sun god. Typically depicted with a hawk's head and associated with Horus, Mont was particularly prominent around Thebes; his cult center was south of the city, at Erment. There the priests kept a bull, Buchis, that was considered a physical manifestation of Mont. Later, after the god Amun supplanted Mont in promi-

nence in Thebes, Buchis (which had a white body and a black head) was said to be a manifestation of the god Amun instead. **See also** Amun.

Montuemhet (ca. 700–650 B.C.)

A Twenty-fifth Dynasty noble, Montuemhet was the fourth prophet of Amun in Thebes during the reign of King Taharqa. However, he held more power than what normally came with the title, effectively controlling the entire city and eventually other parts of Upper Egypt as well. Evidence of his power comes from the fact that he built numerous temples in Thebes as well as a large tomb for himself at Deir el-Bahri. Inscriptions in his tomb indicate that when the Assyrians invaded Thebes, Montuemhet negotiated the peace treaty between them and Egypt without consulting the king. **See also** Amun; Deir el-Bahri; Taharqa; Thebes.

Montuhotep

Several Middle Kingdom kings of the Eleventh Dynasty had the birth name of Montuhotep ("[The God] Montu Is Content"), although some were more commonly known by their throne name. Egyptologists disagree on the order of their rule, so while some refer to them as Montuhotep I, II, III, and so forth, others prefer to call them by their throne name. These kings and their major accomplishments are as follows:

Nebhetepre ("Pleased Is the Lord Re"), Montuhotep I or II (?– ca. 2010 B.C.), was crowned king in approximately 2060 B.C. and reigned for fifty years, during which he built a magnificent funerary palace near Thebes. Although this structure has been almost completely destroyed by erosion and other forces—both natural and human—Egyptologists can tell that it once had an underground tomb most likely topped by a pyramid, with terraces, trees, and gardens. Nearby are the tombs of the king's many wives, as well as the bodies of approximately sixty soldiers displaying battle wounds. Archaeologists have concluded that these soldiers were killed in one of Nebhetepre's many military campaigns. Nebhetepre fought in several battles that resulted in the taking of the city of Heracleopolis from a rival line of kings and the expulsion of Libyan invaders from Egypt. He also reestablished a strong centralized government and subdued various nomarchs who were threatening the crown. After his success in unifying Upper and Lower Egypt under one rule, an accomplishment that ended a division that began at the end of the Old Kingdom, he changed his Horus name (another name, aside from the throne name, given to the king at his coronation) from Horus Netjeryhedjet ("Lord of the White Crown [Upper Egypt]") to Horus Smatowy ("Uniting the Two Lands").

Sankhkare ("Giving Life to the Soul of Re"), Montuhotep II or III (?–ca. 1998 B.C.), took the throne in approximately 2010 B.C., when he was most likely an old man, and reigned for approximately twelve years. During this time, he initiated trade with people in the Red Sea region and encouraged an increase in trading with the land of Punt. He was also active in mining and quarrying operations, particularly in the Wadi Hammamat region of the Eastern Desert, and built several structures, including a temple or festival shrine to the god Thoth and the beginnings of a mortuary temple at Deir el-Bahri.

Nebtawyre ("Lord of the Two Lands of Re"), Montuhotep III or IV (?–ca. 1991 B.C.), assumed the throne in approximately 1998 B.C., after which he founded an important town on the Red Sea, Kuser, with a harbor used for shipbuilding and launching voyages to Punt. He also encouraged mining, quarrying, and trading expeditions. In such endeavors, he was assisted by his vizier, Amenemhet I, who succeeded him on the throne. However, some modern scholars believe that

Amenemhet played some role in the end of Nabtawyre's reign, because the king suddenly and inexplicably disappears from all records after a reign of only approximately six years. **See also** Amenemhet I; Libya; Middle Kingdom; Punt.

monuments

Egyptologists use the term *monument* to refer to structures that serve as memorials. Some Egyptologists use a narrow definition of the term, considering only tombs, pyramids, and temples to be monuments. Others define monuments more broadly, including cemeteries, cities, towns, villages, and fortresses—in short, any structure that shows evidence of an ancient person's life—in their definition. **See also** cemeteries; fortresses; houses; pyramids; temples; tombs.

mummification

Mummification is the process of embalming and wrapping a body in order to preserve it. Such preservation was important because, according to ancient Egyptian religious beliefs, the body needed to be intact for the deceased to enjoy the Afterlife. Only two ancient Egyptian texts, papyri from the first century A.D., explain the process of mummification, and both are incomplete and badly damaged; therefore Egyptologists have had to learn about mummification from studying the mummies themselves. Egyptologists know that the ancient Egyptians first attempted to preserve corpses in about 2600 B.C. Their first efforts involved wrapping bodies in strips of linen soaked in resin, thereby creating a cast around the body as the resin hardened. However, even though this made a permanent representation of the body's shape, the body itself would still eventually decay. As a result, the Egyptians began to experiment with various techniques to dry out the corpse so it would not decompose. By the Fourth Dynasty, they had figured out that removing the internal organs and treating the body with salt would preserve it. Over time, this process was refined, and specialists in mummification (embalmers) became more skilled. Their goal became to do as little damage to the body as possible, while still removing all of its fluids so it would not decay.

As the first step toward mummification, the body was taken to a building called an *ibu,* or "purification house," for an initial washing. Probably located on the Nile River or some other water source, this structure was used for a variety of rituals associated with purification. Once purified, the body was taken to an embalming house, which was at first a linen tent but by the Late Period a mud-brick structure. In the embalming house, the body was placed on a wooden or stone table that had grooves to direct fluids away from the work area. There the body's blood was drained and its abdominal organs and entrails removed through an incision, which might run from the navel to the left hip bone. Archaeologists have found knives made of volcanic glass that were apparently made specifically for embalmers. The lungs and the esophagus were also removed through the incision, with the embalmer reaching up through the diaphragm to grab them. Egyptologists disagree on whether the heart was removed as well, but if it was, then it was subsequently replaced to accompany its owner's body into the Afterlife.

Once removed from the body, the internal organs were washed, typically in palm wine, and packed in salts that drew all the liquid from them over several days. Meanwhile the brain, which was thought to have no value, was extracted using a hooked wire inserted through the nostrils and discarded. (Sometimes the eyes were cast away as well.) After the brain was discarded, the embalmers flushed out the cranial cavity and filled it with a liquid resin that soon hardened. They then washed the body with palm wine, stuffed its empty cavities with aromatic spices and bundles of cloth or other packing material, sewed any incisions closed, and buried the body in a bed of natron. This composition of mineral salts, found primarily in Egypt's Natron Valley (the Wadi Natron) in the Western Desert, not only drew water from body tissue but also broke down and drew out fat deposits. It took approximately forty days for the entire dehydration process to be completed.

During this time, the embalmer turned his attention back to the body's organs, which had already dehydrated. They were covered with a liquid resin, and after the resin hardened, the organs were wrapped in linen and placed in containers called canopic jars, in a box or miniature coffin called a coffinette, or back

These mummy cases, of two kings named Intef, date from about 1600 B.C.

into the body once it had been fully dehydrated. The treatment of the internal organs could be quite elaborate. In the case of King Tutankhamun, for example, his lungs, liver, stomach, and intestines were each placed in a separate coffinette made in his likeness, decorated with gold, and stored in an elaborate canopic chest.

After it was thoroughly dehydrated, the body was removed from the natron, washed, and positioned so that its arms were folded over its midsection. Once properly arranged, the body was ready to be wrapped in linen strips. The linen that would rest against the body was of the best quality, whereas outer wrappings were coarse. Both types of linen were soaked in or coated on the underside with either liquid resin or gum prior to wrapping in order to completely seal the body.

Within the wrappings, in between the many layers of linen, the embalmers tucked jewelry, charms, and other small treasures. Sometimes the number of these items was great. King Tutankhamun's mummy, for instance, contained over 150 pieces of jewelry and amulets.

Mummification involved more than just a physical process. At various steps in the procedure, priests performed rituals and ceremonies designed to help the spirit of the deceased reach and succeed in the Afterlife. No one knows exactly what these rituals and ceremonies were, but they differed according to the rank of the deceased and the historical period in which they took place. In general, though, as the body was being wrapped, a priest chanted magic spells over it to ensure that the deceased would one day be reanimated. The priest wore a mask with the face of a jackal, representing the god of embalming, Anubis, and was perhaps assisted by another priest dressed to look like Osiris, chief god of the dead. During the New Kingdom, sometimes the priest placed amulets or prayers from

the *Book of the Dead* (a guide to the Afterlife that included not only prayers but also magic spells and hymns) in with the body's organs to protect them. After the required number of days for the mummification process, which ranged from forty to seventy days but in one case took 274 days, the body was taken to its resting place, where more rituals were conducted as part of the deceased's funeral. **See also** Afterlife; funerals; natron; religion; tombs.

mummy panel portraits
During the Greco-Roman Period of Egyptian history, the Greeks and Romans living in Egypt adopted the Egyptian practice of mummifying the dead. However, instead of placing masks over the mummies' faces, as was the Egyptian custom, they used mummy panel portraits, wooden boards on which a likeness of the deceased had been painted.

The biggest discovery of mummy panel portraits was in a Roman cemetery in the Faiyum at Hawara. Found by British archaeologist Sir William Matthew Flinders Petrie in 1887, its brick tombs contained dozens of mummy panel portraits apparently painted during the third or fourth century, as indicated by the clothing, hair, and jewelry styles of the subjects. Here and elsewhere, the paintings on mummy panel portraits are highly detailed. The paint used was tempera, a mixture of various pigments, animal glue, and wax.

Most of the Hawara portraits are of young men and women. This leads some Egyptologists to believe that they were painted long before the subjects' deaths and were used as household wall paintings until they were needed. Other experts, however, argue that the portraits were painted at the time of death and that the reason the subjects appear young is because they died young. In either case, the shape of the wooden panels was sometimes altered to conform to the outline of the mummy. Fortunately this did not damage the central image in the painting, because it was surrounded by a painted background that could easily be trimmed. **See also** Hawara; mummification.

music

Egyptologists do not know what ancient Egyptian music might have sounded like, since no written musical scores have ever been found. However, they generally believe that music was featured in temple ceremonies and festivals and as part of the entertainment at various public and private gatherings. The oldest known instruments, dating from predynastic times, were wooden or reed flutes and clarinets; trumpets, castanets, cymbals, bells, and handheld harps were used during the Old Kingdom. By the Middle Kingdom there were standing harps as well, along with guitars, tambourines, and various types of rattles. In subsequent periods, foreigners entering Egypt brought new instruments, including the lute, lyre, and oboe. The main goal of temple music was to create rhythmic sounds rather than tunes.

The musical instruments selected for use during a particular religious ceremony most likely depended on the deity or deities they were meant to invoke. For example, the sistrum, a ceremonial rattle typically made of bronze, was said to be the instrument of the goddess Hathor and was often associated with fertility rituals. However, this instrument was also employed by the Divine Wife of Amun (a position held by a royal Egyptian woman that came with religious duties) in the Temple of Amun at Karnak in ceremonies designed to honor the god Amun. Even household deities, who were typically the focus of personal worship rather than large temple ceremonies, might be associated with certain instruments. For example, Bes (a deity connected to childbirth) was associated with the harp, the tambourine, and several other instruments.

In some cases, the objective of the music was apparently to raise a cacophony that would scare away evil spirits; in others, it was to please the gods. Because the ancient Egyptians believed that most music pleased the gods, they incorporated it into as many daily rituals and activities as possible. Workers on building sites often sang while they labored, and people of all classes were encouraged to play instruments. However, it appears that only blind musicians were allowed to play in temple sanctuaries, because no one but a priest or a king was allowed to view some of the items there, such as the sacred statues of the gods. **See also** Bes; dancing; Hathor; songs.

Mut

Mut was an ancient Egyptian goddess whose body formed the sky, although she was believed to manifest on earth sometimes as a vulture. In mythology she was the wife of Amun, a solar deity, and the mother of his son Khons, a lunar deity. (According to some myths, she was Khons's adoptive rather than natural mother.) Mut was also associated with Sekhmet, a goddess who often represented the warrior aspect of female deities. Egyptologists believe that a temple dedicated to Mut at Karnak that had over three hundred statues of Sekhmet is evidence of this association. **See also** Amun; Karnak; Sekhmet.

Mutemwiya (dates unknown)

An Eighteenth Dynasty queen circa 1400 B.C., Mutemwiya was the wife of King Tuthmosis IV. Mutemwiya was possibly a foreign princess, perhaps from Mitanni, sent to the king as a tribute. She probably acted as regent to the king's heir, Amenhotep III, during the early years of his reign, although some Egyptologists believe that the regent was someone from the family of the young girl who became the young boy's wife Queen Tiy, in the second year of his reign. What is not in dispute is that Mutemwiya was Amenhotep III's mother, because he depicted her in that role in wall reliefs in a temple complex that he built at Luxor. In these reliefs, Amenhotep III is shown as an infant being formed by the god Khnum, after which he is born to Queen Mutemwiya; the god Amun is depicted as the father. Amenhotep III also built Mutemwiya a tomb at Thebes, and probably thanks to his efforts, she was honored in Egypt long after her death. **See also** Amenhotep III; Amun; Luxor; Tiy; Tuthmosis IV.

myths

Egyptologists believe that the ancient Egyptians primarily passed on their myths orally rather than through written texts, because relatively few written versions of myths survive today. The ancient Egyptian myths that have survived are contradictory, which means that two gods might be brothers in one myth, for example, and father and son or uncle and nephew in another. Most of the surviving myths discuss the gods in their role as creators and maintainers of the world, and as part of this maintenance they were often called upon to battle evil gods or monstrous Underworld creatures. **See also** Creation myths; literature; Scorpion King; Underworld.

names, royal

Most people in ancient Egypt had only one name, but kings might have several. In fact, by the Eleventh Dynasty, the king had five names, the first a name given to him at birth and the remaining four names given to him when he assumed the throne. Each name was also associated with a royal title. The birth name, or nomen, came with the title "Son of Re." The throne name, or prenomen, came with the title "He of the Sedge and Bee" (sedge and bee were symbolic terms for Upper and Lower Egypt). The Horus name, sometimes referred to as the golden Horus name, came with the title "Golden Horus," while the *nebti,* or two ladies' name, came with the title "He of the Two Ladies" (the two ladies were goddesses Wadjet and Nekhbet of Upper and Lower Egypt, respectively). The last name, the Horus name, came with the title "Horus."

From the Twelfth Dynasty on, all five names were used as the king's official signature and in association with coronations and other major events in a king's rule. However, the kings themselves preferred to refer to themselves simply by one of their names—in order of preference, the Horus name, throne name, or birth name. **See also** Horus.

Napata

From the Nineteenth Dynasty on, the town of Napata in Nubia became an important center of Nubian civilization and eventually the capital of Upper Nubia (which was also called Napata or Napata-Meroe), a kingdom that had gained its independence from Egypt. In the Twenty-fourth Dynasty, military forces from this kingdom moved north into Egypt, where one of Napata's kings, Piankhy-Piye, established the Twenty-fifth Dynasty. Although this Nubian dynasty lasted less than one hundred years, Napata survived as an independent kingdom until sometime during the fourth century A.D. **See also** Nubia.

Napoléon I (1769–1821)

Napoléon Bonaparte, the man who became Emperor Napoléon I of France, is best known in connection with Egyptology for having led an expedition of twenty-five thousand soldiers and an assortment of scholars to Egypt in 1798. The purpose of his expedition was twofold: first, to challenge British power in the region by conquering Egypt and, second, to study the Egyptian culture, both ancient and contemporary.

The military aspect of Napoléon's expedition failed, but the research aspect was a success. It was the largest and most extensive study of ancient Egypt ever undertaken. Archaeologists, architects, artists, surveyors, engineers, mathematicians, botanists, and other experts spent three years investigating and reporting on Egypt's culture, history, flora, fauna, monuments, artifacts, and other features. They also mapped the location of both contemporary and ancient cities, buildings, and monuments. Perhaps the most important

Narmer—and by extension kingship in general—became associated with Horus.

Narmer might also have been the first king to unite Upper and Lower Egypt, although this is by no means certain. Support for this theory comes from a dark green slate palette (a slab used as a mixing surface to turn powders into paints and cosmetics) known today as the Narmer Palette; dating from Narmer's reign, it has decorations showing the king wearing both the White Crown of Upper Egypt and the Red Crown of Lower Egypt, suggesting the he controlled all of Egypt. However, according to a third-century-B.C. Greco-Egyptian priest, Manetho (who apparently relied on ancient records as his sources), a king named Menes was the ruler of a united Egypt. Some Egyptologists therefore believe that Menes and not Narmer brought Upper and Lower Egypt under one rule. Still others think that Narmer's successor, Aha (also known as Hor-Aha), was the true unifier but gave credit to Narmer, who was probably his father.

There is also evidence that Narmer fought in some major battles. His ceremonial macehead indicates that he took over the Delta by capturing 120,000 men, 400 oxen, and nearly 1.5 million goats. He might also have married a Memphis noblewoman or princess, possibly Neithotpe, as part of a political alliance between his city and hers. **See also** Aha; Manetho; Scorpion King.

Napoléon's 1798 expedition to Egypt had both military and scholarly objectives.

discovery made during Napoléon's expedition was that of what came to be called the Rosetta Stone, a piece of rock that had what turned out to be the same text in three different languages—hieroglyphic, demotic, and Greek—inscribed on it. This discovery eventually helped scholars learn how to translate ancient Egyptian hieroglyphics. **See also** Rosetta Stone.

Narmer (dates unknown)

Apparently the last king of the Predynastic Period, Narmer ruled around 3000 B.C. from the city of Hierakonpolis, a cult center for the god Horus. Narmer's choice of Hierakonpolis as his capital had lasting consequences for Egyptians' attitudes and beliefs about their kings' relationship to the gods. By establishing the royal capital in the god's cult center,

natron

Natron (or *net-jeryt,* "of the god," in ancient Egyptian) is a mixture of sodium carbonate and bicarbonate with salt, sodium sulfate, and other substances. In ancient times, it was primarily found in the Wadi Natron (Valley of Natron) in Egypt's Western Desert, left behind on the valley floor when a series of lakes evaporated each summer.

The ancient Egyptians used natron to dehydrate the tissues and organs of bodies during the mummification process. First, the body's internal organs were removed and placed in containers of natron; then natron was stuffed inside the body and placed around it. Over the following days—possibly as many as forty—the natron worked to break down fat and grease and draw it from the body and its organs. After this, the natron was washed off and other steps in the mummification process took place.

The natron used for mummification was solid and dry but sometimes mixed with liquid or semiliquid resin. The ancient Egyptians also used liquid natron to bleach cloth and possibly to make soap. **See also** mummification.

Nauri Decree

King Seti I issued what is now known as the Nauri Decree during the Nineteenth Dynasty in an attempt to control workers constructing his mortuary complex at Abydos. The document established guidelines for how workers should behave and outlined various punishments for crimes committed at the site. It also addressed issues related to the care of the king's mortuary complex and its estates. **See also** Abydos; Seti I.

Necho II (Nekau I; Wahemibre) (?–595 B.C.)

Also known by his throne name, Wahemibre ("Carrying Out the Wish of Re Forever"), Necho II began his reign in 610 B.C.—during the Twenty-sixth Dynasty—when Egypt was relatively free of internal political and social problems. As a result of this period of calm, the king had enough money and military power to conquer other lands, most notably Syria and Palestine. He also built up trade with Greece, established a navy for Egypt, and created a canal that enabled ships to travel from a branch of the Nile River to the Red Sea. In addition, Necho II sponsored seagoing expeditions. In fact, some

Egyptologists believe that sailors serving Necho II were the first to circumnavigate Africa. **See also** travel.

necropolis

Egyptologists and archaeologists use the term *necropolis,* the Greek word for "cemetery," to refer to large, important burial areas that were in use for so many years in ancient Egypt that they contain burials from different eras of history. The term *cemetery* is reserved for smaller burial areas or for sections of a necropolis where all burials are from the same dynasty or other unified period of history. **See also** burial sites; cemeteries.

Neferhotep I (dates unknown)

During the Thirteenth Dynasty, King Neferhotep I controlled the Nile Delta except for lands held by a foreign people, the Hyksos. Neferhotep I, apparently the son of an Abydos priest, was not of royal blood, and it is unclear how he became king. Nonetheless, he ruled approximately nine years, sometime around 1740 B.C., and his accomplishments were considerable. During this time, he became preoccupied with his country's religious activities, overseeing various ceremonies, festivals, sacred plays, and other events, particularly at Abydos, and built his pyramid at el-Lisht. However, he also built up foreign trade, encouraging strong relationships with Nubia and Lebanon. Neferhotep I's son, Wahneferhotep, by his principal queen Senebsen, apparently died before he could assume the throne, so the king was succeeded by his brother, Sobekhotep IV. **See also** Hyksos.

Nefertari (Nefertari-Mery-Mut) (?–1250 B.C.)

Nineteenth Dynasty queen Nefertari was the principal wife of Ramses II. Her father was probably Bakenkhons, an important official, and her brother was apparently Amenmose, the mayor of

Thebes. Queen Nefertari had several children, including Princes Amonhirwonmef and Prehirwonmef and Princesses Merytamon and Mertatum, none of whom lived long enough to inherit the throne.

Exactly what became of Nefertari is a mystery. She probably died in the twenty-fourth year of her husband's reign, whereupon another wife, Istnofret, took her place as principal wife. However, some Egyptologists believe that Nefertari did not die at this point but merely retired from public life. In either case, there is no record of her from this point on, and her disappearance roughly coincides with the dedication of her temple.

Queen Nefertari's temple was constructed in Abu Simbel, beside that of her husband. Scenes in her temple feature the goddess Hathor, with whom Nefertari was associated throughout her life. The queen's large rock-cut tomb contains many such paintings as well, and is considered by most Egyptologists to be one of the most beautiful tombs in the Valley of the Queens. **See also** Bakenkhons; Ramses II.

Nefertem

Nefertem was an ancient Egyptian god associated with the lotus flower and its fragrance. Because in some myths the sun was said to have originally emerged from such a flower, Nefertem became known as a sun god in various places and times. At Memphis, however, he was worshiped as the son of the creator god Ptah and the lioness-headed goddess Sekhmet. Consequently, in Memphis, Nefertem was often depicted with the head of a lion. Elsewhere, Nefertem was worshiped as the son of the cat goddess Bastet or the cobra goddess Wadjet. In myths featuring the sun god Re, Nefertem was sometimes said to have comforted Re by giving him a lotus flower when he was upset, and some Old Kingdom texts refer to Nefertem as the lotus flower before Re's nose. **See also** Bastet; lotus; Ptah; Re; Sekhmet; Wadjet.

Nefertiti (dates unknown)

Eighteenth Dynasty queen Nefertiti was the wife of King Amenhotep IV, who eventually changed his name to Akhenaten. She was also possibly the niece of Queen Tiy, her husband's mother. Queen Nefertiti apparently had six daughters with Akhenaten but no sons, leading some Egyptologists to argue that the king took a second wife, Kiya, who most likely produced the king's eventual heir, Tutankhamun.

Some Egyptologists contend that when her husband died, Nefertiti took over the throne by impersonating a man and taking the name Smenkhkare, who is listed in some ancient sources as having reigned for a few months in between the reigns of Amenhotep IV and Tutankhamun. The theory that Nefertiti and Smenkhkare were the

Some scholars believe that Eighteenth Dynasty queen Nefertiti, portrayed in this painted limestone bust, briefly ruled Egypt following the death of her husband, Amenhotep IV.

same person is based on several facts. First, upon assuming the throne, Smenkhkare adopted many of Nefertiti's names and titles. Second, in a painting that is labeled as Smenkhkare and his wife, the wife is Nefertiti's daughter Merytaten and she is shown seated on the king's lap, which is the traditional pose in such artwork for daughters, not wives. (An earlier queen who usurped the throne, Hatshepsut, and her daughter were depicted this way in a similar painting.) Finally, during her husband's reign, Queen Nefertiti seems to have been the power behind the throne, so it is likely she would have wanted to continue controlling Egypt.

Nonetheless, most Egyptologists believe that Nefertiti was not Smenkhkare. Instead, they theorize that Smenkhkare was another son of King Akhenaten, either by Kiya or some other, as yet unidentified, wife. In support of their position, they note that a mummy found in the Valley of the Kings has been proven through testing to be that of a brother or half-brother of King Tutankhamun.

Queen Nefertiti's mummy has never been found. However, archaeologists have found numerous paintings and reliefs, not only in her husband's city of Akhetaten but also in his buildings at Karnak, that depict the queen. In one of the most famous wall paintings, the queen is shown grieving over the death of her daughter Merytaten. In others, she is shown participating in ceremonies honoring the god Aten and performing many rituals normally reserved for the king, including one symbolizing her physical attack on Egypt's enemies. Queen Nefertiti is also the subject of one of the most famous ancient Egyptian works of art, a painted portrait bust probably crafted by Thutmose, King Akhenaten's chief sculptor. It is currently in the Egyptian Museum in Berlin. **See also** Amarna; Amenhotep IV; Kiya; Smenkhkare; Tutankhamun.

Neferure (Nefuru-Re; Nefrura) (ca. 1492–ca. 1470 B.C.)

Neferure, an Eighteenth Dynasty princess, was the daughter of Queen Hatshepsut, who took over as ruler when Neferure's father, King Tuthmosis II, died. During Hatshepsut's reign, Princess Neferure held the title "Divine Wife of Amun." This was usually reserved for the queen, but since Hatshepsut could not have a wife, she gave the title to her daughter instead. Princess Neferure was also apparently a favorite of her mother's vizier, Senenmut, because she is often depicted with him; some Egyptologists therefore believe that she might have been his daughter instead of the child of King Tuthmosis II. Egyptologists also suspect that Nefurure married her half-brother Tuthmosis III, who eventually became king, because a tablet found in the Sinai lists her as "king's daughter, king's wife." However, it appears that she died in the eleventh year of her mother's reign, so she never actually held the title of queen. **See also** Hatshepsut; Senenmut; Tuthmosis II; Tuthmosis III.

Neith

Called Nit in ancient Egypt but renamed by the Greeks, Neith was a goddess first worshiped in predynastic times. Her cult center was at Sais (on a branch of the Nile in the Delta northwest of Cairo), but worship of the goddess eventually spread to the Faiyum and other parts of the Delta. During the Twenty-sixth Dynasty, when Sais was Egypt's capital, Neith was considered one of the country's most important deities.

Because she was also one of Egypt's oldest deities, Neith had many associations, with various ones being prominent at different times and places. Neith was variously said to be the mother of the crocodile god Sobek, the wife of the destroyer god Seth (although more commonly the goddess Nephthys was depicted in this role), and at times a creator goddess thought to be an aspect of Nun, the primordial waters from which the earth arose. Neith was also a funerary goddess who watched over the canopic jar that held the stomach. In addition, she was connected to linen mummy bandages, which is probably why in some parts of Egypt she was associated with weaving and weavers. The Greeks viewed Neith as the equivalent of Athena, their warrior goddess. Indeed, even before the Greeks gained influence in Egypt, certain Egyptians also associated her with warfare and hunting, and she was often depicted holding a bow and arrow and usually wearing the crown of Lower Egypt. **See also** canopic jars and chests; Nun; Saite Period; Sobek.

Nephthys

Called Nebt-Hut by the ancient Egyptians but renamed by the Greeks, the goddess Nephthys was the sister of three other prominent ancient Egyptian deities: Osiris, Seth, and Isis. She was also said to be the wife of Seth (although in a few myths, Neith filled this role). Nephthys was considered the protectress of the canopic jar holding the lungs. She was associated with the head of the deceased as well, with her sister, Isis, associated with the feet. In some myths, Nephthys acted as Isis's assistant; for example, she helped Isis collect the pieces of Osiris after Seth hacked him apart, in order to provide the deceased with the proper burial rituals. (In some versions of this myth, however, Isis acted alone.) Nephthys was usually depicted as a woman but sometimes as a kite, a bird in the hawk family. **See also** canopic jars and chests; Isis; Osiris; Seth.

Netjerwymes (dates unknown)

A Nineteenth Dynasty official who served as the envoy of King Ramses II, Netjerwymes is of particular interest to twenty-first-century archaeologists because they only recently discovered his cliff tomb at Saqqara and have just begun excavating it. Inscriptions there indicate that Netjerwymes negotiated an important peace treaty between Egypt and the Hittites, then one of Egypt's most powerful enemies. The tomb also provides evidence that Netjerwymes earned the king's approval for his deeds, as one sculpture in its mortuary chapel depicts Ramses II welcoming his envoy to the Afterlife. The chapel also contains painted reliefs showing Netjerwymes in prayer as well as images of the goddess Hathor. An unexcavated section of the tomb is believed to contain Netjerwymes' burial chamber and perhaps his mummy, since the tomb seems not to have been disturbed by robbers. **See also** Ramses II; Saqqara.

Neuserre (Niuserre; Ini; Izi) (?–ca. 2422 B.C.)

Neuserre ("Possessed of Re's Power") was the throne name of the sixth king of the Fifth Dynasty, but he was also known by his birth name, Ini or Izi. He left behind a solar temple at Abu Ghurob and a pyramid at Abusir; near the latter are the tombs of his two known queens, Reputneb and Khentikus. Reliefs in the solar temple depict Egyptians sailing merchant ships—among the earliest such scenes related to foreign trade—and reliefs in the pyramid show the king fighting Asiatics and Libyans. In addition to these activities, Neuserre promoted mining expeditions to obtain copper, turquoise, and other minerals from the Sinai. **See also** Abu Ghurob; Abusir.

New Kingdom (ca. 1550– ca. 1069 B.C.)

Lasting from approximately 1550 B.C. to 1069 B.C., the New Kingdom was a period of ancient Egyptian history characterized by prosperity and political stability following the chaos of the Second Intermediate Period. Its founder, King Ahmose I, expelled the invading Hyksos, who had established a kingdom in the eastern Delta, thereby unifying Egypt once more. Under successive kings, Egypt also began expanding its territory into foreign lands. The military grew stronger, and with it the central government. Moreover, art and architecture flourished. A series of rulers launched major building projects, providing Egypt with some of its most significant ancient architecture. In addition, temples became larger, with workshops, storehouses, and fields.

The New Kingdom was characterized by changes in worship practices as well. In particular, kings lessened their connection to the god Horus while elevating the god Re, worshiping the solar deity first as Horus-Re and then, after Egypt's capital was moved to Thebes (a cult center for the god Amun), as Amun-Re. However, the stability of the New Kingdom was also briefly threatened by a break in traditional religion during a period now known as the Amarna Period. At this time, King Amenhotep IV (also known as Akhenaten) decided to make Aten the national god of Egypt and force his subjects to worship this deity exclusively. This period of forced monotheism ended as soon as the king died, and the country returned to its former gods and worship practices.

Other problems existed in the New Kingdom as well. Several rulers, most notably Queen Hatshepsut and several kings of the Ramessid Period, usurped the throne, and periodically a weak king would cause Egypt to lose prestige and power both abroad and at home. In fact, the New Kingdom ended when such a king, Ramses XI, essentially abdicated his power to two high priests who split the country between them. **See also** Ahmose I; Amenhotep IV; Hatshepsut.

Nile River

The longest river in the world, the Nile River is the dominant geographical fea-

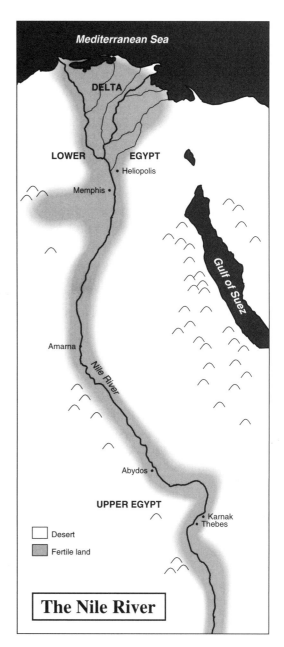

The Nile River

ture in Egypt. The river flows north approximately forty-five hundred miles from the heart of Africa to the Mediterranean Sea. Shortly before reaching the sea, it splits into several channels whose number and precise course have varied over time. This region where the river splits is known as the Nile Delta.

South of the Delta of the Nile is the Nile Valley, a fertile valley bordering the river for approximately 560 miles and providing a thirteen-thousand-square-mile corridor of greenery. Approximately 3 million people lived in this area during the peak of population in ancient times. The Nile Valley is flanked by limestone cliffs, some right next to the river and some set back from it, and beyond these cliffs lies desert which is dotted by oases.

Every year the Nile River and its tributaries would flood and deposit thick, black, highly fertile silt over much of the valley. The ancient Egyptians never understood why the river flooded. Nonetheless, because this event—which they called *akhet,* or inundation—was so important to their livelihood, they kept track of the Nile's water level to predict how extensive inundation would be by placing measuring devices called Nileometers at key points along the river.

The Nile River's flood was very regular, beginning in July and then gradually receding in September and October, so the ground was exposed for planting in October and November. Crops grew from this point until May, when the Egyptians harvested them prior to the next inundation. During the growing season, the ancient Egyptians carried water from the Nile or from reservoirs to the crops, because rainfall in the Nile Valley and the Delta is almost nonexistent. Beginning in the Twelfth Dynasty, they built dams and canals and more reservoirs to control and channel the water so that the river's silt reached a larger area and so that they could store water for dry times.

In addition to providing water and nutrients for crops, the Nile was also a key source of food (primarily in the form of fish and waterbirds) and building material (Nile mud), and served as a transportation route. Because it was so central to life in ancient Egypt, the river was also a focus for religious worship. Various festivals revolved around the inundation and the Nile itself. One such festival was the Night of the Tears, which marked the beginning of the inundation. Its name comes from the Egyptians' belief that the goddess Isis created the overflowing waters of the inundation by crying over her dead husband, Osiris.

The Egyptians also had various beliefs regarding the Nile's source. The most prevalent belief was that the Nile originated beside one of its islands, Elephantine, where it was thought that an underground stream linked the Nile with the realm of the gods. This idea was probably based on Elephantine's location at a key geographical point along the Nile: the First Cataract. This was a stretch of rocks and fast-moving water, and there were nine more rapids farther south. These whitewater areas were so difficult to navigate that Elephantine marked the natural southern border of ancient Egypt in most eras. In keeping with their view of Egypt's importance in the world, the ancient Egyptians found it difficult to believe that the source of the Nile would be outside of their own boundaries. **See also** agriculture; Elephantine; irrigation; Isis; Osiris.

nobles

Nobles in ancient Egypt enjoyed a considerable amount of autonomy and power. The first ancient Egyptian nobles were relatives or associates of the king whom he rewarded for their loyalty with gifts of land, valuable goods, high-ranking government jobs, and tombs near his own. Over time, these men amassed great wealth and corresponding power. Meanwhile, with each succeeding generation, a family's personal link to the king grew more distant, so later generations of nobles did not necessarily feel any personal loyalty toward the king and some even began to challenge his rule. In fact, during the First Intermediate Period, several nobles vied to become kings of Egypt themselves. Consequently King Senwosret I moved to reduce their power by curtailing their rights, although Egyptologists disagree on exactly what the nature of this curtailment was. Nonetheless, the nobility continued to enjoy a privileged position in society, and their hereditary jobs, status, and estates continued to provide them with great wealth. They lived in the best houses, ate the best food, wore the best clothes, and had numerous servants; they sometimes paid their servants to stand in for them when the king asked them, as he had the right to do by a practice called corvée, to work on government projects such as quarrying, mining, or building construction. **See also** kings; peasants; slaves.

nomes and nomarchs

Called *sepat* in ancient Egyptian, a nome (a word first applied by the Greeks) was a territory headed by a local governor, or nomarch. Nomes were not just administrative units but cultural entities. Each nome had its own capital city, which was also a cult center with a priesthood dedicated to serving a particular deity or deities. Each nome had its own festivals, sacred animals, sacred trees, taboos, and emblems.

Egypt was divided into forty-two nomes, twenty-two in Upper Egypt and twenty in Lower Egypt, although the borders of these geographical regions and perhaps also their number occasionally shifted. The nomarch system originated during predynastic times, as communities headed by tribal chiefs combined to create small kingdoms. When Egypt was first united to form the Old Kingdom, the nomes became the basic unit of government, each with its own administrative system for collecting taxes (in the form of grain and other goods), which were passed along to the central government. The central government in turn supported works that benefited the nomes, such as the building of monuments and the construction and maintenance of irrigation systems.

Certain nomes and their rulers were more powerful than others, and when a weak king was on the throne, a nomarch or alliance of nomarchs from the most powerful nome(s) sometimes tried to usurp the throne. In fact, during the First Intermediate Period, several nomarchs essentially turned their nomes into independent kingdoms. One of these was Ankhtify, a nobleman whose tomb inscriptions identify him as the "great chieftain" of the Heracleopolitan nome. Autobiographical writings in this tomb further state that he had absolute power over the people of his nome. **See also** Ankhtify; cult centers; government.

Nubia

Nubia was a land south of Egypt; Lower Nubia was between the First and Second Cataracts of the Nile River and Upper Nubia south of the Second Cataract to the border of modern-day Sudan. Certain regions within Nubia were sometimes referred to by their regional names, such as Kush and Wawat.

Beginning in the First Dynasty, Egypt's kings were determined to control Nubia, primarily because it provided valuable resources like building stones, copper, amethyst, and gold. The region was also the conduit through which goods from southern Africa, such as ivory, ebony, certain spices, leopard skins, and ostrich feathers, passed into Egypt. Consequently, during the First and Second Dynasties, Egypt's kings conquered several Lower Nubian settlements and established trading posts in the area, with the most important such post being Buhen near the Second Cataract. They also established colonies near mining and quarrying sites. By the Fourth Dynasty, there were several Egyptian fortresses in Nubia as well.

The Nubians fought these encroachments and developed great skill as warriors. Because of their growing military prowess, during the last stages of the Old Kingdom the Nubians took back control of their country from the Egyptians.

A wall relief from the entrance of the Temple of Ramses II at Abu Simbel portrays Nubians captured in one of Egypt's campaigns against its southern neighbor.

During the Middle Kingdom, Egypt's King Montuhotep II, of the Eleventh Dynasty, decided to move against the Nubians in a show of military force and to gain territory and natural resources. He stationed a garrison at Elephantine from which he could more easily attack Lower Nubia, and soon he had taken much of the region. Throughout the remainder of the Middle Kingdom, Egypt established a string of fortresses along the Nile River in Nubia and increased its Nubian mining, quarrying, and trading activities. Nonetheless, Egyptian interest in Nubia largely ended with the beginning of the tumultuous Second Intermediate Period. Nubians once again controlled their own country, and the Egyptian people remained uninterested in Nubia even after the military strength of the New Kingdom once again provided Egypt with the means to control the region. **See also** Elephantine; fortresses; mining and metalworking; quarrying; trade.

Nun

According to certain ancient Egyptian myths, Nun was an ancient being that manifested itself as the primordial waters out of which the earth (the primordial mound), the first god, and various other components of Creation arose. **See also** Creation myths.

Nut

Nut was a goddess of the sky, daughter of Tefnut (a goddess of moisture), and the granddaughter of Re (the sun god); however, Nut's name means "one made of water" rather than "sky" because the Egyptians believed that the sky was made of water. Nut was worshiped first in Heliopolis but eventually throughout Egypt, along with her brother and lover, Geb, god of the earth. In some regions, however, particularly Hermopolis, she was paired not with Geb but with Nu, and together the two represented the primeval waters as part of the Ogdoad, a group of eight primordial deities that had to come together for Creation to occur.

In Heliopolis, Nut was a key figure in a Creation myth in which her father, Shu, god of air, pulled her from atop a reclining Geb and raised her up so that her arched back formed the heavens. Before this separation, Nut and Geb created four children, each one born on successive days: Osiris, Isis, Seth, and Nephthys. As this Creation myth spread beyond Heliopolis, a fifth child was sometimes added to the list: Horus the Elder (an aspect of the god Horus). In addition, Nut was thought to give birth to the sun each morning. Her womb was called the Duat (or Underworld), and just as the sun awaited its rebirth there each night, so did the stars reside there during the day.

Because of her importance to ancient Egyptian cosmology, Nut was portrayed often in Egyptian art, appearing on sarcophagi, coffins, papyri, and tomb and cenotaph walls and ceilings. For example, one sarcophagus, which now resides in the New York Metropolitan Museum of Art, is decorated with a scene of Nut bending over to touch the earth with her hands, with the resulting arch of her body forming the sky. In other scenes, such as one painted inside the coffin lid of a woman named Soter, the goddess is depicted beside figures that personify the signs of the zodiac and the hours of the day. **See also** Geb; Isis; Nephthys; Ogdoad; Osiris; Re; Seth; Tefnut; Underworld.

oases

Oases (the plural form of oasis) are fertile regions, usually depressions in the land, that are surrounded by desert sands. In ancient times, a string of oases ran roughly parallel to and to the west of the Nile River within the Libyan Desert. The fifth-century-B.C. Greek historian Herodotus once referred to these oases as "Islands of the Blest," so impressed was he with their lushness. This greenery was made possible by a vast supply of underground water that came to the surface via springs or wells. As a result of this water supply, the Libyan Desert oases were among the earliest inhabited regions in Egypt, first by nomads and then by permanent residents. Much of the archaeological record of these first settlements has been lost to erosion, however. **See also** Bahariya Oasis; Dakhla Oasis; Kharga Oasis; Libya; Siwa Oasis.

obelisk

An obelisk (known as *tekhen* in ancient Egyptian) is a four-sided stone pillar, often as tall as one hundred feet, with its top shaped like a small pyramid. Obelisks were made of granite quarried at Aswan or of basalt or quartzite taken from various other sites in Egypt's desert regions. The tips of obelisks, known as *benbenet,* were usually gilded so that they would reflect the sunlight. This was an important feature to the ancient Egyptians, who believed that obelisks were sacred to solar deities, particularly Re. For the same reason, the Egyptians sometimes put other symbols of the sun, such as carvings of baboons (associated with mornings because they always greeted the dawn with screeches and posturing), on the sides of the obelisk, which might also have hieroglyphs referring to sun gods. Sometimes, temples dedicated to the worship of other gods, such as Thoth, Isis, Ptah, and Osiris, might have an obelisk incorporated into their design as well.

The ancient Egyptians believed obelisks such as this one were sacred to the sun gods.

The cities of Heliopolis, Thebes, and Memphis were particularly noted for having many fine obelisks. Obelisks often came in pairs, and according to some Egyptian mythology, for every pair on earth there was a corresponding pair in the celestial realm. Heliopolis once was home to what is perhaps the most famous pair of obelisks, known as Cleopatra's Needles. Today, however, Cleopatra's Needles have been separated, with one in New York and the other in London.

From inscriptions and wall art, Egyptologists know that large obelisks like Cleopatra's Needles were carved at quarries and then transported via sledges to ships that would carry them along the Nile River to their final destination. The stones were so heavy that thousands of men were needed to pull the sledge, and the ships had to be out of the water during loading or they would tip. As a result special dry docks were constructed beside the Nile River in which water could be drained and then reintroduced once the obelisk had been loaded. However, an obelisk would typically still be so heavy that its vessel would have to be towed by as many as nine others, each with over two dozen oarsmen.

Given this massive weight, Egyptologists disagree on how an obelisk might have been raised into position once it reached its final destination. Some theories involve the use of ropes and levers pulled by slaves to elevate the stone. Others theorize that an obelisk could have been laid atop a high sand embankment and the sand gradually removed from beneath the foot of the obelisk. This would have caused the obelisk to gradually tip and virtually raise itself. Proponents of this idea have managed to raise their own obelisk in this way. **See also** architecture; Cleopatra's Needles; quarrying.

offerings

The ancient Egyptians believed that the *ka,* or spirit, of the deceased needed nourishment after death or it would cease to exist, and offerings were the means of providing that nourishment. Family members would take food to the tomb—which they considered the spirit's home—on a daily basis. If family members could not do this themselves and they were wealthy enough, they often hired a *ka* priest to feed the *ka* each day. As payment, this priest was usually given a tract of cultivatable land that would produce the food for the offerings as well as extra food that the priest could trade for a profit. This property was transferred to the priest's heirs—along with the responsibility of feeding the *ka*—when the priest died via a legal document that spelled out the terms of the agreement between the family and the priest.

Over time, priests gradually developed more and more rituals related to the *ka* offering, eventually performing as many as 114 daily rituals involving magic spells intended to make food suitable for the *ka.* Evolving from the earliest lists of offerings, this collection of rituals was known as the Liturgy of the Funerary Offerings, believed to transmute meat, bread, and wine into divine ethereal substances.

The offerings were left on tomb altars, often beside a false door (a stone carved to look like a door) that supposedly allowed the *ka* to move from within the burial chamber to the area where the priest performed his ceremonies. The *ka* would then nourish itself on the essence of the food, in the process making it necessary to place new food on the altar the next day. The old food was then subjected to a reanimation ritual whose intention was to make it once again fit for human consumption. Meanwhile, the old food was eaten by temple workers because, even with its essence depleted, it was still considered nourishing enough for mortals.

As offerings became more complex, ordinary Egyptians looked for relief from these daily obligations. By the Middle Kingdom, they had decided that servants could work for the *ka* in the Afterlife to produce food much the way they did for living people. Consequently, they placed models of servants and food-producing equipment in tombs with the idea that, if the proper rituals were conducted upon the tomb owner's death, these figures would magically come alive, full-sized, in the Afterlife as industrious workers. Carved out of wood and painted to look as real as possible, these models included representations of servants using beer-making equipment, plowing a field, working in a granary, or taking care of various aspects of the tomb owner's estate. **See also** Afterlife; funerals; *ka;* models, tomb; priests.

Ogdoad

In the ancient Egyptian mythology of certain regions, particularly Hermopolis, the Ogdoad was a group of eight primordial deities, paired into male-female couples, that had to come together in order for Creation to occur. These male-female pairs were Nu and Nut (or Nun and Naunet), who represented the primeval waters; Heh and Hehut (Huh and Hauhet), who represented endless space; Kekui and Kekuit (Kuk and Kauket), who represented darkness; and Kerh and Kerhet (Amun and Amaunet), who represented the unknowable. The males were typically depicted with frog heads, the females with snake heads. According to some mythology, the death of these deities supposedly occurred at the moment matter was created, whereupon together they became the soul of the god Thoth. However, during the Old Kingdom, they were said to be the deities who made the Nile River flow and the sun rise; by the Middle Kingdom, other gods had taken over these duties. A New King-

dom inscription in the Temple of Hatshepsut at Medinet Habu claims to have been built on the site where the Ogdoad were buried: Primeval Hill, where matter was formed from chaos. **See also** Creation myths; Nut; Thoth.

oils

The ancient Egyptians used a wide variety of oils from various plants and trees, such as balsam, cedar, and moringa. Oils were used to make skin treatments and perfumes and as part of the embalming process and certain religious rituals. For skin treatments, the oils were typically mixed with solid animal fats and fragrant substances like flower petals. Flowers and other fragrant substances would be soaked in oils and the mixture then squeezed through cloth to separate the scented oil from the plant matter to make perfume. Oils intended for religious rituals might be scented in the same way. These oils were used to anoint cult statues and other religious objects; they also might be placed around the temple in bowls to scent the air. Exotically spiced oils from Syria, Libya, and Lebanon were used during the embalming process to cover up offensive odors and to cleanse the body and make it easier to manipulate. **See also** cosmetics and perfumes; mummification; plants and flowers.

Old Kingdom (ca. 2686– ca. 2125 B.C.)

Lasting from approximately 2686 B.C. to 2125 B.C., the Old Kingdom was a period of ancient Egyptian history that followed the Early Dynastic Period and began with the Third Dynasty. However, the division of the Old Kingdom and the Early Dynastic Period—and the name *Old Kingdom* itself—was established by nineteenth-century historians; many modern historians see little difference between the two periods, viewing the Old Kingdom as the natural outgrowth of developments during the Early Dynastic Period.

These developments include an increase in the power and scope of the central government and notable advances in art, architecture, agriculture, and technology. In addition, most Egyptologists believe that ancient Egyptian writing first appeared during this time, although recent discoveries indicate that it might have appeared much earlier, during the Predynastic Period. The Old Kingdom was a time of prosperity and security, with no serious challenges to the throne from foreign powers, and the king was viewed as a god on earth (perhaps the mortal manifestation of the god Horus or the son of the solar deity Re). During the Old Kingdom, since the Egyptian people generally believed that they would continue to prosper only if they helped their kings ascend to the heavens after death, they built them lavish tombs and pyramids.

Many of the earliest tombs of this period were of a style called mastaba, in which the aboveground part of the structure was shaped like a mound, representing the primordial mound of earth from which all life was believed to have arisen. Gradually, the exterior walls of these tombs were made to resemble stairs, in the belief that this would help the king ascend to heaven after death. This led to the development of the pyramid, an extremely tall structure with four triangular sides that rise into the sky to form a point. The largest of the pyramids, the Great Pyramid of Fourth Dynasty king Khufu at Giza, was originally 460 feet tall (it is now 450 feet, due to subsequent damage).

Eventually, however, the prosperity that made such elaborate projects possible waned. The kings of the Old Kingdom had large numbers of relatives because they had multiple wives. Over time, these large families placed a drain on the royal treasury, as did the construction projects themselves. In addition, the king often rewarded nomarchs (governors of local districts called nomes) with wealth, which enabled them to rise in power and prestige. By the end of the Old Kingdom, the nomarchs had become Egypt's nobility, and as their power increased they increasingly challenged the king's authority. The Old Kingdom ended when several nomarchs created independent states with themselves as ruler. This ushered in the period of chaos known as the First Intermediate Period. **See also** Early Dynastic Period; First Intermediate Period; nomes and nomarchs.

oracles

The ancient Egyptians often consulted oracles, which were believed to have the ability to predict the future. The most common form of oracle was a cult statue, a statue of a deity worshiped in a temple dedicated to that deity. At festivals, such statues were brought out of their temples in small shrines and taken on processions—through the streets or down the Nile River by boat—that stopped intermittently at select spots, or stations. At these stations, people could stand before the portable shrine and ask a cult statue about the future, usually using yes-or-no questions. Sometimes the answer was given in words that only the petitioner could hear, but on most occasions the statue's answer would be deduced from certain signs in the environment that were attributed to the deity the statue represented.

During the Nineteenth Dynasty, the belief that cult statues could provide the answers to questions put before a god led to a new judicial practice: Statues of gods began judging defendants' guilt or innocence. To determine a verdict, members of the court would conduct certain rituals before the statue and then ask it whether the defendant was guilty. Alternatively, a list of the suspects might be read aloud and the statue asked to give a sign upon hearing the name of the guilty person. In either case, the verdict was rendered by looking for and interpreting subtle changes in the environment.

In addition to cult statues, various animals were believed capable of serving as oracles. For example, sacred bulls were thought to be connected to the gods and capable of being oracles. A sacred bull was housed in a special stall in a temple but led out periodically into a large hall where it could act as an oracle. In the hall were doors leading to chambers where food offerings for the bull had been placed. The doorways were marked with certain standard answers (such as "yes" and "no" if there were only two doors), and after the bull was asked a question, he would be released; the answer to the question would be determined by which doorway the animal walked through. **See also** bulls, sacred; festivals; legal system.

Osiris

Osiris was an ancient Egyptian god of the dead, the Afterlife, and rebirth, and given the Egyptians' preoccupation with mortuary rituals it is understandable that Osiris gradually became one of their most important and popular deities. In fact, he eventually rivaled Horus as the god most associated with kingship, with Horus being connected to the living king and Osiris to the deceased one.

Egyptologists believe that Osiris was first worshiped during the Old Kingdom, since he is first mentioned in the Pyramid Texts that appear on the walls of Fifth and Sixth Dynasty pyramids. Among other things, the Pyramid Texts recount a mythical story about Osiris that features his death and resurrection. However, because the Pyramid Texts were heavily damaged over time, Egyptologists have very little of the original version of this

An illustration from the Book of the Dead *depicts the deceased standing before Osiris, who was said to be the judge of souls in the Afterlife.*

myth. Instead they have to rely on subsequent versions and variations such as those that appear in the Coffin Texts of the Middle Kingdom and the writings of Plutarch (ca. 46–ca. 126), a Greek who visited Egypt and wrote about Egyptian culture.

The most common version of the myth in these texts features an Osiris who began his existence in mortal form as the king of a town in the Delta during a time of chaos. Shortly thereafter, he united all of Egypt under a strong, orderly, and prosperous rule. However, Osiris's brother, Seth, was jealous of Osiris's success and plotted to kill him, with the help of seventy-two cohorts. These men tricked the king into climbing into a coffin and trapped him inside, where he soon died. Seth then disposed of the coffin in a branch of the Nile River, which carried the coffin to what today is the Mediterranean Sea. Eventually, it came to rest in the roots of a tree at the port of Byblos.

By this time, Osiris's sister and wife, Isis, had learned that he was dead and had begun searching for his body so that she could give it a proper burial. Before embarking on her search, however, she left her son Horus hidden in some reeds, fearing that Seth would kill him too. Eventually the queen ended up in Byblos, where, with the help of her magic skills, she found the coffin and brought it back to Egypt, hiding it in a marsh while she went to get her son. While she was away, Seth found Osiris's body and hacked it into at least fourteen pieces. This still did not end Isis's determination to give Osiris a proper burial. With the help of her sister, Nephthys (or alone, according to some versions of the myth), she found all of the pieces. In some versions of the myth, she buried each piece where she found it, conducting proper burial rites at each site. In other versions, she reassembled the body and wrapped it in linen for burial. In either case, because Osiris's body was given the proper mortuary rites, he was able to reach the Afterlife and become a god.

Some versions of the myth end with a trial among the gods in which Osiris accuses Seth of treason. Perhaps because Osiris was associated in this myth with an Afterlife legal system, the ancient Egyptians believed that Osiris judged souls in the Afterlife, with the help of other deities, in a place called the Judgment Hall of Osiris. Consequently, many mortuary rituals involved spells that would ensure that the deceased would do well when coming before Osiris. The *Book of the Dead* offers many such spells, and also includes many accounts of the soul's trial in the god's judgment hall. Osiris is featured prominently in the Coffin Texts as well.

Osiris was worshiped throughout Egypt, but his main cult center was in Abydos, where during the Early Dynastic Period he merged with a god called Khentiamenti, by whose name he was sometimes called. While Khentiamenti was usually depicted as a black dog, Osiris was always depicted as a man, though often a mummified one. He usually held two symbols of kingship, the crook and the flail, and wore a crown, because of his association with Egypt's deceased kings. His skin was typically green or black, the colors of fertility and the rich Nile soil, or sometimes white, the color of linen used for mummy wrappings. His main symbol was a hieroglyph known as the *djed* pillar, a column that stood for strength and stability and was said to represent the god's backbone.

In Abydos, Osiris was worshiped with Isis and Horus, his wife and son, while in the city of Heliopolis, he was worshiped as part of the Ennead, a group of nine gods associated with Creation. In Memphis, he was worshiped as Ptah-Sokar-Osiris, a god created when Osiris merged with the creator god Ptah and the funerary god Sokar. Osiris was also associated with those aspects of the natural world—specifically, the Nile River and the moon—that had regular cycles of rebirth and renewal.

Various festivals dedicated to Osiris, varying according to region, were held throughout the year. One that was widely celebrated was the Fall of the Nile, which equated the drying up of the river's floodwaters with Osiris's death; another festival to Osiris was held when the inundation returned. Osiris remained popular through the Greco-Roman Period. **See also** Abydos; Creation myths; *djed;* Isis; Seth.

Osorkon I (?–ca. 889 B.C.)

A king of the Twenty-second Dynasty, Osorkon I ruled during the Third Intermediate Period. His father, Sheshonq I, had united Egypt after several years in which there were two thrones, one in Upper Egypt at Thebes and one in Lower Egypt at Tanis. Osorkon I ruled from Tanis but continued to maintain Egyptian unity. In his later years, he coruled with his oldest son, Sheshonq II, but because Sheshonq II died before his father, the throne passed to a younger son, Takelot I, upon Osorkon I's death. Takelot I proceeded to lose control of Upper Egypt, and soon the country was once again divided in two. **See also** Tanis; Third Intermediate Period.

Osorkon II (?–ca. 850 B.C.)

Twenty-second Dynasty king Osorkon II succeeded his father, Takelot I, to the throne in 874 B.C. during the Third Intermediate Period. Shortly thereafter, his cousin Harsiese became high priest of Amun at Karnak (a village that was part of Thebes), a position he too inherited from his father, Sheshonq II. However, Harsiese was not content to be only a high priest, so in the fourth year of Osorkon II's reign he declared himself king of southern Egypt. Osorkon II could do nothing to break his rival's control over the south

until Harsiese died without leaving an heir. At that time, the king appointed one of his sons, Nimlot, to be the new Theban high priest of Amun, thereby ensuring the region's loyalty to his throne. He then did the same thing in Memphis, appointing another son, Sheshonq, high priest of Ptah there. This gave Osorkon II control of two of Egypt's most important cities and enabled him to hold the country together. At the same time, to lessen the risk of invasions from outside Egypt, the king made friendly overtures to other countries in the region, including Israel and Assyria, putting himself on good terms with his foreign neighbors. Osorkon II also launched several building projects within Egypt to honor the gods. For example, he built a temple to goddess Bastet at Bubastis, as well as other structures at Tanis, Memphis, Thebes, and elsewhere. **See also** Bastet; Memphis; Ptah; Thebes.

Osorkon III (?–ca. 759 B.C.)

A king of the Twenty-third Dynasty, Osorkon III ruled during the Third Intermediate Period, a time when Egypt was fractured into several kingdoms. His main area of control was the central Delta, which he ruled from Leontopolis; his main rival, King Sheshonq III, was located in Heracleopolis to the south. Although as a prince Osorkon III had been a military commander, as well as high priest of Amun, he was apparently unable to expand his territory until fourteen years into his rule, when his rival died. At that time, Osorkon III placed his son Takelot III in Heracleopolis as its ruler and chief priest. Six years prior to his own death, Osorkon III began sharing his rule with Takelot III. However, because Osorkon III lived to be quite old, Takelot III reigned for only two years on his own before he too died. **See also** Heracleopolis.

Osorkon IV (?–ca. 715 B.C.)

Osorkon IV was a king of the Twenty-second Dynasty who ruled the area around Tanis during the tumultuous period known as the Third Intermediate Period, when various individuals vied for control of the country. Osorkon IV had at least four rivals within Egypt, and he was threatened by foreign rulers as well, such as King Sargon II of Assyria. In fact, his reign ended abruptly shortly after he sent a dozen horses as a peace offering to Sargon II, which has led some Egyptologists to suspect that he was assassinated as part of an Assyrian plot against him. **See also** Assyria; Third Intermediate Period.

ostraka

Ostraka (the plural form of ostracon) is a Greek word for small, relatively flat shards of pottery or flakes of stone that students used for practicing writing and drawing; scribes, architects, draftsmen, and others made notes on them. Letter writers also used ostraka, as did artists planning their works. The most common type of script found on ostraka was hieratic, probably because it was generally quicker to produce than hieroglyphics. **See also** hieroglyphics; papyrus; writing, forms of.

Overthrowing Apophis

The Ramessid Period ritual known as Overthrowing Apophis required priests to assemble at night to recite the various names of a serpent demon whose primary name was Apophis. It was believed that this ritual would aid the sun god Re on his journey to the place where he would rise each morning. The priests also made and destroyed wax images of Apophis to celebrate his demise.

Overthrowing Apophis was based on an ancient Egyptian myth generally referred to today as *The Journey of the Sun Through the Netherworld.* This myth concerns the sun god Re's nightly travels through the Netherworld to reach the spot where he arose each morning. Re made this journey in a boat with several deities as companions. At various points en route, the group had to perform certain tasks and/or face certain dangers. One of these dangers was the serpent demon Apophis, whose aim was to swallow the sun and destroy Re. Re had magical powers that could protect him from this threat, but only if various measures were taken to lessen Apophis's power. These measures included sticking knives into Apophis and reciting all of the demon's names. A Ramessid Period religious text also known as *Overthrowing Apophis* lists all of these names, as well as hymns that were to be sung when Re safely passed Apophis. **See also** Ramessid Period; Re.

painting

Beginning in the Predynastic Period, the ancient Egyptians painted decorations on pottery, leather, and walls. Over time, wall art became more and more prevalent, and paint was used either alone or as part of carved reliefs to decorate tombs, temples, and residences of all types. In addition, paintings began appearing on coffins, papyri, and a variety of household and tomb goods. Wall paintings were usually applied onto a coating of gypsum plaster rather than directly onto the mud bricks and clay plaster used to build the structure.

To create paintings, artists used brushes made of reeds and palm fibers, which they dipped in water and glue or gelatin before adding pigment stored on a palette. (Using such adhesives is known as tempera painting.) Pigments were minerals or mineral substances that had been ground into powder and fashioned into cakes, with the color dependent on the type of mineral used. Black, for example, was made from ground charcoal or some other type of carbon, while green was usually made from powdered malachite, white from gypsum, and red from red iron oxides and ochers. To obtain various shades, the Egyptians either mixed two colors together prior to painting or painted one color atop the other to produce a new color. **See also** art; colors.

palaces

Typically made of mud brick or of mud brick and wood rather than stone (because they were not intended to last for eternity), palaces were used not only as kings' residences but also as places where government business was conducted. In fact, the palace—or *per-a'a* (Great House), as it was called during ancient times—was divided into two sections, one for each purpose. Rooms related to government work were located around the perimeter of the palace; the inner area was for the private use of the king, his family, and perhaps his harem, although in many cases the harem was housed in a separate palace (sometimes only a short walk away from the king's, but other times in a separate city). Above the private rooms of the palace was a balcony that could be seen from the street, which the king used for public appearances. Government rooms included a large hall for public meetings and audiences and a smaller room where the king might meet privately with individuals he wanted to see. Palaces had wall decorations—especially paintings on stuccoed walls—and decorative columns, and by the New Kingdom they had become quite grand. One of the largest palaces of this period was that of Amenhotep III, which had not only living quarters but also shrines, chapels, and its own specially constructed lake. **See also** Amenhotep III; architecture; harem; houses.

palettes

Known as a *mestha* in ancient Egyptian, a palette was a wooden or stone slab that was used as a grinding and mixing surface and had recesses to hold pigments, paints, cakes of ink, and powders intended for practical, cosmetic, or ceremonial purposes. Ceremonial palettes might feature elaborate carvings of mythical beasts, deities, symbols of power and kingship, and scenes depicting a king in battle or killing or escorting prisoners. Palettes for everyday use, however, had few decorations, if any.

Palettes of scribes had grooves and slats to hold fine brushes for writing on papyrus; these were substituted with reed pens during the Ptolemaic Period. Scribes' palettes also typically held at least two cakes of ink, a red one made from ground red ocher and a black one made from carbon, as well as other writing tools. The ink cakes were transformed into liquid ink by mixing them with water using the brush. Because scribes relied so heavily on their palettes for their work, the image of the palette was their symbol. **See also** art; cosmetics and perfumes; painting; scribes.

Panehsi (Panehesy; Panhey) (?–1069 B.C.)

A series of men with the name Panehsi, all related to one another, served in prominent government positions during the New Kingdom. The most significant of these men was the viceroy of Nubia, stationed at Elephantine during the Twentieth Dynasty reign of King Ramses XI. The king put Panehsi in charge of quelling a rebellion in Thebes that was being led by its high priest of Amun. The viceroy succeeded in this endeavor and assigned one of his officers, Herihor, to take command of the city so that he could return to Elephantine. Soon, Herihor had become the Theban high priest of Amun as well as the king's vizier. Meanwhile, Panehsi gained control of much of Upper Egypt, and the king essentially gave over his power to him and Herihor. When Ramses XI died, Panehsi and Herihor officially divided the country between

them. **See also** Herihor; New Kingdom; Ramses XI; Third Intermediate Period.

papyrus

Papyrus is a plant that grows naturally along the Nile River and its tributaries because its roots require soft soil and need to be entirely underwater. During the Old Kingdom, the Egyptians began to cultivate papyrus as well. The outer fibers of this plant provided the ancient Egyptians with the material for mats, baskets and other containers, some furniture and clothing, boats, ropes, sandals, hut walls and roofing, and many other items. Its pith—a soft, spongy substance in the center of its stems—was used to manufacture thin sheets used as a writing surface. For this reason, the word *papyrus* refers not only to the plant but to the writing material and the ancient manuscripts made from papyrus.

To make papyrus (i.e., the writing material), the Egyptians gathered stems from harvested papyrus plants and cut them into pieces. They then stripped off the outer rind of each stem, separating it from its soft, spongy interior (the pith), and the pith was cut into thick slices. These slices were then laid side by side on a table, first in one layer and then in another that was turned crossways over the first. The two layers were then hammered and pressed until the papyrus was a thin sheet. Sheets were then joined, using an adhesive, to make a roll long enough to hold a desired amount of text, and trimmed along the edges to make them even. This manufacturing process was controlled by the government, which is probably why the Greeks first coined the word *papyrus,* meaning "royal," for the resulting paper.

Archaeologists have found rolls of papyrus dozens of feet long; however, the standard roll had only twenty joined sheets. In addition, while sheets were made in varying sizes, depending on the length of the cut papyrus that went into their manufacture, the average sheet was roughly twelve inches by five inches. Both sides of a sheet could be written on, but because the papyrus was always rolled up, writers used first the inside of the roll, or recto, and then the outside of the roll, or verso.

In addition to its role as a writing medium, the papyrus plant was featured in many myths, said to have grown from a mound of soil that arose from the primordial waters at the time of Creation. This plant was also associated with fertility, the Nile River, and youth. Several gods and goddesses, including Horus, Hathor, and Bastet, were sometimes shown holding or wearing a papyrus plant or a scepter shaped like a papyrus. **See also** plants and flowers; scribes.

Paser

Two men named Paser are significant to ancient Egyptian history. The earliest of the two (?–ca. 1279 B.C.) served Nineteenth Dynasty king Seti I, first as a priest who cared for the Two Crowns of Upper and Lower Egypt (which were worn by the king during certain ceremonies and events) and then as vizier. He also served as vizier for Seti I's successor, Ramses II, with whom Paser had been a close friend ever since childhood. Paser supervised many building projects for both kings, and when his father, who was high priest of Amun, died, Paser assumed this position while still continuing to be Ramses II's closest adviser.

The second Paser of importance (?– ca. 1108 B.C.) was the mayor of eastern Thebes during the Twentieth Dynasty reign of Ramses IX. At some point during this reign, Paser accused his rival Pawero, the mayor of western Thebes and the guardian of its royal tombs, of being involved in a tomb-robbing ring after encountering people who claimed to have seen tomb guards helping robbers enter the tombs. Paser told this to the highest local authority, Kha-em-wese, who established a commission to look into the matter. The commission discovered that several tombs previously certified by Pawero's men as being unviolated had in fact been robbed. However, all of Paser's witnesses changed their stories, so Paser could no longer prove that tomb guards were involved nor find the robbers. As a result, the commission abandoned the investigation.

Paser was furious over this, certain that Pawero had bribed or threatened the witnesses into silence. Meanwhile, Pawero threw a large party to celebrate the outcome of the investigation. This angered Paser even more, and over the next year he persisted in trying to get the investigation reopened. Shortly thereafter, Kha-em-wese was replaced with Nebmare-nakht, a man willing to listen to Paser. The official launched a new investigation and eventually arrested and tried forty-five robbers, using torture on the first few arrested to obtain the names of others. However, historians have found no records that indicate Pawero was among those arrested, although they have found many other details about the investigation in ancient Theban papyri. **See also** Ramses II; Ramses IX; robbers, tomb; Seti I.

peasants

Peasants made up approximately 80 percent of Egyptian society, and their lot was a hard one. The work, which was primarily agricultural, was backbreaking. All tasks were done by hand, although a few tools were developed to make work somewhat easier. Of these, the most important was the *shaduf,* a pole with a bucket on one end and a counterweight on the other that enabled peasants to draw water from the Nile River with less physical effort. But even with such devices, ancient Egyptian farmers still had to labor all day in the hot sun during the growing and harvesting seasons.

Peasants were also subject to corvée, according to which the king had the right to enlist any of his subjects for a mandatory period of duty as a laborer on building, irrigation, mining, quarrying, or other projects. Theoretically, an Egyptian from any class of society could be forced to leave his home at any time to work for the king, but peasants were far more likely to be called on to serve, particularly since it was a practice of the wealthy to pay someone else to fulfill their corvée duties for them. A peasant's period of service typically took place during times when farmers were not needed to plant or harvest crops, because the government recognized the importance of these duties to the country's well-being. In addition, during times of political instability, the king rarely exercised his right of corvée because it was highly unpopular. However, even in these times, a peasant might still be called on to serve as a soldier. Until the New Kingdom, when Egypt established a professional standing army, peasants were the foundation of the Egyptian military just as they were the foundation of Egyptian agriculture. **See also** irrigation; nobles.

Penno (Penni; Penne) (?–ca. 1136 B.C.)

Penno was an important official in Nubia during the Twentieth Dynasty reign of Ramses IV, serving as an administrator at the Nubian city of Derr and as the controller of its Temple of Horus. He was eventually named deputy governor of Lower Nubia and in that position controlled the quarrying activities in the Wawat region below the First Cataract. As a reward for his service, King Ramses IV gave him silver urns, as indicated in inscriptions on a statue that Penno erected to honor the king. Penno also apparently profited by obtaining administrative positions for close family members; for example, the mayor of Derr was one of his younger relatives, as were several scribes and treasurers. **See also** Nubia; Ramses IV.

Pepy I (ca. 2346–ca. 2287 B.C.)

A king of the Sixth Dynasty, Pepy I ruled for approximately forty years despite many difficulties. He first became king as either a boy or a young man, assuming the throne after King Userkare, although he was probably a son of Userkare's predecessor, King Teti. At the beginning of his reign, Pepy I had to quell uprisings in his own land, and subsequently he was forced to deal with uprisings in Egyptian-held territories in Palestine. His initial response to such problems was reactive, taking no action unless threatened. Gradually, however, he became an aggressive king, attacking and acquiring foreign lands without provocation.

Pepy I was also a prolific builder, commissioning the construction of temples dedicated to various deities at Abydos, Bubastis, Coptos, Dendera, and Tanis as well as a pyramid at Saqqara. At some point during his reign this pyramid came to be called Men-nefer (or Mn-nfr) Mare, meaning "Pepy Is Established and Good"; over time, this name became Menfi and was used for the king's nearby capital city, which the Greeks later renamed Memphis. Here and elsewhere, archaeologists have found various statues of the king, and several life-sized statues of Pepy I are the earliest such works to be made in copper.

Archaeologists have also found records indicating that sometime during his reign Pepy I was the target of an assassination plot launched against him by one of his lesser wives, Weretyamtes. The king's general, Weni, was given the responsibility of investigating and trying the case against her and her son (whose name is unclear from ancient records), whom she had wanted to place on the throne, but records fail to indicate what became of them. Pepy I had several wives, his primary ones being two sisters, Ankhnesmery-Re I and

Ankhnesmery-Re II, whose brother was the king's vizier, Djau. Each woman bore a son who would later rule Egypt: Merenre I and Pepy II, respectively. **See also** Ankhnesmery-Re II; Merenre I; Userkare; Weni.

Pepy II (?–ca. 2184 B.C.)

A king of the Fifth Dynasty, Pepy II succeeded to the throne after the death of his older half-brother Merenre I, who in turn had succeeded their father, Pepy I. When Pepy II became king he was only six years old, so his mother, Queen Ankhnesmery-Re II, served as his regent. Both mother and son were surrounded by a number of powerful men, including a nomarch named Harkhuf and Pepy II's vizier and uncle, Djau. Nonetheless, once he assumed full power, Pepy II apparently showed considerable initiative, launching a number of trade expeditions to Nubia and Punt and commissioning several building projects. In fact, these trade expeditions were specifically intended to acquire gold and jewels to decorate buildings he had commissioned, including his pyramid at Saqqara.

These building projects, however, depleted the royal treasury, as did Pepy II's practice of buying loyalty by giving land and tax exemptions to various nobles, priesthoods, and towns. Over time, this had the effect of lessening the strength of the central government because the nobles and priests were able to parlay these grants into fortunes so large that they no longer needed to be loyal to their king. By the end of Pepy II's reign, several nomarchs (governors) wielded power comparable to their king's. As a sign of their growing independence, these nomarchs constructed rock-cut tombs in their own district, rather than next to the king's tomb at Memphis.

But despite this dilution of power and prestige, King Pepy II reigned for either ninety-four or, more likely, sixty-four years, according to various ancient and classical records. In the process, he outlived his many queens. These included Nit (or Neith), who was his brother Merenre's widow as well as Pepy II's half-sister and cousin, and Ipwet, who as Merenre's daughter was Pepy II's niece. **See also** Ankhnesmery-Re II; Merenre I; nomes and nomarchs; Pepy I; Saqqara.

Pepy-Nakht (Hekaib) (dates unknown)

During the Sixth Dynasty reign of Pepy II, Pepy-Nakht was the nomarch of Elephantine circa 2200 B.C. He held several important positions during his lifetime, including viceroy of Upper Egypt and governor of Egyptian territories below the First Cataract. According to inscriptions and depictions in his cliff tomb at Aswan, Pepy-Nakht met with some resistance from the Nubians when he tried to impose Egyptian control over the area. He apparently killed several of their rulers and took others to the city of Memphis as tribute to Pepy II. Pepy-Nakht's inscriptions further extol his devotion to duty, because he traveled to a port on the Red Sea (probably Kuser) to recover the body of an official slain during a rebellion there.

After Pepy-Nakht's death, he was deified in Elephantine, where a cult was established to worship him. This cult continued to exist for hundreds of years. During this time, Pepy-Nakht's tomb was restored at least once. **See also** Elephantine; Pepy II.

Per-Ramses (Per-Ramesses)

Located near the modern village of Qantir in the northeastern Delta, Per-Ramses ("House of Ramses") was the capital city of Nineteenth Dynasty kings Seti I, his son Ramses II, and several of their successors. As such, it had a huge palace, several temples, an administrative building, a military base, and many homes and other structures. However, when nearby Tanis became the capital of Egypt at the beginning of the Twenty-first Dynasty, the structures in Per-Ramses were used as a source of building stones for the new city. In fact, archaeologists found so many inscriptions, carved reliefs, and statues related to the Ramessid kings—particularly Ramses II—who lived at Per-Ramses that the first archaeologists excavating Tanis thought that they had found Per-Ramses instead. **See also** Ramses II; Seti I; Tanis.

Persia and Persian Periods

Located on the high central plateau of what is now Iran, Persia was a powerful empire that ruled Egypt during the Twenty-seventh and Thirty-first Dynasties. As a result, some historians call the Twenty-seventh Dynasty the First Persian Period and Thirty-first Dynasty the Second Persian Period. During these periods, Egypt was overseen by a satrap, or provincial governor, appointed by the Persian king. The satraps apparently took on all of the trappings of an Egyptian king, even to the point of honoring Egyptian religious rituals, so Persia's control of the nation had little influence on ancient Egyptian culture.

The First Persian Period began with the Persian conquest of Egypt in 525 B.C. and lasted until Prince Amyrtaeus of the Egyptian city of Sais retook the country in 359 B.C. Persia reconquered Egypt in 343 B.C., ushering in the Second Persian Period. It lasted until a Macedonian king, Alexander III (Alexander the Great), took control of Egypt in 332 B.C. after conquering Persia. Both the First and the Second Persian Periods were part of a broader era of ancient Egyptian history known as the Late Period. **See also** Alexander the Great; Late Period; Saite Period.

Peru-Nefer

Located near Memphis with access to the Mediterranean Sea, Peru-Nefer was the main port for Egypt's navy during the New Kingdom. Consequently, it had repair facilities for ships as well as extensive docks, both of which were frequented by both merchant and military vessels. **See also** military; travel.

Petosiris (dates unknown)

Petosiris was the high priest of Thoth at Hermopolis during the reign of Ptolemy I. However, his significance to modern scholars lies in his tomb at Tura el-Gebal, the necropolis for Hermopolis. In this tomb, which was built around 300 B.C., wall reliefs blend Old Kingdom Egyptian religious motifs with Greek artistic and religious features, the earliest true merging of the two cultures in tomb art. **See also** Hermopolis; Ptolemaic Period.

Petrie, William Matthew Flinders (1853–1942)

British archaeologist and Egyptologist Sir William Matthew Flinders Petrie developed many new excavation techniques as the first person to apply truly scientific methodology to Egyptian archaeology. Other Egyptologists soon adopted his methods, abandoning their use of dynamite and other heavy-handed techniques in favor of excavating ruins with painstaking care. Because of his contributions to Egyptian archaeology, Petrie has been called the father of modern Egyptology. Petrie also pioneered the method of dating ancient ruins by matching pottery fragments found there to patterns known to have been associated with particular periods of Egyptian history.

Petrie began studying archaeology with a private tutor as a boy, and by the age of twenty-four he was writing about ancient ruins in Britain such as Stonehenge. In 1880 he went to Egypt to survey and excavate the Great Pyramid at Giza. He continued to excavate in Egypt and other areas of the Middle East for the next forty years, sponsored extensively in his early years by the Egypt Exploration Fund (now called the Egypt Exploration Society). During his lifetime, Petrie made many major discoveries as he visited Egypt's most important archaeological sites. For example, he excavated much of Abydos as well as the city of Akhetaten (also known as Amarna), the capital established by King Akhenaten. He also excavated more than three thousand predynastic graves at Naqada northeast of Thebes, and in the Faiyum he explored the pyramid of Amenemhet III and found a nearby tomb with a large amount of Twelfth Dynasty jewelry. Meanwhile, Petrie continually criticized other archaeologists who did not treat their own excavation sites with care. For example, he accused Swiss archaeologist Edouard Naville, also sponsored by the Egypt Exploration Fund, of being too hasty in his excavations, thereby damaging precious artifacts, and of being foolish for ignoring small objects and shards during his excavations.

In addition to undertaking archaeological expeditions, Petrie served as Professor of Egyptology at University College in London from 1892 to 1933. In 1894 he established an institution that just over ten years later became the British School of Archaeology. In 1904 he published *Methods and Aims in Archaeology,* which provided thorough information about excavation methods and then-unique tips about how to incorporate photography into archaeological fieldwork. Toward the end of his life, Petrie conducted a series of excavations in Palestine, discovering ten cities and establishing guidelines for other excavations in the area. **See also** Abydos; Amarna; archaeological expeditions.

pharaoh

The word *pharaoh* is a Greek derivation of the ancient Egyptian word *pero* or *per-a'a,* meaning "royal residence." At first, the word was used to refer to the king's palace, but later it was used to refer to the

king himself. *Pharaoh* continues to be used in preference to *king* in popular literature, although modern Egyptologists typically refer to Egypt's rulers as kings. Among both scholars and nonscholars, the word *queen-pharaoh* is typically used to refer to any queen who served as Egypt's independent ruler rather than just a king's consort. **See also** palaces; queens.

Philae (Jazirat Filah)

The island of Philae (also known today as Jazirat Filah) at the First Cataract of the Nile River once held numerous monuments and temples that were built throughout the Ptolemaic Dynasty, beginning with King Ptolemy I. According to ancient records, there was apparently some construction earlier on the island, but the oldest building material to survive is from the time of the Nubian king Taharqa (around 690–664 B.C.); these stones were incorporated into the foundation of a monument built sometime after 380 B.C. by King Nectanebo I (also known as Nakhtnebef).

Temples on the island were dedicated to a variety of Egyptian deities, including Osiris, Isis, Nephthys, Hathor, and Khnum, as well as the Nubian gods Arensnuphis and Mandulis. Among the structures were the Temple of Isis, considered to be one of the most beautiful ancient temples, and the Temple of Hathor, which has columns with inscribed depictions of the god Bes accompanied by musicians (because Bes was believed to play music regularly to soothe Hathor). There was also a temple dedicated to Imhotep, a Third Dynasty vizier deified after death as a god of healing, and another temple honoring Emperor Augustus of Rome, who took control of Egypt after the death of Queen Cleopatra VII in 30 B.C. The southeast end of the island apparently once had housing for people visiting the temples there.

The Temple of Isis on the island of Philae was built during the Thirtieth Dynasty (380 to 343 B.C.).

Although abandoned, many of the island's structures remained relatively intact for centuries. Consequently, in the nineteenth century, Philae became a popular stop for British tourists visiting Egypt. This remained true even after the British built a dam at Aswan in the early twentieth century that caused the Nile River to flood the island during certain times of the year. At those times, the tourists simply rode in boats around the tops of the temple columns. In the 1960s, however, a new Aswan Dam project was expected, upon completion, to result in the island buildings being totally and permanently submerged. To prevent a permanent loss of the buildings, an international team of archaeologists dismantled and relocated all of Philae's structures to the nearby island of Agilikia, which was substantially higher than Philae. The job was completed so carefully that today it is difficult to tell that the temples were ever located anywhere else. **See also** Bes; Hathor; Imhotep; Isis; Khnum; Nephthys; Osiris; Ptolemaic Period.

Piy (Piankhy; Piankhy-Piye) (ca. 747–ca. 716 B.C.)

Piy was a ruler of Kush, a region in Nubia, who marched his army northward in approximately 727 B.C. to take over Egypt. During this time, which Egyptologists call the Third Intermediate Period, there were four Egyptian kings controlling various parts of Egypt amid much disorder. Consequently Piy's troops easily conquered Thebes and eventually, with some difficulty, Memphis, thereby gaining what were then the two most important Egyptian cities. He took other cities as well, until both Upper and Lower Egypt were his. As the first king of Egypt's Twenty-fifth Dynasty, he took the Egyptian throne name of Menkheperre, "The Manifestation of Re Abides." Piy was an absentee ruler, preferring to have his capital at Napata in northern Nubia, and under his rule Egypt retained its traditions and customs. He was buried in Nubia in a pyramid at el-Kurru alongside his favorite horses. However, his body was embalmed according to Egyptian practices, setting a precedent that was followed by four Kushite successors (Shabaka, Shabataka, Taharqa, and Tanutamani). **See also** Memphis; Nubia; Thebes.

plants and flowers

Blessed with highly fertile soil in the Nile Valley, the Delta, and the Faiyum, ancient Egypt produced a wide variety of plants and flowers that could be used for food, seasonings, medicine, perfume, ointments, and oils. Plant fibers went into the production of a variety of items such as baskets, brushes, pillows (which were often stuffed with herbs), ropes, and even boats. For most ancient Egyptians, gardening was both a functional activity and a pleasurable hobby, providing not only food but also decorative and symbolic plants and flowers for household use. In addition, ancient Egypt had government-run gardens to provide plants for various royal craftsmen and flowers for festivals, religious ceremonies, and other state functions.

However, Egyptologists have yet to determine exactly which plants, herbs, and flowers were available to Egyptians in different eras of their history, although botanists have identified various species by studying artwork and by examining plant matter entombed in ancient trash heaps. Botanists in the field of Egyptology have found valuable information in the tomb of King Tutankhamun, which included many specimens of plants and flowers, including a wreath placed on one of the king's coffins. From such information, Egyptologists know that the lotus flower was among the most important ancient Egyptian plants, because its scent was believed to soothe the gods. Indeed, all fragrant flowers were particularly important in ancient Egyptian life, used as a sign of greeting and for a variety of religious rituals. **See also** agriculture; cosmetics and perfumes; food; gardens; Tutankhamun.

police

Ancient Egypt's police were responsible for capturing and punishing wrongdoers either on their own authority or as authorized by the courts. Individual policemen could even mete out punishment, usually in the form of beating wrongdoers to prevent a recurrence of bad behavior. Repeat offenders or those accused of serious crimes might be driven from town or taken to jail to be tried in the court system.

In administering justice, police officers worked as part of individual police forces that maintained law and order in specific cities or regions and had additional responsibilities depending on their assignment. For example, during the New Kingdom, the Medjay, a police force consisting of men of Nubian descent, primarily protected building sites in Thebes, preventing the theft of tools and supplies, dealing with worker disputes, keeping the peace both at the building site and at the nearby workers' village, and overseeing the distribution of pay. Police in rural areas oversaw the collection of taxes, while police assigned to temple complexes maintained order in the temple and upheld its religious practices, ensuring that all of its priests obeyed the rules related to proper conduct. Border police protected trading caravans traveling in and out of Egypt, and cemetery police prevented tomb robbing. **See also** legal system; Medjay.

polygamy and kingship

Ancient Egyptian kings were apparently polygamous from at least the Early Dynastic Period, primarily because having multiple wives was a way to ensure the availability of male heirs to the throne. When the king died, the oldest surviving son, no matter how young, of the king's principal wife would become king, followed by his brothers should he die before producing a male heir of his own. However, if the principal wife had no sons at the time of the king's death, then the oldest son of the king's secondary wives would rule.

Only when a king had no male heirs among any of his wives did his rule pass to someone else, typically another male family member or some other strong male figure (often the king's top military commander) appointed heir by the king prior to his death. During the New Kingdom, the king typically shared his rule with his designated heir during the final years of his reign in order to cement his chosen successor's claim to the throne. On a few occasions, however, a strong queen controlled the throne of a weak king, particularly if that king was a child, or even usurped the throne for themselves, as happened in the case of Hatshepsut, who usurped the throne from Tuthmosis III. **See also** harem; kings.

positions and titles

In ancient Egyptian society, a man's status was clearly defined by his position, or job, and his titles. However, even though a man's position was affected by his parentage—which is why, for instance, the son of a military commander usually became a soldier himself—a person could achieve a more prestigious position by displaying special skills or moral character. In this way, soldiers could work their way up to commanders, and a low-ranking priest who was particularly clever and loyal to the king could become a high priest or even a vizier, who oversaw all aspects of Egyptian government.

In the First Dynasty, titles merely reflected a person's social status; for exam-

ple, those nobles who were closest to the king always held the title of "seal bearer," in reference to the clay seals that were used among the wealthy to identify the owner of various goods. Toward the end of the First Dynasty, however, titles became more specialized to reflect a person's duties for the king. For example, a person with the title of "chancellor" dealt with the royal treasury and the Granaries of the Two Lands (the central repository for Egyptian food collection and distribution). Someone with the title "master of largess" was in charge of distributing food and goods during times of hardship to those who needed them most. In the Old Kingdom, the number of titles proliferated at a rapid pace, yet one title might carry with it multiple duties. For example, the "royal herald" carried messages for the king during times of battle, organized and supervised the details of public ceremonies, and often acted as a foreign diplomat as well. The title of "overseer" was given to the head of any one of the many departments within Egypt's large bureaucracy. In addition, one person might hold many titles all at the same time, provided that he could do the work associated with each one. **See also** scribes; viziers.

pottery

The ancient Egyptians used mud from the Nile River to make items such as dishes, bowls, and a variety of jugs, jars, and other containers. From scenes depicting the craft on the walls of Old and Middle Kingdom tombs, Egyptologists know that there were four basic steps to pottery making. First the clay was kneaded, either with the hands or with the feet, as pieces of straw and/or animal dung were added to it to alter its texture. Next, it was fashioned into its desired shape, either with the hands or on a potter's wheel. At first, this wheel was turned by hand, but by the New Kingdom it was powered via a foot pedal, although even after the wheel was first introduced, some pottery continued to be shaped with the hands.

After shaping, certain substances might be added to the clay to change its color. For example, red ocher might be added to make the red of the clay more intense. Pottery might be red, black, black and red, or gray depending on the composition of its clay and the methods used to prepare and finish it. The final stage of pottery making, either sun-drying or baking the piece, could also affect color depending on the heat's intensity.

Once the pottery was finished, it might be painted or left plain. Initially, painted decorations were geometric in design, but later other types of designs and symbols and then scenes were featured, particularly on vases. Glazing, however, was unknown in Egypt until the Greco-Roman Period. **See also** art; paintings; vases.

Predynastic Period (ca. 700,000–ca. 3000 B.C.)

The Predynastic Period is a span of time from prehistory to the establishment of the First Dynasty in approximately 3000 B.C. Scholars know little about the Predynastic Period in comparison to other eras of Egyptian history. However, archaeologists generally believe that the first humans in Egypt probably migrated there from East Africa as early as 700,000 B.C. Archaeologists refer to the culture of these prehistoric people as Paleolithic, and other than the remains of stone tools, they have found little to indicate how these Egyptians lived.

However, excavations of Paleolithic sites suggest that the earliest Egyptians were hunter-gatherers who subsisted on edible plants, fish, and some game animals, particularly gazelle, hartebeest, and a species of wild cattle. Most of the population was concentrated along the Nile River, because this is where the animals were concentrated. However, for reasons

unknown, in approximately 12,000 B.C. all evidence of human life disappeared from the Nile River Valley, leading archaeologists to suspect that a massive flood made the area uninhabitable. It appears that when this happened the Egyptians fled to the Western Desert, not returning to the Nile Valley until 8000 B.C., in what archaeologists call the Neolithic Period.

As with the Paleolithic, most of what is known about the Neolithic comes from tool artifacts. From these, archaeologists surmise that the earliest Egyptian Neolithic cultures emerged in Lower Egypt in the Western Desert and that human occupation reached its peak there in the late Middle and late Neolithic Periods. The first Neolithic Egyptians were desert nomads, moving from place to place to find water and food. By 7500 B.C., however, they had begun digging wells, enabling them to establish permanent settlements, and building simple homes of twigs covered with mud. They also began growing crops in desert oases.

Shortly thereafter, around 7000 B.C., settlements appeared in the Nile Valley of Lower Egypt, where there were apparently two distinct cultures that archaeologists call the Elkabian and the Qarunian, which subsisted on hunting, fishing, and gathering but still had no agriculture. Only much later, in approximately 4400 to 3900 B.C., did an agriculturally based civilization develop. Located in the Faíyum oasis, its people lived in mat or reed huts as part of small farming communities, where they stored emmer wheat and barley in underground pit granaries. They also wove baskets, made linen and pottery, and had tools that included flints and arrowheads set in wooden handles or poles. A nearby culture, the Merimda, soon developed agriculture as well, but their granaries were simply clay pots buried in the ground and their huts were made of wooden poles and reeds.

Two other cultures that developed in Lower Egypt during the Predynastic Period, the el-Omari (ca. 3700–ca. 3400 B.C.) and the Ma'adi (ca. 4000–3200 B.C.), gradually developed more sophisticated architecture. At first their oval huts were simple, with walls of reed mats or twigs covered with mud. Then they progressed to buildings with underground chambers reached by carved stairs. In addition, three cemeteries (which included the bodies of animals as well as people) found near a Ma'adi site in a dry riverbed yielded a copper axhead and bits of copper ore, which some archaeologists believe represent the first manufacture of this metal in Egypt.

Some archaeologists, however, believe that the axhead was acquired from a foreign land and suggest that the Ma'adi were the first Egyptians to engage in trade. In support of this theory, there are objects at the site, primarily pottery, that many archaeologists believe were acquired from Palestine and other parts of the Near East. Furthermore, animal remains show that the Ma'adi culture was heavily dependent on the donkey, an animal commonly used later in Egypt to transport people and goods on trading expeditions.

Even with these advances, the predynastic cultures in Lower Egypt never became as sophisticated as the predynastic cultures in Upper Egypt. For example, the Upper Egypt culture known as Badarian (ca. 4400–4000 B.C.), initially found at the base of cliffs at el-Badari but later at various other sites near the Nile River as well, made clay pottery that was much more delicate than that of their Lower Egypt counterparts. In addition, the Badarians made clay and ivory figurines; bone and ivory jewelry, hairpins, combs, and other personal items; and tents and leather and fur items from the skin of domesticated cattle, sheep, and goats. They also cultivated grains, wove clothing, and

had many stone weapons and tools. Their grave sites held bodies lying in pits on their left sides, facing west and covered with mats or hides, which suggests that some sort of ritual accompanied disposal of the dead. The fact that the bodies were found with offerings of food and personal and ceremonial items, including stone palettes, seems to support this conclusion.

Two other complex Predynastic Period cultures in Upper Egypt were the Naqada I and Naqada II cultures, both found at Naqada in the late nineteenth century by archaeologist and Egyptologist Sir William Matthew Flinders Petrie. The Naqada I (ca. 4000–3500 B.C.) was located from Nubia north to Deir Tasa. The Naqada II (ca. 3500–3200 B.C.) covered much of the same territory but stretched farther north along the Nile River. However, both cultures had the largest number of settlements around Abydos and Hierakonpolis.

Like the people of the Badarian culture, the people of both Naqada cultures made far more sophisticated pottery than did their counterparts in Lower Egypt. Naqada I craftsmen made polished pottery that was red with black rims and painted with white decorations, while Naqada II craftsmen primarily made coarse, cream-colored pottery painted with brown decorations. With both cultures, initially the decorations painted on pottery were geometric patterns but later they became pictures, first of animals and then of boats, hunters, warriors, and other people and objects. Naqada II craftsmen also worked in a wider variety of materials, including copper, gold, and many types of stone.

Naqada II agriculture exhibited a similar sophistication, with people cultivating several species of barley and wheat, many types of fruits and vegetables, and several types of domesticated livestock. Dogs had been domesticated by this time as well. Buildings appear to have included mud-brick palaces as well as rectangular houses, and there might also have been temples.

In fact, it appears that both Naqada cultures had the most complex religious beliefs of the Predynastic Period. Evidence for this complexity comes from numerous burial sites. As is the case with Badarian graves, bodies at Naqada I sites were buried in pits on their left sides facing west. Clad in loincloths of cloth or animal skins, these bodies were laid on a mat, their heads sometimes resting on a straw or leather pillow, and covered with either another mat or the skin of a goat, gazelle, or other animal. Covering the mat or skin was a layer of offerings, and additional offerings might be placed nearby. Artifacts found at these grave sites included a variety of stone knives, figures of animals and humans fashioned out of clay or ivory, and decorated slate palettes and maceheads.

Naqada II sites show more variation, with the elaborateness of burials apparently determined by the deceased's wealth and status. They also provide evidence of more complex burial rituals. Some graves were small round or oval pits with a few plain offerings, while others were large rectangular pits divided into chambers with mud-brick walls with the body in one chamber and funerary goods in others. The body in such a grave was usually within a wood or pottery coffin, perhaps wrapped in linen. In most cases, there was only one body per grave, but larger graves might hold up to five bodies. At some Naqada II sites, bodies were dismembered, with parts arranged in the tomb in an apparent ritualistic fashion. For example, in a five-body tomb, the five skulls were lined up along one wall.

A few corpses in multiple-body graves appear to have been the victims of ritualistic sacrifice, and some Egyptologists believe that this is the first evidence of servants being sent to accompany kings to the Afterlife. Decorations on tomb goods appear to foreshadow later beliefs regarding the Afterlife. For example, the main image is the boat, and the Nile River appears to be a religious symbol. Many archaeologists see this as the first step toward the later view that the Nile River connected the mortal realm with the realm of the gods.

Over time, the people of Naqada II spread north and south along the Nile River, establishing settlements to an area south of Abu Simbel and to the north well into the Delta. In doing so, the people of the Naqada II culture assimilated those in the Ma'adian culture. Shortly thereafter, new cultural developments led to an era that archaeologists call the Naqada III phase, which lasted from 3200 to 3000 B.C. This phase of development has been called the foundation of the First Dynasty because it featured the creation of a political entity that united several communities under one ruler. In fact, the last two rulers of the Naqada III phase, the Scorpion King and Narmer, controlled so much territory and had so much power that some archaeologists have reclassified the period of their rule as Dynasty Zero, and a few suspect that one of these two kings might have been the unifier of all Egypt.

Naqada burials of this period show that Egyptian society had become highly stratified by this time, which means that there was a wide difference between the lifestyles of the rich and the poor. This is evidenced not only by the value of funerary goods buried with the rich as opposed to the poor but also by the fact that some cemetery sites had both simple graves and mud-brick tombs, the latter of which were for the elite. **See also** Narmer; Petrie, William Matthew Flinders; pottery; Scorpion King.

priests

Although certain Old and Middle Kingdom temples had priestesses (called *hemet netjer,* or "wife of the god"), the ancient Egyptian priesthood was primarily male, and its focus was to serve the gods. There was no public ministry, which means that the priests did not go out into the community to preach. Moreover, temples—which were considered the private homes of the gods—were not open to the public.

The priest's main job was to help the king maintain his connection to the gods, performing various rituals and ceremonies within a temple to honor the particular deity or family of deities believed to live there. Priests might also serve as educators, teaching students who intended to be priests and/or scribes or doctors. The largest temples also functioned as educational institutions, libraries, and archives, employing hundreds of scribes to write and copy both sacred and secular texts. Temple institutions that housed centuries of accumulated knowledge were usually called the House of Life.

Priests assigned to work in this area of the temple spent their days studying, writing, and discussing various texts, and on occasion they were also called upon to draw up a calendar of festivals using astronomical charts. Meanwhile, other priests spent their days anointing statues and other ritual objects with oils, cleaning and purifying temple sanctuaries and water sources, preparing for upcoming religious festivals, and performing a variety of daily rituals. However, not all priests were allowed to enter every room of a temple; certain inner sanctuaries were reserved for the highest-ranking priests and/or for those who had undergone intense purification rituals.

Both large and small temples were staffed by a hierarchy of priests. At the bottom of this hierarchy were priests-in-training, but with diligence they could quickly work their way up the ranks. As they did so, they received titles that came with specific duties. For example, priests who conducted ceremonies related to pu-

rification were called *web* or *wab* priests; in smaller temples, these priests might conduct most other rituals as well. Priests in charge of mortuary rituals (i.e., those related to embalming) were called *sem* priests. Those who conducted funerary rites (i.e., those conducted as part of the funeral) were called *hem-ka* priests.

Still other priests were in charge of other ceremonial functions at a temple. For example, the stolist priest was in charge of washing, feeding, and dressing the temple's cult statue of the god, while the lector priest was in charge of reciting the words of the god (i.e., magic spells) during temple rituals. There were many other types of priests as well, but Egyptologists are unsure what all of their functions were.

At the top of the temple hierarchy were senior priests, each with specific titles and duties, who usually worked in the temple full-time. Of these, the two most important were the high priest, who supervised all of the other priests in the temple, and his deputy, the second prophet, who was in charge of the day-to-day functioning of the temple community, which included temple bakers, butchers, florists, and farmers. Temple complexes were often like small cities, producing all of the food and supplies for the people who lived and worked there. Consequently, the largest temples had extremely large staffs. For example, during the New Kingdom, the Temple of Amun at Karnak had more than eighty thousand workers, over seven hundred square miles of agricultural land and gardens, and thousands of domestic animals.

In such large temples, priests with different duties would be grouped together to form teams. Each team would then dedicate itself to performing all temple rites and rituals for a period of one month, living full-time at the temple until their period of service ended and the next team took over. At that point, the priests who had been released from duty would begin working as scribes, doctors, or in some other profession, either while still living within the temple complex or at home with their wives and/or families.

Only gradually did the priesthood become a full-time vocation. At first, priests were laypeople who served only occasionally in the temple. But by the New Kingdom, the priesthood was a social class in its own right, and fathers passed their positions down to their sons. Because of the hereditary nature of their positions, priests were not only allowed but encouraged to marry. However, priesthoods had rules governing when a priest could be with his wife. Specifically, a priest could not be with his wife during periods when he would be serving the gods.

Priests also had to adhere to dietary and clothing restrictions. There were certain foods that a priest could never eat, although Egyptologists disagree on what these were. Priests also had to dress only in clothes made of white linen and sandals made of plant fibers, with leopard skin cloaks for those of highest rank. Hairstyles were also indicative of certain ranks. Priests involved with purification ceremonies, for example, had to have shaved heads and bodies; they also had to wash in the temple's sacred lake or other purified water several times a day and night and rinse their mouths with a natron (salt) solution. Priests who would be handling the god's cult statue had to follow these guidelines as well.

During the New Kingdom, politics became increasingly associated with the priesthood, and this in turn affected priestly duties. Titles might be awarded more on the basis of family connections than on merit, and some priests were far more interested in serving their own interests than in serving their gods. The practice of passing temple jobs on from father to son had created priestly clans, and those connected with the largest and wealthiest temples became extremely powerful. The most influential of these temples during the New Kingdom was the Temple of Amun, which eventually succeeded in having all other temples placed under its control. Moreover, at the time, the high priest of Amun was said to have divine knowledge of whether a particular king or crown prince was truly the chosen representative of the gods. This power, combined with great wealth, gave the priesthood control over Egypt's kingship, and the New Kingdom ended with a line of priests usurping the throne. **See also** Amun; *ka;* New Kingdom; positions and titles; Third Intermediate Period.

Psamtik I (Psammetichus I) (?–610 B.C.)

Psamtik I was a king of the Twenty-sixth Dynasty during the tumultuous transition from the Third Intermediate Period to the Late Period. He reigned for fifty years, largely because at the beginning of his reign, when the country was at its most unstable, he had the support of a powerful ally, the Assyrians. He added to his power by awarding his daughter the honorific title Divine Adoratrice, or Divine Wife, of Amun in Thebes, a title that came with great wealth and estates as well as religious duties. When the Assyrians began having problems in their own lands, Psamtik I moved to expel them from Egypt, then brought all rival kings and chiefs in the Delta under his control. He then began opening Egypt up to foreign trade, thereby stimulating the economy. With this new wealth, he supported art, architecture, and religious institutions, particularly in his home city of Sais. (Indeed, this period of history is sometimes called the Saite Period or Saite dynasty.) By the end of his reign, Psamtik I had restored Egypt's stability and traditional religious values. **See also** Divine Wife of Amun; Third Intermediate Period.

Psamtik II (Psametik II; Psammetichus II; Neferibre) (?–589 B.C.)

Also known by his throne name, Neferibre ("Beautiful is the Heart of Re"), Psamtik II was the third king of the Twenty-sixth Dynasty. During his six-year reign, from 595 to 589 B.C., he engaged in at least two military campaigns, one in Nubia and one in Palestine. Otherwise, little is known about his reign.

Psamtik III (?–ca. 525 B.C.)

Twenty-sixth Dynasty king Psamtik III had been on the throne for only a year when the Persian army, under the command of Persia's King Cambyses III, attacked Egypt at its eastern city of Pelusium. The Persians were well armed and well trained, and within a short time they had overcome Psamtik III's army. Meanwhile, the Egyptian king escaped to Memphis, where the Persians eventually captured him. Soldiers took Psamtik III to the Persian capital of Susa, where he was executed. **See also** Late Period; Persia and Persian Periods.

Ptah

One of the oldest of ancient Egypt's creator gods, Ptah was the main deity of Memphis. Consequently, Memphis was sometimes called Hiku-Ptah or Hat-Ka-Ptah, which translates as the "Palace of the Soul of Ptah." However, Ptah was typically worshiped in conjunction with his consort, the goddess Sekhmet, and their son, the god Nefertem.

Ptah was said to have directly made all life. All deities, towns, people, animals, and everything else in existence formed first within his heart; he spoke their names to call them into being. He created not only all inanimate objects and living things but also personified concepts such as Truth and Order. Ptah was typically depicted as a semimummified man carrying a staff with three important Egyptian symbols: the *was* (a staff with an animal head), the *djed* (a pillar with three horizontal lines at the top), and the ankh (shaped like a capital letter "T" with an inverted teardrop atop it), representing power, stability, and life, respectively. Ptah was also associated with architecture, undoubtedly because in his role as creator he produced all buildings. In addition, Ptah was honored as the source of creativity, no matter what its form.

Beginning in the Old Kingdom, Ptah might appear as Ptah-Sokar, incorporating Ptah's characteristics with those of the god Sokar, who personified the darkest parts of the Underworld. The main role of this composite god was as the guardian of Memphis tombs. During the Late Period, Ptah usually appeared as Ptah-Sokar-Osiris, placing even more emphasis on the god's funerary aspects in a way that Egyptologists do not quite understand, although they do know that beliefs related to Ptah-Sokar-Osiris involved the concept of resurrection. **See also** ankh; *djed;* Memphis; Osiris; *was* scepter.

Ptolemaic kings

In 323 B.C., when Alexander III, the Macedonian conqueror of the Persian Empire (which included Egypt), died, a coalition of his generals took over rule of the vast area under his control. Ptolemy I Soter was one of these generals and by 305 B.C. was in complete control of Egypt. Declaring himself king, Ptolemy I established what historians sometimes call the Ptolemaic dynasty, a series of kings named Ptolemy who ruled Egypt from 305 B.C. to 30 B.C. The time when these kings ruled is often referred to as the Ptolemaic Period, or as the beginning of what is known to historians as the Greco-Roman Period (because it was an era of Greek and Roman influence). The Ptolemaic kings, the dates of their reigns, and the main accomplishments and/or events of their reigns are as follows:

Ptolemy I Soter (305–285 B.C.) As king, Ptolemy I continued to build in the capital city of Alexandria, founded by Alexander the Great, turning it into a major center of Greek culture. He placed his son Ptolemy II on the throne in 285 B.C., spending the last two years of his life in retirement.

Ptolemy II Philadelphus (285–246 B.C.) Ptolemy II added works to a library and museum established by his father at Alexandria and built many additional structures in the city. He also encouraged the establishment of many new Greek settlements and supported a major expansion of the Faiyum irrigation system. He promoted the arts, and through military conquest, Egypt gained land in Syria and took all of Phoenicia.

Ptolemy III Euergetes I (246–221 B.C.) Ptolemy III continued his predecessors' building projects. Pursuing an aggressive policy of expansion, Ptolemy III fought several battles in Syria and conquered the city of Babylon. He also expanded Egypt's navy.

Ptolemy IV Philopator (221–205 B.C.) Ptolemy IV's major accomplishment was defeating King Antiochus III of Syria during a series of battles that culminated in a major victory in Palestine in 217 B.C. However, at home, Egypt experienced great unrest as native Egyptians rebelled against Ptolemy's rule. Some Egyptologists believe Ptolemy IV's death was the result of foul play, while others believe his dissolute lifestyle was responsible.

Ptolemy V Epiphanes (205–181 B.C.) Ptolemy V assumed the throne as a boy when his father died suddenly. Ptolemy V's rule was extremely weak, with continuing internal unrest as well as attacks from foreign powers. He stayed on the throne only by allying Egypt with Rome.

Ptolemy VI Philometor (181–145 B.C.) Like his father, Ptolemy VI also assumed the throne as a boy. But whereas Ptolemy V ruled under the supervision of his ministers, Ptolemy VI's mother ruled as regent. Later, Ptolemy VI was captured during a Syrian attack on Egypt but was eventually released; upon his release, he ruled jointly with his younger brother Ptolemy VIII from 170 to 164 B.C. When Ptolemy VIII usurped the throne, Ptolemy VI petitioned Rome for help and the Romans restored his crown, sending Ptolemy VIII into exile.

Ptolemy VII Neos Philopator (145 B.C.) The son of Ptolemy VI, Ptolemy VII ruled less than one year before being murdered by his uncle, Ptolemy VIII, who then declared himself king.

Ptolemy VIII Euergetes II (145–116 B.C.) After murdering his nephew, Ptolemy VII, and assuming the throne, Ptolemy VIII forced the young man's mother to marry him so he could strengthen his claim to the throne. Ptolemy VIII is widely considered to be one of the most publicly hated ancient rulers; the Egyptians typically referred to him as *physon*, or potbelly, and not only refused to accept him as their king but drove him into exile on the island of Cyprus. (This was actually his second exile there; he had previously been expelled from the country by his brother, Ptolemy VI, whose throne he tried to usurp.) When Ptolemy VIII eventually returned to Egypt, he killed his eldest son in order to prevent him from holding on to the throne.

Ptolemy IX Soter II (?–80 B.C.), Ptolemy X Alexander I (?–88 B.C.), and Ptolemy XI Alexander II (dates unknown) These three kings accomplished little during their reigns, which were fraught with family intrigue and murder. When Ptolemy XI was murdered by an Alexandrian mob because he had killed his popular wife, he left no legitimate heir.

Ptolemy XII Auletes (80–51 B.C.) The illegitimate son of Ptolemy IX, Ptolemy XII was a puppet controlled by Rome and therefore was disliked by the Egyptians.

Ptolemy XIII Theos Philopator (51–47 B.C.) and Ptolemy XIV Theos Philopator II (47–44 B.C.) Each of these kings, who were both brothers of Queen Cleopatra VII (as well as her husbands), ruled jointly with her in succession; Ptolemy XIV took his older brother's place after Ptolemy XIII drowned in the Nile River.

Ptolemy XV Caesarion (44–30 B.C.) Cleopatra's son Ptolemy XV, fathered by the Roman emperor Julius Ceasar, coruled with his mother. He was the last of the Ptolemy line. **See also** Caesar, Julius; Cleopatra VII; Late Period.

Ptolemaic Period

Some historians use the term *Ptolemaic Period* to refer to a period of ancient Egyptian history immediately following the Late Period. The name of this period, which lasted from 332 B.C. to 30 B.C., was derived from the fact that fifteen of its kings bore the name Ptolemy. Historians differ over the exact beginning date for the Ptolemaic Period. Some date the beginning from when Ptolemy declared himself king, while other historians include years when he was still a general in the period. **See also** Greco-Roman Period; Late Period; Ptolemaic kings.

Punt

Ancient Egyptian writings often mention the land of Punt, but modern scholars are unsure of where it might have been located. In fact, a few Egyptologists believe that Punt was a mythical land because it was depicted in popular stories and love songs as an exotic utopia. The majority view, however, is that, although the ancient Egyptians exaggerated its qualities, Punt did exist and was probably someplace in East Africa. More specifically, since the Egyptians reported reaching Punt either by sailing from an Egyptian port located on the Red Sea or by traveling from the Near East down the Euphrates River to the Persian Gulf and around the Arabian Penin-

sula, the most likely location for Punt was the eastern coast of modern-day Ethiopia near where the Red Sea meets the Gulf of Aden. Alternatively, some scholars suggest that Punt was across the water from this area, on the southwestern coast of what is now Yemen.

The reason that the ancient Egyptians traveled to Punt—a journey that took no less than a month—was to acquire a variety of goods, including myrrh and myrrh trees (which provided incense), spices, ivory, resins and gums, and animal skins. The first expedition to Punt apparently took place in the Fourth Dynasty, and throughout many reigns, kings continued to send trading expeditions there.

Because Egyptologists do not know where Punt was (or even if it was a real place), they do not know what life there was like. However, wall reliefs in a temple built by Queen-Pharaoh Hatshepsut that show an Eighteenth Dynasty Punt expedition depict the people of Punt as dwelling in huts near a beach. These huts were unusual in that they were raised up off the ground and required ladders to enter them; modern scholars surmise that this might have been done to protect the inhabitants from wild animals. **See also** Hatshepsut; incense; trade.

purification practices

Purification practices and rituals were an important part of ancient Egyptian worship. Incense was burned prior to temple ceremonies and rituals in order to purify the air. Most priests ritualistically washed themselves as often as four times a day (twice at night and twice during daylight hours) in order to purify themselves for temple work. Indeed, the word for the type of priest most numerous in a temple was the *wab,* or "purified," priest. Such priests also shaved all of the hair on their heads and bodies, kept their nails cut short, rinsed their mouths in a natron (salt) solution, and followed rigid rules regarding what they could eat, drink, wear, and do prior to engaging in religious ceremonies. Ritual washing was conducted in a temple's sacred lake, if it had one, or in rectangular or T-shaped limestone troughs. Such troughs have been found not only in temple complexes but also near smaller temples and shrines.

Purification or cleansing rituals were probably conducted in households as well, since ancient Egyptian texts mention women engaging in such activities after childbirth and menstruation. In fact, the ancient Egyptian word for menstruation, *hesmen,* also means "to purify oneself." In addition, a few New Kingdom texts mention that eating fish caused a person to be impure, so households might have been subjected to dietary taboos prior to purification rituals. The most important function of purification rituals and practices, however, was still in the domain of priests: to make spells and rituals more powerful. Indeed, ancient Egyptian magical texts suggest that certain spells and rituals would not work at all unless the person performing them was in a purified state. **See also** magic; priests; sacred lakes; temples.

pyramids

Pyramids are ancient Egyptian monuments that have a square base with four triangular sides rising to form a point. A total of 110 pyramids have been found in Egypt, along with twenty tombs atop which pyramids probably once sat, and more are being discovered all the time. The most recent discovery is that of a pyramid belonging to an unidentified queen. This structure is located in Abu Roash, near the pyramid of King Djedefre. Of the pyramids that have been found, forty-two are known to have belonged to kings. Scattered from north to south along the Nile River and into the Faiyum in the cities of Abu Roash, Giza, Zawiyet el-Aryan, Abusir, Saqqara, Dashur, Mazghuna, el-Lisht, Meidum, Seila, Lahun,

and Hawara, Egypt's pyramids are of four types: the step pyramid, which has sides terraced to look like steps; the true pyramid, with smooth sides; the bent pyramid, which has a change in the angle of each side's face midway up the pyramid; and the sarcophagus-shaped pyramid, which has no point and therefore is classified by some Egyptologists as a mastaba tomb rather than a pyramid. Of these, the true pyramid is the most numerous, with thirty-five known to exist. Egyptologists have determined that the step pyramids, of which there are five, were precursors to the true pyramids. Egyptologists disagree on why the other two types of pyramids exist, but there is only one of each.

Exactly why the Egyptians built pyramids has been debated for centuries. Given the immense size of the pyramids and the amount of labor and materials that went into their construction, and considering the precise measurements and architectural skills necessary to build a true pyramid, some Egyptologists argue that the view of pyramids as royal tombs or places to stage mortuary rituals is too simplistic. What archaeologists have found—or more accurately *not* found—supports this view: While it is true that Egypt's kings built impressive tombs to hold their remains, some of the pyramids show no evidence of having held a sarcophagus, and others contain a sarcophagus that was clearly never used. In addition, some kings built more than one pyramid, which suggests that pyramids were perhaps intended as false tombs, much as cenotaphs were, or that they might have served some other purpose entirely.

Over the years, many alternative theories have been proposed for why pyramids might have been built. Entire books have been written on these theories, with little agreement among the proponents for each theory. Among the most widely held beliefs are that the structures were intended as astronomical observatories or

The pyramids of Giza. The ancient Greek historian Herodotus claimed that the Great Pyramid (far right) took twenty years to build, but modern scholars believe that construction took much longer.

that they served some science-related purpose that is not yet understood. Another theory is that the pyramid was connected to an initiation into some secret mystical society or performed some other function related to magic and/or religion. Supporting this view is the fact that a pyramid was often part of a complex of buildings that included at least one temple.

There are also many theories regarding how the pyramids were built. In writing about their construction roughly two thousand years after the fact, the fifth-century-B.C. Greek historian Herodotus reported that the Great Pyramid took twenty years to build. Modern scholars, however, believe that Egypt could never have gathered the workforce necessary to complete such a structure in that amount of time, given that all work was done by hand and involved massive stones. By some estimates, in fact, 240,000 to 300,000 men would have been needed for the Great Pyramid project to be completed in twenty years, and even in this scenario some Egyptologists wonder how they could have accomplished this task—unless they had some special construction techniques that modern scholars know nothing about.

The ancient Egyptians never depicted or wrote about how they constructed their pyramids, despite the fact that they have revealed many other aspects of their life in artwork and texts. Consequently, Egyptologists have had to guess about the building techniques they might have used, and these conjectures have caused many disagreements. For example, Egyptologists suspect that ramps were used to drag stones up the face of the pyramid, but they disagree on how these ramps might have been arranged and manipulated. Disagreements have also raged over how the stones were moved and lifted.

had usable chambers within them, often decorated with scenes and funerary inscriptions such as the Pyramid Texts.

Just as Egyptologists disagree on why and how the pyramids were built, no one knows why their construction ended. The prevailing theory is that Egypt's kings realized that such prominent structures provided an obvious target for tomb robbers and therefore switched to building easily concealed rock-cut tombs. However, if pyramids were not intended to be tombs, then this argument would not have merit. Alternatively, Egypt's kings might have decided that the pyramids were too costly to build, or they might have run out of money, building materials, and/or an adequate supply of laborers. **See also** architecture; mastaba tomb; tombs.

Pyramid Texts

The Pyramid Texts are a collection of inscriptions found in Fifth and Sixth Dynasty pyramids, beginning with that of King Unas. However, most scholars believe that they date from an earlier time and that the inscriptions from the Fifth and Sixth Dynasties are actually copies of materials from some earlier dynasty.

The Pyramid Texts have many confusing or nearly incomprehensible sections featuring obscure religious symbols or phrases. However, their nature seems clear; they consist of spells, incantations, and prayers that were probably recited during mortuary rituals and myths, information, and instructions intended to help the spirit of the deceased make the transition to the Afterlife. Some of the material in the Pyramid Texts later appeared in the Coffin Texts, the *Book of the Dead*, and other funerary texts. However, in these later texts the material was intended for nonroyals as well as royals, whereas the Pyramid Texts were only for kings. **See also** Afterlife; *Book of the Dead;* Coffin Texts; Unas.

Many pyramids' smooth outer casings have disappeared, revealing the stone blocks that make up their basic structure.

While the earliest pyramids were entirely of stone, some later ones combined mud-brick core elements with a limestone outer casing. In most of the true pyramids, coatings of masonry surround a central core to form a series of interior buttresses that decrease in height as they rise, so beneath the outer casing of the true pyramid is the form of a step pyramid. In some pyramids of the Twelfth or Thirteenth Dynasty, internal chambers were filled with rubble or mud to support the structure, but these did not hold up well over the centuries. All pyramids also

quarrying

The ancient Egyptians quarried stones for building and sculpting projects, variously choosing white limestone, sandstone, alabaster, red granite, black granite, diorite, and schist. During the Old Kingdom, most stones were obtained from blocks that were easily broken off or already on the ground, but by the Middle Kingdom this supply had been seriously depleted and extensive and aggressive quarrying began.

White limestone came from quarries at Tura (called Roan in ancient times), which was near Memphis. The Tura quarries were the first large-scale operations, and they required stoneworkers to tunnel deep into the ground, creating large caverns in which they could stand to chisel out the best limestone.

Sandstone was quarried primarily at Gebel el-Silsila. Alabaster (used mostly for dishes and statues) and schist (many sculptors' choice for small statues) were both quarried in the Eastern Desert, alabaster mostly at Hat-nut and a quarry site near Amarna, and schist in the Wadi Hammamat, located between Coptos and the Red Sea. Black granite came from the Wadi Hammamat as well, while red granite came from quarries at Aswan and diorite came from a region south of Aswan.

Quarries were usually abandoned for periods of time and worked only when stones were needed for a particular building. With distant quarries, major expeditions were required to transport the necessary workers and tools to the site and bring back the quarried material. For example, an expedition launched by King Ramses IV to the Wadi Hammamat required nearly eighty-five hundred people and ten ox-drawn wagons filled with food and other supplies. Approximately eight hundred of these people were soldiers, two thousand were mercenaries and slaves, and the remainder were military commanders, project leaders, priests, stonemasons, and other craftsmen. To travel to the quarries, the expedition had to journey for two to three days across land after leaving their boats on the Nile River.

Bringing stones back to a building site, from this and other quarries, could be extremely difficult, because the largest stones—particularly those used for obelisks—could weigh hundreds of tons. In fact, one obelisk abandoned at Aswan weighs over one thousand tons. Whenever possible, such large, heavy objects were transported by ship along the Nile River, but even then they had to be transported from the quarry to the river; they were placed on wooden platforms, or sledges, with rollers beneath and were dragged overland by teams of men with ropes. Loads of stones or even single stones might be so heavy that thousands of men were needed to pull the sledge, and when they reached the river, the ships had to be out of the water during loading or they would tip. Special dry docks were constructed beside the Nile River in which water could be drained and then reintroduced once the stone was loaded. However, some of the largest stones, such as obelisks, were typically still so heavy that the vessel would have to be towed by as many as nine others, each with over two dozen oarsmen. To make stones as light as possible before transport, rough carving was done at the quarry so that all unnecessary sections of the stone were cut away. **See also** art; obelisk; statues; stoneworking.

queens

Although most ancient Egyptians were monogamous, a king had several wives in order to increase his chances of having a male heir. Egyptologists generally reserve the title of "queen" for the woman the king had designated his principal wife, with lesser wives called consorts. The principal wife lived at the palace with the king, while lesser wives lived in the harem, which was often in another location altogether. If the principal wife produced no sons, the king would customarily designate an heir from among the sons of the lesser wives in his harem, and that child's mother would receive the title and status of queen as well. However, a queen who came from humble beginnings never achieved the same prestige as a queen who had been the daughter of a king.

A queen's role in the royal household was determined by her husband. Although in Egyptian society women were considered equal to men, the position of the queen was unique in that she was thought to be married to a physical manifestation of a god, and of course even as a man the king had ultimate power. Therefore, some queens subjugated themselves to the whims and wishes of their king or, if he was young, to those of other powerful people at court. However, there were also queens who had nearly as much power as a king, and in a few cases they became independent rulers of Egypt.

There were three basic ways for a queen to achieve such power. First, a king might simply turn his responsibilities over to a particular queen. For example, although Amenhotep III was a strong ruler in his youth, in his later years he left his official duties to his wife, Queen Tiy. Second, a queen might gain power as regent for an heir who was too young to rule on his own. This was the case with Queen Hatshepsut, who became the regent of young King Tuthmosis III (the son of a lesser queen) upon the death of her husband, King Tuthmosis II. Third, a very few queens, all of whom were the daughters of kings, claimed the throne as their own, ruling as queen-pharaoh. This was the case, for example, with Hatshepsut, who eventually usurped the throne from the boy king for whom she was regent.

Queens who did not long for the throne might still be involved in government affairs. Generally well educated, some queens helped royal scribes at court or participated in other palace activities. In addition, queens and princesses might be honored with titles that came with specific duties. One of the most important titles that a queen could receive during the New Kingdom was "Divine Wife of Amun." This position came with religious duties associated with the powerful Temple of Amun at Karnak and Luxor and also conferred wealth, honor, and political clout to the title owner. In the Twenty-first Dynasty, however, the title was changed to Divine Adoratrice of Amun so that the king's daughter could hold the position, provided that she remain unmarried. **See also** Ahmose-Nefertiry; Divine Wife of Amun; harem; Hatshepsut; Tiy.

Qurna

On the Nile River near Thebes, Qurna (also known as Abd el-Qurna) is the location of the mortuary temple of Nineteenth Dynasty king Seti I. It also contains tombs of nobles from the Eighteenth and Nineteenth Dynasties. However, only a small part of the king's temple remains today. **See also** Seti I.

Ramessid Period (1295–1069 B.C.)

The Ramessid Period is the name commonly used by historians to refer to a period within the New Kingdom during which eleven kings sharing the name Ramses (sometimes spelled Rameses or Ramesses) ruled Egypt, along with several of their relatives. There is little that can be said to characterize this period in Egyptian history. Some of its kings were among the strongest in Egypt's history, while others were among the weakest. In fact, the last king of the period, Ramses XI, effectively gave over his rule to two powerful high priests, thereby ending the unity of Egypt and ushering in the chaotic time known as the Third Intermediate Period. **See also** Ramses I; Ramses II; Ramses III; Ramses IV; Ramses VI; Ramses IX, Ramses XI; Third Intermediate Period.

Ramses I (ca. 1343–ca. 1294 B.C.)

Founder of the Nineteenth Dynasty, Ramses I was a military commander, vizier, and perhaps also high priest of Amun under King Horemheb. He assumed the throne when the king died without an heir. By that time, however, Ramses I was already an old man, so he reigned only sixteen months before dying and leaving his throne to his son Seti I. Ramses I's tomb was near Horemheb's in the Valley of the Kings, but some years after his entombment, priests moved his mummy, which had been damaged by tomb robbers, to a royal cache at Deir el-Bahri for safekeeping. **See also** Deir el-Bahri; Horemheb; Seti I.

Ramses II (ca. 1303–ca. 1213 B.C.)

Nineteenth Dynasty king Ramses II is also known as Ramses the Great because of his many accomplishments during his sixty-seven-year reign. He assumed the throne at age twenty-five after the death of his father, Seti I. Even before this occurred, however, he had distinguished himself on the battlefield, participating in a military campaign with his father against the Hittites in Syria. As king, he again went up against the Hittites in Syria, leading over twenty thousand men in an attack on the Hittite-held city of Kadesh in the fourth year of his reign. Known as the Battle of Kadesh, this war—which involved approximately forty thousand Hittites with twenty-five hundred chariots—resulted in a draw, although Ramses II later claimed a victory. After a few subsequent campaigns, Ramses II signed a treaty with the Hittites, which he later inscribed on walls at the temple of Karnak and at the Ramesseum, the king's mortuary temple at Thebes.

Ramses II was an active builder: He added to existing temples at Karnak and Luxor; completed mortuary temples begun by his father at Abydos and Thebes; planned and constructed a new Delta city, Per-Ramses, as his capital; and built a tomb for himself in the Valley of the Kings. In addition, Ramses II built two huge temples at Abu Simbel in Nubia. Carved out of the side of a mountain, they featured several colossal statues of the king and some of his family members. To fund such projects, Ramses II exploited many gold mines in the Eastern Desert and demanded tributes (i.e., payments of gold) from his nobles and those foreign princes under his control.

Ramses II was reputed to have at least eight principal wives, countless lesser wives, and over one hundred children, some of whom he placed in positions of power within his administration. His favorite principal wife appears to have been Nefertari, because she is the queen most often featured in artwork and statuary he commissioned.

When Ramses II died, he was entombed in the Valley of the Kings. However, several years later that tomb was discovered to have been robbed, so priests relocated the mummy of Ramses II to a royal cache at Deir el-Bahri, which remained undisturbed until it was found by archaeologists in 1881. **See also** Abu Simbel; Karnak; Nefertari; Seti I.

Ramses III (ca. 1218– ca. 1153 B.C.)

Twentieth Dynasty king Ramses III apparently began his reign with a coregency with his father, Sethnakhte, a few months before Sethnakhte died. Ramses III's independent reign lasted thirty-one years, during which he had to deal with invasions by Libyans and Sea Peoples. After one of the resulting battles, Ramses III reported that his forces had killed more than two thousand Libyans in the Delta.

Ramses III was the target of an assassination plot, which was timed to coincide with coups within his government and military. Fortunately for the king, an informant revealed the plot before it could be carried out. Today, this plot is known as the Harem Conspiracy because

its apparent instigator was one of the king's lesser wives, Tiye, who wanted her son to gain the throne. (In court records, the son's name is given as Pentewere, but since the records use pseudonyms for many of the major participants, it is doubtful whether this was really his name.) More than forty people were ultimately arrested for their involvement in the conspiracy, prosecuted, and found guilty in a series of trials. **See also** harem.

Ramses IV (ca. 1197– ca. 1147 B.C.)

A Twentieth Dynasty king, Ramses IV reigned for only six years. During that time, he was primarily concerned with building monuments (most of which have been destroyed) and restoring and decorating temples. To acquire building and decorative stones, he sent several large mining and quarrying expeditions to the Wadi Hammamat. One such expedition involved over eight thousand men, two thousand of whom were soldiers sent along to keep order at the work sites. Much of what is known about Ramses IV comes from what is now called the Harris Papyrus, a 133-foot-long papyrus found in a tomb at Deir el-Medina that lists all of the annual temple festivals during the reign of Ramses IV's father, Ramses III, and the gifts he gave to temples during his thirty-one-year reign. The document also tells of Ramses IV's military campaigns, including information on their cost and the profits they brought. In fact, the Harris Papyrus is as much an accounting document as it is a testament to King Ramses IV's accomplishments. **See also** Deir el-Medina; Harris Papyrus; Ramses III.

Ramses VI (?–ca. 1136 B.C.)

A king of the Twentieth Dynasty, Ramses VI probably usurped the throne from his uncle Ramses V, who reigned only four years, apparently during a time of civil war. Ramses VI himself reigned only eight years, and he seems to have accomplished little during that time. In fact, under his care, Egypt lost both power and territory abroad. When he died, Ramses VI was entombed in the Valley of the Kings, where tomb robbers found and savagely assaulted his mummy with an ax; Egyptologists have yet to determine a specific reason for their fury. Toward the end of the New Kingdom, priests tried to repair this mummy, although clumsily, and reentombed it as part of a royal cache in the tomb of Amenhotep II, where it was found by archaeologists in 1898. **See also** caches, royal; Valley of the Kings.

Ramses IX (?–ca. 1108 B.C.)

A Twentieth Dynasty king, Ramses IX ruled for seventeen years, during which Egypt was peaceful and stable; however, the king accomplished little during his reign. The most notable aspect of his reign, in fact, was not an architectural or military accomplishment (although he did build extensively in Heliopolis) but an investigation into a tomb robbery ring. The king's officials were prodded into this investigation by Paser, the mayor of eastern Thebes, who thought that his rival Pawero, the mayor of western Thebes and the guardian of its royal tombs, was helping robbers invade the tombs under his care. Records of the ensuing investigation have provided archaeologists with a list of the kings whose tombs were inspected for evidence of robbery, thereby providing Egyptologists with information that helped them identify various ancient Egyptian rulers. **See also** Paser; robbers, tomb.

Ramses XI (?–ca. 1069 B.C.)

Ramses XI, the last king of both the Twentieth Dynasty and the New Kingdom, reigned for twenty-seven years. During that time, Theban priests challenged the king's rule, and he proved himself a weak king by giving two of them, Herihor and Smendes, the position of vizier, one in the south and one in the north. Ramses XI then retired to his palace, leaving the two men effectively in charge of the country. After the king died, these two men officially divided Egypt's rule between them, thereby ushering in the disunified Third Intermediate Period. **See also** Herihor; Smendes I; Third Intermediate Period.

Re

Re was an ancient Egyptian solar deity first worshiped in Heliopolis in the Early Dynastic Period and possibly even earlier. From the Fifth Dynasty on, to enhance their own authority, kings associated themselves with this god, beginning one of their five royal names with the phrase "son of Re." In fact, even after Theban kings elevated their city's god, Atum, above all others during the New Kingdom, they could not bring themselves to lessen Re's power, and so Atum became Atum-Re, a combination of the essences of both gods. In most cases, Atum-Re was considered to be the sun in its setting form, while Re was considered the form the sun took as it traveled across the sky during the day, and another god, Khepri, was the sun at dawn. At other times, Re merged with another solar deity, Horus, whose name was also a part of kings' royal titles, to become Re-Horakhty. In addition, because the sun was believed to continue its journey throughout the night in order to reach the point of dawn again, Re was associated with Osiris, god of the dead (in some myths the father of Horus), who was connected to darkness.

Mythology related to Re varied according to time and place. In many eras and places, he was said to travel across the sky each day and through the Underworld each night using two different solar barks and accompanied by a retinue of lesser deities. Alternatively, he was thought to spend each night within the sky goddess

Nut, who swallowed him at sunset and spit him out at dawn. Various myths tell of Re's struggles to reach the place where he would rise each morning; the Underworld was fraught with monsters, such as the serpent Apophis (featured in a ritual to protect Re called Overthrowing Apophis). Other myths focus on Re's creation, according to which he emerges from a lotus flower that in turn has emerged from the primordial waters. Still other myths describe Re's creation of other deities as the father of Geb, the earth god, and Nut, the sky goddess (although in other myths the father of Geb and Nut was the god Shu).

Re was typically depicted as a man with the head of a falcon or a ram. In a myth in which he plots the destruction of humankind (and then changes his mind), he is described as being very old, with bones of silver, flesh of gold, and hair of lapis lazuli (all very valuable materials in ancient Egypt). Other myths depict the sun as being Re's eye and the moon as Horus's eye, so for much of Egypt's history, the Eye of Re and the Eye of Horus were two of Egypt's most sacred symbols, representing supreme power. However, the Eye of Re was sometimes said to belong to Shu, the god who sometimes took Re's place in myths related to Creation. **See also** Atum; Horus; Nut; Osiris; Overthrowing Apophis.

Red Land

Ancient Egyptians called the deserts surrounding their country the Red Land, or Deshret. The Black Land, or Kemet, was their name for Egypt. Both of these terms came from the color of the ground. Whereas the soil in areas watered by the Nile was rich and black, the desert glowed red in the morning sun. **See also** Black Land.

Rehu-erdjersenb (Rehu'ard-jersen) (ca. 1985–ca. 1955 B.C.)

Rehu-erdjersenb was a Twelfth Dynasty official who is known from a stela at Abydos, which was then the cult center of Osiris. According to its inscriptions, Rehu-erdjersenb served King Amenemhet I as overseer of sealers and chancellor of the court. The stela tells of Rehu-erdjersenb's activities and responsibilities and also lists the members of his family, of which there were many. Rehu-erdjersenb's mastaba tomb, located at el-Lisht, provides additional information about his activities. Elaborate wall reliefs there show him hunting fowl in the marshes of the Nile River and boating on the Nile with his son Nefry. **See also** Abydos; Amenemhet I; el-Lisht.

Rekhmire (ca. 1479–ca. 1400 B.C.)

Rekhmire was one of two viziers during the Eighteenth Dynasty reigns of King Tuthmosis III and Amenhotep II. His father, Nefer-weben, was a priest of the Temple of Amun and his uncle, Woser, was vizier for a previous king. Much of what is known about Rekhmire himself comes from his tomb in the Valley of the Nobles at Thebes. The tomb's texts, reliefs, and paintings have provided Egyptologists with important information about Eighteenth Dynasty life in general and the life of a noble in particular. The main corridor and burial chamber of the tomb are laid out in a T shape, as are many noble tombs of the period, and along its walls is a series of scenes. Some of these scenes show Rekhmire at work, acting as a judge in a court of law, inspecting foreign tributes, inspecting the collection of Lower Nubian taxes, inspecting temple workshops, attending a banquet, and attending an audience with the king. Inscriptions accompanying these scenes tell of Rekhmire's fine character, morals, and ability. Others show various tradesmen and farmers working and giving the fruits of their labors as a gift to Rekhmire. There are also scenes of him and his wife Meryt enjoying leisure activities in the Afterlife. **See also** nobles; viziers.

religion

Much of what remains of ancient Egyptian culture—tombs, temples, and writings and art that feature the gods and the Afterlife—relates to religion. Therefore, many Egyptologists have assumed that religion was interwoven into every aspect of Egyptian life. However, it is impossible to know exactly how much and how often the average ancient Egyptian thought about religion, particularly since much of what remains relates to the dead and not the living. Moreover, Egyptologists admit that there is much about the nature of ancient Egyptian religion that they do not understand, because it involves complex beliefs, confusing and often contradictory associations between various gods and their symbols and manifestations, and strange references to unfamiliar forms of magic.

In trying to understand ancient Egyptian religion, Egyptologists have had to rely on myth and symbolism, primarily as found in tomb and temple art, because the ancient Egyptians left behind no record of discussions or explanations of their religious beliefs. The most confusing of these sources are funerary texts like the Old Kingdom Pyramid Texts and the New Kingdom *Book of Aker* and *Book of Caverns,* all of which incorporate a great many images whose meaning Egyptologists do not understand.

More accessible are ancient Egyptian myths related to Creation, with four main versions coming from the cities of Heliopolis, Memphis, Elephantine, and Hermopolis. These myths tell of a time when all existence was water, out of which a creator god eventually arose. In the Creation myth of Heliopolis, the creator god was Atum, who made two deities who then united to give birth to others. In Memphis, the creator god was

Ptah, who directly made all gods, all life, all towns, and everything else in Egypt within his own heart. In the Creation myth of Elephantine, the god Khnum made all beings, fashioning them on a potter's wheel using Nile River clay. In the Creation myth of Hermopolis, four frog-headed gods (Nun, Amun, Kuk, and Huh) united with four snake-headed goddesses (Naunet, Amaunet, Kauket, and Hauhet) to create the sun, which then brought about human and animal life.

As evidenced by these myths, however, even the clearest material does not provide a coherent view of ancient Egyptian religion, because various mythologies and deities were prominent in Egypt at different times. In the Old Kingdom, Ptah and Re were the most prominent deities, because their cult centers were located in the most prominent cities of the time, Memphis and Heliopolis, respectively, and the same was true for the most prominent Middle Kingdom god, Amun, whose cult center was Thebes. Moreover, the prominence of a particular god was affected by the king, because whenever a king moved Egypt's capital to a new location, the deity of that location typically became a national god as opposed to a local one. The same situation sometimes occurred when a particular area became popular as the royal necropolis. For example, Osiris, who was originally associated with the royal necropolis of Abydos, became a national god during the New Kingdom.

With the rise of Osiris came many myths related to that deity's life, death, and resurrection in the Afterlife. Belief in resurrection goes back to the very beginning of Egyptian civilization, however. At first, this belief applied only to the king, whom the Egyptians considered the physical manifestation of a god on earth—a view the king encouraged because it provided legitimacy for his rule. During the Old Kingdom, the Egyptians believed that when a king died he re-joined his fellow gods in the celestial realm. In subsequent periods, they believed that all other people could enjoy an Afterlife as well, although not necessarily as an associate of the gods. Although some Egyptologists have suggested that it is impossible for any person today to know what ancient Egyptians thought about the Afterlife, from tomb art and goods it appears that the prevailing belief was that when people died their souls (which had three aspects—the *ka,* the *ba,* and the *akh*) would be able to enjoy the same activities through eternity as before death, providing the proper rituals were conducted after death. Moreover, it was believed that certain tomb goods could be made into Afterlife versions of things the person had employed in life, providing the right spells were incorporated into their construction.

Because they believed in an Afterlife that allowed for the enjoyment of personal possessions, part of Egyptian religious practice involved making offerings to the dead. Ancient Egyptians arranged for their relatives or priests to bring food to their tombs after their death to nourish the *ka* aspect of their souls, which was thought to need the essence of food in order to survive. In keeping with their beliefs regarding resurrection, ancient Egyptians also preserved their relatives' bodies via mummification so that they would function in the Afterlife as well. Reanimation rituals were conducted for the deceased, not only at funerals but afterward as well. Egyptologists do not know the details of many of these rituals, but they do know that they involved symbolic gestures and movements, the recitation of spells and incantations, and the offering of various foods and items such as meat, bread, beer, and linen.

Much of ancient religious practice consisted of offerings and rituals to honor certain deities—in cult temples, household

shrines, and elsewhere. In addition, many festivals and processions featured cult statues of the most prominent Egyptian gods, and these statues were treated as though they were the deities they represented. In between their public outings, the statues were cared for on a daily basis by temple priests; temples were considered the gods' homes and priests their household servants. Religion even entered ancient Egypt's system of justice. Statues of the gods were sometimes used to proclaim someone's guilt or innocence in a legal trial, with the help of priest-judges who claimed to be able to hear the gods' verdicts. **See also** Afterlife; cult centers; deities; offerings; priests; temples.

robbers, tomb

Because of the many valuable items placed in tombs, tomb robbers were likely to descend on a burial site almost immediately. They not only stole the possessions of deceased royals and nobles but also unwrapped mummies in search of amulets and jewelry hidden in the linen wrappings. When tomb robberies were discovered, priests rewrapped the bodies and reentombed them, usually at a different site. For example, in approximately 1000 B.C. priests reentombed two large groups of royal mummies, one near Deir el-Bahariat in Thebes and the other in the tomb of Amenhotep II in the Valley of the Kings.

To discourage tomb robbers, the Egyptian government posted guards at the country's most important burial sites, but even this did not deter some robbers. In fact, many had informants, either tomb builders or bureaucrats, who helped them find their way past guards and into tombs.

To foil tomb robbers, kings stopped entombing themselves in highly visible structures and turned instead to concealed rock-cut tombs among the cliffs of the Valley of the Kings. Not only were tomb entrances easy to hide there, but the valley was also easy to guard because it was rimmed with high cliffs and had only one easy entrance and exit point. In addition, kings tried various construction techniques to prevent tomb robbers from finding burial chambers. For example, King Tuthmosis II built his tomb in the Valley of the Kings with an entrance corridor featuring a sharp left turn; tomb builders sealed this corridor at the turn so that any tomb robber digging toward the burial chamber would assume he had to keep going straight. Despite such tactics, tomb robbers continued to violate ancient Egyptian tombs long after they were built and sealed. In fact, during the nineteenth century, many ancient Egyptian artifacts reached the antiquities market specifically through the efforts of nineteenth-century tomb robbers. **See also** caches, royal; tombs; Valley of the Kings.

Rosetta Stone

One of the most important ancient Egyptian artifacts, the Rosetta Stone was found in 1799 within an old stone wall by a soldier on Napoléon's archaeological expedition. It is a roughly 4-foot-by-2.5-foot fragment from a black basalt stela commemorating an anniversary of the reign of King Ptolemy V Epiphanes. The stone's importance lies in the fact that it was inscribed with three forms of writing—hieroglyphic (fourteen lines of text), demotic (thirty-two lines), and Greek (fifty-four lines). When linguist Jean-François Cham-

The Rosetta Stone bears (top to bottom) hieroglyphic, demotic, and Greek text, making it the key to understanding ancient Egyptian writing.

pollion realized that the blocks of text were all saying the same thing in three different languages, the Rosetta Stone became the key to understanding ancient Egyptian writings. Champollion was able to translate Egyptian hieroglyphics, whose meaning had been lost by the end of the ancient Egyptian civilization, and eventually he and other scholars were able to translate demotic script as well. **See also** Champollion, Jean-François; hieroglyphs; writing, forms of.

Sabu family (Fifth and Sixth Dynasties)

Father and son Ibebi Sabu and Thety Sabu were important officials during the reigns of Fifth and Sixth Dynasty kings Unas and Teti, respectively. Ibebi Sabu served King Unas as the high priest of Ptah, aided at some point by his son Thety. He also oversaw the work of all of Egypt's principal artists and craftsmen. After Ibebi's death, Thety inherited the position of high priest of Ptah, as stated on a false door from Thety's tomb in Saqqara. **See also** Ptah; Saqqara; Teti; Unas.

sacred lakes

All major ancient Egyptian temples had a sacred lake. Its waters were used for certain rituals, particularly those related to purification. The main purpose of such lakes, though, was to symbolize the primordial waters from which all life arose. Because some myths claimed that a mound formed in these waters just prior to the creation of life, some sacred lakes featured an island in their midst. In some places, sacred crocodiles or hippopotamuses were kept in sacred lakes; in others, the lake was used in festivals and a

The sacred lake at the Temple of Amun at Karnak is fed by the Nile through underground channels.

bark of the gods was floated across its surface. Most sacred lakes were outdoors, but sometimes a series of canals channeled water to form a small sacred lake inside temple walls. **See also** Creation myths; crocodiles; hippopotamuses.

Sahure (?–ca. 2475 B.C.)

Fifth Dynasty king Sahure was a strong leader who was directly involved in the command of his military troops during his approximately twelve-year reign. He led his forces into battle against Libyans in the Western Desert and established the Egyptian navy, which engaged in both military and trading expeditions. He also established a diorite quarry near Abu Simbel and built a pyramid complex at Abusir, thereby founding a new royal necropolis. This pyramid complex had many painted low reliefs on its walls, most of them depicting the king's military exploits and his navy. Some Egyptologists think that Sahure also built a sun temple at Abusir, but no trace of this structure has been discovered. It is clear, however, that the king actively supported the sun god Re, elevating him to a more prominent position than other gods. Sahure's mother was apparently Queen Khentkawes I, the wife of Kings Userkaf and Shepseskaf. **See also** Abu Simbel; Abusir; Kakai; Khentkawes I; Shepseskhaf; Userkaf.

Saite Period (664–525 B.C.)

Also called the Saite dynasty, the Saite Period is another term for the Twenty-sixth Dynasty, during which a series of kings ruled Egypt from the city of Sais (modern-day Sael-Hagar). Located in the western Delta, Sais had long been the capital of the fifth nome of Lower Egypt and a cult center for the goddess Neith. In approximately 665 B.C., however, Necho I, the ruler of the Sais nome, united the country against invading Assyrians and eventually came to a peaceful understanding with them. As a result,

he soon ruled the Western Delta and all lands around Heliopolis and Memphis. When the Kushite king Tanutamani invaded Egypt and killed King Necho I in an attempt to impose Nubian rule on the country, the Assyrians came to the rescue of Necho I's son Psamtik I, and the Saite Period continued until the Persians conquered Egypt seventy years later.

The Saite Period featured a renaissance of Egyptian art and architecture harking back to more ancient times. Specifically, Saite artists looked to Old Kingdom forms for their inspiration, creating some of the finest works since that period. In addition, the Saite kings gave new life to religious cults in Egypt, supporting various cult centers and adding to, refurbishing, or creating new religious structures. **See also** Late Period; Psamtik I; Psamtik III; Third Intermediate Period.

Salitis (dates unknown)

Fifteenth Dynasty king Salitis was a Hyksos warrior who took command of Egypt sometime around 1650 B.C. following the Hyksos capture of Memphis. Some ancient records suggest that his peers chose Salitis to rule Egypt, but this might have just been a boast by the king. In either case, he was apparently the warrior with the most forces under his command. Soon after establishing Hyksos control over Memphis and the surrounding area, Salitis took the northern Egyptian city of Avaris as his capital, from which his messengers had an easy trip to Hyksos lands in Palestine. Salitis then fortified Avaris and, according to some reports, stationed over 250,000 men in the area to protect his interests there.

Salitis reigned for at least thirteen years and perhaps as many as twenty-three years. During his reign, he adopted many aspects of Egyptian culture as his own. For example, upon declaring himself king of Egypt, he took a typical Egyptian throne name, Mayebre, or "Seeing Is the

Heart of Re." **See also** Hyksos; Second Intermediate Period.

Sallier Papyrus

The collection of texts in the Sallier Papyrus includes copies of several important New Kingdom texts. Of these, among the most significant are the "Poem of Pentaur," a poem about the Battle of Kadesh (between the forces of Ramses II and the Hittites) that first appeared as a hieroglyphic text on a temple wall at Luxor, and *The Satire on Trades,* a literary work of the instruction genre that appears in other New Kingdom papyri as well. Additional texts in the papyrus relate to various military campaigns from the reign of Ramses II and include an account of a battle between Hyksos king Apepi and Theban king Tao II at Avaris. **See also** admonitions and instructions; *Satire on Trades, The.*

Salt, Henry (1780–1835)

During the nineteenth century, Henry Salt was the British consul general in Egypt, a position that afforded him access to valuable antiquities. He was appointed to the position in Alexandria in 1816 and was immediately approached by Sir Joseph Banks, a trustee of the British Museum, to acquire museum-quality Egyptian artifacts. A similar request soon came from Sir William Hamilton, the undersecretary at Britain's Foreign Office. Both men assured Salt that they would pay well for such items, so Salt began hiring men to acquire artifacts for him, either on the antiquities market or through excavation of ruins. Salt also supervised archaeological expeditions himself, using his position to gain access to the best sites, workmen, and supplies. At some of these sites, Salt and his agents caused considerable damage to fragile structures, particularly at Thebes, because their goal was recovering artifacts, not scientific archaeology. Salt spent most of his life collecting and selling antiquities, not only for the British Museum but also for private collectors, including the king of France and Londoner Sir John Sloane, the latter of whom bought the sarcophagus of King Seti I. After Salt's death his estate continued to sell pieces from his collection. As a result, Salt was indirectly responsible for many Egyptian antiquities ending up in other countries, among them a valuable king list discovered in Karnak that is now in the Louvre. **See also** archaeological expeditions; Belzoni, Giovanni Battista.

Saqqara

Part of a series of cemeteries associated with the city of Memphis, Saqqara was a necropolis containing burials from thirty-one dynasties, including both royal and nonroyal tombs. Together with another necropolis site nearby, Abusir, archaeologists consider Saqqara among Egypt's most important archaeological sites. Research is still ongoing at the site, which locals call Abwab el-Qotat, or "Doorways of the Cats," for the thousands of cat mummies buried in the area. Archaeologists are currently focusing on excavating and studying tombs of officials who served King Teti, which seem to suggest that the king was assassinated. Specifically, the officials' names were intentionally defaced in a way that suggests they were guilty of conspiring against the Sixth Dynasty king.

Also of interest to archaeologists is that Saqqara provides an historical progression of tomb-building techniques, giving numerous examples of each stage of development. The earliest tombs in Saqqara, which are from the First Dynasty, are of the mastaba style and were built for nonroyals; there is also a cemetery nearby with many simple Early Dynastic burials. The first royal tomb at Saqqara, probably built for King Khasekhemwy, dates from the Second

Saqqara is the site of the Step Pyramid of Third Dynasty king Djoser.

Dynasty. There are also fourteen royal pyramids at the site, some unfinished, from the Third to Thirteenth Dynasties, most of which have eroded to look like the surrounding hills. Saqqara is also the site of the oldest pyramid, the Step Pyramid of King Djoser.

Other pyramids at the site are striking because of their unusual design. For example, the pyramid of Fourth Dynasty king Shepseskhaf is referred to as a pyramid by many Egyptologists but does not have a point; instead, it was made to look like a sarcophagus. Because of its shape, modern Egyptians call it the *Mastabat Fara'un,* or Pharaoh's Bench.

Important for the ancient writings it contains is the pyramid of Fifth Dynasty king Unas, which was apparently the first pyramid to display the funerary inscriptions known to Egyptologists as the Pyramid Texts. Other pyramids at Saqqara include those of Fifth Dynasty kings Userkaf and Djedkare; Sixth Dynasty kings Teti, Pepy I,

Merenre I, and Pepy II; Eighth Dynasty king Ibi; and other unknown kings.

Saqqara also has many examples of nonroyal tombs from the Old, Middle, and New Kingdoms, most belonging to administrators and other people somehow connected to the kings who built the pyramids. There are also several examples of rock tombs that are cut into a rock face above a valley temple built by Unas. There are other Old, Middle, and New Kingdom and Late and Greco-Roman Period temples in the area as well, along with nonroyal tombs dating from the Late and Greco-Roman Periods.

Another important structure at Saqqara is the Serapeum, a complex of chapels and temples. Included in this complex is a series of catacombs with niches in which mummified sacred bulls were placed. Known as the Apis bulls, these animals were associated with the worship of the god Ptah in Memphis. Other mummified remains buried in the area include cats, jackals, cows, falcons, ibises, and baboons, all animals associated with various deities. **See also** architecture; mastaba tomb; pyramids; Teti I; tombs.

sarcophagus

A sarcophagus is a coffin made of stone such as granite, basalt, limestone, or calcite. Sometimes carved with some of the common architectural features of a palace, such as recessed wall paneling, these coffins were used only by royalty or the extremely wealthy. Moreover, beginning in the Middle Kingdom, they were used as an outer coffin, holding several nested wooden coffins with a mummy in the innermost one. The word *sarcophagus,* Greek for "flesh eater," was first applied to the stone coffin because the Greeks believed that the type of stone that the Egyptians used for these boxes damaged corpses. **See also** coffins.

Satire on Trades, The

Also called *The Instructions of Dua-Khety, The Satire on Trades* is a literary text from a genre of works known as admonitions and instructions in which an older man gives advice to a younger one. Normally, the older man is royal, noble, and/or considered a sage. In the case of *The Satire on Trades,* however, the speaker is a common man, Khety, who advises his son, Pepy, to become a scribe rather than go through the hardships of working at a trade. The occasion of Khety's speech is Pepy's admission into a prestigious educational facility, the Residence School, where he will learn alongside the sons of more prominent men. In telling Pepy to become a scribe, Khety not only extols the job's virtues but also denigrates a variety of other professions. *The Satire on Trades* appears on various ostraka (pieces of stone or pottery that schoolboys used to practice writing) and in papyri, including the Sallier Papyrus. **See also** admonitions and instructions; literature; Sallier Papyrus.

Satirical Papyrus

The Satirical Papyrus is a Nineteenth Dynasty papyrus that contains a collection of satirical writings addressing the problems within Egyptian society during the late Ramessid Period. To this end, it sometimes uses animals to make certain points about these problems. For example, it depicts cats being placed in charge of some baby mice, illustrating the view that the wrong people were being placed in charge of certain vulnerable aspects of the country. The Satirical Papyrus is now in the Egyptian Museum in Cairo. **See also** papyrus; Ramessid Period.

scarab

The scarab (*Scarabaeus sacer*) is a species of dung beetle that was considered sacred by the ancient Egyptians. In particular, the insect symbolized rebirth and was commonly associated with solar gods of creation, such as Khepri and Re. For example, the hieroglyphics representing the name "Lord of the Manifestations of Re" (Neb-Kheperu-Re, the throne name of King Tutankhamun) contained the image of a winged scarab.

The reason for the association between the scarab and rebirth has to do with the beetles' reproductive processes. Dung beetles encase their eggs in a ball of dung or mud, where they remain until they hatch, so a person might see a young scarab emerge from this ball fully formed. This image of Creation was strengthened by the fact that the Egyptians equated the ball both with the sun and with the Nile River from which its mud came. In addition, dung beetles push balls of dung or mud along the ground, and the Egyptians saw this as mirroring the solar deity's moving the sun across the sky.

Beginning in the Middle Kingdom, scarabs were a popular symbol on bracelets, necklaces, and other jewelry. Scarab images were also carried as amulets, objects believed to confer magical protection or other qualities on their owner. In addition, a large scarab amulet called a heart scarab was placed over a mummy's heart (which, unlike other internal organs, was not taken from the body as part of the mummification process) within its linen wrappings. Made of one of several dark—usually green—stones or glass, this amulet might carry an inscription from the *Book of the Dead*, a New Kingdom funerary text, telling the heart how to behave when it was weighed in the Judgment Hall of Osiris. Specifically, the heart needed to remain silent when asked to recount the deceased person's sins. **See also** amulets; *Book of the Dead*; Osiris; Re; symbols.

scepters

Scepters are staffs that were often shown in ancient Egyptian artwork in the hands of kings and gods because they symbolized divinity. In particular, the *was* scepter, which had one end shaped like the head of a gazelle, lion, or other animal, was thought to confer ruling power on its owner, particularly in the divine realm, much the way an amulet would.

A scepter might be made of faience, wood, or other materials, and it was sometimes shown along with two other symbols of divine kingship, the crook and the flail. In addition, scepters might have been employed by kings or high priests during certain temple rituals involving gods associated with kingship, such as Horus. **See also** amulets; flail; Horus.

Scorpion King (dates unknown)

Until recently thought to be a mythological ruler, the Scorpion King—so named because his symbol was a scorpion, although his name has not yet been discovered—is now thought to have been a late Predynastic Period king who apparently ruled the cities of Abydos and Hierakonpolis in around 3250 B.C. The Scorpion

King's existence was confirmed in 1998 when archaeologist Gunter Dryer of the German Archaeological Institute found his twelve-room tomb near Abydos. Although tomb robbers had stolen its mummy and tomb goods, they left behind an ivory scepter dating from about 3250 B.C., making it the oldest such item ever discovered. In addition, one of the tomb's chambers had 160 small bone and ivory labels that appear to be notes and records (primarily of linen and oil deliveries, though there are other types of material as well) written in a very primitive form of hieroglyphics. If these markings are proved to be hieroglyphics, archaeologists will have to revise their conclusions regarding when this type of writing began in Egypt. (Scholars currently say that the first hieroglyphs appeared on clay seals used to mark First Dynasty tombs with their owners' names.)

Even more recently, archaeologist John Darnell of Yale University found a rock-carved scene near the site of Naqada that appears to show the Scorpion King's conquest of that city. If this is indeed determined to date from the Scorpion King's reign, then it would be the oldest known historical document.

In both this scene, which has been dubbed the Scorpion Tableau, and on a mace discovered at Hierakonpolis in Upper Egypt in 1898 (which, although labeled as being the Scorpion King's, was not considered by nineteenth-century Egyptologists as proof of his existence), the Scorpion King is shown wearing the crown of Upper Egypt rather than the double crown of both Upper and Lower Egypt. Therefore, most Egyptologists do not believe that he was the same king as Menes, mentioned in ancient writings as being the ruler who first unified Egypt. They reserve this distinction for Narmer, who is shown in artwork wearing the double crown, or perhaps Narmer's successor, Aha. Nonetheless, there is still much to be learned about the Scorpion King, and some Egyptologists believe that other artifacts may be found to prove that he and Menes are the same person. **See also** Aha; Early Dynastic Period; Narmer; Predynastic Period.

scribes

Called *sesh,* meaning "he who writes," in ancient Egyptian, scribes were learned men who performed a variety of esteemed governmental, religious, and scholarly duties. In fact, scribes were so esteemed that two literary texts of the period, *Amunnakhte's Instructions* and *The Satire on Trades,* focus on the virtues of the profession, explaining that scribes were among the most vital of Egypt's workers and as such were the recipients of good clothes, good food, and the people's respect. So valued were they that many scribes were also exempt from paying taxes.

Most scribes were educated in temple schools run by priests. Any literate male could be considered for education as a

A painted limestone figure of a scribe from the Fifth Dynasty.

scribe, but since a higher degree of literacy was more common among upper-class Egyptians, scribes tended to come from the upper levels of society. In fact, many of them were princes or the sons of viziers and other high-level officials. Their education included not only developing their reading and writing skills but also studying Egyptian literature, law, government, religion, mathematics, and other subjects deemed part of being a well-educated man. After four or more years of study, scribes were typically assigned to work in various branches of various temples, in jobs in government, or on private estates; apprenticeships in these positions lasted as long as eleven or twelve years. Scribes employed in temples primarily spent their time composing and copying various texts, keeping records and accounts, and acting as librarians and archivists. Those in government might collect taxes, control court dockets, maintain army records and the census, measure the water level of the Nile River, and supervise various professionals and expeditions, among other duties. Those employed on private estates were typically record keepers, administrators, and secretaries in charge of correspondence.

Because scribes were among the best-educated and most intellectual men in Egypt, they had access to the highest positions in Egyptian bureaucracy. However, they were also held to a higher standard of behavior than other men. Scribes learned and adhered to a strict code of conduct during their training, and they were expected to continue adhering to this code long after they achieved political power.

Scribes had their own patron deity, Thoth, who was the god of writing, education, and wisdom. Another deity associated with scribes was Seshat, a goddess of writing and mathematical measurement. The symbol of the scribe was the palette, or *mestha,* because scribes used this wood or stone container to carry their writing tools and mix their inks. Scribes most commonly wrote on papyrus and stone, but they also carved their writing on stone. **See also** Thoth; writing, forms of.

Sea Peoples

The ancient Egyptians used the term *Sea Peoples* to refer collectively to several tribes of people who attacked Egypt's northwestern territories during the Nineteenth Dynasty reign of King Merneptah and attacked Egyptian settlements on the Mediterranean coast during the Twentieth Dynasty reign of Ramses III. Most of these people apparently came from different parts of the eastern Mediterranean, where a decreasing food supply motivated them to invade several ancient lands in addition to Egypt. The ancient Egyptians listed the names of these tribes as the Akawasha, the Peleset, the Teresh, the Sheklesh, and the Sherden, providing a physical description of them but not saying where each tribe originated. Consequently, Egyptologists have had to make guesses regarding the Sea Peoples' ethnicity, and there is much disagreement over the various theories. More is known about one tribe of Sea Peoples than the others, however. The Sherden probably came from Cyprus or Sardinia and were first described as being pirates during the Eighteenth Dynasty reign of Amenhotep III, after which they worked as mercenaries in the Egyptian army. Unlike other Sea Peoples, they were apparently assimilated into Egyptian culture. The rest of the Sea Peoples were expelled from Egypt over time, whereupon they moved on to invade other lands. As with the Sea Peoples' origins, modern scholars disagree widely as to where the various tribes ended up. **See also** Amenhotep III; Merneptah; Ramses III.

seasons

The ancient Egyptians recognized three seasons: *akhet, proyer* (or *perit*), and *shomu* (or *shemu*). *Akhet* was the time of inundation, when the Nile River flooded the lands. *Proyet* was the time of sowing crops, which occurred when the Nile waters receded. *Shomu* was the time when crops were harvested. In texts from throughout ancient Egyptian history, there are references to festivals and other events tied to each of these seasons, which lasted roughly 120 days each. **See also** calendars; festivals; Nile River.

Sebni (ca. 2278–ca. 2184 B.C.)

A noble of the Sixth Dynasty, Sebni served Pepy II as the leader of various expeditions. One of these was to bring back the body of his own father, Mekhu, who had been killed during a campaign against Nubians at Wawat, on the coast of the Red Sea. Sebni not only ensured that his father's body was embalmed and transported home but also took command of Mekhu's soldiers and successfully completed the expedition. King Pepy II recognized Sebni for his valor by giving him land. **See also** Nubia; Pepy II.

Second Intermediate Period (ca. 1650–ca. 1550 B.C.)

The Second Intermediate Period was a time of chaos that was brought about when migrants from the east invaded the Delta. Within a short time, the leaders of some of these people, the Hyksos, came to power, conquering Egypt's northeastern territories and setting up their Fifteenth and Sixteenth Dynasties in the city of Avaris in the eastern Delta. Meanwhile, the Egyptian kings, as the Seventeenth Dynasty, continued to make their capital at Thebes. At first, the Hyksos kings and the Theban kings were on fairly good terms, but when Hyksos boats began traveling south along the Nile River past Thebes to trade with Nubia, tensions developed between the two groups, and eventually the Theban kings declared war on the Hyksos. After a series of battles in which two Theban kings, Tao II and Kamose, died at the hands of the Hyksos, Theban king Ahmose I finally laid siege to Avaris and drove the Hyksos from the country, thereby reuniting Egypt under one rule and founding both the Eighteenth Dynasty and the New Kingdom. **See also** Ahmose I; Hyksos; Kamose; New Kingdom; Tao II.

sed festival

First appearing in predynastic times, the *sed* festival was traditionally held every three years of a king's reign beginning with Year 30. However, some kings held them more often, because the festival was an opportunity to prove the king's physical prowess and show that he was fit to rule. For example, Amenhotep III apparently celebrated three *sed* festivals during his thirty-eight-year reign.

Egyptologists disagree on exactly what the various rituals of this festival were, but apparently the king had to run great distances to demonstrate that he was healthy. There might also have been a display of the king's magical powers, as well as rituals designed to symbolize the unification of Egypt. For example, the king might run around his palace enclosure in a way that stood for the encircling of all of Egypt under his control, or he might run between markers symbolizing Egypt's borders. Some Egyptologists believe that the *sed* festival also included symbols related to the king's rebirth in the Afterlife; in fact, a few modern scholars believe that this symbolism, rather than a display of the king's prowess, was the true purpose of the festival.

One of the earliest depictions of a king's *sed* festival was found at the Abydos tomb of First Dynasty king Den. He is shown both sitting on a throne and running between two sets of three markers. Archaeologists have found the remains of such markers at the pyramid of Third Dynasty king Djoser at Saqqara, and inside the pyramid complex there is a relief showing the king running between these markers. **See also** Abydos; Den; Djoser; festivals; Saqqara.

Sekhmet (Sekmet)

Sekhmet was a goddess typically considered to be a manifestation of the warrior aspect of other goddesses, particularly Hathor, Mut, or Bastet. Sometimes, however, she was viewed as a manifestation of the warrior aspect of the sun that made its rays create fires of destruction. Probably because of this association, at various times Sekhmet was also thought to cause destructive plagues, and often she was said to have helped one king or another destroy his enemies during battle.

In the mythology of Memphis, Sekhmet was the wife of the creator god Ptah and the mother of Nefertem, the lotus blossom deity from which the sun first arose. Elsewhere, however, Sekhmet was identified through solar disk symbolism in artwork as the daughter of the solar deity Re, although she was most typically depicted as a lotus. **See also** Bastet; Hathor; Mut.

Semna

The settlement of Semna was located at the south end of the Second Cataract of the Nile River, on the border between Egypt and Nubia near the modern-day town of Gamai, and was therefore in an important position in terms of the country's military strategy. By establishing forts on the cliffs near this site, King Senwosret III was able to prevent his enemies from navigating the river north into Egypt. Because he provided this protection, Senwosret III was revered in Semna, and a subsequent king, Tuthmosis III, eventually built a temple at Semna dedicated to the worship of Senwosret III. **See also** Senwosret III; Tuthmosis III.

Sendjemib (Sennedjem; Senedjemibmehy) clan (Fifth Dynasty)

The Sendjemib clan was a prominent family in Egypt beginning in the Fifth Dynasty. It was apparently established by Inti Sendjemib, vizier and architect for King Djedkare (also known as Izezi). Inti Sendjemib held the title of "overseer of all works," and his most ambitious project was the construction of a small lake that the king used for pleasure boating. After Inti Sendjemib died, his son Mehi Sendjemib probably took over his position, or at the very least held another prominent government job, as did successive generations of the Sendjemib clan. Mehi built a tomb for his father at Giza with numerous scenes and inscriptions that stress the importance of Inti Sendjemib's work for the king. **See also** Giza.

Senenmut (?–ca. 1458 B.C.)

Senenmut was a valued administrator and close confidant to Eighteenth Dynasty queen-pharaoh Hatshepsut, holding dozens of titles and positions during his career at court. His most prominent role was as the steward of the royal family, although he was also a skilled architect. Among his architectural projects was the queen's mortuary temple at Deir el-Bahri, part of the Theban necropolis on the western shore of the Nile River, where Senenmut also built his own tomb. Senenmut's tomb was found to have several interesting features, including an astronomical ceiling and the mummies of Senenmut's horse and an ape that might have been his pet.

In addition to his other activities, Senenmut tutored the queen's daughter Neferure and was depicted in block statues with her on his lap. However, this pose was usually reserved for a parent and child, so there has been much speculation over whether Senenmut was the girl's father, particularly since his tomb and the queen's tomb are side by side. Further fueling this speculation is the fact that Hatshepsut's successor, King Tuthmosis III, defaced parts of Senenmut's tomb and many of his statues. Tuthmosis III had been previously kept from the throne by Hatshepsut and clearly disapproved of both her and her confidant. **See also** Deir el-Bahri; Hatshepsut; Neferure; Thebes; Tuthmosis III.

Sennefer (?–ca. 1400 B.C.)

Sennefer was the mayor of Thebes during the Eighteenth Dynasty reign of Amenhotep II. He was also apparently a favorite of the court, because a sculpture of him and his wife was placed in the king's temple at Karnak. Moreover, Sennefer was buried in a tomb originally intended for the king's grandfather, Tuthmosis III. Across the Nile River from Thebes, this tomb has a wall scene showing him in the Afterlife on a sailboat beside his wife Meryt. However, it was his other wife, a royal nursemaid named Senetnay, whose mummy was found beside his. Egyptologists have speculated that Sennefer might have been the recipient of the king's favor because of this wife's relationship with the royal household. **See also** Amenhotep II; Karnak; Tuthmosis III.

Senwosret I (Senusret I, Sesostris I) (ca. 1966– ca. 1911 B.C.)

Twelfth Dynasty king Senwosret I served as coruler with his father, Amenemhet I, for ten years before assuming the throne after the king's assassination. At that time, Senwosret I had to rush back to Egypt from a military campaign against the Libyans. He continued to participate in military campaigns throughout his reign, extending Egypt's border south almost to the Third Cataract of the Nile River and establishing a series of at least thirteen forts along the river. He also sponsored numerous building projects, including a huge pyramid complex at el-Lisht that included his own pyramid, nine smaller pyramids for royal women, and several tombs for his highest-ranking officials. Excavation uncovered many of the officials' tombs between 1908 and 1934, but Senwosret I's burial chamber is inaccessible because of severe ground-water seepage.

According to ancient records, Senwosret I also built a temple dedicated to Atum-Re in Heliopolis and erected two 66-foot-tall red granite obelisks there weighing 121 tons each; however, no sign of the structure or obelisks has ever been found. In addition, some scholars believe that the king built a capital city, Itj-tawy, although many credit his father with having built it instead. It too has never been found, but archaeologists believe that it is very near el-Lisht. To obtain building and decorative stones for these and many other projects, Senwosret I launched numerous mining and quarrying expeditions, acquiring granite and other hard stones from the Wadi Hammamat, gold from around Coptos, and copper from the Sinai and elsewhere.

During the last three years of his reign, if not longer, Senwosret I allowed his son Amenemhet II to rule with him. Senwosret I died after forty-five years on the throne and accomplished so much during that time that he is considered one of Egypt's greatest kings. In addition, in some places in Nubia, the deceased king was eventually worshiped as a god. **See also** Amenemhet I; Amenemhet II; el-Lisht.

Senwosret II (Senusret II) (?–ca. 1870 B.C.)

A Twelfth Dynasty king, Senwosret II assumed the throne as the son and heir of Amenemhet II, with whom he was coregent for at least three years before his father died. Senwosret II was a forceful and productive king, both at home and abroad. He conducted military campaigns in Nubia, strengthening existing fortresses and taking measures to protect Egypt's mining concerns there as well as in the Sinai. His major accomplishments, however, were related to construction projects in the Faiyum. In particular, Senwosret II built the town of Hotep-Senwosret ("Senwosret Is Satisfied"), also known as Kahun, at the mouth of the Faiyum for workers building him a nearby pyramid complex. This town has proved invaluable to archaeologists, because after the completion of the pyramid complex its workers abandoned Kahun and left many artifacts behind, including hundreds of papyri.

The most important legacy of King Senwosret II, however, was not his pyramid complex but an irrigation system in the Faiyum. Under his command, his engineers built dams and canals to redirect Nile floodwaters and reclaim thousands of acres of land, turning marshlands into rich agricultural fields. Subsequent rulers added to and/or maintained this system, thereby further enriching Egypt's storehouses of food. **See also** Amenemhet II; Faiyum; irrigation; Lahun and Kahun.

Senwosret III (Senusret III) (?–ca. 1831 B.C.)

A Twelfth Dynasty king, Senwosret III succeeded to the throne upon the death of his father, Senwosret II, and reigned for thirty-seven years. During that time, his main priority was the establishment of order (Ma'at) within his society and government rather than the creation of monuments to glorify himself. Toward this end, he reorganized the Egyptian bureaucracy, dividing it into three departments: the North, the South, and the Head of the South (with the "head" being Elephantine and Lower Nubia). The administrators of each of these divisions reported directly to the king's vizier, who in turn reported directly to the king. This system strengthened the central government by lessening the power of local nomarchs (who were nobles) and giving the king more control over his bureaucrats. Also to lessen the power of the nomes, the king encouraged the rise of a middle class composed of various artisans, tradesmen, and large-scale farmers.

Senwosret III further strengthened his control over the country by building a strong military and fortifying his borders. He set up a stela at Semna to mark Egypt's southern border and built many fortresses in the area to defend it. He also fought many battles against the Kush in Nubia to protect Egypt's trade routes, mines, and quarries in the region. Also in the south, he supported a major construction project that reopened a canal originally built by King Pepy I and Merenre I at the Nile River at Aswan to allow Egypt's ships to bypass the whitewaters of the First Cataract. In addition, Senwosret III built, refurbished, or expanded several temples, and he built a mortuary complex at Dashur for himself and his family. His pyramid there was the largest of similar Twelfth Dynasty structures (350 square feet at its base), although today it is badly damaged.

When archaeologist Jacques de Morgan excavated the complex at Dashur in 1894–1895, he discovered the tombs of two of Senwosret III's queens, Mereret and Sit-Hathor (who was also his sister). These tombs had been robbed of all but a large stash of jewelry. Senwosret III's other wives included Neferhent, Neferu, Merseger, Merysankh, and Sebekshedty-Neferu, the mother of his heir, Amenemhet III. **See also** Amenemhet III; Elephantine; Ma'at; Merenre I; Pepy I; pyramids; Senwosret II.

serekh

A *serekh* was a particular brick Early Dynastic palace façade whose image, which included a surrounding rectangle, was used to enclose the king's name during this period, much as a cartouche would surround the king's name during later periods. Accompanying the name within the *serekh* was the image of the falcon representing Horus. The first king to use the *serekh* was Djet of the First Dynasty, placing it around his name on a stela. The image also appeared as a decorative feature, without the king's name, on tombs, coffins, and sarcophagi. **See also** cartouche; Horus.

Seshat

Seshat was an ancient Egyptian goddess associated with writing, measurement, recordings of deeds, and time, and in some periods architecture and builders as well. In mythology, she was the wife of Thoth, the god of wisdom and patron of scribes. Seshat was typically depicted as a woman wearing a dress made from the skin of a panther and a headdress featuring a large seven-pointed star. Another symbol associated with Seshat was the *ished,* a sacred tree in the mythology of Heliopolis. Beginning in the Eighteenth Dynasty, Seshat was said to have used the tree's leaves to create a record of the reigns of Egypt's kings, inscribing each king's name and the years of his reign on a separate leaf to produce the first king list. **See also** Heliopolis; king lists; Thoth.

Seth (Set)

In many parts of ancient Egypt, Seth was considered a destroyer god who represented evil. He originated at least as early as the Early Dynastic Period as an enemy of the god Horus. In mythology, he was most often the brother and murderer of Osiris, with Horus typically portrayed as Osiris's son and heir. In some of these myths, Horus was an infant who was hidden by his mother, Isis, so Seth would not find him; in others, Horus was an adult fighting Seth in a series of battles over the throne left vacant by Osiris's death. Other myths, however, feature Seth as the foe of Re, trying to prevent the solar deity from reaching the point where dawn begins, and Horus as Re's protector and perhaps his son.

In the Creation myths of Heliopolis, Seth was the son of Geb, a god of earth, and Nut, a goddess of sky. His birth occurred after his mother bore two other children on successive days, with Osiris being born on the first day, Horus on the second, Seth on the third, Isis on the fourth, and Nephthys on the fifth. These days constituted a period of the Egyptian calendar known as the Epagomenal Days, and this period's third day, when the destroyer god Seth was said to have been born, was considered the most unlucky day of the entire year.

Even though Seth was associated in most places with destruction, chaos, infertility, and desert wastelands, in some places he was honored. The reasoning behind this usually had to do with two concepts: that order is born out of chaos and that desert wastelands can produce precious minerals and rich oases. In fact, many oases had cult centers dedicated to Seth, and he was also worshiped along desert caravan routes. His main cult center was in Naqada, just north of Thebes, and during the reign of Ramses II, he was elevated to a national god and honored at the king's capital, Per-Ramses. During this brief period, Seth was sometimes considered a god of love and his image appeared on amulets. Seth was typically depicted as a strange beast with a doglike body and a long reptilian snout, although occasionally he might take the form of a hippopotamus or some other animal as a man with his traditional beast's head. **See also** calendars; Creation myths; Horus; Isis; Osiris; Ramses II.

Sethnakhte (dates unknown)

A Twentieth Dynasty king, Sethnakhte reigned for only approximately three years sometime around 1186 B.C. He assumed the throne after the unpopular corule of Queen Twosret (widow of King Seti II) and her adviser (and probably lover), Bay. However, it is uncertain how Sethnakhte came to be their successor. Probably an old man when he became king, he was nonetheless a strong enough ruler to subdue several rebellions, reopen several temples closed by his predecessors, and generally bring order to all of Egypt. At some point during his brief reign, he named his son Ramses III (by Queen Tiy) his heir, so when Sethnakhte died suddenly there was an orderly succession. However, his tomb was unfinished at the time of his death, so his family apparently placed him in the tomb of Queen Twosret, removing her mummy in the process. (By this time her name had been erased from many records, leading some Egyptologists to conclude that Sethnakhte ruled immediately after Seti II.) In 1898, Sethnakhte's coffin and, contained in a wooden boat, a mummy thought to be his were found in the Valley of the Kings tomb of Amenhotep II, where they had been placed as part of a royal cache designed to protect them from tomb robbers. **See also** Amenhotep II; caches, royal; Ramses III; Twosret.

Seti I (ca. 1316–ca. 1279 B.C.)

Nineteenth Dynasty king Seti I was the son of Ramses I. By the time he ascended the throne, Seti I already had extensive military experience, having led several foreign campaigns, particularly against the Hittites. After becoming king, Seti I continued an aggressive military policy. One of his Asian campaigns as king, involving three divisions of twenty thousand men each, resulted in the Egyptian army reoccupying certain areas of Palestine and Syria previously lost to the Hittites. Accompanied by his heir, Ramses II, Seti I also fought a major battle at Kadesh. Other accomplishments of Seti

I's reign include establishing rules to govern Eastern Desert mining operations, moving Egypt's capital to Memphis, and ordering the creation of a king list that has been invaluable in helping archaeologists determine which Egyptian kings ruled during which periods of time. Known as the Royal King List of Abydos or the Abydos King List, it was inscribed within Seti I's mortuary temple at Abydos.

Seti I's tomb, located in the Valley of the Kings, features one of the most impressive Egyptian astronomical ceilings and also includes material from the *Book of the Dead*. Cut into cliffs to a depth of three hundred feet, the tomb also has numerous passages and chambers. Seti I's mummy was not found there, however, but at Deir el-Bahri, where it had been reentombed as part of a royal cache after robbers broke into his tomb. In spite of this previous break-in, when Seti I's mummy was found, it was still surrounded by over seven hundred *shabti* figures made of stone, wood, or faience. **See also** Abydos; Eastern Desert; Hittites; Ramses II.

Seti II (?–ca. 1194 B.C.)

Seti II was a Nineteenth Dynasty king who ruled for approximately six years, although Egyptologists disagree on when his reign occurred and how he gained the throne. The prevailing theory, however, is that he followed King Amenmesses, who like Seti II was a grandson of Ramses II. Seti II had at least three wives: Takhat II, Tiaa, and Twosret, the latter of whom appears to have been his principal wife. Little is known about Seti II's reign, but because of its short duration, he seems to have accomplished little. After he died, his second son, Siptah, ascended the throne because Seti II's eldest son, Crown Prince Seti-Merneptah, had died young. Because of her position as chief wife, Twosret became Siptah's regent, even though Queen Tiaa was his mother,

and eventually Twosret usurped the throne with the help of her counselor, Bay. **See also** Amenmesses; Ramses II; Siptah; Twosret.

shabti (*shawabti; ushabti*)

First used during the Middle Kingdom, a *shabti* was a small human-shaped figurine made out of wood, stone, pottery, faience, bronze, glass, or wax that was placed in a tomb to serve its occupant in the Afterlife. The ancient Egyptians believed that, given the proper magic spell, *shabtis* would become animated in order to fulfill certain tasks. This magical spell (also found in Chapter 6 of the New Kingdom's *Book of the Dead*) was inscribed on each figurine. Once animated, a *shabti* could perform any work that the tomb's occupant might be called upon by the gods to do and engage in activities that would nourish the occupant's spirit. To this end, some *shabtis* were representations of servants, possibly holding tools or baskets or standing beside models of the equipment necessary to make bread or beer. Others representing work supervisors were placed beside a group of similar figurines and shown holding a whip to keep the others in line. Still others might represent soldiers, sailors, or other people who served kings and nobles. The more important the tomb's occupant had been in life, the more *shabtis* he or she generally had. Some people were entombed with as many as four hundred figurines of various kinds, housed in special boxes, and one king's tomb had seven hundred. **See also** *Book of the Dead*; models, tomb.

Shepseskhaf (ca. 2518–2498 B.C.)

Fourth Dynasty king Shepseskhaf reigned for only four years during a time of turmoil in the Old Kingdom. His rule was made difficult by nomarchs who challenged his authority and priests who disagreed with him in religious matters.

Consequently, he accomplished little during his brief reign other than the building of his mastaba tomb (which some Egyptologists classify as a pyramid because of its immense height) in Saqqara. Constructed of mud brick in the shape of a giant sarcophagus, this structure is now known as the *Mastabat Fara'un,* or Pharaoh's Bench, because the Arabs who named it many centuries later thought its eroded form looked like a mounded-earth bench.

From the writings at Shepseskhaf's tomb and elsewhere, modern scholars believe that he was the son of King Menkaure. However, they disagree on whether his mother was Menkaure's principal wife, Khamerernebty II, or some lesser wife. If Shepseskhaf was not Khamerernebty II's son, then he probably inherited the throne only because Menkaure's oldest son, Khunere, who was the crown prince, died before his father and the queen had any other male children.

It appears that Shepseskhaf had at least two queens, Bunefer and Khentkawes I, the latter of whom might have been his half-sister, sister, or daughter. Shepseskhaf apparently had only one daughter and no male children. After Shepseskhaf's death, his successor, King Userkaf, married the late king's wife Khentkawes to legitimize his claim to the throne. **See also** Khentkawes I; mastaba tomb; Saqqara.

Sheshonq I (ca. 974– ca. 924 B.C.)

The first king of the Twenty-second Dynasty, Sheshonq I succeeded to the throne after the death of his father-in-law Pseusennes II. He was an aggressive military campaigner, fighting in Israel, Judah, and Nubia. Sheshonq I himself was from Libya; he had been a chief there before marrying a daughter of the Egyptian king. He probably first came to Egypt to command a division of its police force, since by the end of the New

Kingdom, Libyans were often being recruited for this purpose. Under Sheshonq I's rule, Egypt grew more unified, largely because he appointed members of his extended family to top positions throughout the country in government, the priesthood, and the military. **See also** Libya.

Shipwrecked Sailor, The Tale of the

The Tale of the Shipwrecked Sailor is a Middle Kingdom story about an apparently failed expedition that unexpectedly turns into a success at the end. The narrator of the story begins telling it supposedly to cheer up a man whose own expedition has just resulted in apparent failure. The narrator says that he was traveling by sea to distant mines when he was shipwrecked on an island, the only survivor of a crew of 120. Also on the island was a huge talking snake, who encouraged the marooned man to remain patient and never lose hope for a positive outcome. The snake then prophesied that in four months the man would be on a ship bound for home. Sure enough, at the prophesied time a ship did appear, and the snake gave the man some parting gifts: various ointments, spices, animals, jewels, and other valuable items. When the man reached Egypt, he gave these treasures to the king, who honored him for his act of tribute. **See also** literature; tales.

Shu

Shu was an ancient Egyptian god who figured prominently in a Heliopolis Creation myth found in a collection of pyramid inscriptions known as the Pyramid Texts. In this myth, Shu was said to have formed the world by fathering the goddess of the sky, Nut, and the god of the earth, Geb, and separating the two (who were not only siblings but lovers) so that Nut was raised above Geb. As the figure who stood between the two lovers, Shu was therefore the god of the region between heaven and

In this Creation scene, Shu lifts the goddess Nut above the god Geb, forming heaven and earth.

earth; his name means "void," "empty," "dry," "air," or "atmosphere," depending on the translation. Shu was not, however, the first god. That distinction was held by his father, Re-Atum or Atum, who also created Shu's sister and wife, Tefnut, goddess of moisture. Re-Atum or Atum was the light of the sun, and he and his children and grandchildren (air, moisture, earth, and sky) made up all of the elements that the Egyptians believed created life.

Shu's children also had children, the deities Isis, Seth, Nephthys, and Osiris. These four deities, along with Geb, Nut, Tefnut, Re-Atum, and Shu, are said to make up the Ennead, which is the term Egyptologists use for the Heliopolis pantheon. The Ennead was established at Heliopolis during the Early Dynastic Period, but it eventually became popular elsewhere in Egypt as well, although sometimes the identity of Shu's grandchildren differed. Because he was the son of Atum, Shu was sometimes shown with the symbol of the sun, a disk, atop his head. Alternatively, he was depicted as a lion, also associated with the sun. **See also** Ennead; Geb; Heliopolis; Nut.

Sihathor (ca. 1922– ca. 1878 B.C.)

During the Twelfth Dynasty reign of King Amenemhet II, Sihathor served as the king's treasurer and the director of some of his mining operations. In the latter capacity, he was said to be an expert at acquiring fine turquoise. Sihathor also oversaw the crafting of statues for the king's mortuary complex and was probably involved in the building of his pyramid. In addition, Sihathor controlled the expenditures from the king's treasury. Sihathor is featured in two important pieces of Egyptian art, a block statue of himself found in his tomb and a stela inscribed with his life story as well as information about Amenemhet II's reign. **See also** Amenemhet II.

Sinai

A peninsula located on Egypt's eastern border, the Sinai was one of ancient

Egypt's most important sources of minerals such as copper, malachite, and turquoise. The first Egyptian mines and quarries were established there in the Early Dynastic Period, and the area was worked intermittently throughout Egypt's history. Among its most important sites were Serabit el-Khadim, which included a Temple of Hathor for its workers, and Maghara, which has inscriptions from mining expeditions of Kings Djoser, Pepy II, Amenemhet III, Amenemhet IV, Tuthmosis III, and Queen-Pharaoh Hatshepsut (and possibly also Ramses II).

The Sinai was also the location of a series of military forts built by Twelfth Dynasty king Amenemhet I in response to intrusions during previous dynasties of foreigners entering Egypt along the Sinai border. These forts were maintained and expanded upon for the rest of ancient Egypt's history. Most of their remains date from the Late and Greco-Roman Periods. **See also** mining and metalworking; quarrying.

Sinuhe, The Tale of (*The Tale of Sanehet*)

First appearing in the Twelfth Dynasty, *The Tale of Sinuhe* was a popular Middle Kingdom story about the adventures of Sinuhe (also known as Sanehet). Sinuhe was an official in the royal court when King Amenemhet I was assassinated, and he was afraid he would be unjustly accused of being one of the conspirators who plotted the king's death. Consequently Sinuhe ran away, crossing the Delta and the Isthmus of Suez to the deserts of Palestine. There he encountered a nomadic tribe, the Bedouins, and among them he became a tribal chief before traveling on to the coastal town of Byblos, where he married the daughter of a sheik, Badu, and made a good life for himself. Nonetheless, he never abandoned his culture, and as he approached death he realized that he had to be buried in Egypt if

he was going to receive the proper rituals and achieve the Afterlife. He wrote to the king, Senwosret I, and asked whether he would be allowed to return. Not only did the king tell him to come home, but the entire royal family gave Sinuhe a joyous welcome, and Senwosret I awarded him with a tomb near his own.

Written in the first person, *The Tale of Sinuhe* was apparently intended as an autobiography for the walls of Sinuhe's tomb, but this tomb has not been found. In fact, some scholars argue that there is no such tomb because Sinuhe was a fictional character, not a real person. Either way, the story was often copied by scribes and schoolboys, and several of these copies survive. The best copies are on two papyri now housed in the Berlin Museum and on an ostrakon (a stone flake) in the Ashmolean Museum in Oxford, England. **See also** literature; ostraka; Senwosret I; tales.

Siptah (?–ca. 1188 B.C.)

A king of the Nineteenth Dynasty, Siptah inherited the throne as the son of Seti II by one of the king's lesser wives, Tiaa. However, when his father died, Siptah was too young to rule on his own, so Seti II's principal wife, Twosret, was named his regent. Soon, she had effectively usurped the throne, along with her close adviser and perhaps lover, Chancellor Bay. Four to six years into the regency, Siptah died, and Twosret declared herself queen-pharaoh. The only official accomplishment of Siptah's reign was a Nubian military expedition launched in his name.

Egyptologists are unsure of what happened to Siptah. It is possible that he met with foul play, but forensic analysis of his mummy reveals no obvious sign of violent death. Moreover, the mummy indicates that he was a sickly boy with a club foot, so it would not be unlikely that he died of natural causes. Siptah's mummy was found in 1898 in the Valley of the Kings cache of Amenhotep II, although he was apparently first entombed with his mother, Tiaa, in the Valley of the Kings. At some point, tomb robbers found and damaged their remains, so priests repaired their mummies and moved them for safekeeping to the tomb of Amenhotep II. **See also** caches, royal; Twosret.

Siwa Oasis

The Siwa Oasis is the largest of Libya's Western Desert oases, roughly fifty miles long and as wide as seventeen miles in parts, but it is the least fertile oasis because its soil and water have a high salt content. Consequently, the walls of buildings in the region, which are made of mud brick, have a high salt content as well; when a heavy rainstorm occurs (which is seldom), the salt dissolves, thereby collapsing the walls. Many important buildings have been damaged or lost this way.

In the oasis town of Aghurmi, an important building still exists, albeit in a highly diminished state: the Temple of the Oracle, built during the Twenty-sixth Dynasty reign of King Ahmose II. This temple was famous in much of the ancient world for the often prophetic messages delivered by its priests. The walls of the temple sanctuary, which is nearly all that remains of this once large temple complex, have depictions of the king honoring various deities. The Siwa Oasis has some decorated tombs as well, particularly at a site called Jabal al-Mawta. Many of the tombs there were built by Greeks who moved to the area during the Saite Period. **See also** oases.

slaves

Ancient Egyptians owned slaves, but in contrast to common practice elsewhere, even a slave had some level of personal and legal rights that protected him from abuse. Moreover, slaves could own land and, if their holdings were profitable enough, could hire servants to do their work. What made someone a slave, then, was the fact that he could not do anything or go anywhere without the permission of his owner.

Most people became slaves by selling themselves into slavery to pay off a debt, but slavery was also used as a means of punishing criminals and as a disposition of prisoners of war. In any case, the slave's legal owner could transfer possession to someone else or rent the slave's services to others. Often, a legal document established a set time when a slave would be released from bondage, although a slave owner could do this early if he chose to. **See also** taxation.

Smendes I (Nesbaneb-Djedet) (?–ca. 1043 B.C.)

Smendes I was a Twentieth Dynasty priest who eventually ruled Egypt as king. He initially served King Ramses XI as the high priest of Amun and the viceroy of Lower Egypt, and perhaps also married one of the king's daughters. Meanwhile, another high priest of Amun, Herihor, was the viceroy of Upper Egypt. (Some Egyptologists believe that Herihor was in command of Lower Egypt as well because Smendes I was under his influence.) When Ramses XI died in approximately 1070 B.C., leaving no heir, Smendes I and Herihor divided the country between them. Smendes I established the city of Tanis as his capital and set about improving it, moving monuments there from other locations. Smendes I made improvements to Karnak as well, fortifying the wall enclosure of its temple to prevent flood damage. By this time, his principal queen was Tentamun, but it appears she provided him with no heir.

Smendes I is also known for being a central figure in a story now known as *The Tale of Wenamun*. In this tale, he pays a man named Wenamun to go to the Levant (a term historically applied to the countries along the eastern Mediterranean shores and still sometimes used for Syria and Lebanon) to get wood to use for repairing the Bark of Amun. While recounting his adventures, Wenamun explains that Smendes I had been chosen to be king by an oracle bringing a message from the god Amun. **See also** Amun; Herihor; Karnak; Ramses XI; Tanis.

Smenkhkare (Semenkhare) (?–1336 B.C.)

An Eighteenth Dynasty king, Smenkhkare succeeded King Akhenaten (known early in his reign as Amenhotep IV), the unpopular king who tried to make dramatic changes in the Egyptian religion. Egyptologists are unsure of how or why Smenkhkare came to the throne, first as a coruler and then three years later, after Akhenaten died, as an independent ruler. Some think that he was Akhenaten's younger brother or oldest son, while others think that "he" was actually Akhenaten's wife Nefertiti in disguise. People who subscribe to the theory that Smenkhkare was actually Nefertiti point out that, although there are many documents mentioning Akhenaten, Nefertiti, and their son Tutankhamun, there is no mention of Smenkhkare prior to his ascending the throne. In addition, one of Smenkhkare's throne names, Neferneferuaten, was very similar to Nefertiti's name, and Smenkhkare was on the throne for only a few months after Akhenaten died, which might suggest that Smenkhkare's claim to the throne was tenuous, as Nefertiti's would have been.

One find argues against Nefertiti as Smenkhkare. In 1907, archaeologists found a mummy in the Valley of the Kings that was later determined to be the remains of a twenty-five-year-old man who, according to scientific testing, was a close relation to Tutankhamun, perhaps a brother or half-brother. The mummy's coffin did not bear its occupant's name, though, and was labeled as being for a royal woman. The fact that the mummy was apparently in a "borrowed" coffin has led some Egyptologists to argue that the remains could not be those of Smenkhkare and instead must belong to some as yet unknown prince. **See also** Amenhotep IV; Nefertiti; Tutankhamun.

Snefru (Snofru; Sneferu) (?–ca. 2589 B.C.)

A Fourth Dynasty king, Snefru succeeded King Huni and was probably either his son or son-in-law. During his nearly twenty-nine-year reign, Snefru engaged in military campaigns against the Nubians and Libyans. He also protected the Sinai by increasing his military presence there, eventually earning the nickname "Destroyer of Barbarians" and being worshiped as a god. Snefru proved to be a prolific builder. He initiated trade with Lebanon to acquire cedar, particularly for shipbuilding and the construction of temple doors, and supported extensive quarrying in the Sinai and elsewhere so that he could construct at least two pyramids. These two structures, at Dashur, are today known as the Red Pyramid and the Bent Pyramid. Snefru might have constructed two other, smaller pyramids as well, or perhaps completed them for his predecessor, Huni. They are located at Meidum and at Seila. **See also** Dashur; Huni; Meidum.

Sobek

Beginning at least as early as the Old Kingdom, the god Sobek was worshiped in the Faiyum, where his primary cult center was at the capital city of Kiman Faras or Shedet (called Crocodilopolis by the Greeks and Medinet el-Faiyum today). During the Twelfth Dynasty, the god gained nationwide popularity, thanks to the devotion of King Amenemhet III. He built temples dedicated to the god not only in the Faiyum but near Thebes and at Kom Ombo just north of Aswan. Perhaps because of Amenemhet III's worship of Sobek, a number of succeeding rulers were named for the god: Twelfth Dynasty queen-pharaoh Sobeknefru (also known as Nefru-Sobek); Thirteenth Dynasty kings Sobekhotep II, III, and IV; and Seventeenth Dynasty king Sobekemsaf II.

The god Sobek was always depicted as either a crocodile or a man with a crocodile's head. His associations within the Egyptian pantheon, however, varied. Sometimes he was connected to the solar deity Re, other times to the moon. Sometimes he was said to be a manifestation of the destroyer god Seth (an association that led to the ritualistic killing of crocodiles), whereas other times he was said to be the son of Neith, a goddess of weaving, hunting, and warfare. Sobek was also sometimes said to have emerged from the primordial water of Nun at the time of Creation. In addition, Sobek was occasionally said to be the father of the god Khons (who was more commonly considered the son of the god Amun and the goddess Mut) with his consort Hathor. **See also** Amun; Hathor; Mut; Re.

songs

Ancient Egyptian songs had three main purposes: comfort, entertainment, and honoring the gods. Songs intended for comfort were sung during funeral processions and funeral rites at the tomb as part of the mourning process; they were also sung to people who were sick and perhaps to women in labor as well. Songs for entertainment were often performed by professional singers at parties, dinners, and other gatherings. However, people who were not professional singers also entertained themselves with music. For example, builders on a job site might sing while working. Songs to honor the gods were primarily chants and hymns that were sung by temple choirs as a regular part of various rituals. Modern Egyptologists, however, have no idea what these songs might have sounded like because no written musical scores from ancient Egypt have ever been found. **See also** music.

Sphinx, Great

Shaped like a lion with a human head, the Great Sphinx is a massive ancient Egyptian sculpture carved out of living rock at Giza. Its distinction comes from its size; at 240 feet long and 66 feet high at its highest point, it is the earliest colossus (colossal statue) in Egypt. However, its image is not unique, as the Egyptians created many such statues, although not necessarily with a human head. Sphinxes can have the body of a lion and the head of a man, god, ram, or hawk. For example, a line of sphinxes with the heads of rams once connected a temple at Luxor with one at Karnak.

The human head of the Great Sphinx wears a headdress with a uraeus, the cobra symbol of kingship, but otherwise there are no identifying markers on the colossus. Consequently, Egyptologists have long debated over who the face of the Sphinx is meant to represent. The general consensus today is that it is King Khafre of the Fourth Dynasty, because a causeway links the colossus with his nearby temple. However, some Egyptologists have argued that the Sphinx was the image not of a king but of a sun god, since in Egyptian mythology the lion is often associated with the sun as well as with kingship and certain deities associated with the sun. Lending credence to this view is the fact that in the New Kingdom the Sphinx was called Horemakhet, or "Horus in the Horizon," after the god Horus. (However, it was also called *shesep ankh,* "living image," which the Greeks distorted into *sphinx,* "the strangler.") Furthermore, when King Tuthmosis IV built a temple dedicated to the Sphinx between its front paws, he oriented its eastern and western sanctuaries apparently to connect them with the rising and setting sun, respectively, perhaps

The Great Sphinx at Giza was created around 2500 B.C., during Fourth Dynasty king Khafre's rule. Egyptologists believe the sphinx's face is a likeness either of Khafre or of a sun god.

indicating that he knew King Khafre had built the Sphinx to honor the sun god.

Adding to debates regarding the Sphinx's origin and meaning are Egyptologists who argue that the Sphinx was built long before Khafre's temple. Scholars like Egyptologist R.A. Schwaller de Lubicz, Mark Lehner (field director for the American Research Center in Egypt), and K. Lal Gauri (director of the Stone Conservation Laboratory at the University of Louisville, Kentucky) have studied geological evidence and determined that the Sphinx shows signs of massive erosion by water rather than sand. Some experts, including Schwaller de Lubicz, argue that the Sphinx existed during prehistoric times, when water covered much of Egypt. Others, saying that no advanced civilizations are known to have existed at that time, insist that the Sphinx is a much more recent construction. They suggest that rising groundwater caused

erosion, although they cannot yet explain how or when it occurred.

In addition to water damage, the Sphinx has experienced other damage since its creation. The colossus rests in a hollow that, if left untouched, completely fills with sand every twenty years, burying all but the Sphinx's head. In addition, when uncovered, the soft limestone composing most of the Sphinx's body is subject to serious wind erosion. The statue's head, carved from an outcropping of harder stone, has experienced far less damage from the elements, but during the eighteenth century the statue was damaged by soldiers and the bodyguards of Egyptian caliphs and sultans, who used it for artillery target practice.

Various projects have been undertaken to restore the Sphinx, with its earliest on record being that of Eighteenth Dynasty king Tuthmosis IV. After clearing the sand from its base, he left a twelve-foot-high, fifteen-ton granite stela reporting on what he had done; its inscription tells of a dream that he had while still a prince in which a solar deity in the form of the Sphinx asked him to clear away its sand, repair the monument, and build a temple between its paws in exchange for the crown of Egypt. Tuthmosis IV's statue provides the only inscription at the site, which includes nearby temples. **See also** Horus; Khafre; Tuthmosis IV.

stations of the gods

Located along procession routes in certain towns and cities, stations of the gods were decorated platforms where the statues, shrines, or barks of the gods were placed so that people could take a moment to honor them. During festivals, various religious ceremonies were performed at each of these stops along the procession route. Sometimes people would speak to the statues of the gods there to ask questions or favors. **See also** barks of the gods; festivals.

statues

Ancient Egyptians created many pieces of statuary of various sizes. The earliest ones were made of wood, but stone soon became the preferred material for all except the smallest statues. To carve stone statues, artisans used a variety of tools, including stone hammers, chisels, drills, and saws, which were made more abrasive by rubbing their blades or tips with wet sand. The largest statues, which were created from huge blocks, were crudely carved where their stone was quarried and then transported to wherever they were to be displayed and finished there. In this way, they were made as light as possible for moving, although they still might weigh several tons.

The size of a statue in relation to others in a display was indicative of the importance of the person represented. Therefore, the statue of a king might be

several times taller than surrounding ones. For example, Abu Simbel has statues of King Ramses II that are approximately sixty-five feet high, and in between these statues' legs are smaller statues of the king's loved ones, including his wife Queen Nefertari, his mother Queen Muttuya, his son Prince Amenhirkhepshef, and several of the king's daughters.

All of these statues show figures at rest, which was common for Egyptian statuary. Only a very few statues show people seemingly engaged in some ordinary daily activity or kneeling in deference, probably to a king or god. In most

A close-up of the Abu Simbel statues of Ramses II reveals the smaller statues at the king's feet.

cases, however, the figure was so rigidly posed that there was no suggestion of movement in its body. The only sign that it was intended to be in motion might be a leg taking a step forward or perhaps accessories such as a basket on the head that suggested the figure might be going somewhere or getting ready to engage in some activity. **See also** Abu Simbel; art; Ramses II; stoneworking.

stelae

The Greeks used the term *stelae* (the plural of *stela*) to refer to freestanding vertical tablets or pillars on which historical or commemorative inscriptions and/or reliefs appeared. Called *wedj* or *aha* by the ancient Egyptians, the earliest of these slabs were made of wood, later ones of stone (particularly limestone or granite) carved into a variety of sizes and styles. Although some stelae were erected to commemorate military victories, most functioned like gravestones; placed near or within tombs or mortuary temples, they provided the deceased's names, titles, and achievements in life. Stelae might also depict the deceased, perhaps showing the person receiving offerings or in the company of deities.

In some tombs and mortuary temples, a stela was not freestanding but was instead incorporated into a wall and carved to look like a door. These false doors were said to be passageways through which the deceased person's spirit could pass to receive offerings. Such stelae were always oriented so that a person facing it to make an offering to the deceased was facing west, the direction one supposedly traveled to reach the land of the dead. In addition, royal false doors were usually made of red granite, while nonroyal false doors were made of limestone, sometimes painted red. This color was associated with the dead, although it had many other associations as well. **See also** false door; temples; tombs.

stoneworking

Ancient Egyptians built many of their mortuary, religious, and royal buildings of stone, beginning with Djoser's Step Pyramid at Saqqara in the Third Dynasty. White limestone was used for pyramids and as a surface for carved reliefs on temple and tomb walls, but in constructing other buildings or stone objects the Egyptians also used sandstone, alabaster, red granite, black granite, diorite, or schist.

Many of the quarries that provided these stones were far from the sites where the stones would ultimately be used. Consequently, ancient Egyptian stoneworkers developed techniques that would make the transport of the largest stones easier. In particular, they planned the construction of their colossal statues well in advance so that they could carve away all unnecessary sections of a stone while it was still at the quarry to make it as light as possible for transport. When carving stones at the quarry, they first separated the stones from the landscape using various sizes of metal or wooden wedges hammered into the rock until it split. Then they roughly created the basic shape of the statue. Once the stone was at its permanent site, they refined their rough carvings to create the desired image using a variety of tools, including wooden mallets and stone hammers, chisels, drills, and saws. They made their blades and the tips of their tools more abrasive by rubbing them with wet sand. **See also** art; quarrying; statues.

Strabo (ca. 63 B.C.–A.D. 21)

A Greek historian and geographer, Strabo visited Egypt in 25 or 24 B.C. and later wrote about his experiences in his multivolume work *Geography.* The main purpose of this work was to provide the most thorough information available about every country under Roman influence during the reign of Roman emperor Augustus, from 27 B.C. to A.D. 14. In discussing Egypt, Strabo not only provided details and facts about Egyptian history, geology, and geography (including the size and location of cities) but also described many aspects of Egyptian life, including politics, religion, and agricultural practices. Book XVII discusses his trip to Egypt, which took him from the Mediterranean Sea up the Nile River to Philae in the company of the prefect of Egypt, Aelius Gallus.

Strabo's work also provides detailed descriptions of the city of Alexandria, then under construction, and the tourist attractions in Upper Egypt that were popular in his day. Strabo describes Alexandria's royal palaces, a museum, a library, and the Temple of Serapis, as well as several Egyptian monuments and statuary. For example, he talks about two statues at Thebes known as the Colossi of Memnon, which were then believed to represent a mythical Ethiopian king named Memnon (they were actually statues of King Amenhotep III). Strabo intensely disliked these statues, not because of their appearance but because one of the statues was said to be able to talk. Strabo attributed these stories to priests who wanted to draw tourists to the site. (In fact, strange sounds do issue from the statue, because of the wind moaning through cracks in the stone.)

In addition to *Geography,* Strabo was the author of an earlier history, a forty-seven-book work called *Historical Sketches.* This work focuses on countries that were influenced by Rome from 145 B.C. to 27 B.C., a period that began with Rome conquering Greece and ended with the beginning of the reign of Emperor Augustus. **See also** Alexandria; Amenhotep III; Philae.

symbols

The ancient Egyptians incorporated a wide variety of religious and magical symbols into their artwork, jewelry, furniture, personal items, and other objects, believing them to have the power to influence reality in specific ways. For example, symbols representing gods or crowns were believed to bring the bearer the power to overcome danger. Among the ancient Egyptian symbols considered the most powerful were the Sacred Eye of Horus, the ankh, the scarab, and the *djed* pillar. Also known as the Wedjat, the Eye of Horus represented wholeness, contentment, and healing. The ankh was a combination of two hieroglyphic symbols, those of air and water, and therefore represented life and the giving of life, because the ancient Egyptians believed that air and water were the two elements necessary to create life. The scarab, or dung beetle, was a symbol of creation, renewal, and the solar deity Re, because such beetles hatch from balls of mud and dung that the Egyptians associated both with the sun and with the Nile River from which the mud came. The *djed* pillar, resembling a tree, was associated with the god Osiris and for this reason symbolized rebirth, strength, and stability. Amulets bearing such symbols usually had a general purpose, offering overall protection and good health. Others, however, were designed for a specific event or problem, such as protecting a woman giving birth. **See also** amulets; ankh; *djed;* Horus; Osiris; scarab.

Syria

Located in southwest Asia, Syria was held first by the Assyrians, then the Babylonians, then the Greeks, and then the Romans during ancient times. In addition, at times some parts of Syria were under the control of Egypt, and the lands along these two countries' shared and shifting border was a frequent place of military conflict. During the First Intermediate Period, a group referred to in ancient Egyptian records as the Aamu, or Asiatics, began invading Egypt from Syria, and these invasions continued into the Twelfth Dynasty. Consequently,

Twelfth Dynasty king Amenemhet I built fortresses in the area to protect Egypt's northeast border. Two other Twelfth Dynasty kings also engaged in Syrian military campaigns, Senwosret I and Senwosret III, and in the Eighteenth and Nineteenth Dynasties, battles were fought in Syria against the Mitanni and the Hittite forces, respectively. The Ramessid Period saw conflicts in the region as well. However, despite these military conflicts the Egyptians traded extensively with Syria, although during some periods far more than others. Timber, metals, semiprecious stones, East Asian spices, and other products all traveled to Egypt by way of Syria. **See also** Amenemhet I; Asiatics; Babylonia and Chaldea; Ramessid Period.

Taharqa (?–664 B.C.)

Twenty-fifth Dynasty king Taharqa was a Nubian from the region of Kush. Of all of the Kushite kings who ruled Egypt, he was the most successful. In particular, art and architecture flourished during his reign. However, he was driven from his capital of Memphis by the forces of the Assyrian king Ashurbanipal and after a series of defeats retired to Kush, where he died in 664 B.C. **See also** Nubia.

tales

Egyptologists use the word *tales* to refer to a series of popular stories that were primarily passed on orally by traveling storytellers. Only the ones that were also recorded in papyri are known today, and few of these have been found in their entirety. For example, *The Tale of the Doomed Prince,* a New Kingdom story about a prince beset by a series of troubles, including attacks by monsters, is recorded in only one known papyrus, and the ending is missing.

Fortunately, a few tales appear in multiple papyri. *The Tale of Prince Setna,* for example, is in several Ptolemaic and Roman Period papyri; it concerns a Nineteenth Dynasty prince who kills his children because of his love for a woman, although later he learns that his experiences were only a dream. Other tales include *The Tale of the Eloquent Peasant* (which appeared during the New Kingdom, and possibly before), *The Tale of Sinuhe* (a Middle Kingdom tale), *The Tale of the Shipwrecked Sailor* (another Middle Kingdom tale), and *The Tale of Two Brothers* (apparently from the Nineteenth Dynasty). **See also** *Eloquent Peasant, The Tale of the;* literature; Ptolemaic Period; *Shipwrecked Sailor, The Tale of the; Sinuhe, The Tale of; Two Brothers, The Tale of.*

Tanis (San el-Hagar)

Called Djanet by the ancient Egyptians but renamed by the Greeks (and now called San el-Hagar), Tanis was an important administrative center during the Twenty-first and Twenty-second Dynasties of the Third Intermediate Period, when it was chosen for the royal residence and burial site. Moreover, in the subsequent Late Period, it became the new capital of the nineteenth nome of Lower Egypt. The tombs of four important Twenty-first and Twenty-second Dynasty kings—Pseusennes I, Amenemope, Osorkon III, and Sheshonq III—have been found nearly intact at Tanis. Other tombs, including some with multiple burials, have also been found there. For example, King Takelot III was in the tomb of Osorkon I, and Sheshonq II was in with Pseusennes I.

These kings built other structures in Tanis as well, as did many other Old, Middle, and New Kingdom rulers. In particular, so many kings added to a Temple of Amun located there that the complex, which was enclosed within a mud-brick wall, is now a jumble of stone blocks, columns, obelisks, and statues, most inscribed and decorated with information and scenes from the reigns of various kings. Because of the richness of the site, several prominent archaeologists have excavated in Tanis, including Auguste Mariette during the second half of the nineteenth century, Sir William Matthew Flinders Petrie from 1883 to 1886, and Pierre Montet, the discoverer of the city's royal tombs, from 1929 to 1951. These men found evidence that not only the god Amun but also Seth was worshiped in Tanis. **See also** Amun; Mariette, Auguste; Petrie, William Matthew Flinders; Seth.

Tao I (Senakhtenre Tao I; Sanakhtenre Tao I) (dates unknown)

A king of the Seventeenth Dynasty at Thebes, Tao I succeeded King Intef VII in Thebes at a time when the Fifteenth Dynasty Hyksos king Apepi I ruled in the Delta, around 1633 B.C. Wishing to restore Egyptian sovereignty in the Delta, Tao I became determined to expel the Hyksos from Egypt, but he died before he could accomplish his goal. He left behind at least two children by his principal wife, Queen Tetisheri, a daughter, Queen Ahhotep (who would later give birth to King Ahmose and possibly Kamose), and a son and heir who would become King Tao II (also known as Seqenenre Tao II). Tao I was entombed in the Theban necropolis. **See also** Ahhotep I; Apepi I; Hyksos; Tao II.

Tao II (Seqenenre Tao II) (dates unknown)

Also known as Seqenenre Tao II, Tao II was a Seventeenth Theban Dynasty king who ruled in Thebes during the Fifteenth and Sixteenth Hyksos Dynasties in the Delta, around 1574 B.C. His father, Tao I, had launched a campaign to expel the Hyksos, and Tao II decided to continue it. However, he must have died during a battle with Hyksos soldiers, because his mummy—found in a royal cache at Deir el-Bahri in 1881—displays horrible wounds from axes, spears, and lances, including fractured bones and a cleaved skull. Given the extent of the injuries he received before finally dying, it is understandable that in life Tao II commonly had the phrase "the Brave" tacked on to the end of his name. Tao II left behind two sons, Ahmose and Kamose, who would both become kings and fight the Hyksos, as well as several daughters, all from his principal wife, his sister, Queen Ahhotep. Tao II's mummy was originally placed in his own tomb in Thebes but was later moved by priests to a royal cache in the same area to protect it against tomb robbers. **See also** Ahhotep I; Ahmose I; caches, royal; Hyksos; Kamose; Tao I.

Taweret (Taueret; Thueris)

Called Thueris by the Greeks, Taweret was an ancient Egyptian goddess primarily associated with pregnancy and childbirth. She was typically depicted as having the body parts of a hippopotamus, a lion, and perhaps a crocodile, with their arrangement varying; the most common appearance was a pregnant hippopotamus with the tail of a crocodile and the muzzle, mane, and front paws of a lion. In sculptures, she is usually standing on her hind legs with her front paws resting on a symbol known as a *sa,* which was often marked on amulets intended to confer protection on women in labor (as well as others in near-death situations). Most Egyptologists believe that Taweret's assemblage of animal parts was meant to depict her as being fierce enough to frighten away evil spirits who might try to prevent a child from being born. On rare occasions, however, Taweret appeared as a woman instead of an animal, perhaps wearing a headdress with horns. **See also** children; deities.

taxation

Egypt's king was considered the owner of all property, people, animals, and goods in Egypt, but by virtue of various royal grants and decrees, some lands were owned by certain temples and individuals and these were subject to taxation. However, many temples were exempt from paying taxes by virtue of royal decrees, and on occasion the king granted this exemption to individual landowners as well.

For tax purposes, landowners were required to register with their nome (administrative district), and if they wanted to transfer their property to someone else, they had to do so via a legal document and an official re-registration of land ownership. The administrator of each nome calculated the worth of the land based on its size and yield and collected property taxes on behalf of the central government. The property taxes that the nomes were expected to pay to the king were based on their surface area and the amount of land that the government estimated would be rendered arable by that year's Nile inundation. In a low-flood year, taxes were lower than in a high-flood year.

In addition to property taxes, every Egyptian household paid a poll tax, a tax based on how many people were discovered living in each household when an annual poll, or census, was taken. Similarly, a census of animal herds was taken each year to determine people's livestock taxes. Taxes were also taken as a percentage of whatever a person produced through hard work. For example, farmers paid a portion of the grain they grew as taxes and craftsmen paid a portion of their creative efforts as taxes.

Since Egypt used the barter system rather than money, payments were made in the form of grain, meat, minerals, or other goods. Taxes collected by local administrators were typically sent from a nome's capital city to the royal treasury for redistribution. For this reason, nome capitals were usually established near waterways that connected them via the Nile River to Egypt's capital, where the treasury was traditionally located. This process was overseen by the king's vizier, who was in charge of the entire tax system.

Anyone who could not afford to pay taxes could take out a loan but was then charged an amount equal to the loan at the end of a year if the debt had not yet been repaid. After yet another year with the debt left unpaid, the debtor would owe double the amount; this amount would be doubled the following year and so on, meaning that the debt could very quickly grow out of control. At any time, the debtor could repay part of the loan to reduce the amount that would be doubled. People in desperate straits could also give their land to the royal treasury in exchange for a reduction or elimination of their taxes, depending on the value of their land. An able-bodied person might also sell himself into servitude in order to pay off a tax debt. **See also** economic system; viziers.

Tefnut

Tefnut was an ancient Egyptian goddess first worshiped in the Predynastic Period. She was originally mentioned only as being the wife of the god Tefen, but later was also said to be the daughter of the god Atum, the oldest of Egypt's earth gods. In many Creation myths, Atum was said to have acted alone in creating Tefnut and her twin brother Shu, who then joined to create their own children, Geb and Nut. Geb and Nut were the god of the earth and goddess of the sky, respectively, while Shu represented air and Tefnut represented the rain or dew or, in some translations, all moisture.

Over time, Tefnut was also associated with creation because of her connection to life-giving rain. This association was particularly strong in the city of Heliopolis, where she was paired with another Creation god, Ptah, who originated in the city of Memphis. Another common association was between Tefnut and Ma'at, a goddess of harmony and balance. Tefnut's connection with Ma'at eventually led many ancient Egyptians to view her as a symbol of spirituality.

Tefnut was often depicted as a woman with the head of a lioness or simply as a lioness with no human features. Another common depiction of Tefnut is alongside her brother, Shu, with the two working together to hold up the sky. In this capacity, Tefnut was viewed as representing the border between heaven and earth. **See also** Atum; Geb; Ma'at; Nut; Ptah; Shu.

temples

There were two main types of temples in ancient Egypt: cult temples dedicated to various deities, and mortuary temples for deceased kings. Most cult temples built prior to the New Kingdom no longer exist, probably because they were made of mud brick and/or of stones that were later raided for other construction projects. Consequently, most of what archaeologists know about cult temples comes from structures of the New Kingdom or later.

The typical New Kingdom cult temple had a line of statues leading up to its entrance, perhaps also connecting it to another temple or some other religious structure nearby. For example, the temples of Karnak and Luxor were linked by an avenue of sphinxes, statues with the body of a lion and the head of a ram (although some sphinxes elsewhere had the head of a man or hawk). The pylon, or gateway, of the temple would usually have towers displaying flags with some image associated with the temple's deity or family of deities, since a temple was believed to be a particular deity's home.

Just outside the temple was a large open court, the peristyle court, that might serve as a public gathering area during festivals. Otherwise the public was not allowed inside the temple complex, nor was it ever allowed through a second pylon to the temple proper. Within this area was a hypostyle hall, which had a roof held aloft by many decorative columns. The walls were decorated as well, with both inscriptions and painted reliefs, but these images could be difficult to see because the design of the hall allowed little natural light to enter. A temple might have several such halls, as well as other courts and numerous chambers, storerooms, offering halls, and shrines. The main shrine was where the cult statue representing the god or goddess of the temple was located. All major temples also had a sacred lake, typically used for purification rituals.

In the Fifth Dynasty, several kings built one type of temple that was specifically dedicated to the solar deity Re. The temple of King Userkaf was apparently the first such temple built in ancient Egypt, and although today it is in extremely poor condition, it once featured a squat obelisk (a stone pillar symbolizing the solar deity) and a stone sun altar, both unique to sun temples. It also had a causeway leading to a mud-brick boat said to belong to Re, as well as many other symbols and architectural and decorative features associated with the sun and sunlight. Another sun temple, that of King Neuserre, had both an upper temple and a lower one linked by a causeway that some archaeologists consider a symbol of making the passage through life. The lower temple was situated in a valley beside a canal so that boats could dock beside it, and the upper temple had a chapel, an eighteen-by-nineteen-foot sacrificial altar of alabaster blocks, and an obelisk. The temple complex also apparently had a brick solar bark nearly one hundred feet long, whose purpose was to carry the king's spirit in the Afterlife.

The public was not allowed inside these temples, nor in any other temple's sanctuaries. Egyptian temples were not intended to be a place where people from the surrounding community went to worship. Instead, they were places where priests dedicated themselves to the care and honoring of certain deities. However, only a few temple priests actually conducted religious rituals; most spent their time maintaining temple structures and estates, which produced food for the gods' offerings as well as for temple residents. The cult temple was also an educational institution where boys who intended to become priests, scribes, government administrators, or other learned professionals were schooled.

Mortuary temples, on the other hand, were strictly dedicated to the deceased kings they honored. Archaeologists have many examples of such structures, dating back to the Early Dynastic Period, because like the kings' tombs these temples were built to last for eternity. In studying structures from different historical periods, archaeologists have seen a steady progression in size and grandeur; later temples are part of complexes of buildings that might be connected to another, nearby temple via a causeway or avenue. The earliest mortuary temples were themselves part of a complex that included the king's tomb, but by the Middle Kingdom kings had begun to have their mortuary temples in a separate structure from the one holding their burial chamber. These first mortuary temples were actually cenotaphs, or false tombs, built as though they were intended to house the king's body but in fact intended only to associate the deceased king with a particular god. By the New Kingdom, all mortuary temples had this purpose, and the kings separated their mortuary temples and their tombs by vast distances; some kings even had a mortuary temple in more than one city. Egyptologists suspect that the driving force behind this change was tomb robbing. By housing the king's body and tomb goods away from his mortuary temple, the king could keep his remains inconspicuous and therefore safe from robbers, yet still glorify himself through a grand structure. **See also** barks of the gods; Karnak; Luxor; Neuserre; purification practices; sacred lakes; Userkaf; Valley of the Kings.

Teti (?–ca. 2323 B.C.)

The first king of the Sixth Dynasty, Teti succeeded King Unas, probably because he married the king's daughter Iput. He had at least two other wives as well, Khuit (also known as Kawit) and Shesheshet. Teti reigned at least twelve years, aided during the first part of his reign by his viziers Kagemni and Mereruka, but few records exist regarding his time on the throne. Apparently, however, his rule was marked by peace and unity between Upper and Lower Egypt, since he took the Horus name Seheteptawy, or "He Who Pacifies the Two Lands." In addition, Teti encouraged trade with Nubia, Byblos, and possibly Punt. He built his pyramid at Saqqara, inscribing material relating to religion and magic on its walls. (Together with similar materials found in other Fifth and Sixth Dynasty pyramids, these inscriptions are known as the Pyramid Texts.)

What became of Teti is uncertain. Nineteenth-century archaeologists found his coffin and sarcophagus in Saqqara, but not his mummy. However, if third-century-B.C. Greek historian Manetho is to be believed, Teti was assassinated by his own guards. Indeed, archaeologists currently excavating the tombs of Teti's officials, located at Saqqara, have discovered signs that some of these men were involved in a conspiracy against the king. For example, the tomb of one of the king's viziers, Hezi, was taken from him; Hezi's name was chiseled off and replaced with the name of a lesser official, Seshemnefer. This was a typical punishment for someone who committed a crime against the country. Archaeologists have also found the burial complex of Teti's intended heir, Tetiankh-Kem ("Tetiankh the Black," son of Queen Khuit), and discovered that he died at around the same time as Teti. Since Tetiankh-Kem's mummy shows he was only twenty-five when he died, Egyptologists suggest that he and his father were both murdered, probably by supporters of the succeeding king, Userkare. **See also** Byblos; Nubia; Punt; Pyramid Texts; Saqqara; Userkare.

Tetisheri (dates unknown)

Seventeenth Dynasty queen Tetisheri was the wife of Tao I and the mother of Tao II, who was killed fighting Hyksos invaders. She was also the grandmother of Kings Kamose and Ahmose I, both of whom continued the war with the Hyksos. Born a commoner, Tetisheri lived with her children and grandchildren around 1580 B.C. in a palace at Deir el-Ballas, and she was apparently particularly close to her grandson King Ahmose. When she died at age seventy, Ahmose built her a large mortuary complex and provided funds for priests to conduct frequent rituals in her honor. He also erected a cenotaph in her honor at Abydos. In subsequent generations, Queen Tetisheri continued to be honored as the ancestress of the Eighteenth Dynasty, and today some archaeologists refer to her as the Mother of the New Kingdom. **See also** Ahmose I; Kamose; Tao I; Tao II.

Thebes

Called Waset by the ancient Egyptians but renamed by the Greeks, Thebes was the capital of the fourth nome of Upper Egypt, and at times served as Egypt's capital as well. Because it was located near Nubia and was therefore close to important mines and trade routes, the city rose to prominence in the Eleventh Dynasty and continued to grow in power and influence. During the Second Intermediate Period, a series of Theban kings opposed the rule of the invading Hyksos, and during the Eighteenth Dynasty, Thebes became both the religious and the administrative capital of Egypt, and its main god, Amun, became Egypt's national god. From this point on, even when Egypt's capital was located elsewhere, the city and its priesthood remained powerful. In fact, the high priests of Amun in Thebes were sometimes the rulers of Egypt, either through their influence on a particular king or after actually usurping the throne.

Given its connection to many powerful men, it is not surprising that Thebes holds some of the most spectacular tombs and temples in Egypt. The areas north of and across the Nile River from Thebes contain a series of necropolis sites and religious centers; these sites include Karnak, Luxor, Deir el-Bahri, Medinet Habu, and the Valley of the Kings. **See also** Amun; Deir el-Bahri; Hyksos; Karnak; Luxor; Medinet Habu; priests; Second Intermediate Period; Third Intermediate Period; Valley of the Kings.

Third Intermediate Period (ca. 1069–664 B.C.)

The Third Intermediate Period is a period of ancient Egyptian history following the New Kingdom and lasting from approximately 1069 B.C. to 664 B.C. At the beginning of this period, Egypt was in decline as a result of a series of weak kings at the end of the New Kingdom. The last king of that period, Ramses XI, had given over control of the country to two high priests, and when he died they divided the country between them, ushering in the Third Intermediate Period. For the rest of this period a series of high priests, weak kings, and usurpers all vied for power, along with Libyan mercenaries who had settled in Egypt during the New Kingdom. This era of chaos drew to a close when a Nubian king, Shabaka, led his forces north to start the process of uniting the country. His successors finally established a centralized government for Egypt by the beginning of the

Late Period. **See also** New Kingdom; Ramses XI.

Thoth

The ancient god of wisdom, learning, and science, Thoth was considered the patron of temple scribes and the protector of priest-physicians. He was usually depicted as an ibis, a long-legged, long-beaked wading bird from the heron family, or as a man with an ibis head. Sometimes, however, he took the form of a baboon, even though the baboon was more typically associated with a solar deity and Thoth was associated with the moon, as evidenced by the lunar disk often shown atop his head. Consequently, he was sometimes called "Beautiful of Night." In certain myths, he was said to participate in an Afterlife ceremony in which the deceased's heart was weighed to determine a person's worthiness; Thoth was the one to record the verdict. Thoth's main cult center, which was the site of a major New Year's festival, was in the city of Khmun, renamed Hermopolis by the Greeks because they connected Thoth to their god Hermes. (Today, the city is called el-Ashmunein.) **See also** Hermopolis; scribes.

Ti (Tiy) (?–ca. 2421 B.C.)

Ti was a Fifth Dynasty official during possibly the reign of King Neuserre but probably that of King Kakai, also known as Neferirkare. According to inscriptions at Ti's mastaba tomb at Saqqara, he held several titles, including scribe of the court, supervisor of works, overseer of the pyramids and sun temple at Abusir, royal councillor, and lord of the secrets, which appears to mean that he held some privileged knowledge, probably related to architecture. More important than Ti's titles, however, are his tomb reliefs and mortuary inscriptions, which feature a variety of scenes from daily life, some with Ti as participant and others with him as a passive observer. For example, Ti is shown watching geese and cranes being force-fed for fattening, shipbuilders and craftsmen at work, boatmen playing a game, and his men hunting a hippo. Ti is also shown riding in a skiff with his wife, performing his official duties, sailing in a boat past wildlife, and enjoying other activities, sometimes with family members and pets. To create these scenes, Ti apparently employed the best artists of his day, because the quality of their work is excellent. The tomb also once contained a painted statue of Ti nearly six and a half feet high, which is now on display in the Cairo Museum and considered one of the masterpieces of Egyptian art. Given such works, Ti was obviously quite wealthy, and his tomb inscriptions record that he had extensive landholdings. He was also married to the king's daughter, so his sons were considered royal. **See also** Kakai; Neuserre; Saqqara.

Tiy (ca. 1400–1340 B.C.)

Eighteenth Dynasty queen Tiy was the principal wife of King Amenhotep III, and some Egyptologists believe that she eventually ruled the country in his stead. Support for this theory lies in the fact that Queen Tiy's signature appears on many official documents, including announcements of her husband's marriages to other women. Queen Tiy appears to have been supportive of her husband's relations with lesser queens, which he undertook in order to produce male heirs; in correspondence with daughters Isis and Sitamun, she urges them to marry their father specifically to give him sons.

Queen Tiy herself did apparently produce a male heir, Amenhotep IV, and another son who died either as an infant or in childhood. She also had at least two other daughters in addition to Isis and Sitamun. Until the king's death in approximately 1352 B.C., when Queen Tiy was around forty-eight years old, she and her children lived with King Amenhotep III's harem in a palace on the western shore of Thebes. When Amenhotep IV assumed the throne, changed his name to Akhenaten, and built the city of Akhetaten (also known as Amarna), Queen Tiy moved there. In fact, some Egyptologists believe that she had a great deal of influence over her son's decision to create Akhetaten, which was his way of honoring the god Aten, because the queen was a major supporter of an Aten cult that had developed during her husband's reign.

No one knows where Queen Tiy was entombed following her death. Some Egyptologists believe it was in Akhetaten but others think that her sarcophagus was placed beside her husband's in his tomb in the Valley of the Kings. At one time, a mummy found in the Valley of the Kings was thought to be hers, because some of the items in its tomb—including part of a sarcophagus—were hers. However, it now appears that the mummy might be that of some previously unknown prince—perhaps Smenkhkare, although this is a subject of much debate among scholars. Some Egyptologists suspect that Queen Tiy's mummy might have been destroyed along with that of her son Akhenaten because of their association with Aten worship.

After Akhenaten's death, the Egyptians returned to worshiping the gods that the king had tried to replace with Aten. They also defaced many of the king's monuments and abandoned his city of Akhetaten. In addition, a small shrine dedicated to Queen Tiy was appropriated for one of Akhenaten's successors, King Tutankhamun. However, Queen Tiy's temple at Sedeinga in Upper Nubia was kept intact, and she was worshiped as a goddess there for many years as part of a royal solar ceremony. There is also a statue of Queen Tiy beside a colossal statue of her husband at his mortuary temple at Memnon. In addition, she is mentioned in a series of correspondence now referred to as the Amarna Letters because they were found in Akhetaten. In one of these letters, which was written to Queen Tiy after she had been widowed, the king of Mitanni, Tushratta, asks about her health and requests that she remind her son, the new king, of Mitanni's close ties to Egypt. **See also** Amenhotep III; Amenhotep IV; Aten; Smenkhkare; Tutankhamun.

tomb goods

The ancient Egyptians placed many goods in their tombs with the belief that these items could be used in the Afterlife. Chosen either before death by the tomb's owner or by surviving relatives, tomb goods included furniture, clothing, jewelry, games, and any other items the deceased enjoyed before death. The selection typically reflected the interests, values, and status in society that the tomb owner held in life. For example, queens and princesses were often entombed with a great deal of jewelry, personal items like combs and cosmetics, and perhaps even lavish furniture. Queen Hetepheres I, the wife of King Snefru and mother of King Khufu, was entombed with a bed that had carved legs, gilded wood, a portable canopy, a box for its curtains, and a curved headrest that functioned as a pillow; her tomb also contained two gilded wooden chairs, a gilded wooden sedan chair with carrying poles for use in processions, and many personal items. Kings were entombed with such items as well, but the emphasis was typically on weapons for hunting and warfare, crowns and other trappings of royalty, and statues and other objects intended to glorify their name. Tombs for couples or families often contained board games for their enjoyment through eternity. In a few cases, someone took a favorite dog, cat, or other animal with them, which was either mummified and placed within the tomb or buried outside near the tomb.

For kings, one of the most important funerary items was a boat, which would be buried near a royal tomb for the purpose of carrying the king on journeys in the Afterlife. Because the Nile River was the main route of travel in ancient Egypt, having a boat was vital to the living, and given ancient Egyptian beliefs about the Afterlife, it was understandable that they would consider it vital to the dead as well. Moreover, according to Egyptian mythology, boats were the means by which the solar deity traveled through the sky each day and through the Underworld each night, and since deceased kings were believed to accompany the god, the funerary boat of a king took on even greater importance. Boats were featured in either symbolic or literal burials beginning in the Early Dynastic Period, when boat-shaped pits were constructed beside several royal mastaba tombs and pyramids. Some of these pits appear to have been for symbolic burials, since no vessels were found inside, but others do have the remains of real boats made of cedar. For example, just south of the Great Pyramid of Khufu, archaeologists found two pits, each holding a boat so large it had to be disassembled to fit inside the pit. The archaeologists reassembled one of these boats, which had 1,224 pieces, into a 142-foot-long craft and built a special museum, the Boat Museum, so they could put it on display. The other boat remains in its pit awaiting excavation.

During the Middle Kingdom, people began using models of boats as tomb goods, placing tiny but highly detailed replicas of boats in their tombs and arranging for spells to be worked after their death that were intended to transform these boats into full size in the Afterlife. This belief extended to other tomb models as well. For example, models of ser-vants engaged in such activities as making beer, plowing fields, working in a granary, or taking care of various aspects of the tomb owner's estate were placed in the tomb for the purpose of providing the tomb owner with their services in the Afterlife.

Other items associated with magic were placed in the tomb as well, although Egyptologists are unsure as to all of their purposes. Some, however, had magical spells on them that give a clue about their function. For example, a pillow-like, disk-shaped object called a hypocephalus, made of bronze or *cartonnage* (linen coated with plaster), was typically marked with Chapter 162 of the *Book of the Dead*, a spell related to keeping warm. During the New Kingdom, many other spells of the *Book of the Dead* appeared in the tombs; during the Old Kingdom, the funerary texts were the Pyramid Texts, and during the Middle Kingdom the Coffin Texts, appearing on walls and coffins, respectively. **See also** *Book of the Dead;* furniture; magic; models, tomb; pyramids; Pyramid Texts; *shabti;* tombs.

tombs

Archaeologists have many examples of ancient Egyptian tombs because these structures were built to last for eternity. To this end, tombs were typically constructed of stone or cut into living rock (i.e., rock areas that are part of the natural landscape). The size of ancient Egyptian tombs changed over time, but every tomb had a burial chamber for the tomb's owner and usually an offering chapel where offerings could be left for the spirit of the deceased. The grandest tombs were always those of kings, followed by those of his family members; the size and decor of the tombs of nobles reflected their status and wealth in life.

The design of tombs also evolved over time. The earliest royal tombs, at Abydos and Saqqara, were of a style known as mastaba, with an underground burial chamber and an aboveground chapel that was shaped like a mound. Over time, the mounds of mastaba tombs housing kings were slightly terraced to look like steps to suggest that the deceased king would be ascending to the heavens to join the solar deity. In the Third Dynasty, the architect and vizier Imhotep based the first ancient Egyptian pyramid, the Step Pyramid of King Djoser, on this structure, beginning with the mastaba design but giving it more pronounced steps and making it much taller. Imhotep also copied the roof style of mastabas, imitating those structures' palm tree logs in carved stone.

From this point on, although nobles continued building mastaba tombs for themselves, kings increasingly chose to construct pyramids, apparently to hold their remains. (There is some disagreement among Egyptologists as to whether pyramids were intended to serve as tombs or to fulfill some other purpose;

however, few alternative burial sites for the pyramid-building kings have been discovered.) Over time, builders smoothed the sides of pyramids rather than stair-stepping them, and they made interiors more complex, with numerous passageways and chambers.

Pyramids continued to be built as tombs by kings until the Second Intermediate Period, when the Valley of the Kings, near Thebes, became the royal cemetery. This region had many desert cliffs into which tombs could be cut, and as a result, rock-cut tombs became the tomb of choice for kings and many nobles. As with pyramid construction, the construction of rock-cut tombs grew more sophisticated over time. The oldest rock-cut tomb yet discovered, that of Eighteenth Dynasty king Tuthmosis I, had only one fairly straight corridor leading to a square burial chamber. However, the next tomb built there, that of Tuthmosis II, had an oval burial chamber with a corridor designed to make a sharp

The use of tomb ornamentation, including columns, reliefs, statues, and paintings (pictured), became more prevalent over time.

left turn in order to foil tomb robbers; tomb builders sealed this corridor at the turn so that any tomb robber digging toward the burial chamber would assume he had to keep going straight. The next tomb, that of Tuthmosis III, added another new feature, a deep trench designed to direct floodwaters down and away from the burial chamber. In addition, his tomb had four storage rooms and an antechamber with pillars. Subsequent tombs, which date until the end of the New Kingdom, had many more rooms and passageways.

Rock-cut tombs remained prevalent until the Twenty-fifth Dynasty, when a series of Kushite kings revived the practice of building pyramids at their capital of Napata in Nubia. They did this out of a desire to identify themselves with earlier, pyramid-building kings. However, the pyramids that they constructed were much smaller and more modest than previous ones, and they lacked much adornment.

Otherwise, however, tombs of all kinds became more highly decorated over time, with the latest ones (except those completed in haste because of an untimely death) having ornate columns, wall paintings, and a great deal of statuary. Religious and magical texts appeared on tomb walls beginning in the Old Kingdom, but they were particularly prevalent in New Kingdom rock-cut tombs. For example, every wall and ceiling in the Valley of the Kings tomb of Seti I, which is over one hundred yards long with three corridors and several rooms with numerous pillars and connecting flights of steps, is covered with reliefs and paintings displaying funerary texts including *The Litany of Re,* the *Book of What Is in the Duat, The Book of Gates,* and the *Book of the Divine Cow,* and one room has a detailed astronomical ceiling. **See also** Abydos; pyramids; Saqqara; Valley of the Kings.

toys and games

Archaeologists have found many ancient Egyptian wall paintings and painted reliefs depicting Egyptians playing games, and excavations have uncovered toys at numerous sites. The most common toys are wooden dolls (sometimes in cradles) and carved animal figures, both with movable limbs and painted features. However, in many cases, it has been difficult to discern whether a particular doll or figure was intended for use as a toy or as a religious or magical object. For example, archaeologists disagree on whether a set of animal figures (e.g., hippopotamuses, crocodiles, and apes) made of Nile River clay that was found at Lahun are toys or whether they were related to worshiping gods that took the form of these animals. However, some objects are obviously toys, including tops, miniature weapons, rattles, woven slingshots, and wooden, leather, linen, or reed balls.

According to depictions in wall art, children in ancient Egypt enjoyed playing games of catch, sometimes with the participants sitting piggyback atop their friends' shoulders. They also played water games, since living next to the Nile River encouraged most Egyptians to become good swimmers. Leapfrog was another popular activity among children, as were walking on tightropes, playing tug-of-war, juggling, wrestling, racing on foot, archery, and horseback riding (the latter of which was primarily enjoyed among the upper classes). Children also played with small animals, as evidenced by the fact that little girls were sometimes depicted in artwork holding a pet kitten.

Among adults, one of the most common activities was participating in or watching sporting events, most of which involved skills used in hunting. Two popular events were javelin-throwing contests and archery. Board games were also very popular. One such game was Senet, which was typically mentioned in Chapter 17 of the *Book of the Dead* as a common way for people to pass the time in the Afterlife. Senet was apparently played by members of every social class throughout Egypt. Playing required a game board and a set of five to seven playing pieces, usually cone shaped. Senet boards found by archaeologists usually have thirty squares arranged in three rows; some of the squares are blank while others are marked with hieroglyphs. Egyptologists disagree on what the rules of the game were, but it appears that the players' goal was to be the first to move their playing pieces across the board to a particular square, tossing some form of labeled stick or bone to determine how many squares a piece could be moved during a turn. As with modern board games, the labels on each square probably gave instructions that affected what happened to a piece that landed on it. Other board games mentioned in ancient Egyptian writings include Serpent and Dog-and-Jackal; however, Egyptologists do not have any idea how these games were played. **See also** animals.

trade

Although ancient Egypt had an ample supply of food, the country lacked some important resources—particularly high-quality timber—that had to be acquired through trade with other lands. As early as the Predynastic Period, Egyptians were trading with Mesopotamia, and with Syria and Lebanon in Early Dynastic times. During the Old Kingdom, the Egyptians also traded with Libya, Nubia, and Punt, and they continued to engage in trading activities with these lands throughout ancient times.

All foreign trade was under the control of the central government. The king sponsored most trading expeditions, and the few private commercial ventures were overseen by government officials and subject to tariffs and other fees. The government also protected trading caravans, establishing fortifications at oases and providing patrols along borders and frontier roads and at trading centers. In conducting trade, Egyptians used the barter system, although certain items were used as standards to help determine value. For example, to establish the price of an item, its weight might be compared to that of gold. **See also** economic system; military.

travel

Because most of the major settlements in ancient Egypt were along the Nile River, the primary means of travel was by boat. Boats and ships came in many sizes and varieties, with some made of papyrus reeds and some of wood. The ancient Egyptians made their reed boats by bundling reeds in layers and tying them together with ropes. Shaped much like a canoe, they were paddled or poled along the shallows of the Nile River. Because the river had many such shallows, wooden boats tended to be flat-bottomed, with little or nothing in the way of a keel. They too were typically paddled or rowed, although many had sails as well. Wooden barges and other vessels used for transporting animals and/or heavy supplies were towed by another boat. Larger boats of all kinds might have a cabin, or perhaps two, constructed of reed mats or linen. From the Middle Kingdom on, large boats also had rudders. Seagoing ships had fixed ones with as many as thirty rowers; these vessels might be over sixty feet long.

For trips on land covering distances too far to walk or involving heavy burdens, most people used a donkey. However, apparently only the lower classes rode astride these donkeys, because although archaeologists have found a donkey saddle, they have not found any scenes in royal or noble tombs depicting a donkey being ridden astride. Instead two donkeys might support poles atop which was a chair for the rider and servants on the ground forced the donkeys to move forward. Alternatively, there might be no donkey but servants simply carrying the chair aloft.

The wheel was known in the Old Kingdom, but wheeled carts were not used until the New Kingdom, because of the problems presented by Egypt's rocky and sandy terrain. The introduction of light, two-wheeled, horse-drawn chariots by the Hyksos helped with these problems, but because only nobility and royalty could afford horses, the masses did not make use of these new vehicles. Large caravans, however, might use ox-drawn wagons to transport their goods. **See also** chariots; Nile River; trade.

Turin Canon

Also known as the Royal Canon of Turin, the Turin Canon is a king list that once offered the largest number of kings' names—over three hundred, from Egypt's first king to King Ramses II—complete with the precise length of each king's reign to the day, although the starting and ending dates of each reign were not given. However, the papyrus on which it was written in hieratic script was seriously damaged by nineteenth-century antiquities collectors and many names were lost, leaving large gaps in information. In fact, fewer than ninety names are legible today. The papyrus now resides in the Egyptian Museum in Turin, Italy. **See also** chronology; king lists.

Tutankhamun (ca. 1345–ca. 1327 B.C.)

A king of the Eighteenth Dynasty, Tutankhamun ascended the throne when he was no more than eight or nine years old and ruled under the close watch of two powerful administrators, a military general named Horemheb and a court official named Ay. Tutankhamun began his rule in a time of great unrest in Egypt. The country had recently suffered under the rule of Akhenaten, who had promoted worship of a new national god, Aten; the Egyptian people hated Akhenaten's religious policies

and practices, and when the king died they pressured his successor, Smenkhkare, to abandon Aten worship. Smenkhkare died before restoring the traditional religion, and it was at this point that Tutankhamun assumed the throne. Under Horemheb's guidance, Tutankhamun returned Egypt to the worship of its traditional gods.

Egyptologists suspect that as Tutankhamun matured he grew restive under the control of Horemheb and Ay, some believe that this opposition led to Tutankhamun's being murdered by one or both of the men. They argue that the king's mummy shows he was killed by a blow to the back of the head, a wound that was probably not received during a military campaign or accident. Supporting this theory is the fact that when Tutankhamun's

The mask of Tutankhamun, made of gold inlaid with glass and semiprecious stones, was just one of a vast number of treasures found in the Eighteenth Dynasty king's tomb.

widow, Ankhesenamun, wrote to a foreign king asking him to send one of his sons to marry her and assume the throne to protect her from unnamed enemies within Egypt, Horemheb ordered the prince killed at Egypt's border. However, other Egyptologists are just as convinced that Tutankhamun was not murdered. They argue that the lethal blow, which was in the region of the left ear, was in a location that no assassin would have chosen to strike. Therefore, some suggest that Tutankhamun died after falling from a moving chariot and hitting his head on a rock.

In any case, after Tutankhamun's death, Ay assumed the throne for a brief time, apparently with Horemheb's blessing, and married Ankhesenamun to solidify his claim to the throne. When Ay died, Horemheb then assumed the throne as his heir, and one of his first acts was to remove all mention of kings associated with Aten worship from Egypt's monuments. This included Tutankhamun, because even though he had rejected Aten worship, he was still the son of its principal proponent, Akhenaten. Consequently, almost all knowledge of Tutankhamun disappeared.

Tutankhamun's tomb, thanks to Horemheb's efforts to alter the historical record, lay undisturbed and was found in the Valley of the Kings by archaeologist Howard Carter in 1922. This tomb, although undecorated except for a few rough paintings in its small burial chamber depicting scenes from the *Book of the Dead*, contained so many treasures that it took Carter the next ten years to remove and catalog them all. The tomb also held Tutankhamun's mummy, which was inside a gold coffin placed in another gold coffin that was inside a gilded wood coffin decorated with precious stones. The mummy had a solid gold mask of the king over its face, wearing a royal headdress decorated with a glass paste imitating lapis lazuli, and its body was decorated with over 150

pieces of jewelry, most of them with symbols related to deities and/or kingship. Near Tutankhamun's remains were those of two mummified human fetuses, probably miscarried offspring produced by him and his wife.

Also in the tomb were hieroglyphs warning that anyone who disturbed Tutankhamun's treasures would meet a terrible end. When Lord Carnarvon, Carter's sponsor, died of a mysterious illness soon after he entered the tomb, the public blamed the death on the "curse of King Tut." When several other people connected with the discovery of the tomb also died in strange ways, the public's fascination with the idea of a curse grew. However, Carter scoffed at the curse and himself lived another seventeen years after entering Tutankhamun's tomb, reaching the age of sixty-six before he died. **See also** Amenhotep IV; Ankhesenamun; Ay; Carter, Howard; Horemheb; Valley of the Kings.

Tuthmosis I (?–ca. 1492 B.C.)

Eighteenth Dynasty king Tuthmosis I ascended the throne as the brother-in-law or perhaps son-in-law of King Amenhotep I, who died without fathering a son. At that time, Tuthmosis I was a military general, and he continued to engage in military campaigns as king, fighting in both Nubia and Syria. He apparently also established the royal burial site in the Valley of the Kings, because his is the oldest tomb that has been found there. Egyptologists disagree on the length of Tuthmosis I's reign, placing it anywhere from six to thirteen years. **See also** Amenhotep I.

Tuthmosis II (ca. 1536–1504 B.C.)

An Eighteenth Dynasty king, Tuthmosis II succeeded to the throne as a son of Tuthmosis I only because his half-brothers, Wadjmose and Amenmose, died before their father. Tuthmosis II was the son of a lesser wife, Mutnefert, who was not of royal blood. Therefore, to strengthen his connection to the throne he married his half-sister Hatshepsut, the daughter of Tuthmosis I and his principal wife, Ahmose Meryt-Amon. A powerful and ambitious woman, Hatshepsut eventually reigned as queen-pharaoh after her husband's death, after usurping the throne from Tuthmosis II's son and heir Tuthmosis III. Prior to Tuthmosis II's death, Hatshepsut probably also had great influence at court, because Tuthmosis II was in poor health for much of his reign. However, he did manage to conduct at least two military campaigns, one in Nubia and one in Syria, during his roughly fourteen years on the throne. **See also** Ahmose Meryt-Amon; Hatshepsut; Tuthmosis I; Tuthmosis III.

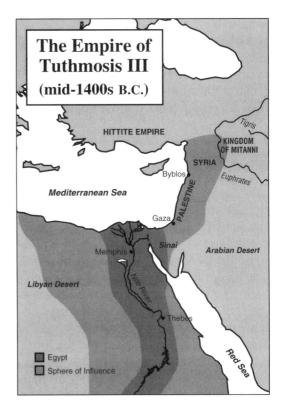

Tuthmosis III (ca. 1510– ca. 1450 B.C.)

Eighteenth Dynasty king Tuthmosis III first succeeded to the throne as a young boy, with his stepmother Hatshepsut as his regent. Hatshepsut quickly usurped the boy's throne, and he did not regain it until she died (possibly of foul play) twenty years later. Upon her death, Tuthmosis tried to destroy every reference to Hatshepsut in monumental inscriptions.

By the time he assumed the throne, Tuthmosis III had military experience, although under Hatshepsut the military had become so weak that Egypt lost much of its power abroad. Tuthmosis III soon regained this power, leading troops into battle repeatedly to reassert Egyptian control over Syria and campaigning extensively in Nubia. Tuthmosis III was also aggressive in supporting Egypt's religious institutions. He built, rebuilt, or added to many temples and supplied them with wealth.

During Tuthmosis III's fifty-four-year reign, Egypt once again became a major power after years of decline. Moreover, art and architecture flourished and the country experienced great prosperity. When he died, Tuthmosis III was entombed in the Valley of the Kings, where tomb robbers stole his funerary goods and damaged his mummy. Subsequently repaired and reentombed, it was found in 1881 in a royal cache at Deir el-Bahri. **See also** Deir el-Bahri; Hatshepsut; Tuthmosis II.

Tuthmosis IV (?–ca. 1392 B.C.)

An Eighteenth Dynasty king, Tuthmosis IV inherited the throne as a young son of Amenhotep II, but some Egyptologists believe that he was preceded by another of the king's sons who has not yet been identified. Tuthmosis IV is best known for clearing away sand from the base of the Great Sphinx at Giza, probably built in the Fourth Dynasty by King Khafre. Tuthmosis IV repaired this colossal statue after having a dream while camped at its base during a hunting trip. Then still a prince, he dreamed that the Sphinx told him he would become king only if he restored the monument to its former glory. Tuthmosis did gain the crown, but he died only nine years into his reign and therefore accomplished little as king. **See also** Amenhotep II; Sphinx, Great.

Two Brothers, The Tale of

Dating from the Nineteenth Dynasty, *The Tale of Two Brothers* is a work of literature that was found in a papyrus known as the Papyrus Orbiney that now resides in the British Museum. The story recounts the details of a fight between two gods who are also brothers, Anup and Bata. The latter was an obscure predynastic god and the former might have been one as well, although many Egyptologists believe that Anup was really Anubis, god of embalming. In any case, by the New Kingdom the Egyptians probably associated the story with brother deities Seth and Osiris, who were the focus of many conflict stories. However, whereas Seth kills Osiris in stories of their conflict, the brothers in *The Tale of Two Brothers* eventually work out their difficulties.

The problems between Anup and Bata begin when Anup's wife flirts with Bata but is spurned by him. Angry and insulted, she tells her husband that his brother raped her. Anup goes after Bata, but before he can kill his brother, the god Shu puts a crocodile-filled river between them. This gives Bata the chance to tell Anup what really happened. Anup then goes home and kills his wife for misleading him. Meanwhile, Bata, unable to cross the river to return home, sets off on a journey of exploration. **See also** Anubis; literature; Osiris; Seth; tales.

Twosret (Twosre; Tausert) (?–ca. 1186 B.C.?)

Nineteenth Dynasty queen Twosret ("Mighty Lady, Chosen of Mut") was the principal wife of King Seti II. After her husband died, she became regent for his heir, her stepson Siptah. In managing the boy's affairs, Twosret was aided by her adviser Bay (who held the official title Great Chancellor), who was vizier first to Seti II and then to Siptah. When Siptah died sometime between the fourth and sixth years of his reign, Queen Twosret took over the throne with Bay as her closest adviser, calling herself pharaoh and taking the throne name Sitre Meryamun ("Daughter of Re, Beloved of Amun"). Twosret and Bay ruled the country for two years, during which the Egyptian people continually expressed their dislike for the two usurpers.

Egyptologists are unsure of what happened to Siptah. It is possible that he met with foul play, but there is no obvious sign of murder on his mummy, which was found in the Valley of the Kings cache of Amenhotep II. Moreover, he was also a sickly boy with a clubfoot, so it would not be unlikely that he died of natural causes. Egyptologists are also unsure what happened to Bay. They have identified his tomb, as well as that of Queen Twosret, but there is no sign that Bay's was ever used. Queen Twosret's tomb was appropriated by her successor, Sethnakhte, who moved her mummy to a small pit tomb. There in 1908 archaeologists found jewelry made for an infant, so perhaps Queen Twosret had a child with Seti II, although no record shows that she bore any children. However, the kings of the Ramessid Period (i.e., those who bore the name Ramses) removed Twosret's name from many royal documents and lists because they believed it was wrong of her to have declared herself pharaoh, so much about her personal life remains unknown. **See also** Ramessid Period; Sethnakhte; Seti II; Siptah; Valley of the Kings.

Unas (Wenis) (?–ca. 2345 B.C.)

The final king of the Fifth Dynasty, Unas reigned for approximately thirty years. During his reign, he built a large funerary complex at Saqqara that includes a pyramid and one of the earliest reliefs showing a military battle. The pyramid also contains the earliest known appearance of the Pyramid Texts, which were spells, incantations, liturgies, and other material that the ancient Egyptians believed would help their king reach the Afterlife. However, Egyptologists believe that the Pyramid Texts were actually written in earlier times. Today Unas's pyramid is in ruins, but its underground burial chamber has been excavated to uncover the king's sarcophagus as well as the Pyramid Texts. **See also** Afterlife; Pyramid Texts; Saqqara; sarcophagus.

Underworld

According to ancient Egyptian beliefs, the Underworld (also known as the Duat) was the otherworldly realm that the solar deity passed through each night in his solar bark (boat) on his way to the point where he would rise in the morning. The Egyptians' view of this realm varied according to where and when they lived, but generally the Underworld was believed to be filled with beasts who sought to stop the solar deity each night before he could reach the end of his journey.

The soul of the deceased was also said to travel through the Underworld on its way to the Judgment Hall of Osiris, where it would learn whether it would be allowed to enjoy eternity. In this sense, the term *Underworld* referred to the physical location of the Afterlife; the Afterlife was a form of existence (i.e., the eternity that comes after life) rather than a specific place. In some mythology, an entrance to the Underworld was said to be located in the city of Memphis. **See also** Afterlife.

Upper Egypt

During ancient times, Upper Egypt was the southern region of Egypt, located between Itj-tawy (now Asyut) in the north and continuing south to the First Cataract of the Nile River at Ta-resu (now Aswan). At various times, this border was even farther south, at either the Second Cataract or the Third. The main features of Upper Egypt were the Nile River Valley and the Western Desert oases of Kharga and the Faiyum, three regions that featured vegetation within an otherwise desert landscape. By the Fifth Dynasty, there were twenty-two nomes in Upper Egypt, and the main areas of settlement were these three regions. **See also** Aswan; cataracts; nomes and nomarchs; oases.

uraeus

A symbol of kingship often displayed on crowns and royal headdresses, the uraeus ("She Who Rears Up") was the image of a cobra about to attack its enemy. The cobra undoubtedly represented the goddess Wadjet, considered the guardian of Lower Egypt, who was believed to manifest as the serpent. Some ancient Egyptian myths mention the uraeus of the god Re, suggesting that, like earthly kings, he too wore the insignia on his crown. **See also** crowns; Re; Wadjet.

Urhiya (?–ca. 1270 B.C.)

A soldier during the reign of Nineteenth Dynasty king Seti I, Urhiya worked his way up to the position of general. He then moved from the military to the administrative branch of government, becoming a steward for Ramses II. Urhiya's progress was unusual because he was of foreign descent (probably Hurrian, Canaanite, or Palestinian), and in earlier times, foreigners were not allowed positions of power. In another break with tradition, Urhiya was even permitted to pass his office of high steward on to his son, Yupa. **See also** Ramses II; Seti I.

Userhet

There were two Eighteenth Dynasty Egyptians named Userhet who left behind notable Theban tombs. One was a royal scribe who lived from approximately 1430 to 1400 B.C.; the other was a man whose title was first prophet of the royal *ka* under King Tuthmosis I. The full import of the First Prophet title is unclear, but some Egyptologists assume that it involved foretelling events related to the king as well as participating in religious ceremonies. Probably for this reason, the images in this Userhet's tomb were symbolic. He and his wife are depicted as human-headed birds (the typical form of the *ba* aspect of the spirit) sitting beneath a sacred fig tree from which the waters of eternity pour. They hold some of this water in their hands so they can drink it. Another scene shows Userhet's heart being weighed in the Judgment Hall of Osiris.

The tomb of Userhet the royal scribe contains scenes that are fairly realistic representations of life at the time. One depicts a large banquet, but its female figures have been defaced; Egyptologists believe that this was done by early Christians offended at the women's apparent wantonness. Other tomb scenes depict hunters with dogs, mourning women, and a barber giving Userhet a shave. In addition to being a royal scribe, this Userhet was a royal tutor who helped raise several princes and as a noble was himself raised in the royal nursery and academy, known in ancient Egyptian as the *kap*. **See also** scribes; Thebes; Tuthmosis I.

Userkaf (Userkhaf) (?–ca. 2491 B.C.)

The first king of the Fifth Dynasty, Userkaf was the grandson of Fourth Dynasty king Djedefre and the son of Queen Neferhotep, but Egyptologists disagree on who his father was. Userkaf apparently claimed the throne through his maternal line and/or as the husband of Queen Khentkawes I. The two most notable accomplishments of Userkaf's reign, which lasted approximately seven years, were his relocation of the royal burial site from Giza to Saqqara, where he built a pyramid and mortuary temple, and his construction of the first sun temple, located at Abu Ghurob. The pyramid's mortuary temple had many wall reliefs, particularly of birds, and a sculpture of the king's head, but the pyramid is so damaged that its interior is inaccessible to archaeologists. The temple at Abu Ghurob had a squat obelisk and a sun altar, with a causeway leading to a mud-brick boat said to belong to the solar god Re. Four of Userkaf's successors would later build similar temples to the sun god. **See also** Djedefre; Khentkawes I.

Userkare (dates unknown)

A king of the Sixth Dynasty, Userkare is an enigmatic figure. For many years, Egyptologists argued over whether he actually existed because his name does not appear on many king lists. Now, however, Egyptologists believe that he ruled for a year, between the reigns of Teti and Pepy I. They also suspect that Userkare took the throne after leading a successful plot to assassinate Teti. They further believe that Userkare was related to a Fifth Dynasty ruler and for this reason thought the throne was rightfully his. Although evidence of Teti's assassination has been found in some tombs at Saqqara, there is no proof that Userkare was involved in a conspiracy to kill the king, and his ties to the royal family are unclear. Moreover, nothing is known of the accomplishments of his brief reign. **See also** Pepy I; Saqqara; Teti.

Valley of the Kings

The Valley of the Kings is a necropolis located on the opposite shore of the Nile River from Thebes that contains the tombs of New Kingdom kings, apparently beginning with King Tuthmosis I. This site was most likely chosen as a necropolis for four reasons. First, the entrances to its tombs, which were cut deep into the living rock of the valley's surrounding cliff faces, could be easily hidden from tomb robbers and protected by guards. Second, the Valley of the Kings was on the west bank of the river, and because the ancient Egyptians associated the west with the land of the dead, almost all of their burials were on that side of the Nile. Third, Thebes was the most powerful New Kingdom city and the capital of Egypt at the time the Valley of the Kings was in use, which made it the

The Valley of the Kings, the burial site used by New Kingdom rulers, is located on the west bank of the Nile, across from Thebes.

logical place for the kings' necropolis. And fourth, given the vast storehouses at Thebes, Egypt's kings had little difficulty constructing and supplying a workers' village, Deir el-Medina, near the Valley of the Kings for its tomb builders.

The Valley of the Kings has two main branches leading through its cliffs, the East Valley and the West Valley; most of its royal tombs are located in the East Valley. The tombs were not carved to place their occupants in any kind of order, nor were they laid out in any sort of row or pattern. Apparently, each king simply picked a spot for his tomb without regard to others nearby. Among the most notable tombs in the Valley of the Kings are those of Tuthmosis III, Amenhotep II, Horemheb, Tutankhamun, Seti I, Ramses III, Ramses VI, and Ramses IX. All of these tombs have decorations featuring funerary texts. For example, the tomb of Tuthmosis III depicts an unrolled papyrus inscribed with the *Book of What Is in the Duat*. The tomb also has a feature that Egyptologists once thought was intended to foil tomb robbers: a deep pit at the end of its downward-sloping entrance corridor. Some Egyptologists now believe that this pit had some other, symbolic purpose, particularly since there is a painted sky right above the pit. Exactly what that purpose was, however, remains a mystery.

Another tomb with unusual features is that of Seti I, which has the most complex design of any tomb yet found in the Valley of the Kings. Over one hundred yards long, the tomb has three corridors and several rooms, and every wall and ceiling within the entire tomb is covered with wall reliefs and paintings. Some of the rooms are actually halls with pillars, and flights of steps connect various rooms with one another. The funerary texts displayed on the walls include *The Litany of Re*, the *Book of What Is in the Duat*, *The Book of Gates*, and the *Book of the Divine Cow*; one room also has a

detailed astronomical ceiling. Also within the tomb at one time was the king's sarcophagus, carved out of a block of alabaster and decorated with blue hieroglyphs and scenes related to *The Book of Gates*. Italian treasure-hunter Giovanni Battista Belzoni, who found this artifact, sold it to a private collector in England, and it is now in a small London museum, the Soane. Different museums also have numerous items from the tomb of King Tutankhamun, which was found in 1922 filled with so many treasures that it took archaeologists ten years to remove and catalog them all.

Despite efforts to hide them, tombs in the Valley of the Kings were opened, even during ancient times. For example, the tomb of Ramses VI has Greek and Coptic graffiti on its walls that was made by visitors during the Greco-Roman Period. **See also** Belzoni, Giovanni Battista; Carter, Howard; Thebes; Tutankhamun.

Valley of the Nobles (Tombs of the Nobles)

Also known as the Tombs of the Nobles, the Valley of the Nobles is a necropolis area near the Valley of the Kings and the Valley of the Queens on the west bank of the Nile River at Thebes where many nobles and high-ranking Middle Kingdom and New Kingdom officials built rock-cut tombs. Many of the tombs have wall decorations, although most are painted rather than carved because the limestone from which the tombs were constructed is so soft that carvings would have quickly crumbled. Scenes in the tombs often come from daily life, and might also include an autobiography of the tomb owner's life. These autobiographies have provided Egyptologists with valuable information about Egyptian officials and military men such as Amenemhab, Menna, Ineni, and Rekhmire. **See also** Amenemhab; Ineni; Menna; Rekhmire.

A relief from a tomb in the Valley of the Queens. Very few of the known tombs in the valley were completed and decorated before being put to use.

Valley of the Queens (Biban el-Harim, Biban el-Sultanat)

Located on the western shore of the Nile River at Thebes near the Valley of the Kings, the Valley of the Queens was an area set aside in the Nineteenth Dynasty for the tombs of queens and other royal family members. Archaeologists estimate that there may be more than seventy tombs in the Valley of the Queens, but they have found just over twenty. Of those found, only a few were actually completed and decorated prior to their use.

Of the tombs that were completed, one is particularly elaborate, that of Nineteenth Dynasty queen Nefertari. Its many painted reliefs relate to Chapter XVII of the *Book of the Dead*, in which the spirit of the deceased is given a recitation necessary to ensure resurrection in the Afterlife. However, as part of this material,

Nefertari is shown playing a game that appears similar to checkers, and archaeologists are unsure of how this scene connects with the rest of the funerary text. In other scenes, Nefertari worships the solar deity, is received by the goddesses Neith and Sekhmet, makes offerings to Osiris, and stands before Thoth.

Not every occupant of the Valley of the Queens is a queen, or even female. For example, one tomb in the Valley of the Queens is that of Prince Amenhirkhepshef, a son of Ramses II who died as a child. In his painted reliefs, his father leads him to various deities, including Ptah, Isis, Shu, and Nephthys. A nearby tomb, that of Queen Titi (whose place in the Ramessid dynasty is not yet known), has painted reliefs showing the goddess Hathor in various forms. **See also** *Book of the Dead;* Nefertari; Ramses II; Thebes; Valley of the Kings.

vases

The ancient Egyptians had many types of vases, made from a variety of materials depending on the era in which they were made and for whom they were made. The earliest vases, in predynastic times, were carved from hard stone, and shortly thereafter alabaster was used as well, but eventually vases were also made from ivory, glass, bone, porcelain, gold, silver, bronze, brass, glazed pottery, or plain earthenware. Pottery and earthenware were primarily used by the lower classes.

Ancient Egyptian vases had one handle, two handles, or none, and some vases had rings instead of handles. Sometimes they had ornamental lids shaped like animal heads, such as the gazelle or ibex; others had lids with more than one animal head, one on either side, or the head of a monster or a person. The sides of the vase might be decorated with patterns, flower images, or other ornate designs. Vases for liquids might be large, while those for ointments might be very small. In either case, a vase might be marked with hieroglyphs, perhaps to label its contents or identify its owner. **See also** art; pottery.

villages, workers'

Archaeologists have found the ruins of workers' villages, the places where the craftsmen who worked on the king's monuments lived, to be particularly helpful in piecing together a picture of daily life in ancient Egypt. This is because such villages were often abandoned once a nearby building project was finished, leaving homes and other structures that then lay undisturbed for thousands of years. Despite having been abandoned, these villages have provided archaeologists with numerous artifacts and papyri, giving glimpses into the lives of the builders and their families.

Two workers' villages were Kahun, where those who worked on King Sen-

wosret II's pyramid lived, and Deir el-Medina, the site of the mortuary temples of Eleventh Dynasty king Montuhotep and Eighteenth Dynasty queen Hatshepsut, a temple complex of Tuthmosis III, and other structures both at Deir el-Medina and nearby. From these and other sites, Egyptologists know that although a few hundred workers might start out on a building project, their number would dwindle to a few dozen craftsmen once the basic structure was erected.

Upon beginning a project, work gangs would be divided into two groups, one for the left side of the building and the other for the right. Each gang had its own leaders and deputies, who settled disputes within the group and provided members with supplies and pay. Bachelors were apparently paid less than men with wives, and men with children were paid even more, with accounts settled at the end of each twenty-eight-day period. Pay usually took the form of grain, which could then be used or bartered for other goods.

Workers generally lived for eight days at a time at the work site, laboring four hours in the morning and four in the afternoon with a meal in between, and then returned to their village to rest for the next two days. Therefore, the village was populated only by women and children for much of the time. However, men often failed to show up for work, due to drunkenness or a variety of excuses ranging from a family crisis to a need to honor the gods. Absenteeism was a major problem on most construction projects, as evidenced by records left by scribes who noted each worker's efforts for payment purposes. There was at least one royal scribe at each site to keep track of such things, as well as messengers and couriers to connect the site with the outside world. In addition, each project had its own police force to guard materials and tools and to ensure the workers' safety. **See also** architecture; building materials; Deir el-Medina; Lahun and Kahun.

viziers

Chosen by the king, usually from the king's family and/or among the most promising royal scribes, a vizier (called a *djat* or *tjat* in ancient Egyptian) was second in power only to the king and acted as his adviser, minister, or deputy. As such, he supervised all government departments and programs, including building and irrigation projects, the census, food storage and distribution, and the tax system. The vizier was also the chief justice of the court system, and he personally sat as a judge on the most important cases of the High Court.

In fulfilling his duties, however, the vizier did not act alone. He had many assistants, including scribes as well as members of the royal family: princes, princesses, and even queens. There were also many lesser bureaucrats involved in the departments overseen by the vizier. For example, the administrators of each nome collected taxes (in the form of grain, meat, minerals, and other goods) on behalf of the central government and then turned them over to the vizier's assistants for redistribution as part of the royal treasury.

During most dynasties there was only one vizier, but sometimes during later periods there were two, one in charge of the affairs of Upper Egypt and one in charge of Lower Egypt. The vizier for Upper Egypt traditionally resided at Elephantine, while the one for Lower Egypt resided in whichever city the king had chosen as his capital.

The most famous Egyptian vizier was Imhotep, who served under the Third Dynasty king Djoser and was deified approximately two thousand years after his death as a god of wisdom and medicine. A skilled architect, Imhotep designed and oversaw the construction of Egypt's first stone pyramid. **See also** Elephantine; Imhotep; nomes and nomarchs.

wadi

A wadi is a valley, gully, or riverbed that remains dry except during times of extremely heavy rain. When dry, wadis in the Eastern Desert served as ancient Egyptian roads, providing relatively smooth, flat passageways to and from cities along the Nile River to ports along the Red Sea. For example, the Wadi Hammamat was part of a major route connecting the city of Coptos with the port of Quseir.

Some wadis might also serve as water reservoirs. For example, Egypt's Wadi Natron filled with water during a period of flash floods every spring, creating a series of lakes on the valley floor. When these lakes evaporated in the summer, they left behind valuable salt deposits known as natron, which the ancient Egyptians used as part of the mummification process. **See also** Eastern Desert; Hammamat, Wadi; natron.

Wadjet (Uadjet)

The ancient Egyptian goddess Wadjet symbolized Lower Egypt and, together with the goddess Nekhbet, who symbolized Upper Egypt, she was said to protect the king from harm and strengthen his rule. In one myth, Wadjet is identified as the sister of Isis, and the two are said to have protected Horus as an infant by covering him with reeds and other plants so his father's killer, Seth, could not find him. In other myths, however, Isis's sister is identified as Nephthys, and Wadjet is not mentioned.

Wadjet was sometimes depicted as a woman, typically wearing a cobra-wrapped sun disk on her head, but she usually appeared as a cobra ready to strike. This image of her was used as the uraeus ("She Who Rears Up"), an insignia on the royal headdress. Her name, however, meant "She of the Papyrus," probably because of her mythological role in concealing Horus with papyrus reeds. Wadjet's cult center was Buto, located in the Delta of Lower Egypt, while Nekhbet's was in Hierakonpolis, Buto's sister city. **See also** Buto; Hierakonpolis; Lower Egypt; Nephthys; uraeus.

Waja-Hur (dates unknown)

A Twenty-sixth Dynasty builder, Waja-Hur lived and worked in the city of Heliopolis. In 2001, archaeologists found his tomb there in what is now the residential Ein Shams (Arabic for "Eye of the Sun") district of Cairo. Inside the tomb was Waja-Hur's sarcophagus, an inscription telling of his profession, and sixteen statuettes engraved with his name. The tomb was located approximately twenty feet below the ground and does not appear to have ever been disturbed by tomb robbers. Archaeologists know that at least one other tomb is located nearby, and excavations continue at the site. **See also** Heliopolis.

wand

Ancient Egyptians who practiced magic used wands, which came in three varieties. The first was the snake wand, made of bronze and shaped like a straight, coiled, or twisted snake. The second was a magic rod, which was a rod or stick made of wood, ivory, bronze, or glazed soapstone with various images on it. These images include religious symbols such as those used on amulets and engravings of animals, with the most popular being crocodiles, cats, lions, baboons, and frogs, all of which were associated with various prominent deities. Occasionally, a small statue of an animal might be attached to the rod as well. The third type of wand was apotropaic—that is, designed to divert evil. Egyptologists believe that ancient Egyptian apotropaic wands were associated with the hippopotamus goddess Taweret because they were usually made of hippopotamus ivory. Apotropaic wands bear imagery similar to that found on magic rods, but they also often include images of fantastical creatures whose symbolism and purpose are unclear. However, given the association with Taweret (goddess of childbirth) and some of the other known childbirth-related images on these wands, most Egyptologists believe they were used during labor in magic rituals to protect mother and child, and perhaps also in subsequent rituals to protect the infant. **See also** amulets; magic; Taweret.

was scepter

The *was* scepter was an ancient Egyptian scepter symbolizing power. Essentially a stick with one end shaped like the head of a gazelle, lion, or other animal, it was thought to confer the right to rule on its owner, particularly in the divine realm. The god Ptah and many ancient Egyptian kings were often shown holding the *was* scepter. In addition, the hieroglyphic image of this animal-headed scepter was sometimes used as a symbol of power, called simply the *was,* in ancient Egyptian artwork. **See also** symbols.

Wawat

Wawat was a region in Lower Nubia whose name was sometimes used to refer to all of Lower Nubia. Its capital was Aniba, alternatively known in some records as Miam. **See also** Nubia.

Way of Horus

During ancient times, the Way of Horus was the road from what is now el-Qantara, located on the east bank of the Suez Canal, to Gaza, on the coast of southern Palestine. From the Middle Kingdom on, the Way of Horus was one of Egypt's most important trade routes but was also subject to attack by nomads from the Eastern Desert and elsewhere. Consequently, the ancient Egyptian military established fortresses along the road, as well as fortified wells where trading caravans could safely water their animals. **See also** Eastern Desert; fortresses; military; trade.

weapons and armor

Ancient Egyptians had a variety of weapons and armor, particularly since mercenaries brought military equipment with them from other lands. For an Egyptian soldier, however, the most important long-range weapon was the bow and arrow. There were several varieties of the bow, including a composite bow introduced from Asia during the Second Intermediate Period; it was constructed with laminated strips of various materials to give it more power and range. Arrows had reed shafts with flint, copper, or bronze tips, and beginning in the Old Kingdom, they were held in a quiver.

During the Predynastic Period, a mace with a stone head was the most powerful close-combat weapon, but it was replaced during the Old Kingdom by the battle-ax, which had a copper head that came in various shapes. The spear and the javelin were used from at least as early as the Old Kingdom on, as were daggers, cudgels, clubs, and throwing sticks. During the New Kingdom, one of the most popular weapons was a scimitar, or sickle sword,

Spears, such as the ones carried by this regiment of tomb models, were used by Egyptian soldiers from at least the Old Kingdom on.

introduced by the Asiatics. A sword with a curved blade, this weapon was called the *khepesh* by the ancient Egyptians. Prior to the Twelfth Dynasty, Egyptian blades were made first of stone and then of copper, but later they were increasingly made of bronze, a material that was probably introduced by the Hyksos. Weapon handles were always made of wood, with leather used to attach the handle to the blade.

From the Predynastic Period on, soldiers used shields, which were made of wood covered with leather. However, they rarely wore helmets until the Late Period, although the king wore a battle crown that has been called a helmet despite the fact that its purpose was not protective but symbolic. A leather apron served as body armor until the New Kingdom, when metal armor was gradually introduced.

Much of the information about what was worn on the battlefield comes from the tomb of Ahmose Son of Abana, a pro-

fessional soldier who fought in wars against the Hyksos at the end of the Second Intermediate Period. His autobiographical wall inscriptions describe his body armor, made of overlapping metal pieces stitched to a linen or leather sleeveless jacket, which he wore over a short kilt and breechcloth complemented by a leather helmet. These inscriptions also tell how he was trained in the use of the bow and arrow as well as several bronze-tipped weapons and blades. **See also** bronze; copper and copper molds; Hyksos; military.

weather

For much of the year, the weather in ancient Egypt would have been fairly predictable, and scientists believe that the modern-day climate is very similar to what it was in ancient times, at least since the Old Kingdom. The Egyptian climate is very dry, with extended periods of rain uncommon except very close to the mouth of the Nile River, near the city of Alexandria. However, on occasion flash floods would occur in certain regions, such as the Valley of the Kings at Thebes. Throughout Egypt, any rainfall that occurred during the year would be seen from October to April. During the winter, temperature highs range from the mid-60s to the high 70s Fahrenheit, but cold winds blow across the deserts at dusk and dawn. In the summer, the temperature highs are in the 80s and 90s in the Delta but average 106 at Luxor and 108 at Aswan. **See also** agriculture; seasons.

weaving

The ancient Egyptians wove linen and wool fibers in order to make cloth. Both were spun first, using fibers from the flax plant for linen and wool from sheep. In either case, the spinning process—performed with a spindle—drew out and twisted strands of fiber to make thread or yarn, which was then woven on one of two types of hand looms to create cloth. The first was a horizontal loom, used during the Old and Middle Kingdoms. It was essentially two wooden poles, parallel to the ground and to each other, that were raised slightly above the ground by four pegs, one at each end of a pole. The second type was a vertical loom—an upright, rectangular wooden frame—first used after the Hyksos invasion of Egypt and therefore probably introduced by them. Both looms required the use of a handheld shuttle to work strands of thread or yarn over and under the thread or yarn already strung on the loom. In addition, at some point during the transition from one loom to another, the Egyptians began using a comb to push the woven strands closer together during the weaving process. **See also** clothing; linen.

weights and measures

To complete their building projects, pay their workers in grain, and collect taxes from landowners, the ancient Egyptians had to develop a standard system of weights and measures. The basic weight units were the *deben,* the equivalent of about three ounces, and the *kite,* about three-tenths of an ounce. To weigh a particular object, that object was placed in one of the two trays of a balance scale, and gold rings weighing one *deben* each were placed in the other until the scale balanced. Grain, gold dust, and other items difficult to weigh in a scale were typically valued and traded according to volume rather than weight.

Units of measurement had been originally established according to the average sizes of human body parts, with the smallest unit being the width of the fingers. Four finger widths equaled a palm, and seven palms equaled approximately twenty inches, or the average distance from the elbow to the fingertips. Numbers to record weights and measurements were written using hieroglyphs, with various pictures of

animals, objects, deities, and other items representing different amounts. **See also** economic system; mathematics; taxation.

Wenamun, *The Tale of*

Dating from the early Twenty-first Dynasty, the story known as *The Tale of Wenamun* was found in a papyrus that surfaced on the Cairo antiquities market in 1891. Egyptologists disagree as to whether it is a true story or a work of fiction. However, they believe that it accurately reflects various truths about the Twenty-first Dynasty, most notably how little influence and prestige a once-mighty Egypt had in foreign countries as a result of King Ramses XI's weak rule.

The story is presented as a report by a temple official, Wenamun, to the king about a trip he took on behalf of his temple to the port of Byblos on the coast of Lebanon. Wenamun was supposed to buy cedarwood to repair the Bark of Amun, a ceremonial boat, and once abroad he expected to receive respect as an emissary of Egypt. Instead, he was treated badly during every step of his journey. Moreover, when he reached Byblos, he found the price of the wood to be excessive and was dismayed that the Byblos king refused to negotiate. The overall tone of Wenamun's story is one of discouragement and frustration. **See also** Ramses XI.

Weni (ca. 2340–ca. 2280 B.C.)

According to a stela at his tomb at Abydos, Weni was a prominent public official during much of the Sixth Dynasty. His career, which spanned the reigns of Teti, Userkare, Pepy I, and Merenre I, began with a job as a soldier when Weni was just a boy. He then worked his way up through the ranks of the military. Among the military expeditions in which he participated were an invasion of north Palestine, several campaigns in north Sinai, and the quelling of five revolts in Egyptian territories. In one of his Sinai campaigns, Weni led an army of several thousand across the desert without anyone dying, despite the fact that the army faced many hardships and had to find its own food and water along the way.

As a military commander, Weni became known as a fierce warrior who attacked his enemies even before being provoked. Yet he also came up with new defensive tactics to protect his men. During the reign of Pepy I, Weni was appointed to serve as a judge in Hierakonpolis. He was also charged with the task of investigating whether a queen in the royal harem, Weretyamtes (also known as Amtes or Yamtisy), was plotting to have Pepy I killed. He placed a record of this trial on a stela, but it has no record of the outcome.

Weni was also responsible for overseeing public works in southern Egypt during the reign of Merenre I when the king appointed him governor of Upper Egypt. In this capacity, he created five channels or canals near the First Cataract of the Nile River so that building stones from quarries near the cataract could be transported more easily to Saqqara, where Merenre I's pyramid was being constructed. Weni's own tomb was probably at Abydos, although some Egyptologists believe that the structure attributed to him there was not a tomb but a cenotaph (a false tomb used as a memorial rather than as a place to hold a mummy). **See also** Abydos; cenotaph; Merenre I; Nile River; Pepy I; Teti.

Wepwawet

Wepwawet was an ancient Egyptian god, typically depicted in the form of a jackal, and during the Old Kingdom he was said to open the road through the Underworld of the Afterlife for the deceased. Later, however, Wepwawet became identified with Anubis, who then took on these two qualities, and Wepwawet became the pilot of the boat in which the sun god traveled through the Underworld each night. **See also** Afterlife; Anubis; Underworld.

Westcar Papyrus

Now in the Egyptian Museum in Berlin, the Westcar Papyrus is a Middle Kingdom papyrus that contains a collection of stories known as the *Tales of Wonder.* One story in particular, "The Birth of the Royal Children," has provided Egyptologists with information regarding childbirth practices in ancient Egypt. In particular, it tells of midwives and dancing girls being present in the birthing room, mentions a fourteen-day cleansing ritual following birth, and says that women were required to drink beer after giving birth because it was believed to be good for both mother and child. **See also** children; medicine.

Western Desert

The Western Desert was a desert region that ran along the Nile River just west of its fertile valley and stretched west to what is now Libya. However, the ancient Egyptians probably considered the Western Desert part of Libya as well. They established forts in this region to protect Egypt from Libyan invasion, usually in or near oases. The landscape of the Western Desert was dotted with oases, the four main ones being Kharga, Dakhla, Farafra, and Bahariya. All of these places produced grapes, dates, and perhaps other crops as well. Outside of these areas, however, the Western Desert was extremely harsh. **See also** Libya; oases.

Wilkinson, John Gardner (1797–1875)

From 1821 to 1833, John Gardner Wilkinson visited every major ancient Egyptian site and many minor ones to copy their inscriptions into notebooks. This material has proved invaluable to modern scholars, particularly since Wilkinson's color reproductions are highly accurate and show some wall scenes that have subsequently been damaged. Wilkinson also produced one of the most important nineteenth-century books on ancient Egypt, which is still used as reference material in many libraries today: *Manners and Customs of the Ancient Egyptians including their private life, government, laws, arts, manufactures, religion, architecture, and early history, derived from a comparison of the paintings, sculptures, and monuments still existing, with the accounts of ancient authors,* published in three volumes in 1837.

wine

Although they did not know how to distill alcohol, the ancient Egyptians were able to make wine, and they drank both red and white. Most wine was produced from grapes, although pomegranate and date wines were also available. The first grape vineyards appeared in Egypt in around 3000 B.C., and within a short time they existed throughout the Delta and in most desert oases. By the Old Kingdom, at least six different types of wine were produced in Egypt, and priests had begun using the beverage as part of temple rituals. During the New Kingdom, different types of wines, spices, and other ingredients were mixed to create new drinks. However, throughout all periods, wine was primarily drunk by the upper classes; the lower classes usually chose beer instead because it was less expensive.

Grapes were handpicked year-round to make juice and to eat as well as to make wine. After they were picked, grapes intended for wine were placed in large winepresses. In these low boxes, up to six men stomped on the grapes while pressing on a wooden framework to extract the bulk of the juice into vats. The remainder, which was the sweetest juice, was squeezed out by putting the grape skins into sacks that were then wrung by four men using two attached twisting poles. All of the liquid was then poured into uncovered stone or pottery jars and left to ferment. Midway through the fermentation process, the liquid might be transferred to new stone or pottery jars for long-term storage, capped with clay stoppers, and labeled according to the origin, quality, and variety of grape.

Because a good harvest and successful fermenting were vital to producing good wine, the Egyptians prayed to the gods to bless their wine-making endeavors. Certain deities were considered particularly important in this regard; the god Shezmu was the patron of winepresses, for example, and the deity of the wine itself appears to have been the goddess Renenutet, who was associated with harvests as well.

Wine was an offering at many temple rituals, but particularly at cult centers dedicated to the goddesses Hathor, Tefnut, Bastet, or Sekhmet. In fact, some myths feature Hathor and Sekhmet becoming drunk on wine or beer. Drunkenness appears to have been a common occurrence at Egyptian festivals, and attendance records from pyramid construction sites indicate that Egyptian men often missed work because of drunkenness and its aftereffects. **See also** Bastet; beer; Hathor; religion; Sekhmet; Tefnut.

women, role of

The role of women in ancient Egyptian society was as an equal partner to men. Women could own property, make their own wills, testify in court, and exercise many other rights that would have been foreign to women in most other ancient cultures (and some modern ones as well). Marriages were conducted only with the consent of both parties, and if the couple subsequently divorced, the wife usually kept whatever goods she had brought into the marriage as well as a portion of whatever she and her husband had earned together. Women also had equal access to the Afterlife, and many tombs have scenes of husbands and wives sharing various leisure activities through eternity, including boating, gardening, and listening to and playing music.

Some roles, however, were largely reserved for women. For example, child care was primarily the responsibility of women, as were food preparation and the manufacture of household items like baskets and reed mats. Weaving of cloth was also the sole domain of women until the New Kingdom, when men might weave as well. In addition, the senior women in the household were in charge of household shopping—in other words, bartering household goods in the marketplace to acquire other items. Other jobs, though, were open to both genders. Women worked alongside men in agricultural fields, bakeries, granaries, and breweries, and a few women even took traditionally male jobs such as florist or boat pilot.

Despite this level of equality, jobs associated with power and prestige were closed to all women, except perhaps a strong-willed queen or princess. For example, women could not work as government administrators, although sometimes a princess might assist a royal scribe in his work. Nonetheless, there were no official female scribes or viziers, nor were there any female soldiers or military commanders. In addition, only four women ever ruled Egypt directly as queen-pharaoh (and even then the public strongly disapproved of such a rule), although a few others were truly the power behind the throne.

The priesthood was also run by men, but a few temples dedicated to goddesses did have priestesses. Moreover, royal women could act as priestesses through a position known as Divine Wife of Amun (later Divine Adoratrice of Amun). Established by King Ahmose I of the Eighteenth Dynasty for principal royal wives and later extended to princesses, this title not only came with religious duties but also with vast estates in Thebes, and women awarded the title quickly became very wealthy and powerful. **See also** Amun; children; Divine Wife of Amun; marriage; priests.

woodworking

The ancient Egyptians used wood to create boats, coffins, furniture, weapons, and various architectural components such as doors and pylons, with different woods

This relief shows ancient Egyptian carpenters at work. The Egyptian craftsmen employed many of the same woodworking techniques used by modern-day carpenters.

being chosen for each purpose. However, Egypt had few trees that were adequate for such applications, so most wood was imported from places like Lebanon, Punt, Assyria, and Mitanni.

Woodworking tools included axes, adzes, saws, chisels, awls, borers, rasps, and mallets. Most tools had a copper blade (or, in later periods, a bronze one) attached by a leather thong to a wooden handle. Prior to the use of copper, tools had stone or flint blades. The ancient Egyptians also employed handmade nails to hold pieces of wood together.

Ancient Egyptians used woodworking techniques that would look familiar even to modern-day carpenters, although lathing (the use of a machine to turn a piece of wood against a cutting or abrading tool) did not appear in Egypt until the Greco-Roman Period. For example, Egyptian craftsmen employed dowels, tongue and groove, mitering, hinges, leather lashes, and copper bands to create furniture joints, and wooden pieces might be finished with various inlays and other decorations. **See also** furniture; trade.

writing, forms of

Modern scholars do not know what the ancient Egyptians' language sounded like because it is not spoken by any modern peoples, but they do have several forms of ancient Egyptian writing to study. The oldest is hieroglyphic writing, used at least as early as the Early Dynastic Period for monumental and ornamental inscriptions. Hieroglyphs continued to be used for such works, and for religious texts on some papyri as well, until the end of the fourth century A.D.; the last known hieroglyphs appeared at Philae in A.D. 394. Read as pictures of the items they represented or as symbols of concepts or sounds related to the image being portrayed, hieroglyphs are a complex form of writing because one hieroglyph can mean more than one thing. For example, a disk symbol might repre-

sent an object, the sun; a concept, the sun god; or the sound made by pronouncing the word for the sun and the sun god, *ra*. The discovery of this aspect of hieroglyphs, made by French linguist and historian Jean-François Champollion, was what finally enabled scholars to begin translating them. This in turn enabled modern scholars to translate other forms of Egyptian writing as well.

Because hieroglyphic writing was cumbersome and time-consuming, ancient Egyptian scribes developed a faster, cursive (flowing) form of hieroglyphs, known as cursive hieroglyphic writing. Because cursive hieroglyphs were more rounded, they were easier to write with a reed pen than were regular hieroglyphs, which were designed to be carved with a chisel. As a result, cursive hieroglyphs quickly spread in popularity, particularly for day-to-day writing such as accounting statements. Temple scribes, however, continued to use standard hieroglyphs for sacred texts.

At first, cursive hieroglyphics were essentially the same as regular hieroglyphs, just easier to write. Over time, however, cursive hieroglyphic writing developed into a truly separate form of writing with its own symbols and meanings. The ancient Egyptians called this type of writing *Kemyt,* but modern scholars call it hieratic writing. By the New Kingdom, hieratic script was being used for religious and other formal texts as well as day-to-day writing, and by the late New Kingdom, it had begun to be used for a few stone inscriptions as well.

In the Twenty-fifth Dynasty, yet another form of writing developed in Egypt, called *sekh shat* ("writing for documents") in ancient Egyptian and demotic script today. Even more cursive than hieratics, it was used for books and documents until the end of the Roman Period. However, when the first Christians, who spoke Greek, began preaching their religion in Egypt, they wrote the Bible in

Coptic script, which used Greek letters to express words from the ancient Egyptian language.

Coptic writing was translated by modern scholars fairly easily, but hieroglyphic and demotic writing were a puzzle to them for centuries. What ultimately helped them solve the puzzle was an ancient Egyptian artifact known as the Rosetta Stone. The Rosetta Stone had three forms of writing on it—hieroglyphic, demotic, and Greek—all representing the same text, so scholars were able to compare the two unknown types of writings (hieroglyphic and demotic) with the known one (Greek) to translate the text. **See also** Champollion, Jean-François; Christianity, spread of; Philae; Rosetta Stone.

Xerxes (ca. 519–465 B.C.)

Xerxes was a Twenty-seventh Dynasty king who came to the throne of Egypt as the successor of Darius I during the First Persian Period, when Egypt was under the control of Persia. His rule was unusually harsh, even for an outsider, and the Egyptians hated him more than any other Persian king of Egypt. He was assassinated by some of his own courtiers in 465 B.C. **See also** Persia and Persian periods.

Yuya (Yuia) and Tuya (Tuia) (both ca. 1400–1352 B.C.)

Yuya was a priest of the god Min during the reign of Amenhotep III, as well as the Master of the Horse for the king's army, which was in Thebes; his wife, Tuya, was a royal nursemaid who first served King Amenhotep III's mother, Mutemwiya. Yuya and Tuya's daughter, Tiy, became queen of Egypt at age eleven when she married Amenhotep III as his principal wife. Tiy's son, Amenhotep IV (also known as Akhenaten), subsequently gave Yuya the title Father of the God, and Egyptologists believe that Yuya and Tuya both had a great deal of influence at court during Queen Tiy's time there. In 1905, an archaeological expedition led by Theodore Davis found the couple's tomb in a wadi near the Valley of the Kings. This structure was undecorated but appeared to have been undisturbed, and Yuya and Tuya's mummies are currently among the best preserved in the Cairo Museum. **See also** Amenhotep III; Amenhotep IV; Tiy.

APPENDIX 1

DYNASTIES OF ANCIENT EGYPT

Scholars disagree regarding the historical divisions and dates related to ancient Egyptian history. Generally, however, they identify the historical periods and dynasties of ancient Egypt (with all dates approximate) as follows:

Early Dynastic Period	3000–2686 B.C.
First Dynasty	3000–2890 B.C.
Second Dynasty	2890–2686 B.C.
Old Kingdom	2686–2125 B.C.
Third Dynasty	2686–2613 B.C.
Fourth Dynasty	2613–2494 B.C.
Fifth Dynasty	2494–2345 B.C.
Sixth Dynasty	2345–2181 B.C.
Seventh and Eighth Dynasties	2181–2160 B.C.
(sometimes these two dynasties are placed in the following period)	
First Intermediate Period	2160–2055 B.C.
Ninth and Tenth Dynasties	2160–2125 B.C.
(in the city of Heracleopolis)	
Eleventh Dynasty	2125–2055 B.C.
(only in the city of Thebes)	
Middle Kingdom	2055–1650 B.C.
Eleventh Dynasty	2055–1985 B.C.
(in all of Egypt)	
Twelfth Dynasty	1985–1773 B.C.
Thirteenth Dynasty	1773–1650 B.C.
Fourteenth Dynasty	1773–1650 B.C.
(sometimes these two rival dynasties are considered part of the following period)	
Second Intermediate Period	1650–1550 B.C.
Fifteenth Dynasty (Hyksos)	1650–1550 B.C.
Sixteenth Dynasty (Theban rulers)	1650–1580 B.C.
Seventeenth Dynasty (Theban rulers)	1580–1550 B.C.
New Kingdom	1550–1069 B.C.
Eighteenth Dynasty	1550–1295 B.C.
Ramessid Period	1295–1069 B.C.
Nineteenth Dynasty	1295–1186 B.C.
Twentieth Dynasty	1186–1069 B.C.

Third Intermediate Period	1069–664 B.C.
Twenty-first Dynasty	1069–945 B.C.
Twenty-second Dynasty	945–715 B.C.
Twenty-third Dynasty	818–715 B.C.
Twenty-fourth Dynasty	727–715 B.C.
Twenty-fifth Dynasty	747–656 B.C.
Late Period	664–332 B.C.
Twenty-sixth Dynasty	664–525 B.C.
Twenty-seventh Dynasty (First Persian Period)	525–404 B.C.
Twenty-eighth Dynasty	404–399 B.C.
Twenty-ninth Dynasty	399–380 B.C.
Thirtieth Dynasty	380–343 B.C.
Thirty-first Dynasty (Second Persian Period)	343–332 B.C.
Greco-Roman Period	332 B.C.–A.D. 395

APPENDIX 2

RULERS OF
ANCIENT EGYPT

Historians disagree on the names and reign dates of Egypt's kings, but generally the kings of thirty dynasties identified by Greek historian Manetho, plus the kings of the "Zero Dynasty" noted by modern historians, are as follows:

Predynastic Period (sometimes called Zero Dynasty or Dynasty Zero): Scorpion King, Narmer.

Old Kingdom:

First Dynasty: Aha (Hor-Aha), Djer, Djet, Den, Mereneith, Anedjib, Semerkhet, Qa'a.

Second Dynasty: Hotepsekhemwy, Raneb, Nynetjer, Weneg, Sened, Peribsen, Khasekhemwy.

Third Dynasty: Sanakhte, Djoser, Sekhemkhet, Khaba, Huni.

Fourth Dynasty: Snefru, Khufu, Djedefre, Khafre, Menkaure, Shepseskhaf.

Fifth Dynasty: Userkaf, Sahure, Kakai, Shepseskare, Neferefre, Neuserre, Menkauhor, Akauhor, Djedkare, Unas.

Sixth Dynasty: Teti, Userkare, Pepy I, Merenre I, Pepy II, Merenre II, Nitiqret.
[Some sources add Merenre II to the end of this list, followed by a queen Nitocris or Nitiqret, who was probably his wife. In addition, some historians place the Seventh and Eighth Dynasties within the Old Period while others consider it a part of the First Intermediate Period. According to the third-century B.C. Greek priest-historian Manetho, there were seventy kings in the Seventh Dynasty, but modern historians believe that number was a gross exaggeration. There were supposedly seventeen kings in the Eighth Dynasty, but only two—Wadjkare and Qakare Iby—are currently known.]

First Intermediate Period (Seventh through Eleventh Dynasties): Various known kings, including Khety I, Khety II, Khety III, Merikare, Neferkare, Montuhotep I and II, Intef (Inyotef I, II, and III).

Middle Kingdom:

Eleventh Dynasty: Montuhotep II, Montuhotep III, Montuhotep IV.

Twelfth Dynasty: Amenemhet I, Senwosret I, Amenemhet II, Senwosret II, Senwosret III, Amenemhet III, Amenemhet IV, Sobeknefru (Nefru-Sobek).

Thirteenth Dynasty: Numerous kings, including Amenemhet V, Sobekhotep I, Sobekhotep II, Awibre Hor, Userkare, Sobekemsaf I, Sobekhotep III, Neferhotep I, Sobekhotep IV.

Fourteenth Dynasty: Names of individual kings unknown, though there were said to be seventy-six.

Second Intermediate Period:

Fifteenth Dynasty (Hyksos kings): Salitis, Yaqub-Hor, Khayan, Apepi I, Apepi II.

Sixteenth Dynasty (Hyksos kings): Names of kings unknown.

Seventeenth Dynasty (Theban Kings): Rahotep, Sekemre, Intef (Inyotef VI), Montuhotep VII, Sobekemsaf II, Sawadjenre Nebiryerawet, Userenre, Intef (Inyotef VII), Tao I, Tao II, Kamose.

The New Kingdom:

Eighteenth Dynasty: Ahmose I, Amenhotep I, Tuthmosis I, Tuthmosis II, Tuthmosis III, Hatshepsut, Amenhotep II, Tuthmosis IV, Amenhotep III, Amenhotep IV (Akhenaten), Smenkhkare, Tutankhamun, Horemheb.

Nineteenth Dynasty: Ramses I, Seti I, Ramses II, Merenptah, Amenmessu, Seti II, Saptah, Queen Tausret (Sitrameritamun).

Twentieth Dynasty: Sethnakhte, Ramses III, Ramses IV, Ramses V, Ramses VI, Ramses VII, Ramses VIII, Ramses IX, Ramses X, Ramses XI.

Third Intermediate Period:

Twenty-first Dynasty: Smendes, Amenemnisu, Pseusennes I, Amenemope, Osorkon I, Siamun, Pseusennes II.

Twenty-second Dynasty: Sheshonq I, Osorkon I, Sheshonq II, Takelot I, Osorkon II, Takelot II, Sheshonq III, Pimay, Osorkon IV.

Twenty-third Dynasty: Pedubastis, Sheshonq IV, Osorkon III, Takelot III, Rudamun, Iuput II, Peftjauawybast, Nimlot.

Twenty-fourth Dynasty: Tefnakhte, Bakenrenef.

The Late Period:

Twenty-fifth Dynasty: Some kings' names are in dispute, but they include Piankhy-Piye, Shabaka, Shabataka, Taharqa, Tanutamani.

Twenty-sixth Dynasty: Necho I, Psamtik I, Necho II, Psamtik II, Apries (Wahibre), Ahmose II (Amasis), Psamtik III.

Twenty-seventh (First Persian) Dynasty: Cambyses, Darius I, Xerxes, Artaxerxes, Darius II, Artaxerxes II.

Twenty-eighth Dynasty: Amyrtaeus.

Twenty-ninth Dynasty: Nefaarud, Hakor.

Thirtieth Dynasty: Nectanebo I, Teos, Nectanebo II.

DEITIES OF
ANCIENT EGYPT

These are the most important deities worshiped in ancient Egypt, along with their main physical manifestations, associations, and any main cult centers that have been indentified:

Gods

Amun—a man, sometimes ram-headed or frog-headed, or a goose; associated with Creation; cult centers at Thebes and Hermopolis.

Anubis—a jackal or a man with a jackal's head; associated with cemeteries and embalming.

Aten—sun disk; associated with the sun; cult center at Akhetaten (also known as Amarna).

Bes—a dwarf; associated with childbirth; a household god with no cult center.

Geb—a man; associated with earth and fertility; cult center at Heliopolis.

Hapi—a man; associated with Nile inundation; cult centers at Gebel el-Silsila and Aswan.

Horus—a falcon or falcon-headed man; associated with the sky and kingship; cult centers at Edfu, Hierakonpolis, and Behdet.

Khepri—a scarab beetle or a man with scarab-beetle head; associated with Creation and the sun.

Khnum—a ram or a man with a ram's head; associated with Creation and fertile soil; cult centers at Elephantine and Esna.

Khons(u)—a boy with a crescent-moon headdress; associated with the moon; cult center at Thebes.

Min—a man; associated with agriculture, fertility, Eastern Desert mining, and travel; cult centers at Coptos and Akhmim.

Nefertem—a man with a lotus headdress or a man with the head of a lion; associated with primeval lotus blossom; cult centers at Memphis and Buto.

Nun—a man, frog-headed man, or baboon; associated with primordial waters; cult centers at Heliopolis and Hermopolis.

Osiris—a mummified man; associated with death, the Afterlife, rebirth, agriculture, and soil fertility; cult centers at Abydos and Busiris.

Ptah—a semimummified man; associated with Creation, architecture, and creativity; cult center at Memphis.

Re (Ra)—a man with a ram or falcon head; associated with Creation and the sun; cult center at Heliopolis.

Seth—strange animal; associated with chaos, destruction, infertility, storms, and the desert; cult center at Naqada.

Shu—a man or lion-headed man; associated with air and divine knowledge; cult centers at Heliopolis and Leontopolis.

Sobek—a crocodile or a man with the head of a crocodile; associated with the power of kings; cult centers at Kom Ombo and the Faiyum.

Sokar—a mummified man; associated with funerary goods and rituals; cult center at Memphis.

Thoth—a baboon, an ibis, or an ibis-headed man; associated with the moon, scribes, and wisdom; cult center at Hermopolis.

Wepwawet—a jackal or a man with a jackal's head: associated with the passageways and gates of the Underworld; cult center at Assiut.

Goddesses

Bastet—a cat or a woman with a cat's head; associated with pregnancy, music, dance, the rays of the sun (as the daughter of Re), and protection from disease and demons; cult center at Bubastis.

Hathor—a cow or a woman with cow features; associated with motherhood, fertility, music, dancing, drinking, and the sky; cult centers at Dendera and Deir el-Bahri.

Isis—a woman; associated with motherhood and magic; cult center at Philae.

Ma'at—a woman; associated with Order, Justice, and Truth.

Mut—a vulture; associated with motherhood; cult center at Thebes.

Neith—a woman with the Red Crown of Lower Egypt; associated with Creation, warfare, weaving, and Lower Egypt; cult center at Sais.

Nekhbet—a vulture; associated with Upper Egypt; cult center at el-Kab.

Sekhmet—a lioness or a woman with a lioness's head; associated with power, healing and the sun (as the daughter of Re); cult center at Memphis.

Seshat—a woman with a panther-skin robe; associated with writing.

Taweret—a hippopotamus with lion and perhaps crocodile features; associated with childbirth; a household goddess with no cult center.

Tefnut—a woman, a lioness-headed woman, or a cobra; associated with moisture and the uraeus (headdress cobra); cult centers at Heliopolis and Leontopolis.

FOR FURTHER RESEARCH

Barbara Adams, *Ancient Hierakonpolis*. Warminster, England: Aris & Phillips, 1974.

Cyril Aldred, *Jewels of the Pharaohs: Egyptian Jewelry of the Dynastic Period*. New York: Ballantine Books, 1978.

Alan K. Bowman. *Egypt After the Pharaohs, 332 B.C.–A.D. 642*. Berkeley and Los Angeles: University of California Press, 1986.

Bob Brier, *Ancient Egyptian Magic*. New York: Quill, 1981.

———, *The Murder of Tutankhamen*. New York: G.P. Putnam's Sons, 1998.

C.W. Ceram, *Gods, Graves, and Scholars*. New York: Bantam Books, 1976.

A. Rosalie David, *Discovering Ancient Egypt*. New York: Facts On File, 1994.

Simon P. Ellis, *Graeco-Roman Egypt*. Princes Risborough, UK: Shire Egyptology, 1992.

Rosalind Hall, *Egyptian Textiles*. Princes Risborough, UK: Shire Egyptology, 1986.

James E. Harris and Edward F. Wente, eds., *An X-ray Atlas of the Royal Mummies*. Chicago: University of Chicago Press, 1980.

R.A. Hayward, *Cleopatra's Needles*. Buxton, England: Moorland, 1978.

Christine Hobson, *The World of the Pharaohs: A Complete Guide to Ancient Egypt*. New York: Thames and Hudson, 1987.

Henry Hodges, *Technology in the Ancient World*. London: Allan Lane and Pelican Books, 1970.

P. Hodges, *How the Pyramids Were Built*. Shaftesbury, UK: Element Books, 1989.

Colin A. Hope, *Egyptian Pottery*. Princes Risborough, UK: Shire Egyptology, 2001.

Geoffrey Killen, *Egyptian Woodworking and Furniture*. Princes Risborough, UK: Shire Egyptology, 1994.

Napathali Lewis, *Life in Egypt Under Roman Rule*. 1983. Reprint, Atlanta: Scholars, 1999.

Miriam Lichtheim, *Ancient Egyptian Literature: A Book of Readings*. 3 vols. Berkeley and Los Angeles: University of California Press, 1973, 1976, and 1980.

Paul T. Nicholson, *Egyptian Faience and Glass*. Princes Risborough, UK: Shire Egyptology, 1993.

R.B. Parkinson, comp., *Voices from Ancient Egypt: An Anthology of Middle Kingdom Writings*. London: British Museum, 1991.

Christopher Pick, *Egypt: A Traveller's Anthology*. London: John Murray, 1991.

Nicholas Reeves, *Akhenaten: Egypt's False Prophet*. London: Thames and Hudson, 2001.

———, *The Complete Tutankhamen: The King, the Tomb, the Royal Treasure*. London: Thames and Hudson, 1990.

Gay Robins, *Egyptian Statues*. Princes Risborough, UK: Shire Egyptology, 2001.

John Rodenbeck, ed., *Reading Egypt: Literature, History, and Culture*. Cairo: American University in Cairo Press, 2000.

Alberto Siliotti, *Guide to the Pyramids of Egypt*. New York: Barnes and Noble Books, 1997.

David P. Silverman, ed., *Ancient Egypt*. New York: Oxford University Press, 1997.

Joyce Tyldesley, *Daughters of Isis: Women of Ancient Egypt*. New York: Penguin Books, 1994.

———, *Hatshepsut: The Female Pharaoh*. New York: Viking, 1996.

Steve Vinson, *Egyptian Boats and Ships*. Princes Risborough, UK: Shire Egyptology, 1994.

Barbara Watterson, *Introducing Egyptian Hieroglyphs*. Edinburgh: Scottish Academic, 1993.

Herbert E. Winlock, *The Rise and Fall of the Middle Kingdom in Thebes*. New York: Macmillan, 1947.

WORKS CONSULTED

Books

Barbara Adams, *Predynastic Egypt.* Princes Risborough, UK: Shire Egyptology, 1988.

———, *Protodynastic Egypt.* Princes Risborough, UK: Shire Egyptology, 1997.

Cyril Aldred, *Egyptian Art: In the Days of the Pharaohs, 3100–320 B.C.* New York: Oxford University Press, 1980.

———, *The Egyptians.* London: Thames and Hudson, 1987.

John Baines and Jaromir Malek, *Cultural Atlas of Ancient Egypt.* New York: Checkmark Books, 2000.

H. Idris Bell, *Egypt from Alexander the Great to the Arab Conquest.* Oxford, England: Clarendon, 1948.

James Henry Breasted, ed. and trans., *Ancient Records of Egypt.* 5 vols. 1906. Reprint, New York: Russell and Russell, 1962.

E.A. Wallis Budge, *Egyptian Magic.* New York: Dover, 1971.

Margaret Bunson, *A Dictionary of Ancient Egypt.* New York: Oxford University Press, 1995.

Peter A. Clayton, *Chronicle of the Pharaohs.* New York: Thames and Hudson, 2001.

A. Rosalie David, *Handbook to Life in Ancient Egypt.* New York: Oxford University Press, 1999.

———, *Science in Egyptology.* Manchester, England: Manchester University Press, 1986.

A. Rosalie David and Antony E. David, *Biographical Dictionary of Ancient Egypt.* London: Seaby, 1992.

Editors of Time-Life Books, *What Life Was Like on the Banks of the Nile.* Alexandria, VA: Time-Life Books, 1996.

I.E.S. Edwards, *The Pyramids of Egypt.* New York: Penguin Books, 1993.

Raymond O. Faulkner, trans., *The Egyptian Book of the Dead: The Book of Going Forth by Day: Being the Papyrus of Ani (Royal Scribe of the Divine Offerings).* San Francisco: Chronicle Books, 1994.

Henri Frankfort, *Ancient Egyptian Religion.* New York: Harper, 1961.

Alan Henderson Gardiner, *Egypt of the Pharaohs: An Introduction.* New York: Oxford University Press, 1969.

Alan Henderson Gardiner, ed., with the British Museum Department of Egyptian and Assyrian Antiquities, *Hieratic Papyri in the British Museum. Third Series: Chester Beatty Gift.* 2 vols. London: British Museum, 1935.

Herodotus, *The Histories.* Trans. Robin Waterfield. Oxford, England: Oxford University Press, 1998.

Michael A. Hoffman, *Egypt Before the Pharaohs: The Prehistoric Foundation of Egyptian Civilization.* New York: Knopf, 1979.

Erik Hornung, *Conceptions of God in Ancient Egypt: The One and the Many.* Trans. John Baines. Ithaca, NY: Cornell University Press, 1982.

Paul Johnson, *The Civilization of Ancient Egypt.* New York: HarperCollins, 1999.

R. Talbot Kelly, *Egypt: Painted and Described.* London: Adam and Charles Black, 1906.

Barry J. Kemp, *Ancient Egypt: Anatomy of a Civilization.* London: Routledge, 1991.

Edward William Lane, *Description of Egypt.* Ed. and Intro. Jason Thompson. Cairo: American University in Cairo Press, 2000.

Kurt Lange and M. Hirmer, *Egypt: Architecture, Sculpture, and Painting in Three Thousand Years.* Trans. R.H. Boothroyd. London: Phaidon, 1961.

Kurt Mendelssohn, *The Riddle of the Pyramids.* New York: Thames and Hudson, 1974.

John F. Nunn, *Ancient Egyptian Medicine.* Norman: University of Oklahoma Press, 1996.

Lorna Oakes and Lucin Gahlin, A*ncient Egypt.* London: Hermes House, 2002.

W.M. Flinders Petrie, *The Arts and Crafts of Ancient Egypt.* Edinburgh: T.N. Foulis, 1923.

———, *Egyptian Architecture.* London: British School of Archaeology in Egypt, 1938.

———, *The Funeral Furniture of Egypt.* London: British School of Archaeology in Egypt, 1937.

———, *Objects of Daily Use.* London: British School of Archaeology in Egypt, 1927.

———, *Royal Tombs of the Earliest Dynasties.* 2 vols. London: Egypt Exploration Fund, 1900–1901.

———, *Social Life in Ancient Egypt.* London: Constable, 1932.

———, *Tools and Weapons.* London: Egyptian Research Account, 1917.

Geraldine Pinch, *Magic in Ancient Egypt.* Austin: University of Texas, 1995.

J.E. Quibell and F.W. Green, *Hierakonpolis.* 2 vols. London: B. Quaritch, with the British School of Archaeology in Egypt, 1900–1902.

Stephen Quirke, *Who Were the Pharaohs? A History of Their Names with a List of Cartouches.* New York: Dover, 1990.

Carol Reeves, *Egyptian Medicine.* Princes Risborough, UK: Shire Egyptology, 1992.

Nicholas Reeves, *Ancient Egypt: The Great Discoveries: A Year-by-Year Chronicle.* London: Thames and Hudson, 2000.

Nicholas Reeves and Richard H. Wilkinson, *The Complete Valley of Kings: Tombs and Treasures of Egypt's Greatest Pharaohs.* London: Thames and Hudson, 1996.

Michael Rice, *Who's Who in Ancient Egypt.* London: Routledge, 1999.

Gay Robins, *Egyptian Painting and Relief.* Princes Risborough, UK: Shire Egyptology, 1986.

John Romer, *Valley of the Kings.* London: Michael Joseph and Rainbird, 1981.

Nancy K. Sandars, *The Sea Peoples: Warriors of the Ancient Mediterranean, 1250–1150 B.C.* London: Thames and Hudson, 1985.

Serge Sauneron, *The Priests of Ancient Egypt.* Trans. Ann Morrissett. New York: Grove, 1960.

Heinrich Schäfer, *Principles of Egyptian Art.* Ed. Emma Brunner-Traut; trans. and ed. John Baines. Oxford, England: Clarendon, 1974.

Ian Shaw, *Egyptian Warfare and Weapons.* Princes Risborough, UK: Shire Egyptology, 1991.

Ian Shaw, ed., *The Oxford History of Ancient Egypt.* New York: Oxford University Press, 2000.

William Kelly Simpson, ed., *The Literature of Ancient Egypt: An Anthology of Stories, Instructions, and Poetry.* New Haven, CT: Yale University Press, 1973.

G. Elliott Smith, *The Royal Mummies.* Cairo: Impr. De l'Institut Français d'Archéologie Orientale, 1912.

G. Elliot Smith and Warren R. Dawson, *Egyptian Mummies.* London: G. Allen & Unwin, 1924.

W. Stevenson Smith, *The Art and Architecture of Ancient Egypt.* New Haven, CT: Yale University Press, 1998.

Steven Snape, *Egyptian Temples.* Princes Risborough, UK: Shire Egyptology, 1996.

Harry M. Stewart, *Egyptian Shabtis.* Princes Risborough, UK: Shire Egyptology, 1995.

John H. Taylor, *Egyptian Coffins.* Princes Risborough, UK: Shire Egyptology, 1989.

Angela P. Thomas, *Egyptian Gods and Myths.* Princes Risborough, UK: Shire Egyptology, 1986.

Angela M.J. Tooley, *Egyptian Models and Scenes.* Princes Risborough, UK: Shire Egyptology, 1995.

Bruce G. Trigger, *Nubia Under the Pharaohs.* London: Thames and Hudson, 1976.

Eric P. Uphill, *Egyptian Towns and Cities.* Princes Risborough, UK: Shire Egyptology, 1988.

W.G. Waddell, trans., *Manetho.* Cambridge, MA: Harvard University Press, 1964.

Philip J. Watson, *Egyptian Pyramids and Mastaba Tombs of the Old and Middle*

Kingdoms. Princes Risborough, UK: Shire Egyptology, 1987.

Barbara Watterson, *The Gods of Ancient Egypt*. Stroud, Gloucestershire: Sutton, 1996.

Kent R. Weeks, *The Lost Tomb*. New York: William Morrow, 1998.

Frances Welsh, *Tutankhamun's Egypt*. Princes Risborough, UK: Shire Egyptology, 1993.

John Anthony West, *The Travelers' Guide to Ancient Egypt*. Wheaton, IL: Quest Books, 1995.

Hilary Wilson, *Egyptian Food and Drink*. Princes Risborough, UK: Shire Egyptology, 1988.

Herbert E. Winlock, *Excavations at Deir el Bahri, 1911–1913*. New York: Macmillan, 1942.

———, *Models of Daily Life in Ancient Egypt from the Tomb of Meket-Re*. Cambridge, MA: Metropolitan Museum of Art and Harvard University Press, 1955.

Periodicals

Ventura (California) Star, "Archaeologists Stumble upon New Pyramid," May 6, 2002.

A.R. Williams, "Death on the Nile," *National Geographic*, October 2002.

Alain Zivie, "A Pharaoh's Peacemaker," *National Geographic*, October 2002.

INDEX

PICTURE CREDITS

ABOUT THE AUTHOR

Patricia D. Netzley is the author of more than thirty nonfiction books on a wide range of topics. Her works include *The Encyclopedia of Special Effects* (Oryx Press Hardback, 1999; Facts On File Paperback, 2001), *The Encyclopedia of Women's Travel and Exploration* (Oryx Press, 2001), *Environmental Literature: An Encyclopedia of Works, Authors, and Themes* (ABC-CLIO, 1999), and *Social Protest Literature: An Encyclopedia of Works, Characters, Authors, and Themes* (ABC-CLIO, 1999). Netzley lives with her family in Southern California, where she and her husband are the proud parents of three children— Matthew, Sarah, and Jacob.

ABOUT THE CONSULTING EDITOR

Michael Berger teaches and lectures for the Oriental Institute at the University of Chicago on the culture of ancient Egypt and the lasting influence of Egyptian art on Western art and architecture. He is one of the developers of the Middle Egyptian Text Editions for On-Line Research (METEOR) Project, a web-based teaching and research resource at the University of Chicago. Berger has a master's degree in Ancient Near Eastern Studies from the University of Michigan and has done advanced graduate study in Egyptology at the University of Chicago. Berger manages the Language Faculty Resource Center, a facility devoted to the development of language teaching materials at the University of Chicago.